The Birth of Ethics

The Berkeley Tanner Lectures

The Tanner Lectures on Human Values were established by the American scholar, industrialist, and philanthropist Obert Clark Tanner; they are presented annually at nine universities in the United States and England. The University of California, Berkeley became a permanent host of annual Tanner Lectures in the academic year 2000–2001. This work is the twelfth in a series of books based on the Berkeley Tanner Lectures. The volume includes a revised version of the lectures that Philip Pettit presented at Berkeley in April 2015, together with a printed response from Michael Tomasello, one of the invited commentators on that occasion (also taking part in commentary and discussion were philosophers Pamela Hieronymi and Richard Moran), with a final rejoinder by Professor Pettit. The volume is edited by Kinch Hoekstra, who also contributes an introduction. The Berkeley Tanner Lecture Series was established in the belief that these distinguished lectures, together with the lively debates stimulated by their presentation in Berkeley, deserve to be made available to a wider audience. Additional volumes are in preparation.

MARTIN JAY AND R. JAY WALLACE
Series Editors

The Birth of Ethics

Reconstructing the Role and Nature of Morality

PHILIP PETTIT

With Commentary by
MICHAEL TOMASELLO

Edited by
KINCH HOEKSTRA

OXFORD
UNIVERSITY PRESS

Oxford University Press is a department of the University of Oxford. It furthers
the University's objective of excellence in research, scholarship, and education
by publishing worldwide. Oxford is a registered trade mark of Oxford University
Press in the UK and certain other countries.

Published in the United States of America by Oxford University Press
198 Madison Avenue, New York, NY 10016, United States of America.

CIP data is on file at the Library of Congress
ISBN 978–0–19–090491–3

9 8 7 6 5 4 3 2 1

Printed by Sheridan Books, Inc., United States of America

Table of Contents

COMMENTS

REPLY

The Birth of Ethics

Editor's Introduction: The View from Erewhon

KINCH HOEKSTRA

In *The Birth of Ethics*, Philip Pettit sets out to provide a naturalistic account of the origins of morality, an account that also allows him to shed light on a number of the central topics of moral philosophy. Starting from a hypothetical community, Erewhon, in which people have language and interpersonal interactions but do not make moral undertakings or judgments, he asks how such people would come to develop the practices of obligating themselves to others and holding others responsible. Our own ethics must have arisen in some similar way, he argues, and this origin story therefore reveals much about the nature of morality. Pettit thus offers an account of ethics that is consistent with a scientific worldview and illuminates philosophical arguments about the metaphysics, epistemology, psychology, and semantics of morality.

In "The Birth of Ethics," his Tanner Lectures at the University of California, Berkeley, in April 2015, Pettit's individual lectures were titled "From Language to Commitment" and "From Commitment to Responsibility." The lectures were commented on incisively by the philosophers Pamela Hieronymi and Richard Moran and the psychologist Michael Tomasello, all of whom took part in a subsequent seminar and discussions. Pettit thereafter substantially revised and extended his argument for this book. Tomasello then provided a commentary on the book version of the argument, and that commentary is now printed at the end with a reply by Pettit.

The naturalistic challenge that Pettit here sets out to meet is to show how moral norms can arise in a world that is in principle fully scientifically describable, without special built-in normative features or supernatural guarantees. Although the inherent normativity of nature was a common ancient idea, attempts to meet the naturalistic challenge are also ancient. So Socrates in Plato's *Republic* sets out to construct a city in speech by positing a community of individuals who cooperate for their own ends, and he aims to locate in its growth the origin and nature of justice and the other virtues. There have been other influential attempts to lay out how morality arises from some such undemanding starting points, from the sophistic view of justice as a self-interested convention that is articulated by Plato's brother Glaucon, to David Gauthier's conception of morals by agreement. David Hume provided a naturalistic account of the origin and nature of morals, and readers have disputed whether in doing so he offered an ethical theory or a descriptive theory about how human beings come to make the judgments that we call ethical. Other figures clearly emphasized naturalistic starting points in their attempts to discredit morality as amounting to an articulation of mere power, for example, or a scheme for the profit of a particular group. This is the strategy of Thrasymachus in the *Republic*, and it still informs the arresting account provided in *On the Genealogy of Morality*, which Friedrich Nietzsche identified as a polemic and has proved enduring more for its provocation than its plausibility.

In *The Birth of Ethics*, Pettit insists on plausibility, attending to naturalistic motivations for morality with a constructive rather than a critical aim. He offers a reconstructive analysis, starting from a narrative about the evolution of ethical practices and concepts, in which each phase must be naturalistically intelligible. In Samuel Butler's 1872 *Erewhon*, from which Pettit takes the name of his imagined community, the principal study in the colleges of Erewhon is that of 'hypothetics.' Pettit's study of his Erewhon is a hypothetical account that is designed to illustrate the nature of morality better than a historical account could, especially given the state of the evidence. Rather than trying to trace how ethics emerged, however unlikely that actual emergence may have been, this account suggests how ethics more or less had to emerge.

For their development of ethics to be relevant to us, the human beings in Erewhon have to be like us; yet they are unlike us at the outset, precisely by being without prescriptive concepts and activities. The ethical nature of humans is not thereby denied, but bracketed, set aside while we consider how people otherwise similar to us would come to think and behave ethically. There would be nothing informative about finding a morality the lineaments of which had been previously stipulated by building in moral emotions or normative considerations or inclinations from the outset.

The theory that emerges is simultaneously a kind of moral realism (for moral properties are really in the world) and a kind of moral conventionalism (as those properties are the product of patterns of human interaction and conventions to facilitate interests). It is through an interactive community that normativity comes to be in the world. Central to this account are the roles of self-interest and of language.

The residents of Erewhon move from strategic commitments to moral commitments. The epigraph on the title page of Samuel Butler's *Erewhon* is a Greek phrase from the first sentence of Aristotle's *Politics*, meaning that everybody undertakes every action for the sake of what appears good to them. Pettit begins with an assumption that the residents of his Erewhon are generally keen to promote the welfare of themselves and those close to them, and that they engage with others in order to further these goals; in the process of that engagement, they find themselves weaving a net of ethical commitments and conceptions.

These engagements are frequently linguistic, and although the residents of Erewhon initially use language without normative freight, it is through language that they can fully develop ethical interactions and ethical thinking. Others, like John Searle, have offered accounts of how language and other conventions embed and entail normativity. Objections to attempts to derive 'ought' from 'is' along these lines focus on suspicions that hidden premises are doing the work, or on the concern that the initial institutional practices (like promising) are already so richly normative that the argument is not ultimately naturalistic. *The Birth of Ethics* would preclude these concerns by proceeding with deliberate thoroughness and by starting with suitably pre-moral institutional practices (like reporting obser-vations). Deliberateness is also Pettit's guard against what is poten-tially a misleadingly clarifying power of knowing how the story ends, and the consequent risk that this dictates what 'must be' the logic of its narrative. Proceeding step by step and showing one's work help to forestall retrojection.

Michael Tomasello has argued that early human beings were less self-regarding and more immediately inclined to cooperation than the residents of Pettit's Erewhon; and in his commentary at the end of this book he also objects to the centrality of language in the devel-opment of ethics in Erewhon. While Pettit focuses on a philosophical explanation of ethics, Tomasello, especially in his recent *A Natural History of Human Morality*, provides a different kind of reconstruc-tion as he sketches the prehistorical rise of ethics. In the concluding ex-change, Pettit and Tomasello engage one another directly on the issues at stake between them, particularly about whether language is required for the development of cooperative norms, and whether starting with assumptions about self-interested agents furthers understanding about the nature of ethics (as a matter of theoretical economy that enriches explanatory power) or misunderstanding (as a foundational empirical mischaracterization).

As Tomasello recognizes, what Philip Pettit provides in this book is one of the most insightful and original accounts of the evolution of ethics. Over his remarkably significant and prolific philosophical career, Pettit has tackled an extraordinarily wide range of subjects, from meta-physics to the philosophy of mind to moral and political philosophy and more, and *The Birth of Ethics* brings together insights from much of his earlier thinking. The result is nothing less than an ambitious and sys-tematic explanation of the nature of ethics.

Introduction: The Guiding Ideas

H.L.A. Hart's (1961) book *The Concept of Law* already caught my fancy as an undergraduate student in Ireland. It seemed to do more in illumination of its theme than most of the tomes in analytical, continental or scholastic philosophy to which I was introduced in a wonderfully idiosyncratic syllabus. What I attempt here, many years later, is guided by a desire to explore the possibility of providing for ethics and morality the sort of perspective that Hart gave us on the law.

As Hart tried to explain what law is by seeing how it might have evolved, so this study tries to provide a similar story—a similar, counterfactual genealogy—for ethics. And as Hart argued that a pre-legal society would have supported practices prompting, even necessitating the emergence of law, so this study begins from an argument that a pre-moral society would also have supported practices sufficient to make ethics or morality relatively inescapable.

This study of ethics is motivated, then, by two theses that *The Concept of Law* underlines. One of them is the methodological claim that a good way to understand any phenomenon—or at least any human phenomenon like law or morality—is to see how it might have come about. The other is the anthropological claim that in a society that lacked the phenomenon there would have been pressures sufficient to bring it about: pressures that would have led, in a series of ad hoc adjustments, to its emergence.

There is also a third thesis that drives the study, although it becomes visible only in the final chapter. This is a metaphysical claim to the effect that morality is not just socially important, as almost all accounts maintain; it is also important in our individual lives. The personal importance of morality derives from the fact that it is only by virtue of immersion in the practices that lie at its origin that we can hope to establish ourselves as persons, in particular, integrated persons, whether in our own eyes or those of others.

The methodological and anthropological theses were central to the Tanner Lectures that I gave at the University of California, Berkeley in April 2015. The present work is an expanded version of the text I relied upon in presenting those lectures and supersedes the text that appears in the Tanner Lectures volume. The text is expanded, in particular, by the addition of a first chapter on the methodology followed and by a final chapter on the significance of the approach for a range of issues in moral philosophy. It is in the course of that final chapter that I introduce the third, metaphysical thesis that guides the inquiry.

The methodological thesis

Stated in general terms, the methodological thesis at the origin of the book is that it may be very useful in seeking philosophical illumination on some phenomenon to try to identify a means whereby it could, and would in all likelihood, be generated de novo. One version of such a methodology has been described as creature-construction, but, as chapter 1 shows, other versions of the approach can also be found, not just in Hart's work, but in the wider philosophical literature.

In this book, this generative methodology assumes a reconstructive form. It consists in exploring social conditions under which creatures of our ilk would have been more or less naturally driven, without conscious planning, to evolve and apply ethical concepts, in particular concepts of moral desirability and responsibility. The methodological assumption is that the availability of such a naturalistic genealogy tells us much about the actual role and nature of morality.

A particularly striking model of the reconstructive approach pursued in relation to morality is provided by a standard genealogy of money. I sketch that genealogy at greater length in the first chapter, but the main elements are straightforward. It begins with an imaginary barter society in which people seek to trade with one another for the goods or services they require. The members of this society will face a problem, however, for no matter how well resourced someone is, they may have nothing to trade that is wanted by those from whom they seek a good or a service. But there is a way out of this difficulty that is more or less bound to materialize, and it points the way to money.

It will become salient at a certain point that one or another commodity—perhaps gold or cigarettes, for example—is particularly attractive for most people. And at that point everyone with access to that good will be able to use it, or to use suitable IOU's, to purchase what they want. Thus, everyone will have a motive to obtain that commodity, using it as a medium of exchange. And once it comes to be used in that way it will count as money. Not only will it constitute a medium of exchange; it will also provide a metric for putting prices on other things and, of course, a means of accumulating wealth or purchasing power. It will serve the role that, on reflection, money plays in our society.

Just as this counterfactual genealogy can be illuminating about the role and nature of money, explaining how monetary practices and concepts might have co-evolved, the methodological thesis behind this book is that a parallel genealogy of ethics or morality can serve a similar function. The methodology employed is described in the first chapter, it is applied in the narrative developed over chapters 2 to 6, and the philosophical lessons of the narrative are sketched in the final, seventh chapter.

The anthropological thesis

The anthropological claim that shapes the book guides the narrative of emergence in chapters 2 to 6. The thesis is that the practices that make ethics inescapable for the protagonists in that narrative—and the practices, presumptively, that make it part also of our destiny—involve special uses of natural language. The protagonists back themselves, on pain of a costly reputational loss, to live up to the words they use in communicating their attitudes, assuming a special authority to speak for themselves and, under suitable conditions, to speak for others as well.

As those practices are described here, the protagonists come to avow and pledge certain attitudes in their own name, and to co-avow and co-pledge certain attitudes in the name of others as well. Putting their reputation up as the stake, they bet on themselves not to prove misleading on either front and, in that strategic sense, they commit themselves both to others and with others.

By the account presented here, any linguistic community that establishes such practices is more or less bound to evolve concepts of moral desirability and responsibility, and thereby enter ethical space. The practices will lead members to think of various standards of behavior as morally desirable—this, as a matter manifest to all—and will encourage them to hold one another responsible to those standards.

The metaphysical thesis

The third, metaphysical proposition is meant to explain why these practices of commitment should play such an important personal role for us. While the relevant assumption is implicit in earlier chapters it is only addressed explicitly in the first section of chapter 7, which deals with the metaphysics of morals. The claim is that in enabling individuals to speak for themselves, inviting others to rely on the persona they present, the social practices provide the infrastructure that makes them capable of being socially functioning persons.

To be a person in this functioning sense is to escape the muteness of other animals. It is to speak for a self that you can invite others, and by implication yourself, to rely on; to enable that self to provide a privileged standpoint for making judgments on the desirability—in particular, on the moral desirability—of how you perform; and to claim and display a capacity to be true to that self, counting as fit to be held morally responsible for what you do. Morality, on the emerging story, goes hand in hand with personhood; they are two sides of the one coin.

But couldn't individuals have become persons in the relevant sense, and couldn't they have developed moral concepts, without having to rely on social interactions of the kind envisaged? No, they could not. You become a person insofar as you are a bespoken, beholden self: someone who is bound by your words to those from whom you invite reliance; and someone who has to struggle, therefore, to live up to what you explicitly or implicitly say for yourself. But you cannot speak for yourself to yourself, you cannot make yourself beholden to yourself. You could always let yourself off the hook, after all; you could always give yourself an easy ride. You can only speak for yourself to yourself when you consciously mimic the already established role of an independent interlocutor.

Why, then, be moral? Why live up to accepted moral norms, when you can get away with flouting them? The upshot of the metaphysical thesis is that, despite being generated by social practices, the aspiration to be a person for whom you can speak without duplicity gains an independent hold; that once it has a hold, it can guide you, even in the absence of reputational incentive—or, in limiting cases, social benefit—to be faithful to it; and that it provides a concern, deeply rooted in the construction of personhood and selfhood, to live up to the demands of morality. The appeal of being moral is nothing more or less than the appeal of being a person with integrity: a person integrated around suitably sustainable commitments.

Acknowledgments

In developing the ideas that appear in this work I benefitted from the comments of many of those who read or heard the original lectures. Among those in that audience, I am especially indebted to the insights of my Berkeley commentators, Pamela Hieronymi, Richard Moran, and Michael Tomasello. The fact that I decided to expand and revise the original text means, alas, that the current volume appears without those three commentaries; the contribution of Michael Tomasello in the exchange that appears later is a response to the new text.

I not only benefitted from the comments of participants in the Berkeley audience; I also benefited greatly from comments made by participants in the audiences at a pre-run of the lectures in the Australian National

University in March 2015 and at a re-run in the Goethe University, Frankfurt in May 2016. I learned much, too, from a number of helpful colleagues and students at Princeton University. But I must mention five people in particular who had a deep impact on the book. Jesse Hambly, Josef Holden, and Cathal O'Madagain provided incisive comments on an early draft, which led to significant revisions. Ralph Wedgwood, a blind referee who identified himself after submitting his report, saved me from making a number of mistakes. And Kinch Hoekstra, the editor of the volume, offered immensely probing and helpful comments on the penultimate text; nobody deserves an editor like Kinch but, ideally, everybody should have one.

The basic text of the lectures was prepared in early 2015 and early 2016 at the Australian National University, where I had the enormous benefit of ongoing feedback from colleagues there. It was essentially completed over a three-month period in 2016, as a Senior Fellow of the *Justitia Amplificata* Center at the Goethe University, Frankfurt and the Free University, Berlin. I am very grateful to the Directors of the Center, Rainer Forst and Stefan Gosepath, and to all of those who made the visit to Germany so enjoyable and profitable. I am most grateful also to my hosts at Berkeley, in particular Kinch Hoekstra and Jay Wallace. And, as always, I am deeply indebted and grateful to my partner, Victoria McGeer, with whom I have thrashed out many of the ideas presented here; in chapter 6, indeed, I draw extensively on our joint work on issues of responsibility.

The Birth of Ethics

Chapter 1: Reconstructing Morality

The aim of this project is to offer an account of ethics or morality—I use the terms here as synonyms—that makes sense of how we come to be an ethical species. This opening chapter offers an account of the reconstructive approach taken to that project. But before developing that account, it will be useful to say a little about what is involved, as I see things, in our being an ethical species.

Being an ethical species

We human beings are ethical creatures insofar as we are affectively and behaviorally responsive to ethical or moral considerations—that is, considerations mobilized by moral concepts—and are disposed, however fallibly, to act as they dictate. The motives and actions that ethical considerations evoke will be generally altruistic, going against the grain of more self-serving inclinations. But even altruistic emotions and actions will not count as moral, unless the considerations that we recognize as supporting them include many of a moral character. The altruistic responses of other animals toward their young need hardly count as moral responses. And that, presumably, is because considerations articulated in moral terms play no part in prompting or in regulating those responses.

The concepts that mobilize ethical considerations come in many varieties. They include concepts of what you ought to do, of the treatment you owe me or someone else, and of what therefore is our due and your duty. Thus, they include concepts of how it would be good or bad for you to behave as an agent—say, of what you are forbidden, required, or permitted to do—as well as concepts of what I, qua beneficiary, can claim as a matter of right or justice or desert: this might be a claim that you should keep your promises or show me a modicum of respect. And, moving from an ex ante to an ex post perspective, ethical concepts also include ideas of censure and commendation, guilt and shame and pride.

Ethics requires that we interact with one another as these concepts dictate that we should interact, but also that we act in that way, at least in some part, because of the considerations that the concepts put within our reach. We must be ready and able to apply the concepts in ethical practices like those of praising and criticizing various types of behavior; granting claims to others and making claims upon them; exhorting ourselves and exhorting others to act appropriately; and censuring or commending one another for how we act. And those exercises must not be irrelevant to how we behave. Even if we are each spontaneously disposed to live up to accepted moral standards, we must be ready to activate the practices, whether in dealing with ourselves or others, in the event of the disposition failing.

Desirability and responsibility

While ethical concepts vary, however, and while they can mobilize a wide range of distinct considerations, they all serve to mark different grounds on which actions count as morally desirable, on the one side, and agents count as fit to be held morally responsible, on the other. This makes it possible to use the concepts of desirability and responsibility to explicate other ethical concepts, or at least to identify the role they play. In order to keep things simple and tractable, this study will concentrate on those two dimensions of morality and reconnect with other concepts only in the final chapter.

This focus does not tilt things in favor of any particular understanding of morality; or at least, as we shall see in that final chapter, not in an independently indefensible manner. Thus, it does not beg the question between rival moral theories like consequentialism and non-consequentialism nor between approaches that differ, as we shall see, on the relative priority of desirability and responsibility. The explanation of ethics defended makes sense of why people should be drawn to one or the other side in such debates but does not provide grounds on which to choose between the sides.

The notions of desirability and responsibility are tightly connected with one another. When you judge that one option in a given choice is morally more desirable than alternatives, then, other things being equal, you explicitly or implicitly recommend or enjoin or prescribe its performance by the relevant agent, be that yourself or another. And when you hold that the agent is fit to be held responsible for the choice, you maintain that other things are indeed equal: the agent has the capacities and satisfies the other conditions required for such fitness. In that case, then, you prescribe the option without reserve or, depending on what was actually chosen, you deem the choice praiseworthy or blameworthy in retrospect: you commend or condemn the action and, if you are the agent, you feel pride or guilt about how you behaved.

Moral desirability

Any concept of desirability, including that of moral desirability, is designed to mediate prescriptions for what we should desire—including, by implication, intend—and in that sense, it is essentially practical. It will mediate suitable prescriptions in relation to agents or agencies who have the capacities required for being fit to be held responsible for the choice made. Thus, any such concept can be used to prescribe for what we should individually do, for how we should individually be, or for what we should collectively establish. It may prescribe for how we should individually make things be in the external world or for what sorts of internal attitudes or states we should cultivate or for how we should coordinate with others.

Prescriptive concepts come in many varieties, of course, and desirability in particular may mean moral desirability or desirability of some other kind: for example, desirability in law or etiquette, epistemological desirability, or desirability as a matter of prudence or patriotism. And, as desirability may assume different forms, so too may responsibility. This may mean, not responsibility for living up to moral demands, but responsibility for living up to the demands of law or etiquette, the epistemological demands of evidence, or the demands of prudence or patriotism.

What distinguishes the concept of moral desirability from such other concepts of desirability? There is no theory-independent characterization that promises to pass muster on all sides, but there are some general orientating remarks that ought to be acceptable on most.

Whenever something is desirable, by all accounts, it is desirable in virtue of having certain properties or, equivalently, in virtue of satisfying certain considerations. And by almost all accounts, the considerations that make an alternative morally desirable, rather than desirable in any other way, are characteristically unrestricted or comprehensive.

Those considerations are unrestricted in two respects. First, unlike considerations of prudence or patriotism, they are not restricted in range to the self-interests of a particular individual or country or whatever. If they argue for the moral desirability of someone's taking a prudent option, for example, they will do so in light of the impact on others as well. Second, the considerations are not restricted in standpoint to considerations about what a code of law or etiquette requires; to considerations about what, in certain cases—for example, cases of belief—the available evidence supports; or to considerations about what promotes a set of projects, perhaps altruistic in character, espoused by some individual or group. If moral considerations converge with any such considerations in supporting an option, they will do so in light of the overall impact of obeying the code, sticking with the evidence, or supporting the projects.

Different theories of ethics or morality are liable to differ on what more can be said about the considerations that are relevant to determining moral desirability; consequentialist and non-consequentialist theories, as we shall see in chapter 7, differ in this way. But one assumption common to many different viewpoints is that, as a result of the relative lack of restriction in range and standpoint, what these considerations support—or at least what they support for agents and agencies that are fit to be held responsible—they support in a comparatively weighty or authoritative manner. The considerations that argue for the moral desirability of one or another option are designed to be trump cards that outweigh competing considerations that reflect just a restricted range of interests or a restricted standpoint of concern.

These remarks should be enough to provide us with orientation for the moment. We return to the issue of how to think about desirability, and moral desirability in particular, at the beginning of chapter 5.

The project in this book is to make sense of how we could have come to be capable of registering matters of moral desirability and responsibility, capable of holding one another to moral account, and capable of regulating ourselves so as to prove accountable. In the three sections of this chapter, we look in turn at the genealogical or reconstructive methodology to be followed in the project; at the different constraints that it must satisfy; and at some precedents for its employment. Readers less interested in methodology may wish to go straight to Chapter 2.

1.1 Reconstructing ethics naturalistically

The naturalistic challenge

Because of being inherently prescriptive, ethics raises a problem for those of us who embrace naturalism, holding that the world we live in is an austere place that conforms to the image projected in natural science. Naturalists maintain that all the properties realized in the actual world are naturalistic in the following broad sense: they are of a kind with the fundamental properties that are liable to figure in natural science—properties like mass and charge and spin—or with properties that are actually realized by one or another configuration of such properties; the latter might be illustrated by properties like being dense or impenetrable, audible or visible, asymmetrical or pear-shaped.[1] And naturalists

1. The properties that are actually realized by one or another configuration of fundamental properties include some that cannot possibly be realized on a different basis, as in the examples given, and some that in principle can (Jackson 1998). For most naturalists, examples of the latter would include a property like holding a belief

hold in addition that everything that happens in the actual world does so under the force of the laws, deterministic or in-deterministic, that operate at the most fundamental, presumably sub-atomic level; no new forces—that is, no new fundamental forces—appear at higher levels of realization.

The fundamental properties recognized in natural science—even natural science extended by mathematics—do not include prescriptive properties like desirability and responsibility. And so, there is a serious question for naturalists as to whether prescriptive properties—and, in particular, the properties of moral desirability and responsibility— really are features of the universe we confront. They will presumably enjoy that metaphysical status, on a naturalistic view, only if they can be realized by one or another configuration of fundamental properties. But how could they be realized by properties that have no connection themselves with prescription? That is the naturalistic challenge. [2]

The assumption of realism

Naturalistic philosophers have sometimes responded to this problem by invoking the possibility of projection or illusion, seeking to debunk the idea that, by naturalistic lights, desirability and responsibility are bona fide properties. They have opted for representing ethical talk as funda- mentally emotive or expressive, for example, rather than taking it to be descriptive of any features in the world (Stevenson 1944; Ayer 1982;

that p, which is actually realized on the basis of a subject's neural or electronic con- figuration, but might conceivably be realized in a Cartesian world where mental states are of a totally different kind.

2. For an excellent discussion of the challenge, see Enoch (2011, 100–109). According to a currently popular version of non-naturalism, there is no need to find a naturalistic grounding for normative truths, because normative discourse enjoys a certain autonomy in relation to naturalistic forms of discourse; see Scanlon (2014), Dworkin (2011), and, for a general version of the strategy, Price (1988). See, too, Gert (2012). This position is bound to be attractive for anyone who despairs of finding a naturalistic account of ethics, but it is hardly going to appeal otherwise. Rejecting such despair, I do not consider it here.

Blackburn 1984; Gibbard 1990).[3] Or they have held that in speaking ethically we treat desirability and responsibility as if they were real properties when actually they are not: consciously or otherwise, so this story goes, we regard them as fictions (Mackie 1977; Joyce 2006).

The idea in this book is to resist downgrading ethical discourse in any such manner and, without forsaking naturalism, to try in the spirit of realism to vindicate the assumption that there really are properties like desirability and responsibility in the world and that they have an impact on our actions. These properties do not belong with fundamental, naturalistic properties like mass and charge and spin that figure explicitly in the basic sciences. But the assumption is that despite being non-prescriptive themselves, those fundamental properties can realize or ground the properties we discern in identifying desirable actions and responsible agents. The fundamental properties can realize such properties, so the idea goes, in the way in which the pixels on a television screen realize the patterns or properties that we register in following any TV program. They ground them in the sense of both guaranteeing and explaining their presence.[4]

The pixels on a television screen differ from the patterns they ground insofar as they are not anthropocentric—they can be defined in electronic terms that make no reference to human beings—whereas the supported patterns are: it is only because of our human interests that the smile on a presenter's face or the handshake of the protagonists in a drama are patterns worth noticing. To hold that as the television patterns are grounded in the pixels, so the properties of desirability and responsibility are grounded in equally naturalistic properties, is to allow that desirability and responsibility may be anthropocentric in a similar fashion. For all that naturalistic realism requires, these properties may

3. The focus has usually been on the expressivist reading of judgments of desirability, but a number of authors have also sought to develop a similar reading of responsibility ascriptions. See, for example, Hart (1948–49).

4. The intuitive notion of grounding presupposed in the text is meant to fit with the more technical notion employed in recent literature. See Rosen (2010) and Fine (2012).

be patterns that deserve notice only from the standpoint of creatures with distinctively human sensibilities, engaged in characteristically human practices.

The standard naturalistic strategy

The standard way to vindicate a naturalistic realism about ethical properties is to try to provide a naturalistic reduction for them. In a familiar, relatively strict form, this reduction would involve two claims. First, that what it takes for an ethical property to be instantiated is that this or that set of non-prescriptive conditions are satisfied. And second, that those conditions can be satisfied in the actual world by one or another configuration of broadly naturalistic properties: that is, scientifically fundamental properties or properties that are realized by one or another configuration of fundamental properties.

The first claim is an analysis of the conditions that make it appropriate to apply the ethical term or concept, by our intuitive understanding; this is usually developed by the method of cases, which involves thinking about the range of scenarios where we would apply the concept, and the range where we wouldn't.[5] The second claim is an empirical thesis to the effect that those conditions can be satisfied in this or that naturalistic configuration.[6]

The two-claim pattern exhibited by such a reductive analysis may be illustrated in the naturalistic reduction of a property like that of believing that p. This might hold, to gesture loosely at a functional style of analysis, that the belief is instantiated in a subject in virtue of a more or less reliable disposition to perform actions and adjust attitudes as if

5. If ordinary usage leaves open the possibility of interpreting the concept in one way or another, as it often will, then it is necessary to decide between the candidates on the basis of which property fits best in our theory of the world; for naturalists, a consideration in favor of one candidate rather than another will be that the grounding conditions involve only naturalistic properties.

6. For this account of reduction see Jackson (1998); see also Jackson and Pettit (1990) and Chalmers and Jackson (2001). For a general account of the methodology, with a comparison to the genealogical method adopted here, see Pettit (2019a).

it were the case that p.[7] And it would maintain, as a matter of empirical grounding, that in the actual world—although perhaps not in every possible world—this disposition consists in the subject's having a suitable naturalistic character: having a neural or electronic configuration—maybe this, maybe that—that generates the required pattern of action or adjustment.

Not all naturalists will agree that this is the way to reduce a property like believing that p. Some may ignore the analytical thesis altogether, and claim only that every instance of the property is just identical with the instance of a naturalistic property (Block and Stalnaker 2000). Others may keep the analytical thesis in a weaker form, treating it as a proposal about how best to understand the property to be reduced, not necessarily as an analysis of how the property is conceptualized in ordinary usage. But the strict form of reductive analysis will serve us well as a foil to the alternative introduced here.[8]

For reasons of convenience, however, this presentation of the strict form of reductive analysis is simplified in one regard. It assumes that there is no difficulty in identifying the precise conditions that make it appropriate to apply the target concept, and to ascribe the target property; and that there is no difficulty, therefore, in identifying the naturalistic configuration of properties that grounds the instantiation of the property. But in practice, there will often be a choice available as to which set of conditions to privilege analytically and which configuration of grounding properties to take as grounding the property to be reduced (Johnston 1992, 221–222). The reductive analysis of causation will assume a different form, for example, depending on whether or not we assume that every cause must take time to have an effect or that it must be connected by intervening factors with an effect.

7. For the materials needed in a full explication of this functionalist sort of analysis, see Stalnaker (1984) and Pettit (1998)

8. Many varieties of a doctrine nowadays known as constitutivism are special forms of reductivism in our sense, although not necessarily naturalistic reductivism. For an overview see Smith (2017).

What set of conditions to privilege, and what naturalistic configuration to take as ground of the property, may be determined in part by external considerations. We may make that determination on the basis that one candidate does better than others in serving the role that the concept plays in ordinary exchanges; in supporting our general theory of the domain in question; or even in making the naturalistic grounding of the property more straightforward (Burgess and Plunkett 2013).[9]

The reconstructive alternative

The alternative approach does not begin with an analysis of desirability or responsibility and then seek to argue that conditions sufficient to realize such properties are satisfied naturalistically in the actual world. It starts rather from a naturalistic story about how recognizably ethical terms and concepts could have emerged among creatures of our ilk and could have played a referential, yet prescriptive role in registering bona fide properties of the world. And then it argues on that basis for a naturalistic realism about desirability and responsibility.

The argument involves two claims. First, that insofar as the terms or concepts that emerge in the story respond to the same sorts of prompts, and serve the same sorts of purposes, as our actual ethical terms, the properties they predicate are good candidates for the properties we ourselves predicate with our terms. And second, that since the appearance of those concepts in a predicative role is naturalistically explicable, the properties they ascribe—and the properties ascribed by our counterpart concepts—must be naturalistic, too; if the concepts ascribed nonnatural properties, after all, then those properties would presumably have played a role in explaining how the concepts came into use.

---

9. In more traditional functionalist terminology, the candidate property, P, that is selected from among multiple candidates, may be treated as the best deserver as distinct from a possible deserver of the name or term at issue: say 'C'. At least that will be so, if selecting that candidate is identified with deciding on the best account of the property, P (Rosen 2010). The exercise of analysis in such a case narrows the field of potential accounts, ensuring that whatever account is adopted, it will identify a property intuitively ascribable by 'C'; it will not change the subject. See Pettit (2019a).

These two claims correspond broadly to the two claims in a strict reductive analysis. The first replaces the analytical claim with a thesis to the effect that ethical concepts are expressively equivalent to the concepts introduced in the story. And the second replaces the empirical claim with a thesis to the effect that the properties ascribed by the concepts introduced in the story—and so, plausibly, by their expressive counterparts in our language—are naturalistic in character. Insofar as the reconstructive analysis pairs in this way with the more familiar reductive model, it can be seen as seeking to realize the same goal by somewhat different means.

Does this account of the reconstructive approach simplify things in a parallel manner to that in which our account of the reductive does so? Yes, insofar as there are plausible variations on the genealogy that would generate somewhat different concepts and somewhat different candidates for expressive equivalence with our own ethical concepts. But any genealogy will tend in the nature of the enterprise to support a more or less determinate set of candidates for the role of expressive counterparts to our familiar concepts. It will correspond to a reductive account that has already selected the intuitive conditions that should be privileged in analysis of the concepts. The narrative developed here is determinate in precisely this respect. It is possible that plausible variations on the narrative might direct us to somewhat different expressive counterparts. But the possibility will not be explored here.[10]

Because of how they correspond, the reductive and reconstructive methodologies share a certain vulnerability. The vulnerability in the reductive case is that for all that has been argued, a property that is shown to be capable of being grounded naturalistically may not actually be

10. For an example of varying a genealogy in order to make better sense, allegedly, of a given concept, consider the variation to Hart's genealogy of law proposed in Pettit (2015c, 105–106). This would introduce a development under which it becomes a matter of common awareness that anyone can presume to speak for the group, without fear of contradiction, when arguing, in defense of the law, that it articulates accepted standards as to how things are done in the society. The variation is designed to make sense of why law is taken, allegedly, to be a system that enjoys widespread endorsement.

grounded in that way. The vulnerability in the reconstructive is that a property that is shown to be capable of having been accessed and conceptualized on a naturalistic basis may not actually be accessed and conceptualized in that manner.

How serious is this vulnerability in the analysis of the target concept and property, whether the analysis be reductive or reconstructive? Not very serious, I think. If we have a naturalistic reduction or reconstruction to hand, it would offend against parsimony to hold that nonetheless the concept refers us to a non-naturalistic property and demands a non-naturalistic analysis. Why multiply entities by positing that property, when by hypothesis the concept makes perfectly good sense in naturalistic terms?

Given the choice between reduction and reconstruction, what reason is there to seek a reconstructive rather than a reductive account of ethical properties, or indeed of any naturalistically problematic properties? There is a consideration of methodological accessibility that argues in favor of the reconstructive approach with problematic properties in general. And, more to the point of the current project, there is a consideration of explanatory value that argues in favor of the approach with problematic concepts and properties of the kind involved in ethics.

The advantages of reconstruction: easing the methodological burden

The consideration of methodological accessibility is that reconstructive analysis is likely in most cases to be easier to achieve than reductive analysis. There are two respects in which this is so, and they are associated in turn with the two claims that each must make.

The first of these claims concerns the shape of the target concept: in the reductive case, the claim is that the concept applies in such and such conditions and does not apply in others; in the reconstructive, the claim is that a concept employed within the story of emergence is expressively equivalent, or more or less equivalent, to the target concept. The advantage of the reconstructive approach on this front is that the exercise it requires is second nature to all of us, adept as we must be in determining whether we are thinking in broadly the same terms as others about any topic: whether we are using those terms under the same prompts and to the same purposes. By contrast, the exercise required by the reductive analysis is notoriously challenging and divisive: as noted, it involves using the method of cases, in which we seek agreement in intuition about the range of possible scenarios where we would apply the concept and about the corresponding range where we would not.

The second claim that each approach, reductive or reconstructive, must make is that there is a naturalistic candidate for the property that the target concept predicates. The advantage of the reconstructive approach on this front is that it only has to show that the story invoked is naturalistic in character, since that implies that there must be some naturalistic property or configuration, maybe this, maybe that, which is ascribed by the target concept. What the reductive approach has to do, however, is to identify the sort of naturalistic property that can serve as a plausible referent for the concept.[11]

The advantages of reconstruction: elucidating practice-dependent concepts

But apart from its greater methodological accessibility, the reconstructive approach also appeals on the ground that it has a particular explanatory advantage in making sense of certain sorts of concepts and properties. These are properties that become salient, and concepts that become accessible, only from within various practices, and include properties and concepts of the kind associated with ethics.

We noted earlier that it is not enough for the appearance of ethics that people generally act in conformity to the demands of moral concepts; it

---

11. This advantage is related to an attractive feature of reconstructive analysis that is not of much relevance in the current context. The approach does not presuppose the availability of a language in which to analyze the target concept. Thus, it is possible to employ reconstructive analysis in making sense of how we use the semantically most basic terms in our language—bedrock concepts, as David Chalmers (2011) calls them—in a rule-following way. See Pettit (2002, Pt 1).

is necessary that they have the concepts that support such conformity and are able to deploy them in typical ethical practices. These practices include the evaluation of various types of behavior as well as exercises like granting claims to others or making claims upon them, exhorting ourselves or others to live up to certain standards, and holding ourselves and one another to those standards.

The concepts and practices involved in ethics are interdependent. The practices presuppose the availability of the concepts, since it would make no sense to imagine people assessing types of behavior, assigning claims to one another, or enjoining one another to act in certain ways, if they did not have access to corresponding concepts. But equally the concepts would scarcely have a role to play in human life unless people were positioned to engage in practices of that kind. The practices are concept-dependent, as we might say, the concepts practice-dependent.

The practice-dependence of a certain class of concepts suggests that in order to gain competence in the use of any concept—in order to be sensitized to the pattern that the concept articulates—you would have to know how to engage in the relevant practices. In order to be sensitized to the pattern articulated among chess players in the concept of check-mating or castling, and in order to have a proper understanding of the property involved, you would have to know how to play chess; you might not have to be an expert, but you would at least have to know the rules: you would have to be on the inside, as it were. The lesson here, in parallel, is that in order to gain access to ethical concepts you have to know how to engage in standard ethical practices. It is only those with inside knowledge of the rules of chess who can properly master the concepts of check-mating and castling. And it is only those with inside knowledge of the practices of ethics who can properly master moral concepts.

This creates a difficulty for the reductive enterprise. A reductive analysis of check-mating or castling would identify the property ascribed by the concept from the outside, as a property that plays a certain role in the course of a game of chess. And a reductive analysis of ethical concepts would identify the properties they ascribe from the outside, as properties that serve in certain roles within ethical practice. But such an outside analysis would communicate only a parasitic understanding of a concept. It would identify the property ascribed by the concept in the way a color-blind person might identify the property of redness or blueness: that is, by the role it plays in the discriminations of those on the inside; in this case, those who can see color. It would not communicate anything like an insider sense of the property at issue.[12]

This limitation on reductive analysis does not affect reconstructive analysis in the same way. A reconstructive analysis of ethics must build on a narrative that explains why ethical concepts and practices should have co-evolved in a series of stages. The reconstructive analysis of money that we mentioned in the introduction does precisely this. It describes how monetary transactions and concepts might have co-evolved in stages, with exchange practices developing only in the presence of suitable concepts and the concepts emerging only in the presence of suitable practices. What we may hope for in the case of ethics or morality is that such a story of co-evolution may be available here as well, in particular a story of co-evolution that invokes only naturalistically intelligible adjustments.

In telling a story of co-evolution, the reconstructive analysis will have to appeal for its confirmation to our capacity to simulate how things would present in the wake of evolving developments of practice, and how insiders to those developments would find certain patterns salient and could evolve terms or concepts to articulate them. This is what happens with the genealogy of money, for example, when we are invited to imagine how gold or cigarettes would begin to present, as they are invoked by people in a barter society to serve as a generalized medium of exchange, and get to be used then as a metric for pricing things and as a means of storing wealth. The role of simulation in reconstructive analysis means that with ethics as with money, it ought to give us a simulated sense of the patterns articulated in moral concepts; and this,

---

12. This is not to suggest that reductive analysis is impossible. For an analysis that fits well with the genealogy developed here, see Jackson and Pettit (1995) and Jackson (1998).

without forsaking the naturalistic ambitions that reconstruction shares with reduction.

This particular advantage in reconstructive analysis should become clearer in the course of this book. It will be addressed again in the final chapter, when we look at the role of various practices in revealing moral properties. And it should be salient at two points in the narrative itself. One is in chapter 5, when we argue that as the protagonists avow desires rather than just reporting them, the patterns associated with various concepts of desirability will assume an inescapable salience for them. And another is in chapter 6, when we defend the view that in virtue of relying on one another's pledges of fidelity to certain standards, the protagonists will have to be prepared to hold one another to account— effectively, to hold one another responsible—for how well they do by those standards.

A social reconstruction

A reconstructive analysis might be developed on a wholly individual-istic basis with certain concepts and properties, even with concepts and properties of an interdependent character. In that case it would consist in a story of how a single individual might adjust to certain circum-stances in a distinctive manner, how that pattern of adjustment might provide a base for thinking in a certain way, how that mode of thinking might create new possibilities of adjustment, how this in turn might lead to a more nuanced form of conceptualization, and so on.

Ethical concepts and properties would scarcely be amenable to such an individualistic account, however. The concept of desirability serves individuals in making sense of their choices to others and in responding suitably to certain complaints. And the concept of responsibility serves people in a parallel way to commend or condemn the choices of others or to express corresponding responses to their own decisions. The so-cial role played by the concepts suggests that if we are to tell a plau-sible story about how people might come to master such concepts, then we must give an account of how they might develop the concepts in tandem with one another: that is, as the members of an interactive community.

This means that our reconstructive analysis has to aim at providing a narrative about how a community of individuals who do not initially employ ethical concepts might evolve communal practices to a point where such concepts would become available to them and corresponding properties become accessible. The narrative would have to start with a possible, naturalistically credible form of human society—ground zero—where the members do not yet have access to any ethical concepts, in particular any concepts in the family of desirability or responsibility. And it then would have to show how naturalistically credible adjustments would give rise to certain patterns of interaction and lead protagonists to develop concepts that can be seen as more or less equivalent to the ethical concepts we routinely invoke.

In order to emphasize that ground zero in the narrative envisaged is not our actual social world, I give it the name of Erewhon. This name, borrowed from a nineteenth-century novel, is an anagram of "nowhere" and may serve as a reminder of the unhistorical nature of the community with which the narrative has to start. The task is to identify naturalistically intelligible and plausible developments among the residents of Erewhon that would lead them, without their necessarily being aware of the process, toward the introduction and mobilization of concepts akin to our concepts of desirability and responsibility.

The narrative about how ethics could emerge in Erewhon will be developed in chapters 2 to 6. There are two goals in this narrative, corresponding to the two claims associated with reconstructive analysis. The first is to tell a story in which the members of Erewhon come to think in broadly ethical terms, using those concepts under broadly the same prompts, and to broadly the same purposes, as we use concepts like those of moral desirability and responsibility. And the second is to give such a manifestly naturalistic explanation of the concepts and practices that appear in Erewhon—and hence of our corresponding concepts and practices—that there is little option but to assume that they are naturalistically intelligible.

Factual history, counterfactual genealogy

Given that the narrative provided offers a history of ethics in Erewhon, a natural question bears on the relationship between the story told and actual histories of ethics. Theories that purport to tell us about the actual history of ethics sometimes offer accounts of broadly ethical patterns of desire and behavior without paying much attention to the emergence of ethical concepts.[13] Those theories are not of much concern from the point of view of the current project, however engaging and even compelling they may be in themselves.[14] But how does our reconstruction relate to histories of ethics in which behavioral and conceptual patterns both make an appearance?

In a prominent example of such a history, Michael Tomasello (2016, 154) offers an "imaginative" account of how ethical ways of acting and thinking emerged, building that story on two sources of data: first, evidence about the stages in which our forebears evolved, especially from about four hundred thousand years ago; and second, evidence about the predispositions present in young children, but not in other great apes, for which our ancestors were likely to have been selected in that period. Tomasello's history is imaginative or speculative because, as he says, there is "little in the way of artifacts or other paleoanthropological data to help" (154). So how is the account developed here likely to connect with his enterprise?

Both projects aim at explaining ethics rather than explaining it away in a debunking fashion. But there is a sharp contrast between them. Tomasello explores the emergence of ethics in the actual conditions in

13. This charge is laid against a range of studies in De Scioli and Kurzban (2009, 2013). For an exception, see Kitcher (2011, 412), who describes ethics as "an evolving practice, founded on limited altruistic dispositions that were effectively expanded by activities of rule giving and governance."

14. For an overview of some currently influential approaches in broadly this category, see Tomasello (2016, 137–143). He divides them into approaches that primarily concentrate on the role of sympathy and reciprocity, on the independent aspects of our psychology that are activated in moral concerns, and on the role of cultural selection.

which early humans presumptively operated—his main focus is on the period between four hundred thousand and one hundred and fifty thousand years ago—whereas ours looks at the emergence of ethics in the conjectural conditions that characterize Erewhon. Given the assumption that actual conditions were as he describes, Tomasello offers an account of how ethics might possibly have emerged there. Given the assumption that ethics evolved socially, we in contrast offer an account of conditions that would have made their emergence more or less inevitable.[15]

This contrast between the projects derives from a difference in their goals. Tomasello's aim is to excavate the origins of ethics by looking at factors that might possibly have given rise to ethical ways of thinking and acting in the actual history of our species. The aim here is to explore the nature of ethics by looking at factors that would almost certainly have given rise to ethical ways of thinking and acting in the conjectural conditions of Erewhon. Where the first aims at an actual history, the second aims at a counterfactual genealogy.[16]

If this account of the relationship between the two projects is correct, then there is room for fruitful exchange between them. In the project pursued in this book, for example, there are assumptions about the mutual reliance essential to the inhabitants of Erewhon that are strongly supported by the argument, prominent in Tomasello, that the early humans among whom morality emerged lived under conditions where, unlike other primates, they were required to forage together or die

15. Rousseau (1997, 132) seems to have thought in this way about his project in the *Second Discourse*: "The Inquiries that may be pursued regarding this Subject ought not be taken for historical truths, but only for hypothetical and conditional reasonings; better suited to elucidate the Nature of things than to show their genuine origin." I am grateful to Alison McQueen for drawing my attention to this. For the various strands in Rousseau's genealogy, see Neuhouser (2015).

16. The genealogy pursued here, as mentioned in the text, aims at explaining ethics, not explaining it away; in that respect it contrasts with the debunking genealogy of ethics offered in the nineteenth century by Nietzsche (1997); see Williams (2002) and Prescott-Couch (2014). Insofar as it is counterfactual rather than historical, it fits with some recent uses of the term *genealogy*, but not with all. See Williams (2000); Craig (2007); Skinner (2009).

alone. And if the project pursued here is sound, then it may be that Tomasello should make more use of the role of language in order to explain how our ancestors came to conceptualize and govern their relationships in ethical terms (Pettit 2018b). But the possibility of such cross-fertilization is not our topic. Putting aside the actual history of ethics, the task is to make sense of the project of reconstructive analysis.

1.2 Conditions on a successful reconstruction

If a reconstructive analysis is to serve the role envisaged for it here, then there are some conditions, as already indicated, that it has to meet. It must satisfy the input condition of starting from a possible society that is naturalistically intelligible and, despite lacking ethical and related concepts, is fairly similar to ours. And it must satisfy the process condition of explaining in broadly naturalistic terms why certain evolutionary developments would materialize in that world. We will examine how far these conditions constrain the genealogy to be presented and look then at the way in which it contrasts with parallel approaches that might be taken in the reconstruction of ethics.

Introducing the input condition

The main input requirement on our narrative has to be that the members of Erewhon initially lack access to ethical concepts like those of desirability and responsibility. But it will be useful to stipulate that they also lack access to other prescriptive concepts, such as those associated with desirability under law or etiquette or epistemology, or with desirability in prudence or in patriotism. This stipulation makes the task more challenging and interesting, since allowing participants access to other prescriptive concepts might make it suspiciously easy to explain their developing a concept of the morally desirable.

In order to have a good chance of being feasible, however, the reconstruction must take Erewhonians to be as close as possible to human beings like you and me, despite not yet having prescriptive concepts at their disposal. Thus, the project would almost certainly be infeasible, if it started with creatures, like some of our evolutionary ancestors, who did not yet form societies, or that did not depend on establishing social relations with one another for achieving individual success, or that did not have the cognitive capacities required for natural language.

Reflecting this constraint, the reconstruction provided here assumes that Erewhonians are very like us on a variety of fronts. First, of course, they have beliefs and desires and act routinely for the satisfaction of their desires according to their beliefs. Second, even if they are moderately altruistic, they primarily desire the promotion of their own welfare and that of their kin. Third, they are able to rely on others, and able to get others to rely on them, as an essential means to promoting that end.[17] Fourth, they have the capacity in pursuing mutual reliance, first, to exercise joint attention, consciously focusing on data they take to be available to all, and second, to act jointly with one another in pursuit of shared goals (Tomasello 2014).[18] And fifth, they are able to build on those capacities and use words in the communicative fashion of natural human language (Scott-Phillips 2015).

While the inhabitants of Erewhon have beliefs and desires, however, these attitudes do not involve any prescriptive properties in their contents: for example, they do not include beliefs about what is desirable or, equivalently, about what there is reason to desire or what they ought to desire. And while they can use natural language to express their attitudes, they use it only for the limited purposes of giving one another reports on how things are in their environment. They communicate about whether the blackberries have ripened on the hill, about what the weather is like farther north, about how the prospects are looking for the big-game hunt. And that is all. Language serves them only as

17. The current text takes the notion of reliance that it employs as fairly intuitive. For a useful analysis, see Alonso 2014.

18. On the notion of joint intention and action see (Bratman 2014). For other approaches to the analysis of this notion, any one of which would work for our purposes here, see Tuomela (2007); Searle (2010); Gilbert (2015).

a means whereby they can trade information, to their mutual benefit, about the world they occupy.

It is unlikely that there ever was a time or place in the trajectory of human development, of course, when members of our species used language solely for making reports on their shared world. But, anticipating later discussion, the claim to be developed in the reconstruction is, first, that if Erewhonians used words to communicate about the world in this manner, they would also use them to communicate about their own attitudes; second, that in communicating about their attitudes they would be more or less bound to rely on speech acts of avowal and pledging, co-avowal and co-pledging; and, third, that with those practices in place, they would naturally use certain terms under such prompts and for such purposes that the terms count as expressively equivalent to our concepts of moral desirability and responsibility.

The world that the story posits is not only meant to be akin in these ways to ours; it is also taken, as a presumptive aspect of that kinship, to be intelligible in naturalistic terms. That means at a general level that it should be a world intelligible on the basis of the properties recognized in natural science or grounded in properties recognized in natural science. And it means, in particular, that it should be intelligible without postulating properties of the kind associated with prescriptive properties.

Interrogating the input condition

We may assume for present purposes that the postulation of intentional and linguistic competence in our protagonists does not offend at a general level against the assumption of naturalism: that whatever form that competence involves, it is grounded in properties familiar from natural science; it does not presuppose a Cartesian, immaterial mind, or anything of the kind. But does the assumption that members of Erewhon have intentional competence, and competence in using natural language to express their intentional attitudes, mean that they are already living under a prescriptive regime? And does it offend in that particular way against the claim to be able to characterize Erewhon in presumptively naturalistic terms?

Intentional competence means competence in the formation of attitudes: that is, a capacity to form attitudes under appropriate conditions—say, to form a belief that p in the presence of evidence that p—and a capacity to meet constraints of consistency and the like in doing so. And linguistic competence means a capacity to meet corresponding constraints on the use of language, in the event of wanting to express those attitudes. Such intentional-linguistic competence may assume a low-grade or a high-grade form: it may involve rational processing or reasoned argument. But, whatever shape it takes, it does not require our protagonists to operate under a prescriptive regime; it does not require them to have access to concepts of desirability, moral or otherwise.

Low-grade competence would require them to conform to suitable constraints or regularities in the formation of intentional attitudes but to do so without any degree of intentional control: to do so in an unconscious, non-intentional form of rational processing. High-grade competence would require them in addition to recognize, now on one occasion, now on another, that this or that response is required under relevant constraints; to have a disposition on suitable occasions to respond as required; and to be able to take measures, however indirect, to promote the likelihood of their responding appropriately. It would require reasoned argument rather than mere rational processing.

In order to display the first sort of competence, our protagonists would just have to be disposed to transition rationally from beliefs about the satisfaction of suitable conditions to the formation of other beliefs and to be disposed, depending on what they desire, to give expression to such beliefs. And they could do this just as unconsciously or sub-personally, and just as automatically, as the well-designed robot. Forming the belief that p and that if p, q, for example, they would automatically conform to modus ponens by forming the belief that q and, if they wished, would express that belief in words. They would do this, in particular, without having any desire to satisfy the requirements of the rule and without having any intentional control over whether or not they do satisfy them.

In order to display the second, high-grade sort of competence, our protagonists would have to be able to reason their way to the conclusion that q, not just transition rationally into holding that belief. In reasoning to the conclusion, they would pay attention to the state of affairs that holds according to their premise beliefs—pay attention to the fact, as they see it, that p and that if p, q—and then form the belief that q in conscious response to that presumptive fact. In such an event, they might think "That implies that q," or simply "So, q." They would not just have a belief in the premises that generates a belief in the conclusion; they would think of the truth of the premises in which they believe as forcing them—as it happens, under the rule of modus ponens—to acknowledge the truth of the conclusion and to form a belief also in it.[19]

This ratiocinative, high-grade competence involves taking relevant rules, if only in a case-by-case way, as normative guides (Brandom 1994; Wedgwood 2007). Those rules will include not just a rule like modus ponens but also rules that express the constraints of evidence, consistency, closure, and the like. The capacity for reasoned argument consists in the ability to take intentional steps—say, in exercises of attention and care—to conform to such rules: to practice rule-following.[20]

Low-grade rational processing would certainly not require our protagonists to operate under a prescriptive regime, deploying concepts like those of desirability. But would the presence of reasoned argument mean that they would have had access to such concepts and would have been positioned to prescribe the satisfaction of relevant constraints to one another and to themselves?

No, it would not. In reasoning in the manner of modus ponens, the protagonists would have to treat the presumptive fact that if p, q and that p as a reason for believing that q; they would do this in registering and responding to the pressure to believe that q—that is, in forming

19. For a theory of reasoning of broadly the sort that is sketched here, see Broome (2013) and Pettit (1993, 2007b); and for a summary of the main points of commonality, see Pettit (2016a).

20. For a naturalistic account of rule-following, see Pettit (1993, 2002, 2007a). With the rules envisaged, there is a further question as to whether at base they are broadly representational rules, as I assume, or inferential rules, as Robert Brandom (1994) and Ralph Wedgwood (2007) argue. The argument developed here is independent of the answer given to this question.

the thought expressed in, "So, q." But they might treat that fact as a reason for believing that q without developing the concept of a reason and without having related ideas about what is evidentially compelling or epistemologically desirable. Thus, it is possible to reason from certain premises to a conclusion without having access to the idea that the premises provide a reason for holding by the conclusion. For current purposes, it is enough to vindicate this possibility only for the theoretical reasoning that prompts the formation of belief; we shall turn later in the chapter to the parallel possibility for the practical reasoning that eventuates in the formation of desire or intention.

The claim that this form of reasoned argument would not put our protagonists within reach of a notion like that of epistemological desirability is supported by later discussion. We shall see in chapter 5 that a concept of the evidentially credible would emerge on the basis of the same sorts of practices supporting the emergence of other concepts of desirability, including moral desirability. The salience that those practices would give to the prescriptive notion of credibility suggests that nothing like it would be salient, or even perhaps available, in their absence.[21]

Introducing the process condition

As the possibility of success requires the satisfaction of various constraints on the input side of the reconstruction, so it also requires the satisfaction of certain constraints by the process that the story describes. If the reconstruction is to be successful, this requires, first, that it does not introduce any non-naturalistic factors into the story: it must not postulate a naturalistic miracle; second, that it does not rely on any

21. Suppose that from the earliest stages our protagonists in Erewhon would have been in a position to spell out a notion of epistemological desirability. That concession would not be destructive of the approach taken, since there is no clear path from epistemological to moral desirability. This remark is made in the spirit of a challenge. It invites those who disagree, and in particular those who reject the sort of genealogy developed here, to tell a purely epistemological story about how we might have become an ethical species.

fortuitous occurrences: it must not postulate lucky flukes; and third, that it is the most economical story available: it must not be an idle wheel. Lacking any of these features, it would not direct us to a naturalistically plausible reconstruction.

In order to be naturalistically intelligible, to take up the first constraint, the process cannot presuppose elements or forces that are ungrounded in natural science. And equally, of course, it cannot presuppose that the protagonists already have access to prescriptive properties. This constraint is as clearly needed, and as relatively unproblematic, for the process condition as it was for the input condition. But why require in addition that the process be non-fortuitous and economical?

If the narrative invoked in explanation of the emergence of ethical concepts in Erewhon relied on the occurrence of something antecedently unlikely and serendipitous—if it relied on a lucky accident—then it would have the character of a just-so story. All that it would establish is that, as naturalistic factors lead by a lucky fluke to the emergence of recognizably ethical concepts in Erewhon, so the concepts that respond to similar prompts and serve similar purposes in our ways of thinking may also have emerged by a lucky fluke under the impact of naturalistic factors. This result might have a certain interest in establishing the possibility that our ethical concepts predicate naturalistic properties, but it could hardly establish that such naturalistic properties are prominent candidates for the properties that those concepts actually ascribe.

This explains why the narrative should be non-fortuitous as well as naturalistic. But, turning to the third constraint, why assume that it must also be economical? Why assume that it must be the most parsimonious narrative available?

The narrative to be presented here makes language essential for morality; it assumes that before developing prescriptive concepts, and accessing prescriptive properties, the protagonists already communicate linguistically. This account would not be parsimonious, intuitively, if there were another equally plausible narrative available under which the protagonists became aware of suitably prescriptive properties without having access to language and without first having terms in which to predicate them.

Assuming that this alternative story offered different candidates for the role of the relevant prescriptive properties, both in the target language and in ours, there would be good reason to prefer it. [22] That account would link prescriptive predicates with properties that would have been salient to the protagonists, even if they had never developed language, and had never introduced terms to predicate the properties. And those properties, presumably, would be salient to us on a firmer basis than the rival set of properties and would be more prominent candidates for the referents of our own terms; they would not depend for their accessibility on the effects of induction in language.

How do the three constraints just rehearsed shape the narrative to be offered here? The first constraint will be satisfied to the extent that none of the developments introduced in the story presupposes any non-naturalistic capacities in the protagonists or access to any prescriptive properties. And the third constraint will be satisfied, at least presumptively, to the extent that no more parsimonious but still naturalistic alternative is in the offing; the narrative is presented under the implied tag line: 'if not this, what?'.[23] But what of the second anti-fortuity constraint, against the introduction of lucky flukes?

Unlike the other two, this constraint has a direct impact on how the narrative is constructed. It requires us to offer a characterization of the psychology and circumstances of the inhabitants of Erewhon that enables us to tell a story as to why they would develop ethical concepts that is not unrealistically rigged in favor of the development. The assumptions it makes should be realistic or, if not fully realistic, they should make it harder rather than easier to explain the emergence of morality; they should posit a worse-case rather than a better-case

---

22. If the two narratives identified the same set of properties as the referents of prescriptive terms, of course, that would increase the plausibility of those candidates; it would suggest that they were doubly salient both for the protagonists in the narrative and for us.

23. In the later exchange with Michael Tomasello, I consider and reject an alternative, presumably more parsimonious story, in which language is not necessary for morality.

scenario for its emergence. The assumptions governed by the constraint bear, first, on the psychological profile of protagonists in the story and, second, on their anthropological circumstances.

Interrogating the process condition: the psychology postulated

The psychological assumptions made in the narrative presented here depict the inhabitants of Erewhon as rational actors who, notwithstanding a degree of altruism, are disposed to try to avail themselves of any salient opportunities—including opportunities involving mutual reliance—for bettering their lot. The reason for relying on this rational, relatively self-regarding profile is that it offers a firm basis on which to predict the actions and adjustments of the protagonists fairly reliably.

But it may not seem realistic to postulate that the inhabitants of Erewhon are rational or that they are self-regarding. Or at least this may not seem realistic in view of the assumption that since they are psychologically like you and me, they must be susceptible to various failures of rationality, on the one side, and that they must be capable on the other of various forms of altruistic concern.

Taking up the rationality issue first, it is now common to observe that human beings like you and me fall short of full rationality in a variety of ways. Thus, for example, we rely on a battery of biases and heuristics that generally made evolutionary sense, at least in ancestral environments. And these lead to irrational responses in a range of familiar circumstances (Gilovich, Griffin and Kahneman 2002).

Despite this consideration, however, there are two features of the rationality on which the narrative relies that make it a realistic postulate. The rationality postulated is limited in degree, appearing mainly in the disposition of agents to prove reciprocally reliable to those on whom they themselves rely. And it is a sort of rationality that agents are required to display in recurrent situations, so that they will be in a position to confirm its benefits, time and time again.

The second reason to doubt the psychological profile ascribed to our protagonists is that human beings are not as self-regarding, by many accounts, as the narrative supposes. It is plausible, as Michael Tomasello (2016) argues, that as a result of their self-regarding needs, Mother Nature selected our forebears for the presence of proximate psychological mechanisms triggering mutual cooperation and reliance quite spontaneously; psychological studies of children show that such dispositions are in evidence even before the age of three. By this account, our ancestors would still have been moved, as we continue to be moved, by self-interested concerns for them and theirs. But they would plausibly have developed a natural disposition to be cooperative, making and living up to joint commitments of various kinds. And, presumably, they would have evolved a disposition to share culturally accumulating customs and skills, passing these on to their young (Sterelny 2012).

Assuming that this is right, it is clear that the self-regarding aspect of the psychological profile ascribed to the inhabitants of Erewhon, unlike its rational aspect, is not fully realistic. But this need not be a problem. For the ascription of a primarily self-regarding profile to our protagonists makes it harder rather than easier to explain why they should develop an ethical mindset. This aspect of their profile means that the world tracked in our narrative is a worse-case rather than a better-case scenario. And so, if a recognizable ethics could have emerged there, it would surely have emerged in the presence of a lesser degree of self-regard. What our nature would have generated in the dry wood of Erewhon, it is all the more likely to have generated in the green wood of our actual history.

The narrative developed later suggests that practices of avowal and pledging will put members of Erewhon within reach of ethics by forcing them to single out properties that are robustly attractive, enabling them to sustain the desires and intentions they avow and pledge. One effect of ascribing a rational, self-regarding psychology to those members—one effect of not presupposing natural, cooperative predispositions—is that it may put limits on the sorts of properties they are individually likely to treat as attractors or desiderata of this kind. If Tomasello is right, for example, they are less likely than our forebears to take a property like that of being helpful or cooperative to serve in itself as an individually attractive desideratum.[24]

But this difference does not put the current project in danger. The limitation on the psychology of members of Erewhon may affect the character of the ethics that evolves among them. But the fact that ethics would evolve among them may still throw light on its role and nature. Certainly, this will be so to the extent that we can recognize the moral terms and concepts they come to employ as expressively equivalent to counterparts in our own moral vocabulary and thought.

Interrogating the process condition: the circumstances postulated

These considerations should help to vindicate the psychological assumptions built into the narrative. But the requirement that the narrative should not rely on lucky flukes puts a constraint, not just on the psychology ascribed to members of Erewhon, but also on the circumstances postulated. As in the psychological case, the constraint requires that those circumstances should be realistic or, if not fully realistic, that they should not rig things in favor of the development of ethical concepts and practices.

In the story told here, Erewhon is an isolated society and a society in which members enjoy relatively equal power. The assumptions of isolation and equality facilitate the narrative in the same way as the assumption of a broadly rational, self-regarding mentality. There are many shapes that external relations might assume, only one that answers to isolation. And there are many forms in which inequality might appear, only one where there is equality. Assuming isolation and equality makes the project undertaken more readily feasible.

---

24. But, to anticipate chapter 5, even the members of Erewhon might valorize a corresponding desideratum—that of people being helpful and cooperative with one another—when thinking, as they are bound in part to do, from a common point of view.

But do the assumptions of isolation and equality rig the books unrealistically in favor of the appearance of ethics? Isolation is certainly not a problem. It is plausible that over long periods of our history, many communities of human beings lived in isolation from others, even in ignorance of the existence of other societies. And in any case the assumption of isolation does not make it easier in any obvious way to explain the emergence of ethics. It may even make it harder to do so, since contact with other societies might foreground the role of ethical standards and highlight the attraction of establishing them across communities.[25]

The assumption that the members of Erewhon enjoy relative equality of power raises a sharper challenge for the process condition than does the assumption that it is an isolated society. For this assumption does seem to make it easier to provide an explanation of ethics, or at least an explanation that does not debunk that which it explains.[26] But there are two things to say in response to the challenge.

The first is that the assumption of relative equality is not unrealistic to the point of positing a lucky fluke. For a high degree of equality appears to have prevailed in most of human history: specifically, in the one hundred thousand years or so prior to the agricultural revolution, which occurred less than ten thousand years ago (Boehm 1999; Boix and Rosenbluth 2014). But even if this claim is put in doubt, there is a second, more important point to make in defense of the assumption.

---

25. Consistently with the line taken in this study, it is possible for two societies to differ in the desiderata that get identified as robustly attractive enough to sustain avowed desires and intentions and, to anticipate, as candidates for making various scenarios desirable. But, assuming they regard one another as conversable, to anticipate an idea introduced later, the members of the different societies may work at achieving mutual understanding; may be able to see why they are moved on each side by the locally favored desiderata; and may come to see those differences, like the differences that may exist within their own ranks, as consistent with realism (Wiggins 1987). For a contrary point of view, see Harman (2000).

26. Beginning from a situation of inequality, Nietzsche (1997) explains the emergence of an egalitarian sort of morality, whereby the weak hold back the strong, but the explanation is debunking in the sense that it makes ethics look unappealing rather than appealing.

While the narrative developed here supposes a society in which all are equals across divisions like those of gender or class or ethnicity, it can serve the purpose for which we employ it under variations on that supposition that might be considered more realistic, if less appealing. I am thinking of the sort of variation in which women are subject to men, the weaker to the stronger, or those in a special enslaved category to a master class. If there is such a division, then the sub-society of the privileged is still likely to display a high degree of equality within it. And the narrative developed here for the inclusive society of Erewhon would be likely to work for such an elite, showing how they would develop ethical concepts—broadly, concepts expressively equivalent to ours—governing their treatment of one another.

How would the elite narrative serve the same purpose as the narrative for Erewhon? It would show that any relatively egalitarian society or sub-society would be likely, starting from something like our ground zero, to develop ethical concepts like ours and to evolve corresponding practices in dealing with one another. And that would support a naturalistic analysis and vindication of ethics, as envisaged here.

The narrative would do this, at any rate, to the extent that it did not essentially depend on the suppression of others outside the elite.[27] If it did essentially presuppose such suppression, then it would debunk morality as we think of it, representing it as a code appropriate only for a dominating elite. But if it did not essentially presuppose suppression, as presumably it need not, then it would present morality as a way of thinking and acting that can—and by our lights should—be extended to all. Or at least it would do this, on the assumption that the concepts employed are expressively equivalent, or more or less equivalent, to our ethical concepts.[28]

27. Assuming that it does not depend essentially on such suppression does not mean denying that suppression occurs: domination will certainly materialize there (Pettit 2014b), no doubt also hermeneutic injustice (Fricker 2007).

28. The set of concepts employed in an elite code that presupposed the suppression of others would be unlikely to count as expressively equivalent to our ethical concepts; and the associated, debunking story would be unlikely to count as a story about the emergence of ethics, as we conceive of ethics.

The characterization of the process condition in this discussion combines with the earlier characterization of the input condition to hold out the prospect of a persuasive narrative of development. If Erewhonians have defined, self-regarding purposes, live in isolation from other societies, and occupy positions of relatively equal power, then it is going to be feasible to think of charting the opportunities they are going to confront; to predict the responses they are likely to make to those opportunities; to see how those responses can aggregate to create further opportunities; to predict how they are likely to respond in turn to these; and thereby to trace a plausible trajectory of development. And that is precisely what a reconstructive analysis must seek to do, aiming to show that the trajectory charted is likely to culminate in the appearance of recognizably ethical concepts.

Three contrasting projects

By the account offered so far, the distinguishing mark of the ethical concepts of desirability and responsibility is that they are prescriptive. If the reconstructive analysis of ethical concepts is going to be successful, therefore, then it must explain the appearance of such concepts in the course of developments in Erewhon. And it must do so without presupposing the earlier presence of any ethical concepts—or, as we postulated, any prescriptive concepts at all.

This requirement implies that the reconstruction to be developed here should be distinguished from three more familiar forms of narrative. These are associated respectively with game theory, contract theory, and the sort of theory that presents ethics as prudence by another name.

The game-theoretical narrative is regularly invoked in computer simulations of the emergence of altruism, in psychological experiments that provide evidence of mutually beneficial adjustments among subjects, and in evolutionary explanations, natural or social, of the emergence of cooperation and altruism.[29] While these projects are often

---

29. For a seminal work on explaining the emergence of cooperation, which had an influence across a range of disciplines, see Axelrod (1984). And for work pursued

of great interest in themselves, none of them aspires to play the role expected here of a reconstruction of ethics, since they do not posit, let alone explain, the emergence of ethical concepts. They focus entirely on explaining the emergence of attitudinal or behavioral patterns and do not attempt to explain how ethical concepts could have emerged and exercised influence in the ordering of people's relationships. In the story told here, attitudinal and behavioral adjustments inevitably have an important place. But they figure in a narrative in which concepts co-evolve with the attitudes and behaviors postulated and interact with them in the maintenance of social life.

The need for a reconstruction to explain the appearance of ethical concepts de novo rules out, not only the game-theoretical alternative, but also the standard sort of contractual story. The narrative is supposed to show that despite not having access to ethical concepts or practices to begin with, the inhabitants of Erewhon would be more or less inevitably pushed toward introducing them. But this means that they cannot establish a use for those concepts on the basis of anything like a contract that is represented as a contract to establish a morality. For in order to form such a contract with one another they would already have to possess the concept of what it is they are contracting into. And that means that the story would not explain the emergence of ethical concepts de novo.

The idea to be defended in the reconstruction, then, is not that the members of Erewhon would have motives to enter a social contract with one another for establishing moral standards, as political theory has often invoked people's motives to explain their entering into a political contract. To anticipate again, the proposal rather is that those individuals would be moved to avow and pledge their attitudes, rather than reporting them, and that with avowal and pledging established as shared activities, they would be moved in turn to develop properly ethical concepts. The narrative has to document an unplanned process of more or less inevitable emergence, not a history of contractual agreement. It has to be scripted in the spirit of David Hume (1978, 3.2.2), when he relied

in a similar vein, see Pettit (1986; Pettit and Sugden (1989); Pettit (1990); Brennan and Pettit (2004).

on such a story to explain how we could have developed the concept and practice of promising and contract, on the one side, and ownership and property on the other.

The requirement of de novo explanation means, finally, that the reconstruction sought here cannot take the form of a story under which individuals each come to reason on prudential grounds—on grounds of their individual, long-term interest—that they should embrace ethical standards of desirability and responsibility: they should recognize, in a variation on a cliché, that morality is the best policy. Such a prudential story would presuppose the availability of ethical concepts; in order to argue that morality is the best policy, after all, you have to have the concept of morality. Hence this approach would fail in the same way as the contractual narrative.[30]

As characterized here, the contractual and prudential stories are stories as to how those who already have moral concepts available might mobilize conformity to moral requirements on a contractual or prudential basis. But might such stories not posit independently intelligible contractual or prudential adjustments—that is, adjustments that do not presuppose access to moral concepts—and argue that those concepts would appear in the wake of the adjustments? Yes, they might. But such alternative stories would be akin to stories of emergence of the kind envisaged here; they would not constitute real alternatives. The prudential story would differ at most in positing access to a prescriptive concept of self-interest; and the contractual story would diverge in positing a more demanding, collective form of agreement than that which is generally envisaged in the current narrative. They would each offer an alternative narrative of emergence, albeit ones of a less parsimonious character.

The role of reasoned, practical argument

The contractual and prudential theories suggest that the parties involved reason their way to a conclusion in favor of ethics. Even if we

---

30. A well-known approach that approximates this sort of narrative, although it also has elements of an emergence narrative, is provided by David Gauthier (1986).

reject those theories, that alerts us to a question that we should address in conclusion. The story represents the protagonists as identifying and exploiting various opportunities for advancing their ends, as we have seen. And so, the question is whether it can countenance the exercise of instrumental reasoning in the process of working out the best means to those ends. Does it allow that in making presumptively rational responses to the opportunities they face, the members of Erewhon may reason their way to conclusions about what to do? Does it allow this, in particular, from the initial stages of the narrative?

We know from earlier discussion what it means to reason theoretically, in accordance with modus ponens, that since it is the case that p and that if p, q, it must be the case that q. But what does it mean to reason practically, in accordance with instrumental rationality, that since the end is E, and X-ing is a way—perhaps the only way—of getting E, X-ing is the thing to do?

In theoretical reasoning, our protagonists do not merely form a belief in the premises and then, as a result of an unconscious, sub-personal mechanism, form a belief in the conclusion; they think of the truth of the premises in which they believe as forcing them to acknowledge the truth of the conclusion, and they form a belief in the conclusion under that perceived pressure. The practical reasoning required in the instrumental case must also involve more than an unconscious form of rational processing. It is not going to be enough that the presence of a desire for E together with a belief in the proposition that X-ing is a way to realize E unconsciously and automatically generates a desire or intention to X.

What happens in the case of reasoned, practical argument must parallel the sort of thing that marks off reasoned argument in the theoretical case. The protagonists presumably have to pay attention to the state of affairs that holds when, for example, they desire E and believe that X is a suitable means to that end; they have to see this as pressuring them to form the desire to X; and they have to respond by forming that desire. They have to form the desire in such a way that they can be represented as thinking something like: "so let me X," or "so X-ing is the thing to do."

Unlike the sketch of theoretical reasoning, however, this schematic account of practical reasoning communicates little or nothing about the state of affairs to which the protagonists are supposed to attend and respond in finding their way to action. What is the state of affairs that holds if they desire E and believe that X is a suitable means of realizing it? That state of affairs cannot involve E's being desirable, since by hypothesis the protagonists do not yet have access to any property of desirability. So, what are we to say? Are we to hold that they exploit the opportunities for advancing their ends solely on the basis of an unconscious, non-intentional form of rational processing?

This would not be an outlandish position to hold, since rational processing is all that agency strictly requires; it is all that decision theory assumes, for example, in characterizing rationality in general (Pettit 1991b). But short of ascribing prescriptive concepts to them, we can still imagine that the members of Erewhon may often conduct a conscious, intentional form of deliberation in exploiting the opportunities they detect and, in that sense, may reason their way to the conclusions on which they act.

Suppose that although they lack prescriptive concepts, the members of Erewhon still identify certain attractors or desiderata; this assumption will be supported in the course of our narrative. These are properties that tend to make any scenario attractive to them: that it would be fun, for example, or a source of food, or a way of protecting their family. The availability of concepts for such attractor properties would enable the protagonists in our story to conduct a sort of deliberation that answers broadly to the schematic notion of reasoning illustrated in the theoretical case. It would enable them to pay attention to the state of affairs that consists in E being fun and, X-ing being a way to realize E, to respond to that situation with an attitude formed in a way that might be expressed in the words: "so let me X."

With these points in place, we can think of the members of Erewhon, even at the start of our narrative, as relying often on reasoned argument, and not just on rational processing, in deciding what to do. They may not have access to prescriptive concepts of desirability, strictly speaking, but that does not rule out the possibility of practical reasoning of the simple kind illustrated and of the many variations it would presumably allow.

1.3 Reconstructive analysis illustrated

In order to make the idea of a reconstructive analysis more vivid and perhaps more acceptable, it may be useful in conclusion to show how it is used elsewhere. Perhaps the most familiar case of reconstructive analysis in roughly our sense is provided by the genealogy of money mentioned in the introduction. But there are also other prominent examples of the approach, including examples within philosophy itself.

The reconstructive analysis of money

The most familiar analogue to the project undertaken is the account of money that is standard in economics (Menger 1892). Where our project seeks a naturalistically intelligible story about the emergence of morality, this account looks for an individualistic story about the appearance of money. The account begins from a conjectural society in which members only conduct barter exchanges—by many accounts, no such society ever existed (Graeber 2011)—and uses that starting point to develop a reconstructive analysis of money in independently intelligible terms.

In the barter society imagined, which is an isolated, relatively egalitarian community like Erewhon, people are interested in exchanging various commodities or services but cannot easily find suitable partners. You want the dog that I can provide, but I do not need the service that you would give me in recompense. I want something that a third person can furnish, but that individual does not want my dog or anything else I can currently offer. People in such a society might improve things by writing IOUs in a suitable domain—for example, in the provision of puppies—but this would have similar, if looser limitations. So, what might relieve them of the problem they face?

The standard story is that at a certain point it is very likely that some commodity like gold or cigarettes or cattle would assume a special status, being recognized as a commodity that a great number of people apparently want. At that point, it would be in the interest of each to gain access to that special good or to IOUs issued by individuals or groups who could provide it. People could be sure of finding suppliers for the things they wanted if and only if they had enough of that good, or at least of reliable IOUs in that good. Even if the suppliers did not want it themselves, they would want it for the fact that they could trade it with customers who wanted it, or with customers who themselves had customers who wanted it, and so on.

With these developments, that good and the corresponding IOUs would come to play a distinctive role in the imagined society. And as we reflect on the role they would play, we readily conclude that this is a role played in our actual society by money, so that to say that something is money—to ascribe that property to it—is just to say that it plays the required role. The role is displayed in the part played by the preferred good, or IOUs in that good, as a medium of exchange, as a metric for putting prices on things and as a means of storing wealth.

As we identify further likely or possible developments in our reconstruction, we can bring out other roles that money might play as well, whether as a matter of definition or as a contingent fact. The government might accept the favored commodity in payment of taxes, for example, giving it the status of legal tender; the issuers of IOUs might be legally recognized as banks; the supply of IOUs might be controlled by a body—in our terms, a central bank—that guards against over-supply and under-supply; and these IOUs might come to be backed solely by their trading value, not by the guarantee that owners can cash them in for a corresponding commodity like gold.

This narrative demystifies the practice and concept of money in independent terms—in the terms of economic theory—as our projected narrative would demystify the appearance of ethics in naturalistic terms. It explains how a practice and a concept would emerge in the envisaged scenario that respond to broadly the same prompts and serve broadly the same purposes as our practice and concept of money. And it explains how this process of emergence would materialize in economically plausible circumstances via economically plausible steps, thereby making it likely that the property that is ascribed in the emerging concept, and presumptively the property ascribed in our counterpart concept, is grounded in economically intelligible properties. It is a bona fide property that belongs in common to coins, notes, checks, and all forms of credit.

A philosophical project

As reconstruction can serve in the analysis of money, so it can serve in analyses that are more characteristic of philosophy. There are a number of philosophical exercises in which we can see the method of reconstructive or genealogical analysis at work.

Think of the example mentioned in the introduction: Herbert Hart's (1961) account of how a spontaneous, social regime of primary rules would have required secondary rules for its maintenance and how this could have generated a recognizably legal form of practice and conceptualization. Think of Wilfrid Sellars's (1997) myth of Jones, according to which we could have developed concepts of mental experience and attitude, and begun to practice folk psychology, by seeking a theoretical explanation for our dispositions to make certain utterances and to take corresponding actions. Think of David Lewis's (1969) demonstration that as self-interested rational agents we could have coordinated with one another in familiar predicaments, and given rise to regularities of the kind that answer to the concept of a convention. Think of Saul Kripke's (1980) story about how we could have introduced names as causally linked tags for the things we name, without sharing any single view of the descriptive character of the things named (Jackson 2004). Think of Edward Craig's (1990) claim that we could have developed the concept of knowledge, and the practice of justifying claims to knowledge, out of an interest in determining who should count as good informants by criteria available to everyone in the community (Fricker 2010). Or think of Bernard Williams's (2002) explanation of how a community of mutual informants could have evolved norms of truth and truthfulness without relying on any prior sense of a truth-telling obligation.

All of these projects, like the narrative about money, identify certain activities or practices that would have pushed participants in a certain direction, would have naturally prompted a cascade of adjustments, and would consequently have provided an occasion for the introduction of certain terms or concepts. The activities that figure in our examples are those of overcoming difficulties in the application of spontaneous, social norms; seeking to explain one another's utterances; coordinating with one another in certain predicaments; finding tags by which to track particular items in conversation; identifying speakers who count as reliable informants; and testing for credibility in exchanges of information.

As in the narrative about money, people would have naturally made certain adjustments in pursuing these activities, would have been exposed as a consequence to corresponding patterns, and would have developed terms and concepts to mark their presence. In particular, they would have developed concepts that function like our familiar concepts of positive laws, mental states, social conventions, proper names, knowledge claims, and truth-related norms. And plausibly, the properties that those concepts are used to ascribe are good candidates for the properties our own concepts predicate.

Being developed on these lines, the projects serve to demystify the concepts they address. They propose respectively that the concepts developed within the narratives they tell—concepts that are taken to ascribe bona fide properties—correspond to our familiar concepts of positive laws, mental states, social conventions, proper names, titles to knowledge, and norms of truth and truthfulness: they respond to similar prompts and serve similar purposes. And they explain the emergence of those concepts in suitably unproblematic terms, thereby supporting the claim that the properties they ascribe—like the properties ascribed in our counterpart concepts—are grounded in unproblematic bases.

What counts as unproblematic varies from case to case, and so the reconstructions also vary in the claims supported. They hold respectively that there is nothing normatively mysterious about how we can appeal to positive laws in assessing and regulating behavior; nothing epistemically mysterious about how we can ascribe mental states to ourselves and one another; nothing individualistically unintelligible about our identifying and conforming to conventions; nothing surprising about our using proper names in common for items that we each are liable to describe in different, even conflicting terms; nothing about states of knowledge that makes them more puzzling than other states of mind; and nothing about our attachment to truth and truthfulness that requires an independent sense of the obligatory.

What these reconstructive stories seek to achieve in their respective domains, the story sketched here aims at achieving in the domain of ethics or morality. The idea is to demystify our ethical concepts naturalistically by explaining how corresponding concepts might have emerged in a naturalistically unproblematic way; and to provide a reason to think, therefore, that the properties ascribed by our concepts, like the properties ascribed by their counterparts in the story of emergence, are grounded in unproblematic, naturalistic properties.

Reconstructive analysis and creature-construction

Not only do we find practitioners of reconstructive analysis among contemporary philosophers, however; we also find defenders of an explicit methodology of philosophical analysis that is close in character to the reconstructive approach. This is the methodology that H.P. Grice (1975b) described as creature-construction. Foreshadowed by Jonathan Bennett (1964) in his study of rationality, it is often invoked in contemporary work. Michael Bratman (2014) applies it in analysis of shared agency, for example, and Peter Railton (2014) in analysis of belief.

To take an example close to the project here, Bratman uses the methodology to make sense of what it is that we human beings ascribe when we speak and think of ourselves—or indeed of others—as acting on a joint intention for the achievement of a shared goal. The goal may be that of dancing a tango together, taking a walk with some friends or cooperating with others to rescue a drowning child. Joint action of this kind may be thought to be problematic in individualistic terms, requiring a plural bearer for the joint intention. But Bratman explains in painstaking detail how individuals might actually come in purely individualistic steps to act on a joint intention and display joint action, with each person identifying the particular part required of them and each playing that part under a shared assumption that others will also play theirs.

This explanation can be taken to show that what we ascribe in postulating a joint action by a number of people may be just the same sort of property that might be realized in the case described individualistically. And it shows this without suggesting that in actual life people only cooperate with one another on the basis of the very exacting thought processes attributed to the participants in the individualistic story. When you and I tango together, for example, we may be incapable of identifying what we each do except in terms that presuppose the joint action; what we each do may be as opaque to us as what our right and left hands do in tying our shoelaces. But the explanation is nevertheless illuminating. For what explicit intentions do in generating the joint action in Bratman's model are presumably done in actual life—certainly in an example like that of tangoing—by more or less unconscious adjustments that take their place (Pettit 2017a).

The reconstructive method followed in this book differs in two ways from that of creature-construction. First of all, it looks back at a possible process of construction in the past rather than describing a possible process of construction that agents might follow in the present. And, second, the process that it looks back on is not an intentional process like the process imagined in creature-construction; rather it involves a series of adjustments among the relevant agents—in our case, a whole community—that accumulate to produce an unplanned and unforeseen effect. But these differences are not of deep significance. The methods of creature-construction and reconstructive analysis are alike in exploring a possible generative process in order to make sense of the nature of an actual phenomenon.

The goal of this book, then, is to pursue a familiar style of philosophical investigation, albeit in an area where it has not been much employed. In the following five, progressively longer chapters, we will try to tell a narrative about our imagined Erewhon that, despite being naturalistic in its starting point and in the successive steps it charts, generates an ethical community like that which you and I inhabit. This is a community, as we shall argue, where people think in terms of desirability and hold one another responsible for living up to desirable standards. When that narrative is complete, we can return in the final chapter to teasing out the philosophical lessons that it teaches about morality.

Chapter 2: Ground Zero

This chapter is meant to introduce the society of Erewhon at a point where members have access to natural language but use it only for exchanging basic information about their environment. The characterization of this starting point naturally falls into positive and negative parts. The positive looks at what has to be present in the beginning of the story presented here, exploring how members of Erewhon use natural language in the exchange of environmental information and looking then at the effects this use is likely to generate. The negative offers a sketch of some speech acts that are saliently absent at this point of the narrative, in particular the committal speech acts of avowing and pledging that will assume prominence in the third and fourth chapters.

Language and communication

The natural language that we in Erewhon use at this initial stage of development—at ground zero—is designed to achieve communication of a relatively sophisticated kind. In the normal case, such communication involves the intentional and manifest transmission of information, or what I as speaker take to be information. To rework one standard analysis of the main conditions, I use my words with the primary intention of conveying that information to an audience and with the secondary intention of achieving that result, at least in part, by making my primary intention salient (Sperber and Wilson 1986; Grice 1989).

Strictly, even these two intentions can be present without an act being communicative in the fullest sense associated with language. Consider a case in which I want you to refill my glass of wine, put the glass where you cannot help but notice that it is empty, and fully expect that you will realize that I want it filled and respond to my desire. Or consider a case illustrated beautifully in a poem of Coventry Patmore's (Quiller-Couch 1922, 1023).[1] The heroine mimics sleep in the hope that her lover will kiss her without her seeming, immodestly, to invite it. She is charged with immodesty by an imaginary interlocutor but has a ready, if ingenuous response:

> "I saw you take his kiss!"
> "Tis true."
> "O, modesty!"
> "Twas strictly kept:
> He thought me asleep; at least, I knew
> He thought I thought he thought I slept."

Do I communicate in the original case that I want a glass of wine? Does the heroine communicate that she wants a kiss? In both cases, arguably not. In the first example, I do not want it to be overt between us that I am seeking (yet) more wine; in the second, the heroine does not want it to be overt that she is seeking a kiss. Each of the agents wants to maintain a façade, in the one case of indifference to alcohol, in the other of sexual modesty. For the full communication associated with speech, I must not hide any of my intentions from you in this way: I must keep them overt, as it may be said (Neale 1992, 550; Moore 2017). It may even be that in full communication the intentions have to be manifest to both of us, being a matter of common awareness or common ground: each of us is in a position to be aware of the intentions, in a position to be aware that each is aware of them, and so on in the usual hierarchy.[2]

1. Cited in Blackburn (1984, 110). I reorganize the lines of the poem, in order to distinguish clearly between heroine and interlocutor.

2. The hierarchy need not be problematic, imposing the impossible requirement that everyone should have formed a positive view on the question that arises at each level: whether everyone is aware, is aware that everyone is aware, is aware that everyone is aware that everyone is aware, and so on. All that need be the case is that each is disposed for any question that may arise at any level—assuming the capacity to understand it—to provide a positive answer. Here and throughout I presuppose

These complexities need not be of further concern here, since the argument can go through under any of a range of accounts. But it is important to recognize that they are in place and that they put Erewhon on a par in that respect with familiar human communities. It is complexities of this kind that distinguish communication in human language, or so at least it seems, from the transmission of information by the signaling systems used among other species (Scott-Phillips 2015).

In this chapter, the story will first sketch the alignment and cooperation we are bound to achieve—the norms we are bound to generate—as speakers who communicate after this fashion in reporting on our common world and, by extension, our attitudes toward it. Then, in a second section, it will identify other modes of communicating our attitudes, involving avowals and pledges, that are absent at this stage. And then in a final section, it will look at reasons why avowing and pledging are not as hazardous as they may at first seem: why the availability of practical excuses, and exemptions, makes them feasible.

The narrative that begins here will continue in the third and fourth chapters, explaining why we will have the means, the motive, and the confidence to go beyond mere reports of attitude and commit ourselves in avowals and pledges, individual and shared. And then in the fifth and sixth chapters, it will show how the practices of avowal and pledging can make concepts like those of the morally desirable and responsible available to us and give them a role in the regulation of our conduct.

The narrative that begins in this chapter and continues to the end of chapter 6 will be presented from the viewpoint that I and you and others purportedly occupy as residents of Erewhon; in this narrative, then, 'we' will generally refer to us in this imagined role. Chapter 7, like chapter 1, will shift the viewpoint back from the narrative that we in Erewhon occupy to the viewpoint we all share in thinking about ethics. With the

the more or less standard account of common awareness or belief, usually associated with Lewis (1969), setting aside any issues about its proper articulation. I assume that whatever revisions may be required, they will not impact on the argument of the book. See Lederman (2018) for an overview of background issues.

reconstructive analysis in place, it will return to a consideration of what that analysis teaches about the moral world that we ourselves occupy.

2.1 On what is necessarily present

Beyond free-riding

The reconstruction of money begins with a purely barter society in which the members perform the most elementary form of in-kind trade, exchanging goods and services with one another. The reconstruction of ethics begins with a linguistic community in which members use language in an equally elementary role, exchanging information about their environment with one another. They exchange information about aspects of the shared world on which the speakers are presumptively more informed than the audience.

Thus, I may report to you, as you may report to me, that the berries on the hill are ripening. Or you may report to me, as I may report to you, that the weather up north is getting better. There is no problem about explaining why we should each be interested in this mutual exchange of information. If I know about the berries and you do not, then you will benefit from learning that they are ripening; this will direct you to a potential source of nutrition and pleasure. If you know about the weather up north and I do not, then I will benefit from hearing that it is improving; that will open up the opportunity for a journey that I might otherwise have thought impossible.

When we take one another's words at face value, believing what we are told, then we rely on one another for the information, or would-be information, that they convey. And that reliance will be personally beneficial and appealing for each of us insofar as the other is a reliable informant.

But while it is going to be attractive for each of us to be able to rely on the words of others, it need not always be attractive to provide information on which others can rely with benefit. The benefit I give you in telling you about the ripening berries comes at a cost to me, since

I could have had all the berries to myself had I said nothing or had I misinformed you: had I told you, for example, that they would not be ripe for another week or so.

Am I likely to be tempted in such a case to free-ride: to rely on the information you give me about the weather but to deny you information about the berries? I may be exposed to the temptation, but I am unlikely to succumb. We in Erewhon, like people everywhere, live our lives in continuing interaction with many of those with whom we have exchanges. And that means that I am unlikely to be disposed to misinform you about something like the berries. For if I misinform you about such a matter, you are unlikely to rely on my words on future occasions and you are unlikely to prove reliable in later interactions, or at least in any interactions in which telling the truth would impose a cost on you. Thus, if I misinform you about the berries, I run the risk of suffering various costs. I am likely to lose the ability to rely on you when I need some information you can provide and, equally, I am likely to lose the ability to get you to rely on me when it is in my interest that you do so.

This is going to be so, at any rate, under certain assumptions about the situation that are likely to be generally satisfied. They include the specific assumptions, first, that in most informational exchanges, as in the one described, the benefits of deception are not important enough to outweigh the costs of being seen to misinform you; and, second, that there is no way of keeping you in the dark, say by equivocation or a pretense of ignorance, that allows me to escape those costs. Equally, they include the more general assumption that the society is small enough, and that I am recognizable enough, to make it impossible for me in most cases to dodge detection if I do misinform you.

The focus in the discussion that follows will be on those cases in which there is no easy way for a deceiver to avoid detection, the expected costs of detection are high in relation to the benefits of deception, and there is no easy way of keeping you in the dark without deceiving you. By assumption, such cases are statistically normal in Erewhon.

As it will be unattractively costly for me to prove unreliable in dealing with others in such exchanges, so it will be unattractively costly for you, or indeed for anyone else in Erewhon; it will reduce your ability to rely on others and to get them to rely on you. Thus, it will be a profitable strategy for each of us to make a habit of proving to be informative and reliable reporters. We may seek to get away with lying occasionally, even in normal cases, but it will generally make most sense to prove reliable.

This lesson is reinforced by a further consideration. Suppose I lie to you about the berries. Not only will I be exposed to the possibility of being unable on future occasions to rely on you or to get you to rely on me; I will also be exposed to the possibility that you will spread the word about my unreliability. It will be in your interest to tell others about my failure, after all, since that information will help you to prove yourself reliable to them. And for parallel reasons it will be in the interest of each of them to pass on the word to their interlocutors. Thus, it may even become a matter of common awareness in the relevant circles that I misled you.

In dealing both with you and with others, then, most acts of deception are liable to trigger a serious reputational setback, leading to my being cast as someone with whom it is hazardous to do business. The prospect of such reputational costs is going to be salient for any one of us in Erewhon, and the desire for reputation is likely to dispose each of us to be speakers whom others can depend upon to tell the truth.

Assuming that I lie occasionally, and only occasionally, may I expect to benefit reputationally from any instances in which I tell the truth? Not in general; and not, in particular, when word gets around about my failures. My performance will tend to generate a general reputation that attaches to me as a person, for two distinct reasons.

One is that it would be unnecessarily difficult for others to record and remember how I behaved, now in this circumstance, now in that, now with this interlocutor, now with another; and unnecessarily difficult for others to form situation-specific expectations about how I am likely to deal with them in particular, or with them in a new context. It will be much easier for them to give me a general label as a person, attributing a general disposition to tell the truth reliably or a general disposition of indifference toward the truth.

The second reason for this reputational focus on the person goes back to "a candidate for the most robust and repeatable finding in social psychology," as E.E. Jones (1990, 138) describes it. This, known as the fundamental attribution bias, is "the tendency to see behavior as caused by a stable personal disposition of the actor when it can be just as easily explained as a natural response to more than adequate situational pressure." The presence of that bias in human beings means that if I ever tell lies in Erewhon, then I am in danger of being dubbed a liar; and that I must reliably tell the truth, if I am to be treated as a habitual truth-teller. In the first case, my behavior will be explained by an imputed indifference to the truth, in the second by an imputed disposition to tell the truth reliably.[3]

The fact that reputation focuses on people across different situations, and not on situation-specific performances, is going to raise the reputational stakes enormously. Since this focus is bound to be a matter of common awareness, it means that I or you or anyone else in Erewhon will face serious costs of a kind that it is hard to undo, assuming detection and publicity, if we fail to tell the truth to others. It means that we will live within an economy of esteem, where our truth-telling status in the eyes of the community is on the line in almost every informational exchange (Brennan and Pettit 2004).[4]

---

3. The finding that people are deeply prone to the fundamental attribution bias means that, even when they are conscious of their own sensitivity to reputational considerations (Miller and Prentice 1996, 804), people will be loath to trace the behavior of others to such a situational pressure.

4. The pattern envisaged here is somewhat different, then, from the pattern of tit for tat characterized and illustrated by Robert Axelrod (1984). Under tit for tat, we will each be disposed to tell the truth to anyone we are dealing with for the first time and to treat anyone else as they treated us in the immediately preceding interaction. If I and you each tit for tat, the upshot will be that we each speak the truth to one another on first encounter and, absent a failure on either side, continue to do so in all future encounters. The esteem-based mechanism is consistent with such tit-for-tat effects but not reducible to them. Generalizing tit for tat beyond two-party interactions brings it closer to the economy of esteem, but has problems of its own: see Pettit (1986).

The norm of truth-telling

If we are to be reliable informants and win out reputationally in Erewhon, then we must prove ourselves reliable in two distinct respects. First, we must be careful in processing information about any issue on which others query us: we must consider all the relevant data and take them properly into account. This is going to be attractive for us independently, in any case, since our own welfare will often depend on getting things right. Second, we must transmit that information truthfully or sincerely to our audience, communicating that things are as we find them to be. Putting these requirements together, the lesson is that we will generally be motivated to be competent or careful observers on the one side and sincere or truthful speakers on the other.

To the extent that in normal cases we each generally manage to prove reliable on these two fronts, truth-telling will become a general pattern or regularity in Erewhon. It will emerge as a result, now in this case, now in that, of our being careful about processing any information sought and truthful about transmitting it. But it may become a general pattern of that kind without our noticing that it is a feature of our society. It may emerge, without our being aware of it, behind our backs. It may be an unforeseen, aggregate consequence of how we are each disposed to behave in our individual exchanges.

Under the story told, there is also another general pattern or regularity that will characterize our society. Other things being equal, we will each be aware in any interaction that by proving reliable and telling the truth, we can win a favorable reputation with our audience and with anyone who learns of our performance. We will each expect, case by case, that by telling the truth we can win the good opinion—or at least, avoid the bad opinion—of those who are directly or indirectly involved.

Thus, there will be a regularity of attitude established in the society— a pattern in our expectations—that goes along with the behavioral regularity of telling the truth. As in the behavioral case, this regularity may also escape our notice in Erewhon. No matter how resiliently established, it may be an aggregate consequence of our individual responses that we do not register as a social fact.

Apart from these behavioral and attitudinal regularities, there is also a third sort of regularity—if you like, an explanatory regularity—that is likely to materialize among us. Not only will I and you and others be each generally disposed to tell the truth in making reports to others, and not only will we be each disposed to expect a reputational payoff from truth-telling. It is also likely to be the case that our disposition to tell the truth will be reinforced, now on this occasion, now on that, by that expectation: it will be boosted by the recognition that it may be reputationally hazardous, now in this exchange, now in that, to mislead our interlocutor. And this may be the case on more or less every occasion, of course, without our registering that it holds as a matter of general regularity; as in the other cases, the regularity may escape our notice.

There are different ways, it should be noted, in which my expectation of reputational rewards may support my telling the truth. It may be a sufficient motive for telling the truth, even the only motive that weighs with me. It may be a motive that supplements a distinct motive to tell the truth, where only the complex of incentives is sufficient to support truth-telling. Or it may play yet a third role if I already have a sufficient motive for telling the truth, and do so as a matter of habit or virtue. In this case, the interest in reputation or esteem can serve to reinforce the independent disposition to tell the truth, being there to keep me on the truth-telling track should that motive or habit fail; in a word, it may serve as a backup to counter the possibility of failure.

The observations made about the general pattern of truth-telling displayed in statistically normal informational exchanges can be summed up in three clauses.

- Almost everyone in the community conforms to the regularity of telling the truth, at least when dealing with those who have not proved deceptive in the past.
- Almost everyone expects such conformity to attract a favorable reputation among others and/or nonconformity to attract an unfavorable reputation.

- Almost everyone is supported in their conformity to the truth-telling regularity by the expectation of such reputational benefits and costs.

The sort of regularity that truth-telling exemplifies is not a mere convention, such as driving on the right- or left-hand side of the road (Lewis 1969). Such a convention, unlike the regularity of truth-telling, is grounded in the attraction for each of us of doing the same thing as others. Thus, the convention does not give rise to free-riding problems of the kind that truth-telling occasions. You will not be tempted in approaching another car to break convention, drive on the same lane, and risk a head-on collision. But absent reputational costs you may be tempted to tell me a lie while relying on me to tell the truth; if you think detection is unlikely, you may well try to deceive me (Ullmann-Margalit 1977).

The three conditions it satisfies mean that the truth-telling pattern is distinct, not just from mere conventions, but also from a number of other social regularities. That it is generally maintained in people's practice, as the first condition stipulates, distinguishes it from a standard honored more in the breach than in the observance, such as a supererogatory ideal that we routinely applaud but rarely realize. That it reflects the mutually expected attitudes of inhabitants toward conformity, as the second condition holds, means that it is distinct from a regularity to which others are manifestly indifferent, such as the regularity whereby most people sleep at night, not during the day. And that it is supported by that expectation, as in the third condition, means that it is distinct from a regularity such as taking steps to guard against penury in old age; it is unlikely that people are motivated in any degree by expecting that others will think well of them for displaying such prudence.

Unlike a convention, then, the truth-telling regularity in Erewhon is not supported just by the wish to do the same as others. And unlike the remaining rivals, it is a pattern that is generally realized in the practice of the society, implicated in the prevailing attitudes of members, and supported, case after case, by the expectation of satisfying those attitudes.

A pre-social norm

This sort of regularity is often described as a norm, albeit with varia-tion in how exactly the conditions are understood. It attracts general conformity among the population and does so insofar as it is supported by the expectation of their having positive attitudes to conformity, and negative attitudes to non-conformity.

As there is almost certain to be a norm of truth-telling in Erewhon, so there is equal reason to expect that there will be similar norms against violence, fraud and other failures of reciprocal beneficence. The mani-fest interest of members in the reliability of others, and the attraction for others of satisfying that interest, explains why there is likely to be a norm of truth-telling. And the manifest interest of members in the beneficial reciprocity of others, and the attraction for others of satis-fying that interest, explains why norms of these distinct sorts are likely to materialize as well. Those other norms will not figure explicitly in the narrative that now follows, but they will figure at a later point as examples of what we in Erewhon, having developed moral concepts, are likely to take as desirable patterns.

A norm in the sense elaborated so far does not constitute a criterion that guides us in our choices: a pattern that we intentionally track. It does not constitute a rule in the sense of being a criterion "consulted by those whose behavior is being assessed" (Brandom 1994, 64). For all the narrative supposes, we may not even be aware of the norm that we bring into existence, let alone take it as a pattern to try to realize in our behavior. For this reason, the sort of norm involved may be described as pre-social only; more in a moment on what may give it the status of a rule to consult, transforming it into a social norm.

It makes sense to say that we inhabitants of Erewhon regulate or police one another into conforming to a pre-social norm like telling the truth. But it is important to realize that this need only be an un-conscious and unintentional mode of regulation. It may exist solely by virtue of the fact, on the one side, that we each look to how reliable any interlocutor is, letting our experience dictate how we treat the person in future and how we testify about them to third parties; and, on the other, that in most cases we each seek to prove reliable as interlocutors ourselves, seeing this as the price to be paid for favorable treatment and testimony by others.

As it makes sense to speak of mutual regulation for truth-telling in the Erewhon characterized so far, so it also makes sense to say that we, the members of the society, cooperate with one another in generally telling the truth. But just as mutual regulation of the kind envisaged may be unconscious and unintentional, so the same is true of the co-operation we can be said to practice. The reason is that under the psychology postulated, each of us may think of what we do in telling the truth merely as a means to gaining or preserving a personal, reputational benefit, not as a means of realizing an aggregate end that is to everyone's advantage. While we align our behavior with one another in telling the truth, we each act for our own ends; we do not necessarily act out of a shared or cooperative intention to play our part in securing a social goal.

These points are meant to emphasize the fact that the truth-telling society of Erewhon, as it has been established so far in the narrative, is very simple. The cooperative patterns into which we members regulate one another do not require an awareness of the regularities or an intention to conform to them. They emerge by a reputational motor whose effects—benign effects, in the case of a norm like truth-telling—are not necessarily visible to us; they appear, in Adam Smith's famous phrase, as by an invisible hand.

A social norm

But is a pattern like general truth-telling likely to remain unnoticed in Erewhon? And is it likely to remain incapable, therefore, of guiding us in the manner of a rule? Or is it going to achieve that recognition and attain that role only at a point, which comes much later in the narrative, where we in Erewhon gain access to ethical concepts?

There is reason to think that the pattern will become visible to all before we develop such concepts, and indeed that it will become visible to all as a matter of common awareness, so that everyone is aware of the visibility, everyone is aware that everyone is aware of it, and so on. The reason to think that this is plausible is, first, that the evidence of the regularity in truth-telling is going to be available to all, thereby making it visible; second, that it is also going to be evident to all that this evidence is universally available, thereby making it visibly visible; and third, that as that is true in the relation between the first and second level, so by an inductive step it is going to hold in the relation between the second and third, between the third and fourth, and so on (Lewis 1969).

Assuming a degree of perspicacity on the part of members, then—and a tendency for perspicacious observations to spread—it is plausible that at some point members will come to share in a common awareness of the truth-telling regularity they sustain. And the same will hold, presumably, for any similar norm against violence or fraud or whatever. [5]

This inductive argument for common awareness of the behavioral regularity involved in the norm of truth-telling, or any similar norm, applies also to the other regularities involved: to the attitudinal regularity according to which everyone expects a reputational sanction for how they behave and to the explanatory regularity according to which this expectation supports conformity in everyone's case. This means that in all likelihood any norm like that of truth-telling will satisfy a fourth condition over and beyond the three already listed:

- Almost everyone believes, as a matter of common awareness, that the first three conditions are satisfied.

If truth-telling satisfies this common-awareness condition, thereby assuming the status of a manifest norm, then sooner or later, that is likely to trigger a certain chain of consequences. And those consequences, which we proceed to review, will make it into a social norm, proper—that is, a norm that can serve for us as a guiding rule.

---

5. As noted previously, I presuppose the more or less standard view of common belief throughout this book and, as the text indicates, I also presuppose a more or less standard view of when common belief is likely to emerge. Whatever amendments are required in a more exact account of common belief and its emergence, they are unlikely to impact on the overall argument. For background, see Lederman (2018).

Manifestly, any member of the society can see the norm, once it is recognized in common awareness, as a pattern such that their full acceptance within the society depends on conforming to it. Manifestly, any member can then communicate that observation to any outsider seeking entrance, to any child at the point of social induction, or indeed to any erstwhile or would-be offender, themselves included. And so, manifestly, the norm of truth-telling—and, by extension, any similar norms like those against violence or fraud—can present as a rule of behavior that each must take as a guide, if they wish to belong properly to the community; indeed, it can present as a norm that we each have an interest in encouraging others to accept and abide by.

When norms of truth-telling, non-violence, non-fraudulence or whatever get established in this way as rules, they count as properly social norms. While they may continue, at bottom, to depend for their maintenance on the engine or motor of reputational pressure, conformity to those norms can now appeal on a new count: that the norms direct us to paths we must follow if we are to remain in good standing within the society. While continuing to rely on reputational pressures for motivational support, the norms can also appeal on this social basis.[6]

With this development, the regulation and cooperation that we in Erewhon exercise over one another in eliciting truth-telling or any

6. For an earlier version of this conception of a social norm, see Pettit (1990) and Brennan and Pettit (2004); the current version appears in Pettit (2008b, 2015c). It is more fully elaborated in Pettit 2019b. This notion of a social norm picks up points made in a variety of approaches. See for example Hart (1961); Winch (1963); Coleman (1990; Sober and Wilson (1998; Elster (1999); Shapiro (2011). For an insightful development of the idea of reputationally supported norms, see Appiah (2010). And for an overarching theory that is reconcilable with that adopted here, although it uses terminology somewhat differently, see Brennan, Eriksson, Goodin and Southwood (2013). Notice that a convention in Lewis's sense may also count as a norm, satisfying the four conditions given, although it need not do so; the conditions that make it a convention do not suffice in themselves to make it a social norm in our sense.

similar pattern will no longer be as blind as it would have been prior to the realization of the fourth, common-awareness condition. But it will still not be a form of prescriptive, let alone moral regulation, for it will not depend on the employment of any concept of desirability. We may treat the social norms of our society as appealing without having any sense of them as desirable norms. Indeed, for all that has been said, we may not even have any idea of what it might be for something to count as desirable. The norms may identify a social payoff for conformity, without giving us a prescriptive attitude towards them.

2.2 On what is saliently absent

Beyond self-reports

To the extent that we are anxious to prove ourselves reliable to others, we must have an interest not just in reliably conveying how things are in our shared environment, but also in reliably conveying that we are reliable speakers. We must want to convey, for example, that we form beliefs as the data and only the data require, that we desire or intend to communicate how things are according to those beliefs, and more generally that we have only desires and intentions of a kind that would make us congenial parties in interaction.

How can we convey this information? How can we communicate about ourselves rather than our surroundings: about our internal psychology rather than our external environment? We can certainly make reports on ourselves in the way in which we make reports on the world around us. But are there any other ways in which we might communicate to others the shape of our personal dispositions, thereby reassuring them about our credentials as parties with whom they can do business?

On the face of it, there are two salient possibilities. In terms of art, which will be explained shortly, these are: on the one hand that we might *avow* some attitudes rather than reporting them; and on the other that we might *pledge* certain attitudes rather than avowing or reporting them. These possibilities become visible, as we shall see, in light of ways in which they vary two striking features of mere reports.[7]

In setting up the contrast between avowing or pledging an attitude on the one side and merely reporting it on the other, there is no suggestion that we are likely in Erewhon to go through a temporal stage at which the established practice is to report on our attitudes to one another without any avowal or pledge. Consistently with the points to be made here, and with the narrative developed in coming chapters, avowing and pledging attitudes may come more naturally to us than reporting them. The point of the contrast is to mark the distinguishing features of avowals and pledges and, as will appear in the next chapter, to show that those features can make it appealing to opt for an avowal and a pledge where a report would have been at least an abstractly possible and acceptable alternative.

Two features of reports

In order to be a reliable reporter on the environment, speaking the truth about how things are, I must process information reliably and I must transmit information reliably. But it will be obvious to those of us in Erewhon, as it will be obvious to any creatures of the human ilk, that I may falter in either of these exercises, while still remaining someone on whom you can generally rely as an interlocutor.

Putting aside practical problems in transmitting information—more on these later—there are two salient epistemic problems that may affect the processing of information. These epistemic problems would explain my failure to tell you the truth but do so in a manner that argues against your keeping me at a distance, refusing to rely on me. If they are accepted as explanations of my failure on a specific occasion, they will save my general reputation as a reliable truth-teller.

The first sort of problem that might serve in this role involves misleading evidence. It will be obvious to all of us in Erewhon, as it will be

---

7. For an independent style of argument in favor of the role of such initiatives in social life, see Zawidzki (2013, Ch 7).

obvious in any human society, that the evidence on which I or anyone else relies in forming and reporting a belief may be misleading. I may have been quite sure that the berries on the hill were ripening. But still I may have been misled. For it may have been that I only had the chance to see them late in the day. And the berries may have looked red and luscious in the fading sunlight, when earlier observation would have shown that they were still relatively green.

In this first type of problem, my words fail to match the world as it was at the time I observed it: my report about the ripening berries did not fit the actual facts. In a second type of failure, my words may have matched the world at the time of the observation but they convey the message that it continued that way afterward when, as a matter of fact, it didn't. In this failure, the world fails to stay matched to those words: the facts observed and reported cease to obtain. Thus, it may be in the case of the berries that a third party went and picked the ripe berries before you made your way to the hill and judged my report inaccurate. The world I observed did not mislead me but it changed or altered between the time of my observation and the time of your acting on my report of that observation.

Under standard psychological assumptions, which we in Erewhon may be expected to endorse, my failure to tell the truth about the berries in either of these cases is due to a factor over which I had no control. It was not because of having been careless in processing information—or, presumptively, in transmitting it—that the report I gave you about the berries turned out to be false. Rather it was due to the world having let me down. In the first case, the world presented itself in a misleading manner. In the second, it changed between the time of the observation that led to my report and the time when you acted on that report.[8]

These observations show that even while we in Erewhon sustain a social norm of truth-telling, reliably communicating about how things

---

8. The focus here is entirely on empirically elusive, logically contingent claims. Suitable adjustments will be needed for reports on self-evident or necessary truths. See the short discussion in the last section of chapter 3 of framework beliefs.

are in our environment, we may see good reason not to impose the usual reputational costs on a speaker who fails to tell the truth. We will suspend those costs, and continue to treat the speaker as reliable, when there is a plausible misleading-reality or changed-reality explanation for the failure. It would not make strategic sense for us to take any other line, since doing so would close down lots of opportunities for profitable, future exchanges; it would eject people unnecessarily from the network of mutual reliance.

From epistemic excuses to avowals and pledges

This being so, it should be clear that when I prove to have made a mis-report, I will be happy if I can explain my failure in one of these ways. If you accept the explanation that I offer, or that someone else offers on my behalf, then you will have every reason from your own point of view to overlook the failure and to continue to relate to me as someone who can generally be depended upon to speak the truth. The explanation will let me off the reputational hook and keep our relationship as mutually reliable and reliant speakers in place.

In letting me off the hook in this way, the two explanations count as excuses for my not having told the truth. They are epistemic excuses insofar as they cite problems in the processing of information rather than problems in its transmission: problems that thwart my best efforts to be careful in recording how things are rather than my truthfulness in conveying how I take them to be. As will appear later, other sorts of excuses cite practical problems in the transmission of information to the same reputation-saving effect.

While such epistemic and practical problems may let me off the rep-utational hook, counting functionally as excuses, they are not excuses that presuppose ethical or moral ideas. They presuppose the social norm of truth-telling, and the reputational discipline that keeps that norm in existence among us. And we may naturally grade them for their explan-atory potential in a way that presupposes a sense of the epistemically plausible. But they do not require that we in Erewhon recognize truth-telling as desirable or that we hold one another morally responsible for telling the truth. If they did, they could not figure at this point in the narrative. [9]

Either of the two epistemic problems envisaged in the example with the berries would provide a full explanation of my misreport, not just a partial one, and let me entirely off the reputational hook. It is possible to imagine other problems that would go only some way toward explaining that departure from truth-telling, however, and go only some way toward letting me off the hook. These might be cast as partial rather than full excuses. In this narrative, the category of excuses—practical as well as epistemic excuses—will be limited to full excuses alone. This will make the story much simpler than it might have been. And yet it should not damage the purpose that the narrative is meant to serve; it will be clear as things proceed that room can easily be made for introducing partial as well as full excuses.

Not only does the narrative focus only on full excuses; it also focuses only on excuses of a purely synchronic character. My being intoxicated may well provide a synchronic, misleading-world excuse for having misread and misreported the ripeness of the berries on a given occasion. But it may not let me off the hook over time. It may be clear that I should be treated as an unreliable processor of information by virtue of the fact that, prior to the observation, I was careless about maintaining my information-processing capacity: I let myself get drunk. This shows that a synchronic excuse will let me off the hook only if it is also satisfactory on the diachronic front: only if it is not undermined by a past performance for which there was no synchronic excuse at the time.

Simplicity argues for keeping this complication out of the narrative, however, and for treating synchronic excuses as the only relevant category; and it argues for this line with practical as well as epistemic excuses. Like the focus on full excuses alone, this simplification need not compromise the purpose of the narrative. It ought to be clear in this

9. For an excellent account of the nature and role of excuses in moral thinking generally, see Kelly (2013).

case too that room can always be made for acknowledging that excuses impose diachronic as well as synchronic requirements.

This account of the epistemic ways in which a misreport can be excused directs us to the two modes of communicating things that count as avowals and pledges. These voluntarily and manifestly foreclose appeal to epistemic excuses in communicating that something is the case. To communicate that something is the case—say, that you hold a certain attitude—while foreclosing appeal to the misleading-reality excuse counts as avowing that that is the case; to communicate that it is the case while foreclosing appeal to both the misleading-reality and the changed-reality excuse counts as pledging that it is the case.

It is a particularly strong requirement on avowal and pledging that they have to be voluntary. I do something voluntarily only if I do it intentionally: that is, roughly, as a means of satisfying my desires according to my beliefs. I may do something intentionally, however, without doing it voluntarily; think of what I do in handing over my money to the mugger. In order to do something voluntarily, it must be that as I saw things—rightly or wrongly— there were alternatives to the intentional action that promised to be broadly acceptable.[10] In requiring that avowal and pledging be voluntary, the idea is that the speaker chooses without pressure to foreclose the misleading-reality and the changed-reality excuses that reporting would leave in place.

10. This account is modeled on that in (Olsaretti 2004), although there are differences between us; one is that on that assumed here, it is possible to do something involuntarily but willingly: that is, roughly, with relish. What makes an alternative broadly acceptable? Perhaps, anticipating ideas not yet introduced in Erewhon, that in a suitable context I could be held responsible for not taking it; the alternative does not hurt or offend or challenge me—it does not involve such a cost or such a difficulty—that I cannot be blamed for avoiding it. Why assume that the alternative need only be an apparent option? Because, to turn to a sort of case made famous by Harry Frankfurt (1988)—for more discussion, see chapter 6, section 1—I may voluntarily do X when, unbeknown to me, a third party would have stopped me from taking the alternative option, Y; in such cases doing Y is merely an apparent option.

Self-access and the salient absence of avowal

The fact that any misreport can be excused after the event by appeal to the misleading character of the relevant domain is bound to be a matter of common awareness: something of which we are each conscious, each conscious that each is conscious, and so on. But that means that in making a regular report in Erewhon, I will do so in a way that manifestly keeps open the possibility of appealing to a misleading reality in excusing a misreport: a misleading world in the case of a misreport about independent facts, a misleading mind in the case of a misreport about my own attitudes. Any such report will embody caution, providing me with possible safeguards against proving to have told an untruth and being consequently ejected from the ranks of those reputed to be reliable.

A reporter's caution is well placed when I communicate about our shared world, or about the world of another's mind, for that reality is an elusive domain about which it is manifestly easy for me to be misled. But things are intuitively different when it comes to communicating about my own mind. There is a long tradition of thinking that I have much more intimate access to my mind than I have to the external world. And if that access is secure enough with a given attitude, so it would seem, then I ought to be able to communicate about that attitude without the same caution: without keeping open the possibility, in the event of a miscommunication, of claiming to have been misled about the attitude conveyed. In our term of art, I ought to be able to avow the attitude rather than just report it.

The intimacy of my contact with myself, so the idea goes, would enable me to communicate that I have the attitude—say, a belief or desire or intention—while making it manifest that should I prove later to have misspoken, I will not seek to get off the reputational hook by appeal to having been misled about my mind. In making an avowal, in this sense, I will not present myself as a mere reporter on my mind—that is, as someone who could later excuse a misreport by saying that appearances were deceptive. Rather I will present myself as being in a position to speak about my attitudes without any possibility—certainly without any real-world possibility—of being mistaken.

Avowing an attitude is a speech act that would voluntarily and manifestly set aside a reporter's caution. It would foreclose the possibility of appealing to the misleading character of my mind in excusing a failure to display the attitude that I communicate. It would reflect a special degree of confidence in the self-ascription of the attitude: an assumption that in speaking about it I enjoy the authority of a privileged spokesperson.[11]

Self-control and the salient absence of pledging

There is no avowal of attitude in Erewhon, as the society has been characterized so far. And neither is there any pledging. The idea of pledging an attitude—say, pledging an intention—mirrors the idea of making a pledge, absent unforeseeable obstacles, to behave in a certain manner; it amounts to making a pledge to behave in a way that reflects the presence of that attitude. Where avowing an attitude would voluntarily and manifestly foreclose the possibility of appealing to a misleading-mind in excusing a miscommunication, pledging an attitude would go one better. It would voluntarily and manifestly foreclose the possibility of appealing to any epistemic excuse, whether of the misleading-mind or changed-mind variety.

The notion of making a pledge to behave in a certain manner is close to that of promising to act in that way. But the pledging of attitude envisaged here does not involve promising in a moral or ethical sense of the term. In that sense, to promise would be to engage or create a moral obligation, other things being equal, not to break the promise. In the sense in which pledging is introduced here, it need have no such connotation. As avowing would foreclose the possibility of getting off the reputational hook by appeal to having been misled about my mind, pledging would also foreclose the possibility of getting off the reputational hook by appeal to having had a change of mind. The crucial point to notice in each case is that the hook in

11. For an extended, broadly congenial, account of avowals in more or less this sense, see Bar-on (2004).

question is reputational in character, and does not involve any idea of moral or ethical censure.

It is understandable that I might claim to know my mind sufficiently well to be able to avow an attitude—this, because of the assumption of self-access—without being sure enough about likely changes of mind to be able to pledge it. Thus, I might claim to know enough about my intention—say, an intention to join you on a hunt—to be able to support an avowal, and yet not know enough about how my plans are likely to change to be able to make a pledge. I might feel that I could assure you of the intention, being quite certain of its existence, without feeling able to make a pledge to go to the event, thereby guaranteeing to continue to have the intention.

Why might the idea of pledging an attitude make any sense, then? And why might its absence from Erewhon be salient? The reason is that by long tradition I not only have better access to my own mind than to the shared world; I also have control over my own mind of a kind that I do not have over our shared world. Assuming that I have special control over some of my attitudes—say, my intentions—as well as special access to those attitudes, it makes sense to think that I might be able to set aside both of the epistemic excuses that reporting the attitudes would keep in place. In the presence of such access and such control, the idea is that I could foreclose the possibility of excusing a miscommunication about an attitude like an intention in either of the two ways that reporting would leave open: by claiming that my mind had been misleading or by claiming that I had changed my mind.

If I avowed an intention to join you on a hunt, as in an earlier example, then I could try to excuse my failing to turn up, and my disappointing you, by the claim that I changed my mind. All that would be precluded is an attempt to explain and excuse the failure by claiming to have been misled about my own mind. But if I pledged the intention, assuring you in that extra manner that I would turn up, then I could not invoke that excuse either. I would have foreclosed both the misleading-mind and the changed-mind excuse and would have claimed to speak authoritatively for myself, not just on the basis of a special form self-access but on the basis of a special self-control as well.

2.3 Excuses and exemptions

Are avowing and pledging feasible?

Avowing and pledging are two sorts of speech act that, by the account presented so far, are saliently absent from Erewhon. We members of Erewhon use language only in the most basic way imaginable as a means whereby to make reports to one another about the world and perhaps even about our own minds. We do not avail ourselves of the communicative options—specifically, options in communicating our attitudes—that would appear to be open as a result of our special access to our own minds and our special control over them.

But let it be granted in principle that we in Erewhon might make avowals or pledges of attitude, despite our not actually doing so—that our self-access and self-control should make this possible. There is still a question as to whether avowals and pledges would represent feasible options for us to take. Would it not be prohibitively risky for me, or for any one of us, to set aside excuses in the manner that they require? Would it not be utterly rash to try to meet their requirements, reducing my ability to explain a miscommunication in a face-saving manner—that is, in a way that would preserve my reputation as a reliable interlocutor?

Various considerations that are relevant to this issue will come up in the next chapter. But for now, it is important to emphasize that the risk apparently associated with avowing and pledging is not as great as it may seem. For even if I foreclose appeal to one or both of the epistemic problems that might save my reputation in the event of misspeaking, I may still be able to appeal with plausibility to certain practical problems or to certain forms of exemption, as it is often called, in order to excuse a miscommunication. Unlike the epistemic problems, these difficulties all involve factors such that I will never be in a position to foreclose the possibility of appealing to them as explanations of a miscommunication.

Practical excuses, and exemptions

The practical problems that might be invoked in excusing a miscommunication affect the transmission of information rather than its processing. Unlike epistemic problems, they jeopardize, not my carefulness in observing how things are, but my truthfulness in conveying how I take them to be.

There are a variety of factors that might explain why I give a misleading account of how things actually are, despite having processed the facts correctly. One problem might be that pressure of time or company leads me to speak without thinking properly and to blurt out a falsehood. And another might be that I am coerced or induced not to tell the truth for fear of the consequences—perhaps my career is at stake or someone has put a gun to my head. Were you persuaded that I spoke falsely as a result of any such problem, then you might well conclude that you should not eject me from the network of those you can rely on.

Practical problems arise in a distinctive way with the transmission of information about how things will be as a result of an intention I avow or pledge. In this case my truthfulness may be affected, not via an obstacle to my saying how things are, but via an obstacle to my causing things to be as I say they will be. Thus, suppose that I make a pledge to meet up with you at sundown but fail to turn up at the agreed meeting place. The fact that I broke a leg, or was forcibly kept at home, will provide a practical excuse for what may seem like my untruthfulness or insincerity in communicating that intention.

The fact that I broke a leg or was forcibly detained will get me off the reputational hook in this way because of two natural and manifest assumptions. First, that I as speaker could not plausibly have taken that possibility into account when I avowed or pledged my intention. And second, that you as audience could not plausibly have taken me to have made the avowal or pledge in a manner that allowed for the obstacle. You could only have taken me to communicate the intention, and predict or pledge the behavior, on the assumption that no hindrance of that open-textured type—no unforeseen obstacle—would get in my way.

Epistemic excuses focus on something that goes wrong in my processing of information and in my effort to be careful about what I report. Practical excuses direct attention to problems or limitations that affect my transmission of information, undermining my effort to be truthful in what I say. While both may assume the form of partial excuses rather than excuses of a complete sort, and while both may be required to satisfy a diachronic as well as a synchronic requirement if I am to be truly off the hook, the focus in the evolving narrative will be on complete, synchronic excuses alone. This focus will make the presentation easier, as noted already, without leaving more complex excuses shrouded in mystery; the amendments required for admitting them should be fairly clear in the different cases discussed.

Epistemic and practical excuses both invoke problems that impede my capacity to use words reliably, whether in making reports, avowals or pledges; both explain why, despite having misspoken, I should still be treated as a reliable interlocutor. But apart from such excuses, it is important to recognize a third category of face-saving explanation that might be offered for a failure to prove reliable, whether in making a report, an avowal, or a pledge. This is the exempting explanation that would suggest that at the earlier time of utterance—or, if relevant, the later time on which the utterance bears—I was not fully adult or able-minded: I was not a functional interlocutor or agent (Watson 1987; Wallace 1996; Gardner 2007).

An exempting explanation might cite the hypnotic influence under which I spoke in my original utterance, a bout of paranoia that affected what I said, or a moment of compulsion that overcame me in trying to live up to my words. It would suggest that I was in some sense out of my mind and not fit to be held to the normal expectations that operate under the discipline of mutual reliance. It would argue for keeping me in the ranks of those reputed to be reliable, at least if the impairment cited ceases to remain a presence or a prospect—if I clearly get over the effect of the hypnosis or paranoia or compulsion.

The idea here is not, as in the case of an excuse, that the exercise of my general capacity to prove reliable was impeded by a problem in the processing or the transmission of information. Rather it is that that capacity itself was impaired, whether for a time or over an extended period, and that I should be exempted from being put on the hook for the associated failure. Such an exemption, like an excuse, may be partial or total, and it may or may not allow me to be put on a diachronic hook. But as in the case of excuses, the focus throughout this study will be exclusively on complete, synchronic exemptions.

Looking ahead

By the account offered, avowals and pledges are saliently and perhaps surprisingly absent in the Erewhon described up to this point in our narrative. Their absence is surprising because of the intuitive idea that we have a special form of access to our own minds that would make avowal possible, and a special kind of control over what we do that would make pledging possible.

Since this project is essentially naturalistic, nothing in the narrative that follows can assume that we have a form of access or control that would be scientifically inexplicable. Thus, the narrative must explain the emergence of avowals and pledges, and of the concepts of desirability and responsibility, without appealing to a non-naturalistic access to the self of the sort that Descartes postulated or to a non-naturalistic control over the self of the kind posited by libertarian accounts of free will.

There is no need to appeal to such ideas, because it turns out that there is a compelling, naturalistically intelligible reason why we inhabitants of the society should be driven to enrich the communication of our attitudes to include both avowals and pledges. The explanation of why we should be pushed in this direction is the topic of chapters 3 and 4, which address the commitments constituted by avowing and pledging attitudes, on the one side, and by co-avowing and co-pledging them on the other.

The notion of commitment introduced in those chapters, needless to say, does not have a prescriptive sense. It does not presuppose that we in Erewhon have access to any prior idea of desirability or responsibility but only that we are capable of betting on ourselves to live up to the words we utter in avowing and pledging attitudes.

This notion of commitment is commonly invoked in game theory and economics and applies clearly to avowals and pledges. These are acts of communication in which speakers voluntarily expose themselves to certain costs that they must bear in the event of failing to speak the truth. In effect, they constitute wagers in which speakers bet on themselves to prove reliable, accepting that they will lose their stake if they fail. They will be unable to access a misleading-mind excuse if they fail to live up to an avowal, and unable to access either a misleading-mind or a changed-mind excuse if they fail to live up to a pledge.

Chapter 3 argues that, starting from Erewhon as it has been characterized so far, we would be individually likely to make such commitments in our own name. And then chapter 4 argues that we would be equally likely to make commitments in the name of others as well as ourselves; in other words, we would be likely to make commitments with others as well as commitments to others.

Chapter 3: Committing to Others

In this chapter, the narrative suggests that having established a practice of reliable reporting, we in Erewhon would find ourselves drawn also into more committal forms of communication. We would be presented with the means of avowing and pledging certain attitudes, not just reporting them; we would have a motive to avail ourselves of that opportunity; and we would have a basis for the confidence that the exercise requires. The chapter starts with the avowal of belief, then moves to the avowal of desire and intention, and turns finally to the pledging of attitudes.

It will sometimes be useful in the narrative that follows to speak as if there is an initial stage at which we merely report our attitudes to one another and that we move out of that stage as the possibility and appeal of avowing and pledging attitudes become salient. But, as already noted, this temporal sequencing should not be taken literally. The point of the story is just to mark the features that distinguish avowing and pledging from reporting attitudes and to show why they are likely to make avowals and pledges into attractive options.

3.1. The avowal of belief

The means of avowing beliefs

I will avow a belief by the account already given if I voluntarily communicate it in a manner that manifestly forecloses appeal to a misleading-mind excuse for any miscommunication. I voluntarily communicate it in the sense that I convey it in the presence, or at least the apparent presence, of acceptable alternatives. And I do this manifestly insofar as it is a matter of common awareness between me and my interlocutors that I do so.[1]

The possibility of avowing a belief is immediately accessible for any one of us in Erewhon. For it turns out that when I report on any state of affairs, say, a fact about the external environment, I convey information about my belief in that state of affairs at the same time that I convey information about the state of affairs itself. I convey that information, moreover, as I convey information about the environment, in a characteristically communicative manner. And, most importantly, I convey it in such a way that I manifestly foreclose the misleading-mind excuse.

Why would my reporting that the berries are ripening, that the weather is improving up north or that an acquaintance is honest convey, not just that fact, but my belief in the fact? The answer turns on the tight connection between report and belief. To report that something is the case is to purport to be disposed, evidence remaining unchanged, to act as if it is the case: to purport, in effect, to believe that it is the case. If you reported that something was the case and failed to display that disposition or belief, then we would treat that failure as a sign that you should not be taken at your word. Thus, if you do take me at my word when I say that the acquaintance—let's call him Mogli—is honest, then you must take my words to convey both that he is honest and that I believe that he is honest.

Not only do I convey the information about my belief when I say that Mogli is honest; the fact that I convey it will be a matter of common awareness between us, and indeed among any knowledgeable witnesses. This is because the evidence that I convey it will be available to all of us, the evidence that that evidence is universally available will be available to all of us, and so on in the usual hierarchy (Lewis 1969). When I make the report that Mogli is honest, then, it ought to be the case that we each believe that I purport to believe that he is honest, that we each believe that we each believe that I speak with this purport, and so on.

If it is a matter of common awareness that in reporting the fact that Mogli is honest, I convey also my belief that he is honest, and if I choose

1. The notions of common awareness and of voluntariness were introduced in Chapter 2.

to make that report, then it is intentional on my part—and this, again, as a matter of common awareness—that I convey the belief as well as the fact. At the least I acquiesce in manifestly conveying that belief. I may not desire or intend to convey that message as such but, manifestly, I foresee that it is a side-effect of conveying the fact that Mogli is honest, which I do intend to convey. I intentionally convey the belief that he is honest even if what I intend as such is only to convey the fact of his honesty.

This means that when I say that Mogli is honest I convey my belief in his honesty in a broadly communicative manner. In communicating a linguistic message of any kind, by the analysis mentioned early in the last chapter, I hold—indeed I hold overtly—by two intentions. I overtly use my words with the primary intention of conveying the associated information to an audience and with the secondary intention of achieving that result, at least in part, by making my primary intention salient to them (Sperber and Wilson 1986; Grice 1989). While my explicit intention in the case of Mogli targets the fact that he is honest, it carries over implicitly to the fact that I believe that he is honest. And so, I may reasonably be said to communicate that I believe that Mogli is honest just by communicating that he is honest.[2]

The difference between these two forms of communication is often cast in terms of a distinction between the semantic and the pragmatic message of an utterance. That Mogli is honest is the semantic message of the words I use; that I believe he is honest is the pragmatic message. While the utterance reports the fact that constitutes the semantic

---

2. This suggests that the standard analysis of communication may be unnecessarily strong. Assuming overtness, all that may be required, as in the communication that I believe what I say, is at the primary level that I convey the information intentionally and, at the secondary, that I intentionally make it salient that I am intentionally doing that. Doing something, Y, intentionally amounts to doing it, roughly, as a means of satisfying my desires according to my beliefs. But doing Y intentionally in that sense does not strictly require having an intention to do it as such. It may only involve having an intention to do X as such, while recognizing that to do X is inevitably do Y (Scanlon 2008, 8). I desire and intentionally realize the X-Y package, but I may do so because of desiring and intending X and despite not having such an attitude to Y (Pettit 2018a).

message, it expresses the fact that constitutes the pragmatic. The semantic message is available to you in virtue of the significance of the words I use in giving my report; the pragmatic message is available in virtue of the significance of my action in making the report.

Why would these observations point the way toward my being able to avow a belief rather than just reporting it? The answer, to come to the crunch point, is that pragmatically or expressively communicating that I believe that Mogli is honest forecloses resort to a misleading-mind excuse for not displaying that belief.

I could invoke a misleading-mind excuse for miscommunicating my belief in Mogli's honesty only if I had presumably reflected on my beliefs—if you like, scanned my mind—before communicating the belief to you. But the presumption is that I did not scan my mind in that way when I communicated the belief. Rather, assuming that I took care over what I said, I scanned the world for evidence of Mogli's honesty, and in reporting that he was honest I expressed the belief that he is honest. But if I did not rely on scanning my mind—if I did not need to look at the evidence, introspective or behavioral, for whether I held the belief in his honesty—in order to communicate the existence of the belief, then I cannot be excused for having miscommunicated it on the grounds that the mind I scanned was misleading. A problem in that scanning procedure could explain and excuse my miscommunication only if the scanning procedure actually played a role in prompting the communication. And in the pragmatic case, it does not.

If it turns out that I do not display the belief that Mogli is honest in my behavior, therefore, I will not be able to explain the pragmatic miscommunication of that belief by appeal to a misleading mind. I may prove to have been wrong in ascribing honesty to him and may be able to excuse the semantic miscommunication by pointing out that the evidence about his honesty was misleading: perhaps I mistook someone's testimony to Mary's honesty as testimony to Mogli's. But if I prove to have been wrong in expressing a belief in his honesty—if I prove not to have had that belief—I cannot excuse the pragmatic miscommunication by holding that the evidence of my having that belief was misleading. The reason is that while I may have reflected on the evidence of Mogli's honesty before communicating semantically that he is honest, I clearly did not reflect on independent, say introspective, evidence about my mind before communicating pragmatically that I believe that he is honest.

By this analysis, and by evidence from the familiar world, it would be laughable to respond to the evidence of such a miscommunication by saying that it seemed clear to me that I held that belief but I was misled by the evidence about my state of mind. This would be laughable because, manifestly, evidence would not have played the sort of role in pragmatic or expressive communication that would allow me later to claim that it misled me.

Even under the narrow characterization of Erewhon offered in the first chapter, then, it should be clear that I and others will have been put in a position where it is possible to avow beliefs. Suppose you ask me whether I believe Mogli is honest. And assume that I am in a position where I might report that I have that belief. I might make an utterance to the effect that I apparently hold that belief, keeping open the possibility of excusing myself, should it turn out that I do not actually have it—should it turn out that I do not act as if he were honest. If I reject that perfectly acceptable alternative and choose to respond to your query by expressing the belief—reporting simply that Mogli is honest—then I must count as avowing the belief. I communicate the belief in a way that forecloses the misleading-mind excuse. And since reporting it instead is an acceptable alternative, I do so voluntarily, not out of any sort of necessity or under any sort of pressure.

The motive for avowing beliefs

Sooner or later we Erewhonians are bound to recognize that communicating a belief by expressing it allows of only one of the excuses that reporting the belief would have permitted and that it exposes us to an increased reputational loss. Might we be tempted in that case to play safe and choose to report our ground-level attitudes of belief about any matter rather than avowing them? Rather than expressing the ground-level belief that Mogli is honest, thereby avowing it, might it push me instead toward reporting that belief in words such as "I apparently believe that Mogli is honest," "I'm pretty sure that I believe in Mogli's honesty," or "My belief seems to be that Mogli is honest?"[3]

It may appear that playing safe in this way would be attractive. In reporting the ground-level belief that Mogli is honest, I would be expressing a higher-order belief to the effect that I have that belief; expressive or pragmatic communication at some level is inevitable. But the cost of my miscommunicating a higher-order belief without being able to invoke a misleading-mind excuse—the cost of miscommunicating a belief about whether I believe that Mogli is honest—would not be very high and would not threaten a heavy reputational loss. It would certainly be much lower than the cost of miscommunicating a belief about the world—a belief about Mogli's honesty—without being able to invoke a misleading-mind excuse. You and others are liable to rely quite heavily on the truth of any such message about how the world lies according to my beliefs.

Notwithstanding this consideration, the resort to higher-order reports about our attitudes of belief about the world would still be unlikely to attract us. For the very fact that the pragmatic or expressive mode of communication allows of only one excuse for error provides a motive for why any one of us should positively cherish it. By communicating a belief in this manner, as emphasized, it is manifest that I take on a greater risk than if I had reported it: I expose myself to the cost of not being able to explain a miscommunication about that belief by recourse to the allegedly misleading character of my mind. And by manifestly taking on such a risk—by opting voluntarily not just to report the attitude of belief—I make my words more expensive and give you and others firmer ground for expecting them to be true. Why, you may think, would I voluntarily take on that risk unless I was pretty sure

---

3. Why report the beliefs in such words? Why not say simply "I believe in Mogli's honesty" or "My belief is that he is honest?" The reason will become clear later: viz., that such self-ascriptions of the belief are likely to be taken as avowals rather than reports.

that I would not have to pay the cost of being unable to excuse a possible miscommunication by appeal to a misleading mind?[4]

Suppose you want to know about my belief about Mogli's honesty. And assume that I am anxious to be able to get you to accept whatever communication I make; I am anxious to be treated as someone whose words are credible, both in this instance and more generally. If I hedge and say that it seems to me that I believe that he is honest, then it will be clear to you that even if I prove not to have that belief, I will be able to get off the hook—and indeed it will be very easy to get off the hook— by saying that I must have gotten my belief wrong. But in that case, it will be clear that my words are pretty cheap and so not very credible. If I refuse to hedge in that reportive manner, however, and say simply that Mogli is honest, then it will be clear that I have foreclosed access to that easy excuse; that I am taking a considerable risk in communicating my belief in that expressive mode; and that my words therefore are more credible than they would otherwise have been.

It is bound to be appealing for each of us in Erewhon to give the words we utter as much credibility as we can, assuming we are pretty confident about what we say. And that means that communicating pragmatically rather than semantically that we believe something is bound to be an attractive option. Or at least that is bound to be attractive with beliefs that are relevant to our relationships with others, bearing on what they may expect of us in interaction. Taking on the risk of pragmatically communicating such a belief should help to ensure that others actually believe what we say, which is bound to appeal on a number of counts. It is likely to get others to rely on us in the instance in question, which may be important for our other purposes. And it will enable us to

---

4. The linkage between expense and honesty in animal signaling, which is a continuing subject of debate, is often expressed in the handicap principle (Zahavi and Zahavi 1999). According to this principle, roughly, the relative expense of a wasteful or handicapping signal—say, the peacock's tail, the exaggerated jump of the gazelle— conveys the wealth of resources at the animal's disposal: to the peahen in the first example, to the predator lion in the second. See Maynard Smith and Harper (2004). In such cases the expense is undertaken non-intentionally by nature; in the case of concern to us it is undertaken intentionally by the relevant individual.

prove reliable in living up to those words, thereby improving our general reputational stock.

To choose the pragmatic or expressive communication of a belief, voluntarily foreclosing the misleading-mind excuse, is to avow that belief by the terminology adopted here. It is to opt for that mode of communication over the salient and acceptable alternative of just reporting it. And presumptively, it is to opt for that form of conveying the belief, at least in part, because it represents a more expensive and so more credible form of communication. Absent this difference, there would be little reason for me or anyone else to opt for avowal; it is the feature that makes an avowal more attractive than a report.

The attraction of avowal in this regard will decrease to the extent that it is an avowal only of a belief in a probabilistically or otherwise qualified content, such as that Mogli is probably honest.[5] The expense associated with the avowal of an unqualified belief that Mogli is honest turns on the fact that if I do not act as if the belief is true, it will be relatively clear that I do not act as if it is true and that I am exposed to the cost of not being able to invoke the misleading-mind excuse. The avowal is expensive, in other words, just to the extent that any failure to live up to it is testable. And so, it is only to that extent that the avowal is more credible than a report of the presence of the belief.[6]

The avowal of a belief that Mogli is probably honest is not expensive in the same degree as an avowal of the corresponding, unqualified belief, because I might fail to act as if he is probably honest without that failure being detectable. It will be clear that I fail in that way only if I refuse to rely on Mogli's honesty across a wide range of scenarios and it is going to be difficult for anyone to survey my behavior in different scenarios.

---

5. The observation also applies if the avowal is expressed as an avowal of a certain, less than full degree of belief that Mogli is honest.

6. This observation has a number of implications that cannot be pursued here. Thus, it may explain why on-off beliefs figure more prominently than credences—degrees of belief—in ordinary discourse. And it may explain why beliefs in religious or broadly transcendental matters, whose presence is not independently testable, are often treated as a matter of personal identity, affiliation or even preference.

Thus, the avowal is only marginally more expensive than a report that I believe that he is probably honest. And so, it is only marginally more effective in raising the credibility of the words I utter. For this reason, the focus in what follows will be on the avowal of unqualified beliefs, and so on avowals of belief that are relatively expensive: that is, on avowals of beliefs such that it is more or less easy to test for whether someone fails to live up to them.

Not all expressions of belief count as avowals, it should be noted, because not all expressions are suitably voluntary. In reporting rather than expressing the ground-level attitude of belief that p, as noticed earlier, I give expression to the higher-order belief that I believe that p. Do I avow that higher-order belief, then, in virtue of communicating it expressively? No, I do not.

I will count as avowing it only if, having opted to report that I believe that p, I can be taken to exercise an unconstrained choice in choosing to express the belief that I hold that ground-level or 0-order belief rather than reporting that 1-order belief as well. But to report the 1-order belief would be to express the 2-order belief that I hold that belief in turn, thereby opening up an indefinite regress. It won't be clear at any level or order, n, why I shouldn't opt for reporting the relevant belief at that level, expressing thereby a belief at level n+1. And the prospect of that regress may be taken to make the alternative unacceptable. In reporting that I believe that p—that I hold the 0-order belief—it is true that I express the 1-order belief that I hold that belief. But the alternative of reporting that 1-order belief in turn is unacceptable—here be tigers—so I do not choose voluntarily to express it and the expression does not count as an avowal.[7]

7. Notice, to return to an observation in Chapter 2, that voluntariness is more demanding than intentionality. Assuming that I report that my 0-order belief that p, it is available as a matter of common awareness that I express and pragmatically communicate the 1-order belief that I believe that p. But while I do not express that 1-order belief voluntarily, for the reasons given in the text, I may do so intentionally. Desiring and intending that I report the 0-order belief that p, I may foresee that reporting that 0-order belief inevitably involves expressing the 1-order belief that I believe that p. And that implies, as we saw earlier, that I may intentionally express

Like any expression of a belief, voluntary or otherwise, an avowal will be more credible for being manifestly more expensive than a report. But the fact that it is a voluntary expression of the belief, adopted on the very grounds of being manifestly more expensive, will make it more credible still. It will show that in taking on that expense I am backing myself not to have to suffer the cost of being unable, as a result of the avowal, to excuse a failure to act on the belief. I bet on myself, as a matter of common awareness, to live up to my words. I put my money where my mouth is, giving you the firmest grounds for taking my words at face value. I commit myself, in the game-theory sense of commitment, to holding by the belief at issue.

The confidence required for avowing beliefs

These observations suggest that given the ready availability of avowing as distinct from just reporting our beliefs, we in Erewhon are likely to cherish the possibility of avowal; we are likely to rely on avowal to give as much credibility to our communications about our beliefs as our confidence allows. This is certainly going to be so with communications where the belief communicated is likely to matter in continuing interaction with others; this might not be true, to pick a random example, with the belief that I once saw clouds take the form of a mathematical equation. But how can we ever be confident enough to put aside the possibility of invoking a misleading-mind excuse for a failure to display a belief avowed? It is one thing for us to have a means of avowing our beliefs, and a motive for doing so. It is quite another for us to be in a position where we have sufficient confidence about what we believe to be able sensibly to take this line.

What might make it possible for me, then, to have the level of confidence required for an avowal that I will continue to hold this or that belief? What might enable me to have sufficient confidence that I believe

that 1-order belief; I may adopt the package deal involved—reporting my 0-level belief and thereby expressing my 1-order belief—as a recognized means of furthering my desires according to my beliefs.

that Mogli is honest, for example, or that the berries on the hill are ripening, or that the weather up north is improving? With any such belief, it is possible that despite appearances I do not actually hold it; holding it is not tied up with who I am, for example, in the manner of religious beliefs or framework beliefs (more on these later). So, what might make it possible for me to be sure enough of holding the belief that I am prepared to put aside the misleading-mind excuse?

This question is challenging, since it may seem that the confidence required could only be available on the basis of a non-naturalistic, Cartesian story about how we know our minds. But it turns out that there is a much more plausible, non-Cartesian answer and that this does not offend in any way against naturalistic assumptions. In order to present this answer, however, it is necessary to turn briefly to more general considerations about language and about what language makes possible.

In order to serve a reporting function in any community, natural language must provide the means for speakers like you and me to communicate how things are, according to our beliefs. And this means that when we take care to determine whether or not it is the case that p, to pick an arbitrary sentence from our language, and then assent to the proposition that p, we must tend in general to hold the belief that p.

If this were not generally the case, then our conscientious, sincere assertions—our careful, truthful reports about the world—would be correlated only contingently randomly with our beliefs and with their evidential inputs and behavioral outputs. And in that case the reports would not serve a useful function in guiding others about what to expect of us. Indeed, the assertions would not even be interpretable. They would not be guided by reliable connections with the prompting conditions that lead me to form beliefs or with the prompted actions that my beliefs occasion; and floating free of such constraints, it would be difficult for others to make sense of them (Davidson 1984).

What is it going to mean, whether in Erewhon or elsewhere, for me to take care about determining that it is or is not the case that p? It can only mean taking evidential care: registering and responding to the data on whether or not p, where these are mediated by perception or memory, existing beliefs or the testimony of others. In particular, it

means guarding where needed against distractions that might lead me
not to register all the data relevant or not to attend to them in the full
manner required for responding as they can dispose me to respond. If
I register and respond to the data in that manner, I will be led to assent
to or dissent from the proposition before me, or to withhold judgment.
And in that case, presumably, the corresponding belief-state will materialize within me.

Thus, if I find myself deferring to the data and assenting to the proposition that p after taking such evidential care, then I will presumably
come to form the belief that p, whether for the first time or in reaffir-
mation of a belief already held. In either case I will now believe that p
in the sense, roughly, of being disposed to act and adjust as if it were
the case that p. Across scenarios where my evidence for 'p' remains
unchanged—and just across those scenarios—I will be disposed more
or less dependably or robustly to take actions and draw inferences as if
it were the case that p.[8]

More specifically, I will be disposed to do this robustly over a range
of variations in the distractions that may lead to oversight or inattention. Evidential care is designed, where needed, to guard against such
distractors. If I did not form a suitably robust or dependable disposition
as a result of carefully assenting to 'p', then the words I used in making
the corresponding report would not be indicative of my attitude or even
intelligibly interpretable by others.

There is no problem about how I and others might acquire the concept of a distractor in Erewhon. For the criteria by which something
counts as a distractor will be available to each of us just on the basis of
understanding our practices of assertion. The role that data or evidence

8. The assumed concept of belief is broadly functional in character, building on
the notion of credence in decision theory; see Stalnaker (1984); Pettit (1998). There is
a serious issue as to how credences relate to acts of assent—and to the states of mind
that those acts express—but in this context, I ignore the problem. See Pettit (2016b).
There is also a serious issue that arises from the fact that beliefs confront evidence in
a network, not one by one; but with the exception of some later comments on framework beliefs, I ignore this as well.

play in relation to reports about the world presupposes that distractions are possible and that reports are guided properly by data only in their absence. That fact is bound to be accessible to me and others in Erewhon insofar as we make reports to one another. And so, the concept of a distractor, with the associated ideas of oversight and inattention, will also be accessible.

The upshot of these general considerations appears to be that I can be very confident that I believe something when I find that I assent to it after taking any evidential care needed over the relevant data. That conclusion is independently plausible, being borne out by the fact that people often answer the question as to whether or not they believe that p by thinking about whether it is the case that p—not whether they believe that p—and answering, when appropriate: "p." In other words, they routinely treat it as a question about whether the data elicit a belief that p in them, not whether introspective or other evidence reveals the presence of the belief (Evans 1982; Byrne 2011).

But still, the conclusion needs to be qualified, for there is one important complexity to be added to the account of how I can be confident enough about whether or not I believe something to be ready to avow it. This, to anticipate, is that I not only seek to overcome potential distractors, paying attention to all the relevant evidence in forming a belief that p; I also try to deal with what may be described as potential disturbers of my performance as someone who avows the belief that p.

The possibility of disturbance arises with at least some beliefs that matter in continuing interaction with others. To illustrate the possibility, suppose I am brought by careful consideration of the data to assent to the proposition that the gambler's fallacy is a fallacy. It may be, first, that the belief is liable to disappear in the excitement of the casino, assuming that there is gambling in Erewhon: when there is a run of blacks, I am likely to commit the fallacy, growing in confidence that a red will come up next. Yet, second, I would certainly not be disposed in the wake of such a performance to invoke the excuse that I temporarily changed my mind about the matter during my visit to the casino. On the contrary, I would continue to maintain that the fallacy is indeed a fallacy and disown my behavior in the casino; treat it as a failure to re-spond to the data that show the fallacy to be a fallacy.[9]

Disturbers of belief, in the sense illustrated, are characterized by three features. First, like the excitement of the casino, they are liable to cause a person not to act on a belief they avow. Second, they do not lead the person to excuse the failure to act appropriately by appeal to a temporary change of mind. And third, there are various executive steps that anyone can take in order to neutralize or avoid their impact; the influence they exercise is not inescapable. Thus, to illustrate this third feature, I can guard against the effect of being in the casino by bringing along a friend to remind me of the fallacy at appropriate points; or, of course, I can avoid casinos altogether.

As in the case of distractors, the criteria by which something counts as a disturber are internal to my practice in assertion. The notion of an assertion or report that is maintained over time, and its connection with the idea of an enduring belief, highlights the possibility of disturbance, and a consequent failure in assertoric practice. That fact is bound to be available to me and others in Erewhon insofar as we make a habit of giving and being given reports.

Disturbers constitute a potential danger with any beliefs that—like the belief that the gambler's fallacy is a fallacy—may be expected to continue over time and to matter in my relationships with others. They may take a variety of forms, ranging from the effects of wishful thinking and gullibility to those of incaution and prejudice and are well illustrated by many of the biases and heuristics that are known to shape human cognitive performance (Gilovich, Griffin and Kahneman 2002).

If I do nothing to guard against it, the prospect of failing in the ca-sino means that I may not be sufficiently confident to avow the belief that the fallacy is a fallacy, inviting others to rely on my displaying it. And so, a more nuanced story is needed for the confidence required for avowing a belief with such a role in relations with others. As someone

9. There are otherwise similar cases, of course, in which I may think of myself as having changed my mind. But in those cases, I will presumably think that certain data—misleading data, as I may judge them later—prompted the change.

competent in the natural language of Erewhon, I can be confident that I believe that p in a suitably reliable way just when I satisfy two conditions. First, I am evidentially careful, in the measure needed, to register and respond to relevant data—to avoid distractions—before I assent to it. And second, I am executively careful, in the measure needed, to maintain my sensitivity to the data: that is, to avoid disturbers.

Suppose I satisfy these two conditions, that the data continue to support a belief that p, and that I continue to be a competent subject. In that case I will sustain the belief robustly over variations in factors other than the support provided by the data, and the competence I display in responding to them. In particular, I will sustain it robustly over variations in the distractions and disturbances that might come into play and affect me.[10]

How can I muster sufficient confidence, then, to be able to avow a belief that p as distinct from merely reporting that I believe it? I must take care, as needed, to register all relevant data without distraction and to nullify potential disturbance—in short, I must take any form of evidential or executive care that is required—and I must find that the data I thereby register elicit my assent to the proposition that p. Evidential and executive care will not be required in many cases, of course. With common beliefs, whether about the character of my neighbors, the layout of my environment or wholly abstract issues, I will not have to worry much about being distracted from relevant data, or about being disturbed in my sensitivity to them. I will take special pains to exercise

---

10. This claim is most readily intelligible on the assumption that the data that support or elicit belief leave only one candidate proposition in place; they do not leave room for me to believe either of a constrained number of alternatives. The assumption that data are determinative in this way, rather than merely constraining, will be maintained for convenience throughout this study. But even if the constraining view were adopted, most of the claims made would survive, albeit in a somewhat modified form. The line taken here means that as I put myself in the position to avow a belief, I put myself equally in a position to provide my interlocutor with assurance that things are as they are represented to be in the belief avowed; on related themes, see Lawlor (2013).

evidential and executive care only when there are independent reasons to be concerned.

Assume that I defer with due care to data that support a claim that p, taking whatever precautions are required against distraction or disturbance. And assume that I can know what I am doing in taking such an action, whether it be described as assenting to the proposition, or making up my mind about it.[11] That knowledge is going to be enough to support a high degree of confidence, arguably indeed a claim to know, that I believe that p. Having made up my mind, I can claim, in a seventeenth-century phrase, to have a maker's knowledge of believing that p, not the knowledge of an observer, even an introspective observer.[12] I can speak for what I believe with an authority of a special, practical sort (McGeer 1996; Moran 1997, 2001; McGeer 2008).

If I have the means of avowing a belief that p, and a motive for doing so, then these observations suggest that I will often go ahead and avow it; I will not be inhibited by a lack of confidence. Avowing the belief will make sense whenever there are no grounds for worrying that I may not be exercising sufficient evidential or executive care. Either I do take pains to exercise such care, or it is clear that no special care is required.

Consistently with this picture, we in Erewhon may not always perform to par. Short of having suitable grounds available for avowing a belief that p, for example, I may be pushed into avowing it by distractions that generate oversight or inattention. Or I might be led to form the belief by disturbing factors like wishful thinking and prejudice; these may affect the formation of beliefs, as well as disturbing beliefs

11. Thus, it may be that I can know what I am doing, not in virtue of scanning my mind for the guiding intention, but in virtue of being able to counterfactualize reliably about how I would respond to various scenarios. I can know that I am going for a stroll rather than going to the library by knowing that if I found the library closed, that would make no difference to what I did. The ability to counterfactualize in that manner, however it is grounded, is necessary for intentional agency. See Pettit (2016b).

12. The seventeenth-century notion of maker's knowledge is prominent in Hobbes and Vico (Pettit 2008a, Ch. 1). Rae Langton (2009, Ch. 13) cites an earlier employment of the idea in Maimonides.

already formed. And if I succumb, I may also manage to persuade myself that suitable grounds for avowal are actually available.

Nothing in this narrative precludes these sorts of self-deceptive possibilities, and nothing, as will appear, precludes parallel possibilities in the case of avowing a desire or intention. All that the narrative assumes is that the possibilities will not be rampant, driving out avowals of the bona fide sort. And that assumption is surely plausible.

3.2 *The avowal of desire and intention*

Desires and intentions

As it is going to be manifestly attractive for me and others in Erewhon to avow our beliefs rather than just report them, so the same is true for the other attitudes we may wish to communicate to one another. Or at least that will be so in the case of attitudes that are important in our relationships with others and that we must want others to recognize in us. The focus in this discussion will be on desires and intentions, but the line taken can be extended to other attitudes as well, such as those, for example, of hope and affection and trust.[13]

There is a difference between desire and intention, as those terms will be employed here. An intention is a final disposition to choose one of a given set of alternatives in a choice, whether the choice be between different act-options, different routines for making decisions, different principles for constraining decisions, or whatever.[14] That it is a final

13. Avowing that I hope to finish this book by year's end, or that I trust someone, or that I love you may involve the avowal, and even the pledging, of a corresponding intention: to act as if I believe I will finish the book, to act as if I fully rely on the person, to act toward you as love requires. And in such cases, part of the motivation may well be that doing this is likely to have a positive effect on my finishing the book, on your proving reliable, or on our maintaining mutual affection. But such complexities are put aside in this work. For related studies, see Pettit (1995, 2004) and McGeer and Pettit (2017).

14. The alternatives that I neglect in favor of intending to do something, X, need only be apparent alternatives. Thus, to return to the Frankfurt cases discussed in the

disposition to choose this or that option will show up in the fact that it makes a fixture of that choice in the further deliberations of the agent; short of second thoughts, the agent may be expected, where relevant, to deliberate on the assumption that the chosen option is going to be in place (Bratman 1987, 1999).[15]

A desire is also a disposition to choose, if a choice is available, but it is not restricted in the objects that it may target. It may be a desire that the world in general be of such and such a character, a desire that other people act in a certain manner, or indeed a desire to pick one or another option in a personal choice. Such a desire will approximate an intention if it assumes the form of a final disposition to choose that option.[16]

The attraction of avowal

Suppose, then, that I am confident that I have a wish to prove reliable to others, a preference that people should talk about differences rather than squabbling over them, or an intention or plan to go hunting tomorrow. Such desires and intentions are likely to be of importance in my interacting with others. They are different in that respect from, for example, a desire I experienced on some particular occasion to fly like a bird or from a policy of reading novels when alone.

last chapter, I may intend to do X rather than Y, even though it is the case that unbeknown to me I would be blocked from doing Y if I opted for it instead..

15. In accordance with this account, my individual intentions are necessarily directed to what I can do; they have essentially centered contents, as it is sometimes put (Perry 1979; Lewis 1983b, Ch. 10). I can intend that I do such and such—or, equivalently, I can intend to do such and such—but I cannot intend, except in the special case of a supervisor, that such and such should be done. Joint as distinct from individual intentions will be discussed in the next chapter.

16. The word "desire" and the like—"prefer,", "want," "seek," and so on—are often used to express intentions. The claim, made later in the text, that I can pledge an intention but not pledge a desire introduces considerations that might suggest that there is a sharp distinction between desires and intentions.

If I want to convey the relevant sort of desire or intention to you with a suitable degree of credibility, it will be useful to be able to avow the attitude rather than just report it. Avowing it will mean communicating that I have it in such a manner that I cannot excuse a failure to live up to it by claiming that I must have been misled about my attitude. And such a mode of communication will give you much firmer ground for taking me at my word, relying on my possession of the attitude, than if I reported on its presence in a way that kept that excuse open.

At least that will be so the extent that a failure to act on the desire or intention avowed is testable. As noted earlier, avowing a probabilistically qualified belief is not going to be much more expensive than reporting it, since it is difficult to test for the presence of such a belief, and is not going to make the communication much more credible. And by the same reasoning, avowing a desire or intention is not going to be much more expensive or credible than reporting it, if it is relatively difficult to test for a failure to act on that desire or intention.

This observation explains why the focus in the evolving narrative is on the avowal of a restricted class of desires and intentions, as the focus is on the avowal of unqualified rather than qualified beliefs. In the case of desire, the focus will be on avowals of desires that connect closely with scenarios for action that the avowing agent is likely to face, not on idle wishes and the like; while the agent may not always act on such a desire, there will normally be a salient consideration in place to explain the failure. And, in the case of both desire and intention, the focus will be on avowals of unconditional desires and intentions, like the desire or intention to do something, X, not on conditional counterparts: not, for example, on the desire or intention, if p or r or s, to X; it will be possible to test for the presence of such attitudes, only when the antecedent happens to be fulfilled.

Given this focus, it is clear why the avowal of desires and intentions is going to be an attractive option for us in Erewhon. It will have the same appeal as the avowal of beliefs, or at least of probabilistically unqualified beliefs. But there is a problem about how we in Erewhon can find the means of avowing desires or intentions and, even if we do find a means of doing so, about how we can have the high level of confidence about those attitudes that is required for avowal.

The means of avowing desires and intentions

I can avow a belief that p, as we know, by asserting that p, thereby expressing my belief-state. But I cannot avow a desire or intention that q by asserting that q; such an assertion would express a belief that q rather than a desire or intention that q. While I may have a strong motive for avowing desires and intentions, then, I may lack the means of doing so. Certainly, I cannot avow a desire or intention that something be the case—say, that it be the case that q—by using a sentence like "q" to assert that that is the case.[17]

Notwithstanding this difficulty, however, it is possible to discern a relatively straightforward means whereby we would be able to avow desires and intentions. In order to make this means visible, however, it is necessary to return briefly to the situation with the avowal of beliefs.

The expressive means of avowing a belief is of fundamental importance because it is going to be saliently available as well as saliently attractive in Erewhon, even at the stage where we are exclusively interested in making worldly reports to one another. But suppose that the expressive avowal of belief has become standard practice in Erewhon, as the preceding argument suggests that it would become standard practice. Suppose that it has become a matter of common awareness, in other words, that in Erewhon we will generally want to avow the beliefs we hold—or at least the beliefs in which others have an interest—and that a standard way of doing this is just to express those beliefs: to say "p" in communicating that we believe that p.

Under those circumstances, it is plausible that we will begin to recognize other means of avowing our beliefs. And it turns out that those other means of avowing beliefs offer us models for the avowal of desires and intentions as well.

The attraction of avowing beliefs that are important in our relationships with others is going to be obvious to all of us in Erewhon. And so, it is likely to be a matter of common awareness that it has this appeal;

---

17. I ignore here the limited expressive possibilities that might be illustrated in an utterance such as "Would that q!" or "Oh to make it the case that q!."

after all, we will each have access to evidence of that appeal, to evidence that we each have access to that evidence, and so on. But if this is a matter of common awareness, then the default assumption we will each make with others is that in communicating relevant beliefs to us they are meaning to avow them. They are meaning to speak for what they believe while putting aside the possibility that they may have been misled about their own minds and gotten those beliefs wrong.

Suppose then that in the presence of that default assumption, I do not say "p" in expressive mode but resort to the ascriptive mode, as in saying "I believe that p." Should I be taken to be merely reporting on my belief rather than avowing it? In many contexts, especially contexts in which I act as if I am willing to avow the belief, it will make sense for you to treat my self-ascription of the belief as if it had the force of an expression, not a report: as if it amounted to an avowal. In those contexts, you would expect me to go out of my way to indicate that I was merely reporting on the belief, if that was indeed my intention. You would expect me to resort to cautious phrasing, as in saying that it seems to me that I believe that p, or something of the kind.

Absent such phrasing, you will naturally take an ascriptive assertion like "I believe that p"—an assertion in which I ascribe the belief to myself—to have the same avowal force as the expressive assertion "p." And equally you are likely to assign the force of an avowal to other remarks, too: say, to an explanatory remark such as "The data explain why it is the case that p." In either sort of case, ascriptive or explanatory, you will expect me to be ready to stand by the belief, and not to hedge in the manner of a self-reporter. Hedging in that manner would be unusual enough for you to expect that I would do more to indicate that I was hedging, if indeed that is what I was wanting to do.

That this is what would happen in Erewhon is borne out by the fact that this is what happens in actual languages. As in actual usage, I could hardly expect to be taken as a mere self-reporter if I said that I believed that Mogli was honest. In order to mark out my utterance as merely reporting the presence of the belief, I would have to say that my own impression is that he is honest, or that I am inclined to credit him with honesty, or something of that markedly cautious kind.

Assuming that this line of argument is sound, consider now the point at which we in Erewhon have established a practice that allows us to avow our beliefs in ascriptive and explanatory assertions as well as in expressive ones. At that point, plausibly, we will also have provided ourselves with a salient means of avowing desires and intentions.

Saying in ascriptive mode "I desire to be reliable"—or, equivalently, "Being reliable attracts me"—is not necessarily going to be taken as a mere report that I have that desire but may be heard in appropriate contexts as an avowal. And the same will be true of saying in similar mode that I prefer talking to squabbling, or that I intend to go on a hunt tomorrow. Again, saying that there are factors that explain why I hold such a desire or intention is not necessarily going to count as a detached explanation but may be taken in suitable contexts as an avowal of the attitude explained. [18]

Or at least this will be so with communications in which the attitudes I convey are likely to be of importance in my interactions with others, unlike the episodic desire to fly or the policy of reading novels when alone. Thus, I will be expected in important cases to go out of my way to indicate that I am hedging my bets if that is what I am doing in communicating the attitude. I will be expected to resort to quaint phrasings, as in saying, "Looking at my behavior, I seem to prefer talking to squabbling,"' or "I'm sure that my intention is to go to the hunt tomorrow," or, of course, "I'll probably go on the hunt tomorrow."[19]

18. In the ascriptive avowal of a belief or other attitude, it is worth noting that I do not just communicate that I have, say, the belief that p or the desire for R; I also communicate that I have the belief that I hold that belief or harbor that desire. But while I give expression to that higher-order belief, to return to an earlier observation, I will not strictly avow it. This is because it is not for the sake of communicating the belief more credibly, only because I have little or no option in the matter, that I choose to express the belief rather than report it.

19. Our observations on the avowal of non-credal attitudes bear indirectly on a familiar debate in metaethics as to what is the relationship between a moral attitude of approval or disapproval and an utterance that communicates the presence

The confidence required for avowing desires and intentions

But it is one thing to show that, like others, I will have a motive and a means of avowing desires and intentions in Erewhon. It is quite another to show that I can be confident enough of having such an attitude to be willing to avow it: to be willing to discount the possibility that I am misled about my own disposition. In the case of belief, I can find a sufficient basis for confidence, absent distraction or disturbance, in the fact that the data to which I defer with suitable care elicit assent to the proposition. In order to avow a desire or intention, I need similar grounds to be confident about holding it. But where might I find an effective basis for confidence in this case?

The most plausible answer, which fits with a long tradition of thinking, is that I can find such a basis in the sorts of properties that typically elicit desire or intention—for short, in the desiderata or attractors present. Thus, I can be generally sure that I desire or intend R insofar as the properties that attract me to it here and now, assuming I have taken care over registering and responding to these, dispose me to act and adjust dependably as if R were suitably attractive. As already registered, I can be generally sure of believing that p insofar as the data dispose me to respond dependably as if it were the case that p. And I can be generally sure of desiring or intending R insofar as a parallel condition is

of that attitude: say, "I approve of X," or "You ought to do X," or "X is obligatory." In their simplest forms, one of the standard approaches suggests that this sort of utterance expresses the attitude in the way that an assertion that p expresses a belief, another that it reports the attitude in the way in which an assertion that it seems to me that I believe that p might report a belief. The first of these alternatives is expressivism, which we discussed briefly in the first chapter, and the second is often described as subjectivism (Moore 1911). Neither is satisfactory, however (Jackson and Pettit 1998). In ignoring the role of the belief, simple expressivism would fail to explain why ethical utterances are voluntary acts of communication. In ignoring the difference between reporting and avowing, simple subjectivism would fail to explain why the utterance forecloses the misleading-mind excuse and helps put the speaker on the hook for any failure to live up to the attitude.

satisfied: the desiderata, carefully rehearsed, dispose me to respond dependably as if R were attractive.[20]

This claim holds true of desire and intention, of course, as the other claim holds true in the case of belief, only in the absence of distraction and disturbance. Thus, in this case, as in the case of belief, I must take evidential care against the distraction that would prompt oversight or inattention in relation to desiderata, and executive care against the disturbance of the desire or intention they lead me to form. Or at least I must have reason to think that no particular care is required.

Disturbers of desire and intention must satisfy three conditions. Their presence can prompt a failure to display the desire or intention communicated; they do not lead me to explain the miscommunication as a temporary change of mind; and I can do something to guard against them.[21] The possibility of disturbance in the case of a belief was illustrated with the illusion that may take hold of me in the casino, undermining the effect of my assenting to the claim that the gambler's fallacy is a fallacy. The possibility of disturbance in the case of desire or intention is even more salient, since psychological factors like anxiety or impulse or sheer laziness provide ready examples.

As the confidence needed for the avowal of belief requires evidential care against distractions and executive care against such disturbers, so the same is true here. I must take precautions, where needed, to register without distraction the desiderata on which I rely and to guard myself against potential disturbers.

20. An assumption made throughout this study is that as data determinatively constrict belief, a point we mentioned earlier, so desiderata determinatively constrict desire and intention. Like the assumption about data, this is one of convenience to the extent that the main claims would survive, albeit in a somewhat modified form, if it were dropped: if it were the case that the desiderata present in any instance may just constrain the alternatives available for me to desire or intend, not reduce them to one.

21. As in the case of belief, of course, there may be some cases where I would say that I changed my mind. But those would be cases where, as I think of it, the desiderata seemed to support the change—wrongly, as I may later judge.

The nature and role of desiderata

The desiderata that serve to elicit desire or intention come in many different forms. They include neutral properties that can make a scenario attractive for anyone in any situation: that it would be fun, that it would secure peace, that it would reduce suffering. They include agent-relative properties that can make a prospect attractive for anyone in a certain relationship or position: that it would create an advantage for my child, for example, or further the prosperity of my tribal group. And they even include agent-relative properties that make things attractive, conditionally on the presence of a contingent need or taste: the property of constituting a drink in the presence of thirst, for example, or of giving me relief in the presence of pain.[22]

All of these desiderata, even those that presuppose a need or taste, reflect properties of the prospects targeted in desire and intention. They are properties that elicit my desire or intention and that dispose me to act and adjust more or less dependably as if the prospects were attractive. Assuming that those desiderata remain in place, and I continue to be a competent subject, I will be disposed in the appropriate way—I will hold the relevant desire or intention—robustly over variation in other factors; in particular, variation in the distractions or disturbances that might affect me.

To hold that desires and intentions can be grounded in desiderata, as beliefs can be grounded in data, is to go along with the idea, long accepted in philosophical tradition, that there are general considerations that lead human beings to form desires or intentions and that agents consciously or unconsciously let such considerations determine their

---

22. This discussion ignores time-relativity as distinct from agent-relativity. But despite this restriction of focus, the examples of needs, tastes, and cravings indicate that desiderata may not just include properties that can make a prospect attractive, even if its realization will come at a time when the desire it currently elicits is no longer there—say, the property of enjoying posthumous fame; they may also include properties that make a prospect attractive only so long as the desire it currently elicits—the hankering it relieves—remains in place: say, the property of satisfying the yen for a cigarette. On these matters, see Parfit (1984); Pettit (2006b).

choices. The attitudes do not appear out of the blue, so this ortho-doxy holds, but are generally elicited by attractive features that people identify in the targets of their desires or intentions: features that they agree in finding attractive, even if they weigh them differently against one another. If someone seeks a particular outcome, so the idea goes, they will always do so, at least absent distraction or disturbance, in explicit or implicit response to the attractive features it promises to realize.

This orthodox view does not hold that it is just a brute empirical fact that human beings are moved to seek one or another prospect by the general desiderata that it promises to realize. The idea is that human beings would not be able to make proper sense of the desires and intentions they ascribe to others, or even to themselves, unless there were desiderata in view—perhaps desiderata weighed in different ways by different people—that explained the presence of those atti-tudes. They would fail to make sense of the ascriptions in the way in which they would surely fail to make sense of the ascriptions of cer-tain beliefs—empirically vulnerable beliefs—if there were no data in view that explained why the beliefs should be maintained. Thus, they would find the person who self-ascribed attitudes of a data-insensitive or desiderata-insensitive kind more or less unconversable—incapable, to put the idea roughly, of being engaged in mutually profitable ex-change (Pettit and Smith 1996).

Elizabeth Anscombe (1957) uses an eye-catching example to argue that intelligible attitudes of desire or intention—that is, attitudes whose ascription to someone would be intelligible—have to be grounded in familiar desiderata. She asks how others would think of a person who seeks something as unlikely as a saucer of mud but cannot do anything to make sense of that desire, presenting it to them under an aspect with recognizable attractor potential. In order to find the person conversable, she suggests, others would have to see some general aspect under which the saucer of mud appeals: say, as an ornament or as a reminder of mor-tality. They would not themselves have to be moved by the prospect of possessing that particular ornament or reminder, but they would have to be able to see why the property of being an ornament or a reminder of mortality might have an appeal: why it might have the capacity to make something attractive.[23]

These observations suggest that when desiderata are invoked to explain why I should desire or intend something, they present me as an instance of a familiar, universal type. If a preference is explicable by such desiderata, then that means that I do not seek the end at issue because of its pure particularity; I seek it because of the type of end in view, or because of the type of relationship I bear to that end. Thus, I seek to reduce someone's suffering because of what the reduction of anyone's suffering involves or, if it matters that the person is a friend, because of what the reduction of that friend's suffering involves. The explanation makes me intelligible to others, then, by presenting me as an instance of a familiar type: I am the kind of person concerned about suffering or the kind of person concerned about the suffering of a friend.[24]

The picture according to which desires and intentions relate to desiderata as beliefs relate to data is not endorsed on all sides. Decision theorists reject the picture insofar as they treat preferences as primitive rankings, ignoring the possibility that reliable attractors or desiderata lie at their origin. But they reject it, arguably, only by way of a convenient simplification, not as a position that is objectionable on independent grounds (Pettit 1991b; Dietrich and List 2013).

Opponents of the picture also include particularists, as they are often known (Dancy 2004). While they agree that the properties of objects of desire or intention may play a characteristic role in eliciting that attitude—this, by extrapolation from the role they are supposed to play in eliciting corresponding moral judgments—they deny that those properties always weigh in the same direction. Thus, in a much-cited example, the pleasure of an innocent activity may weigh in its favor,

23. A similar example in the philosophical literature is Warren Quinn's (1993) "radio-man": a character who is disposed to turn on radios but without any even minimally intelligible rationale; certainly without any that he can invoke.

24. In helping a friend, of course, his or her identity will also matter to me. I will be fastened on them in particular, albeit under their aspect as a friend. On related questions, see Pettit (1997b, 2015c).

the pleasure of doing something noxious, like torturing another, may weigh against.

Particularism of this kind is counterintuitive, since it has to reject the common-sense idea that in deliberation about choices, we human beings explicitly or implicitly weigh the pros and cons attaching to each option and form a desire or intention on the basis of the resultant effect. The main arguments in its favor draw on examples such as the pleasure case. But those examples need not be taken to undermine our standard view of deliberation and argue for particularism. On a rival interpretation, they demonstrate that it is not pleasure as such that counts as a desideratum with us but, rather, innocent pleasure.[25]

Back to the confidence issue

It is time to return, finally, to the issue of confidence. As I can form a belief by deferring to relevant data, so I can form a desire or intention insofar as I defer to corresponding desiderata. Thus, I can have confidence that I hold the belief in question, whether for the first time or not, by virtue of knowing that I am deferring to the data and am on guard against distraction and disturbance. And I can have confidence that I hold the desire or intention, whether for the first time or not, by virtue of knowing that I am deferring to the desiderata and am on guard in a parallel way against distraction and disturbance. In this case, as in the other, the confidence needed for avowal materializes by virtue of having a maker's knowledge of the attitude I hold.

The observations rehearsed identify grounds sufficient for me to have confidence enough about desiring R or intending to X to be ready

25. For a critique of particularism on these general lines—and for a critique of the closely related doctrine I call "interpretivism,"—see Pettit (2015c). For a deeper-running complaint about particularism, see Jackson, Pettit and Smith (1999). The line taken in the text would be consistent with thinking that properties can have an aggregate weight in combination that is not just a function of their individual, independent weights; in that sense, it can be moderately holistic. The approach is inconsistent, however, with the radical, particularistic holism that would not recognize any role for individual weights.

to avow that attitude. But, as in the belief case, it is important to recognize that things may not always match this ideal. Thus, I might avow such a desire or intention, and even think I had grounds for doing so, without actually having access to such grounds. The attitude might be one that I embraced, not because of the attraction of the object, but rather because of the sort of oversight or inattention that distraction can produce, or because of the disturbing influence of impulse or whim or the like.

As in the belief case, nothing in the narrative precludes these sorts of self-deceptive possibilities. All that the narrative assumes is that in Erewhon the possibilities will not swamp the bona fide cases. And that assumption is as plausible in this case as in the other.

3.3 The pledging of intention

The idea of pledging

By the definitions given earlier, to make a pledge as distinct from an avowal in communicating an attitude is to go one stage further in reducing possible ways of excusing a miscommunication. It voluntarily and manifestly forecloses not just the possibility of excusing a failure to live up to it by reference to a misleading mind but also the possibility of doing so by reference to a changed mind. If I avow the intention of going with you on a hunt, as in an earlier example, then I can scarcely excuse my failure to turn up by saying that I was misled about my intention. But in that case I can certainly excuse it by saying that I changed my mind since speaking to you. If I pledge the intention to join you on the hunt, however, then I cannot avail myself of this excuse, either.

It should be clear that we are each going to have a motive in Erewhon for pledging attitudes to one another, if pledging is indeed possible. In particular, we are going to have a motive for pledging the congenial or collaborative attitudes that matter in building or maintaining relationships with one another. Pledging an attitude is even more expensive than avowing it, since it exposes me to a greater risk of not having any excuse for failing to act on the attitude. The pledge will be highly credible because of the risk that I choose to take in making it. And it will be all the more credible because of the fact that in opting for it voluntarily and manifestly, I convey the message that I fully recognize the cost of failure but nevertheless back myself not to incur it; I commit myself to being someone who lives up to the attitude I convey.

As it will clearly be attractive in many cases to pledge our attitudes to one another in Erewhon, so it should be clear that if we are bent on doing so, then we will be able to find a linguistic means of signaling that we are making a pledge and not an avowal or report. The fact that, absent expressive possibilities, I can avow a desire or intention in an ascriptive or explanatory fashion shows just how flexible and multifunctional our utterances can become. It argues plausibly that in the presence of an assumption that it is possible and attractive for me to pledge an attitude rather than just avow it, there will be forms of utterance I can invoke to communicate that I am indeed making a pledge.

But even if there is no problem about how we may have a motive for pledging any attitudes and may be able to construct a suitable means of doing so, there is still a question as to whether we could ever garner enough confidence about our attitudes to be able to pledge them. It turns out that while we may be able to have confidence enough to pledge an intention, we could never have enough confidence to be able to pledge other attitudes.

The problem with pledging a belief or desire

Might I be able to pledge a belief? In particular, might I be able to pledge a regular, empirically vulnerable belief of the kind that I recognize I might not maintain? We live in a changing, incompletely grasped world and although I may think that the data are sufficient to elicit belief in an empirical proposition 'p', enabling me to avow a belief in it, I can never be sure that the data will not later be overturned or outweighed. Indeed, for me to consider pledging such a belief would betray a misconception about the very attitude of belief. It would show that I did not treat it as responsive to potentially changing data.

As against this, however, aren't we in Erewhon likely, in a fashion familiar from the actual world, to pledge religious or political beliefs or even beliefs that define the framework in which we think, such as beliefs in principles of classical logic like those of non-contradiction and excluded middle? Yes, but the best gloss on such a pledge is that it involves pledging an intention: say, the intention to treat certain texts or authorities or frameworks as definitive, letting them shape the construal to be given to any other sources of evidence. In particular, it involves pledging the intention of continuing to take that line, conditionally on the absence of a radical conversion or disruption in our way of thinking; while we may think that this is extremely unlikely, we can hardly discount the possibility altogether.

Might I be able to pledge an attitude, not of belief, but of desire? In order to do so, I would have to be able to identify relevant desiderata or attractors in the object of desire. And in deferring to those desiderata, I would have to be confident enough about their remaining effective—and about my ability to guard against distraction or disturbance—to be able to foreclose the changed-mind excuse as well as the misleading-mind excuse. Is there any desideratum that might help me to muster such confidence?

Surprisingly, there is. If I pledged a desire, then the very fact of making the pledge would bring a desideratum or attractor into existence that might serve in the required role. It would make it the case that sticking with the attitude has at least this appealing feature: that it would show that I can be relied upon to keep my word. The question, then, is whether I could rely on that feature to enable me to pledge a desire for hunting, for example; that is, an attraction to hunting that is based on the pleasure it provides.

The answer is that I could not. Suppose that I pledge a desire for hunting; that many of the desiderata that attracted me to hunting cease to be appealing; but that I continue to choose hunting because of wanting to show that my word is my bond. Would the desire for hunting remain in place as a result of the pledge?

No, it would not. I cannot count as desiring to hunt in the relevant sense when I only continue to choose it because of having given my word. Desire in the sense at issue requires me to be attached to hunting on the basis of desiderata other than the attractor that a pledge would put in place. It requires me to like hunting for the sport or recreation it offers, for the chance it gives me to get out into the country, or something of that sort. If hunting were to lose those attractions for me, then even if I continued to hunt because of having given my word, I would not continue to desire or like hunting in the relevant sense. And so, I cannot pledge to hold by a desire any more than I can pledge to hold by a belief.

The possibility of pledging an intention

This problem does not arise, however, with an intention or plan or anything of that kind. Suppose that in speaking with you I pledge an intention or plan to join you on the hunt—equivalently, I pledge to join you—wanting the thrill of chasing prey over open sunny spaces. And imagine that it rains heavily on the appointed day, but that I turn up nevertheless because of having given you my word. Do I count as still holding and acting on the intention pledged? Yes, I do. With an intention as distinct from a desire or preference, the attitude does not have to be sourced in certain sorts of desiderata in order to count as remaining in place; that I act as the intention requires—presumably because it requires it—is enough to establish the presence of the intention.[26] And so, the attractor that pledging an attitude creates in favor of maintaining the attitude can serve in this case—although only, it appears, in this case—to give me the confidence required for being able to make a pledge.

The possibility of avowing beliefs and desires was defended earlier on the basis, not of a Cartesian form of self-access, but of a naturalistically intelligible form of maker's knowledge. What now transpires is that the possibility of pledging attitudes, in particular intentions, is defensible

---

26. This will be so, strictly, only insofar as the intention does not cause the behavior by a deviant chain; it causes it robustly over cases in which the behavior is required by the intention. See Pettit (2018a).

in a parallel way without recourse to a non-naturalistic, libertarian account of self-control. All that needs to be presupposed in order to make sense of how I can pledge an intention is that I can recognize the motivating effect of certain desiderata, in particular the desideratum of proving faithful to my word.

According to previous arguments, I put myself in a position to avow a belief or desire or intention on the basis of consciously deferring to a suitable body of data or set of desiderata, where I am careful to register the data or desiderata without distraction and to guard against the possibility of disturbance. I know that I believe or desire something with sufficient confidence to be able to avow that attitude by virtue of knowing that I defer to those data or desiderata: this gives me a maker's knowledge of the attitude avowed. The same sort of maker's knowledge will enable me to recognize that I intend something with confidence sufficient to be able to pledge the intention; that is, to pledge to act as the intention requires. In consciously recognizing and deferring to the desideratum that the very act of pledging brings into play—the desideratum that consists in proving to live up to my word—I can achieve the degree of confidence required.

As in the case of avowing, the sort of pledging that will be relevant in the narrative constructed here involves pledging an intention of an unconditional kind—say, an intention to X—not a conditional intention: not an intention, if p, to X; not for example an intention, if the weather is good, to join you on the hunt. The same considerations apply here as with the avowal of desire and intention, and with the avowal of belief. To the extent that the intention I pledge is conditional, it will often be hard to test for whether I fail to display it; testing for it will require the satisfaction of the antecedent. And to the extent that that is so, the pledge will involve less risk and expense, and will boost the credibility in a lesser measure.

It is worth noting that conditional intentions would allow us to make pledges that involve beliefs and desires indirectly. Thus, consistently with the narrative presented, I might pledge an intention, if the evidence is supportive, to believe that p or, if suitable desiderata are in place, to desire R. It is in this sense, to revert to an earlier comment, that I might pledge to hold by a framework belief, such as a belief in classical logic, treating it as necessary or self-evident. What I pledge in such a case is the intention, if this does not lead to problems of a kind I can barely foresee, to stick with classical principles in organizing my responses to data (Quine 1970).

Pledging versus promising and predicting

The notion of pledging an intention to X—pledging to act on the intention—corresponds to the more regular idea of promising to X. But the notion of promising in ordinary usage has a strong moral or ethical flavor, as remarked earlier. It is represented as an act such that if I make a promise to do something, then I have an ethical obligation, however defeasible, to do it.

Pledging, as introduced at this point, has no such ethical connotations. When I make a pledge in Erewhon, as when I make an avowal, I back myself to act as thereby advertised, manifestly exposing myself to serious reputational costs in the event of failure. What I do is more akin to making a side-bet that I will hold and act on the intention pledged—a side-bet strategically designed to entice you and others to rely on me—than it is to giving you a promise in the ordinary, moralized sense of that term.

As pledging to act on an intention should be distinguished from the moral possibility of promising to act that way, so it should be distinguished from the empirical possibility of predicting the action. It may be that certain intentions or plans, perhaps again of a religious or political or framework kind, are relative fixtures in my psychology such that I can be fairly well assured—if you like, assured in the way an observer might be assured—that they will continue in place and I can predict with confidence that I will behave as they require. But pledging in the sense introduced here is quite distinct from such prediction, as it can materialize with intentions that are not rooted in the same way in my psychology. Indeed, pledging assumes that the intention it supports is not a fixture of that kind; it serves a useful purpose just to the extent that the attitude pledged is one that I might fail to maintain in the absence of a pledge. [27]

Pledging an unconditional intention, by the account offered here, is more costly, and hence more credible, than merely avowing the intention. If I pledge to act on a certain intention, as in pledging to join you on the hunt, then my stake in living up to those words is higher than my stake would have been, had I merely avowed an intention to join you. And hence you can rely with greater assurance on my joining you than if I had just made an avowal.

As in the case of avowal, of course, the cost of pledging need not make the act prohibitively expensive. If I fail to join you on the hunt but can invoke the practical, unforeclosed excuse of a broken leg in explanation of the failure, then I do not lose my stake. And the same is going to be true when I can plead an exempting disability like a temporary bout of amnesia to explain the failure. Any such factor can persuade you that, despite the failure, you need not despair of me as a cooperative and reliable interlocutor.

27. I am grateful for a discussion of this issue with Pamela Hieronymi and Jay Wallace.

Chapter 4: Committing with Others

The previous chapter shows that it is likely to the point of being more or less inevitable that we in Erewhon will go beyond reporting our attitudes to one another and engage in practices of avowal and pledging. We will find ourselves pushed by the desire to communicate our attitudes as credibly as possible into conveying them in a manner that forecloses various excuses for any miscommunication: in the case of an avowal, the misleading-mind excuse; and in the case of a pledge, the changed-mind excuse as well. We will be drawn into a committal form of self-communication in which we back ourselves to live up to the words we utter in attitudinal self-ascription, displaying our reliability in the degree of reputational risk we are willing to undertake.

This sort of commitment between individuals has a face-to-face character in the sense that we each individually commit to others, inviting them to rely on our words and to enter into one or another form of relationship. But commitment may also have a side-by-side character, requiring us to commit with others as well as to others. I may speak in a way that commits you and me to third parties, for example, putting both of us at reputational risk, should either not live up to the words I utter on our behalf. And what I may do in respect of you, so, of course, you or anyone else may do in respect of me. We may involve one another in a form of plural commitment—in a form of co-avowal or co-pledging—rather than each addressing others in singular commitment. We may commit ourselves with one another as well as committing ourselves to one another.

On the face of it, the possibility of side-by-side as distinct from face-to-face commitment may seem remote and unlikely. The idea of my committing to others, as in avowing or pledging my attitudes, is salient and familiar. The idea of my committing with others—my committing both myself and others to third parties—may look downright exotic. But it turns out that such commitment is accessible and unavoidable in Erewhon, as it is accessible and unavoidable in any communicative society, and that its accessibility is crucial to the prospect of our developing ethical notions, in particular the notion of the morally desirable.

This chapter explores the evolution of the narrative in which this form of plural commitment is likely to come on stream. The chapter is in five sections. First, it looks at the means whereby we as individuals can speak for a group, committing all the members and not ourselves alone; this section addresses in particular the way we avow shared attitudes of belief and desire without explicit, prior authorization. The second section explains why we would be motivated to evolve such a practice of plural commitment, arguing that the co-avowal of attitudes is as unavoidable as the practice of conversation. The third section goes on to explain why we are likely to be confident enough about one another's attitudes to be able to engage in such co-avowal. And the fourth section presents an important distinction between two forms, bounded and unbounded, that co-avowal may assume, which is important in the next chapter. While the focus in the chapter is on the co-avowal of belief and desire, the fifth section seeks to restore the balance with a short discussion of the possibility of co-avowing and co-pledging intention.

4.1 The means of co-avowing attitudes

Speaking for myself

When I avow or pledge an attitude, I play the role of spokesperson rather than reporter in relation to myself. I speak for myself, as we might say, rather than speaking about myself. Thus, I do not convey the attitude in the way in which I might try to communicate the attitude of another, reporting on it in a manner that keeps both epistemic excuses alive. In an avowal, I assume the authority to voice an attitude while closing down the possibility that I may have been misled about my own mind. In a pledge, I assume the authority to voice an attitude while closing down the possibility both that I was misled about my mind and that I might yet change my mind.

In speaking about your attitudes as an arbitrarily selected other, there is a distance between me in the interpreting role and you in the role of the interpreted. In speaking for myself in avowals and pledges—in assuming the role of spokesperson for myself—I reduce or remove that distance. I present myself as the person spoken for and speak, therefore, with a high degree of confidence: with confidence in the case of an avowal that the data robustly support a belief, the desiderata a desire or intention; and with confidence in the case of a pledge that the desideratum of living up to my word robustly supports my maintaining and acting on the pledged intention.

Uttered with the authority of a spokesperson, my words are not supported by my skill as the person speaking to track the independently formed attitudes of the person spoken for. They are supported rather by a dual commitment: as the person spoken for, to conform to what the person speaking says; and as the person speaking, to ascribe only such attitudes as the person spoken for is likely to be willing to display.

Speaking for myself and others

As it is possible for me to speak for myself in this way, so it is possible in certain contexts for me to speak for a plurality. Others may authorize me to make avowals—better, co-avowals—on behalf of all of us, or indeed to make pledges or co-pledges on our behalf. In authorizing me to do this, they will explicitly or implicitly agree as the individuals spoken for to live up to my words. And in acting on that authority, I as the individual speaking will have to stay within the bounds set for me: if I speak for them on matters in which they have not authorized me to speak, then I cease to act as their spokesperson.

There is no reason in principle why I should not be enabled to speak for such a plurality in Erewhon. Two conditions will make this possible. First, that each individual in the group pledges to live up to the words I utter on their behalf, whether in co-avowing or co-pledging.

And, second, that I pledge for my part to speak only within the bounds set by their pledges. They may pledge to let me speak for them without limit, but more likely they will allow me to speak for them only within certain explicit or implicit constraints.

When I co-avow a shared attitude of belief or desire or intention on this basis, I will rely on these pledges by others to foreclose the possibility of anyone's invoking a misleading-mind excuse—anyone's claiming that I got them wrong—in order to excuse their not displaying the attitude avowed and not living up to my words. And when I co-pledge a shared intention on this basis, I will foreclose also the possibility of anyone's invoking a changed-mind excuse—anyone's claiming that they had altered their allegiance—in order to excuse a failure to act on that intention. This is not to say that someone may not decide to overturn the pledged arrangement and reject my authority to speak for them in such respects. I foreclose the possibility of the person's appealing to the relevant excuse only on the assumption that their pledge, and the arrangement it helps to support, remains in place: that we remain a unity.

Co-avowal and co-pledging can mean avowing and pledging attitudes in the name of an incorporated agent, as when I act as spokesperson for a corporate body like a company or church or state; such a body will be organized to act as a single agent with the purportedly coherent web of attitudes that any agent must be expected to display (List and Pettit 2011). But when I speak for the attitudes of a group, we need not be organized to form such a corporate agent; we may be a mere plurality. And it is that sort of speech act that will be of interest here.

This mode of speaking for others is more general than the mode in which I speak for an incorporated agent, since it may occur both with the members of unincorporated and with the members of incorporated groups. But not only is it more general; it is also more fundamental. For unless a group of people had individual beliefs and desires of a sort that might be co-avowed, and individual intentions of a kind that might be co-pledged, it is hard to see how they could be able to form an incorporated body—say, a commercial company, or a political party—in which the members acquiesce in acting together as if they were an individual agent. If they manage to form such a body, that is presumably because of their holding individual beliefs, desires, and intentions of the sort that make incorporation attractive and feasible.

The focus on speaking for a plurality rather than for an incorporated group makes it natural to restrict attention to beliefs and desires rather than intentions, as we shall see in the final section of the chapter. And since it is not possible to co-pledge beliefs and desires, for the same reason that it is not possible to pledge them individually, this means that attention will be restricted to the co-avowal of such attitudes. Apart from the discussion in the final section, then, references to my speaking jointly for myself and others will generally refer only to my making co-avowals on behalf of a group, and indeed to my making co-avowals only of belief and desire, not of intention.

Speaking without prior authorization

It might seem that co-avowal in this sense requires the prior authorization of the spokesperson by other members of the group. That is what Thomas Hobbes (1994, Ch. 16) assumes when he suggests that the paradigm of authorization is my being appointed by you and others to speak for all of us as "a representer, or representative" or indeed, he adds in elaborating the role, as "a lieutenant, a vicar, an attorney, a deputy, a procurator, an actor." Hobbes is particularly concerned with the case in which I speak for all of us as an organized group agent—say, a corporation or commonwealth—and not as individuals. But his assumption about the need for prior authorization might be taken to apply to any case of co-avowal, not just to the case in which the individuals involved constitute an organized agency.[1]

1. Hobbes (1994, Ch. 16) argues that a multitude can become a group agent, being "made one person," by means of advance authorization. He thinks that that is the way that a private body may form—say, a company of merchants, in an example he uses elsewhere—with members authorizing some one officer to make avowals, and indeed pledges, in their collective name under a limited "commission" from them. And he thinks that that is the canonical way in which a commonwealth or state may come into existence, with members authorizing a sovereign spokesperson "without

Advance authorization of the kind at issue may obviously be appropriate in special circumstances in which I speak for all of us in a more or less formal capacity. But the authorization on the basis of which I can co-avow certain attitudes in common with you and others need not have its origin in any such ex ante arrangement, however tacit. I may presume on being authorized by you and others, as when I presume to avow a belief in the name of all—when, as we might say, I essay a co-avowal. I may then claim to have my presumption vindicated—claim to succeed in co-avowing the belief—if none of you lodges an ex post protest at my pretension.

On this picture, I will signal that I am claiming to speak for what each of us in a certain group thinks or feels, whatever form that signal takes, and I will take the claim to be vindicated—to have my authority as spokesperson accepted—insofar as neither you nor anyone else objects to what I say in that role. I do not speak with your advance license, your prior authorization. Rather, I speak on the presumption that no one will reject my authority and that if no one rejects it, then the absence of rejection will have the same effect as ex ante authorization.

Prior authorization of me as the spokesperson of many, as already noted, consists in a pledge by members of the group to live up to my words, displaying the attitude ascribed, so long as I operate within the mandate given. There is no prior pledge involved in the case of ex post authorization, or at least none of an explicit kind. So, what entitles me to make a claim to such authorization when none of you objects to what I say on our behalf?

You and others do not say "Yea" in advance to my playing the role of spokesperson, as an actual pledge would require. But neither do you say

---

stint." The commission in this case is unlimited, he holds, since he defends an absolutist view of the power that a sovereign has to enjoy. He acknowledges that the entity whose voice a group authorizes may be a committee that operates by majority voting but denies that it can be a set of mutually constraining individuals or committees such as the competing branches and offices of government that a mixed constitution would allow. He is mistaken on both of those counts, but this is not the place to explore such issues. See Pettit (2008a, 2014a) and List and Pettit (2011).

"Nay" in the wake of my presuming to act in such a role; in particular, you do not say "Nay" when there was nothing to prevent or inhibit you from doing so. You authorize me, not by what you said, but by what you might saliently have said and chose not to say. You do not explicitly pledge to go along in advance but neither do you balk at my acting as if you were pledged to go along. Thus, you pledge yourself to go along by allowing me to treat you as if you were pledged, when you have every opportunity to object to that presumption. The pledge takes a virtual rather than an active form; it exists as a result of what you could have done and fail to do, and not as a result of a positive action.

The target of concern

The observations made so far are designed to narrow down the target of concern in the remainder of the chapter. The narrative will address the possibility of my speaking for a group, not in all the forms that such speech might take, but only in a form that is restricted in three ways. First, the group for which I speak is any plurality of individuals, not an organized corporate body. Second, the mode in which I speak is limited to the co-avowal of belief and desire as distinct from the co-avowal or co-pledging of intention. And third, the authorization on the basis of which I speak is ex post or presumptive in character rather than prior or ex ante.

The observations made show that the means required for co-avowal in this sense are already going to be available in Erewhon; they involve an active or virtual pledge on the part of each of those spoken for and a corresponding pledge on the part of their spokesperson. But that leaves two other questions open of a kind with questions that arose in the case of individual avowal and indeed individual pledging. First, is there a motive that might make co-avowal attractive for us in a group of individuals? And second, could I ever muster confidence enough about the attitudes of other people to be prepared to essay a co-avowal of purportedly common attitudes? The following two sections address those questions in turn.

4.2 The conversational need to co-avow

The appeal of conversation

In considering the motives that each of us has for individually avowing or pledging attitudes, the assumption has been that in communicating with one another in Erewhon we trade independent utterances in a series of exchanges; we each pay the cost of reliably communicating information to others for the reward of being generally able both to rely on others and to elicit their reliance on us. On this picture, the main concern on my side, exactly analogous to the main concern on yours, is to prove sufficiently reliable in conveying those messages to be able, as occasion demands, to rely on you and to get you to rely on me. As argued in chapter 2, I can generally expect to be able to rely on you in the future, and to be able to get you to rely on me, just in case I have proved reliable in the past.

This assumption about communication is fine for the purposes pursued in the discussion so far. But the appeal of co-avowal is going to be obvious only in light of a further assumption. This is that in reaping the benefits of mutual reliance, we in Erewhon are bound to pursue exchanges of information that have a more complex, conversational structure. The further assumption is crucial, because it turns out that conversationally structured exchanges inevitably involve co-avowal.

In the trading of information envisaged in earlier chapters, I convey some would-be facts about our shared environs and about my particular attitudes. And whether or not I undertake the risks associated with avowing or pledging as distinct from reporting, I do so in the expectation that you will generally respond by taking me at my word and relying on the facts being as I communicate them to be. But it is inevitable that our exchanges will take a more complex form than this communication, now about one purported fact, now about another. In any exchange, you are likely to want to seek further information from me, and I in turn am likely to want to seek further information from you, as we try to build up a more detailed picture of the facts in which we are interested. And we may even want to draw third parties into the exchange as we construct a picture that is adequate to our particular interests.

When our exchanges of information have this interlocking structure, they constitute a conversation. Turn and turn around, we contribute to the picture of things—the picture of our shared world and our respective outlooks—that we each require for the purposes we have in hand. Those purposes may be psychologically independent, as when I seek to learn more about the options and prospects I face, and you seek to learn more about the options and prospects that you confront. Or they may be socially shared, as when we envisage a form of cooperation that promises to be beneficial for both of us and that would require each of us to avow or pledge an individual intention to play our part.

The conversation envisaged here, of course, is the very austere and purposeful sort of exchange in which we have something significant to resolve for ourselves, whether individually or collectively. Concentrating on conversation of this kind is not meant to suggest that we in Erewhon do not go in also for playful banter, idle chatter, and indulgent gossip. Nor is it meant to imply that such exchanges are not important in building up individual relationships. While the narrative constructed here requires only the presence of purposeful conversational exchange, it does not presuppose the absence of its more entertaining, communally enhancing counterparts.[2]

From conversation to co-avowal

Suppose that you and I and others exchange information in this conversational mode, say with a view to resolving problems we face individually or together: perhaps a problem about how to resolve a conflict, what to believe about something, or what to do in pursuit of some cooperative end. If I am to contribute usefully to a conversation like this, I must speak on the basis of presuppositions about what we each believe and want and intend; if I am wrong about the shared presuppositions, then what I say will not engage the concerns of others properly. But in

---

2. The narrative also assumes that conversations are not warped by the effects of power and domination—or hermeneutic injustice (Fricker 2007)—in driving conversations. This fits with the assumption of equality of power discussed in chapter 1.

speaking on the basis of such presuppositions, I presume to co-avow them in the name of each of us in the conversation. Given my presumption that I will not be opposed, it will be manifest to all that I avow the beliefs or desires, not just as personal attitudes, but as attitudes that we are each prepared to accept.[3]

When the presuppositions are unopposed, the contribution I make to the conversation in expressing a belief or desire will be to propose, again assuming no opposition, that that attitude is also one that we each manifestly accept or can be expected to accept as members of the group. If you and others go along with the presuppositions I make and the proposal I put forward, this will establish between us a richer, manifest base of shared presuppositions. And at that point it will create a new opportunity for you or someone else to presume to co-avow yet another attitude and, assuming that your proposal is accepted, to add further to that base.

If things proceed smoothly along this path, then we may each hope to reach a point where our manifestly shared set of presuppositions is extensive enough to be able to solve the problem with which we started. It may be enough to eliminate or corral potentially dangerous conflicts, for example, to establish a common belief about some contentious issue, or to make possible the various forms of coordination or incorporation in which we avow or pledge an intention to take part.

The presuppositional base built up in such a smoothly progressing conversation is well-described as common ground that we manage to establish between us (Stalnaker 1978; Sperber and Wilson 1986; Tomasello 2008). It consists in a set of attitudes such that it is a matter of common awareness among those of us engaged in the conversation that we are each prepared to treat those attitudes as properly co-avowed in our name; in that sense, we each co-accept the attitudes.

---

3. The things I presuppose—or more generally "implicate"—are plausibly going to be identifiable on the assumption that I satisfy constraints like the maxims of conversation—quality, quantity, relation, and manner—analyzed by Paul Grice (1975a). For a more general perspective, in which relevance is the crucial factor, see Sperber and Wilson (1986).

When we go along with a conversation, accepting the different elements in the common ground, we each foreclose the possibility of excusing our failure to live up to the co-avowed attitude by claiming that the co-avower—this may be me or you or anyone else—got our attitude wrong.

The attitudes that are built into the common ground evolving between us are likely to include desires as well as beliefs. In contexts in which any action is envisaged, after all, our co-accepted presuppositions will need to identify presumptive objects of common attraction as well as presumptive matters of common acceptance. But it is worth noting at this point that there is a great difference between the ways in which the two sorts of attitudes lend themselves to co-avowal.

With anything I have solid ground for believing, there will be others who share that ground so that I may presume to co-avow it in their name as well as in mine. But that is not so with all the things I have solid ground for desiring. With some of those things, there may be many people who share that ground, but with other things, there may be few or no people who do so. Desires that prove resistant to co-avowal will typically be grounded in agent-relative desiderata to do with what will facilitate my success, help my children, enable me to keep my pledges, or whatever. The difference between belief and desire in these respects will be at the center of concern in the next chapter.

The emerging image of conversational exchange is easily illustrated. I tell you that there are deer gathering on the southern side of the woods, presupposing that we each want to join in a hunt and that we each know how to get to the woods. You go along with that presupposition, accept my assertion and add, on the basis of the now richer common ground—and perhaps on the basis of the further presupposition that three makes for a better hunting party—that a certain friend is available to join us. As the conversation progresses, perhaps now including the friend as well, we each end up co-avowing a desire to join in a hunt, and a belief that that requires an expedition to the southern side of the woods. And at that point we each explicitly or implicitly avow or pledge an individual intention to take part, building this too into the common ground between us.

Not all conversations will progress as smoothly as this, of course. Even if my presuppositions are accepted, someone may reject the addition to the common ground that I propose in my initial contribution to the conversation, or indeed in any later contribution. Or someone may seem to go along with a particular contribution but register an objection later when they see where it would lead. And what goes for me in this regard goes for each of us; none of us can be assured that our contribution at any point will be accepted by others. But when rejection occurs, this will presumably trigger a round of rejoinders and revisions—it would be in no one's interest just to walk away from every divergence of attitudes— and this can eventually put things back on a progressive path. The most purposeful conversations may sometimes fail in Erewhon, as they may fail in any society. But, plausibly, they will often succeed.

In Erewhon, as already noted, we will each have a motive for taking part in serious conversations of this kind; after all, they are essential for mutual reliance, enabling us to form, maintain, and develop peaceful, helpful, and collaborative relationships. What the analysis shows is that there is no useful conversation of this purposeful kind without a pattern of co-avowal and co-acceptance. Contributors each avow attitudes in the name of all those involved, putting them forward as attitudes that everyone avows or can be expected to avow from the standpoint they share. And, whether or not they make any active contribution, participants each accept that any attitude proposed for co-avowal that no one opposes is one that they are individually prepared to accept as a member of the group.

What forms should we expect essays at co-avowal to take? The conversational context will presumably make it possible to presume to co-avow a belief that p by simply saying 'p', since it will often indicate that I am speaking for all of us, not just myself. And with desires as well as with beliefs, we can rely on ascriptions and explanations to serve also as means of presuming to co-avow those attitudes. Thus, I can presume to co-avow by resorting to an explicit or implicit statement about what we believe or desire: this, as in declaring that we all favor going on a hunt. Or I can achieve the same effect by invoking relevant data or desiderata to explain why the belief or desire is intelligible—say, the belief that the southern woods are a good location for a hunt—relying on the context to indicate that I am speaking for all, not speaking for myself alone.

The orthodox character of this analysis

This analysis of conversation connects closely with the work of Robert Stalnaker, David Lewis, and others on assertion and related topics.[4] Stalnaker (1978, 86) emphasizes that "the essential effect of an assertion is to change the presuppositions of the participants in the conversation by adding the content of what is asserted to what is presupposed." And he also recognizes that in presenting certain presuppositions and assertions as expressive of the attitudes of each, every participant presumes on the authorization of others for doing this and is ready to retreat if ex post authorization is denied. Thus, he adds that the effect of assertion in changing presuppositions, reshaping the common ground between parties, "is avoided only if the assertion is rejected."

What holds about the content of an assertion holds equally, as Stalnaker (1978, 87) stresses, with any presuppositions that an assertion puts in place less obtrusively; an utterance can change common ground, not by just asserting something, but also by intruding a would-be presupposition of all parties. Suppose I say in a conversational context, "The present king of Erewhon is bald." I thereby identify as a would-be presupposition co-accepted among us the claim that Erewhon currently has a king, as well as proposing for co-acceptance the further claim that the king is bald. But you or others can play the same role in rejecting my would-be presupposition as you can in rejecting the proposition I propose as an additional element in the common ground. If you each let that would-be presupposition pass, then the utterance will count as co-avowing the belief that there is a king of Erewhon, as it will count as co-avowing the belief that the king is bald. You must reject my

4. See Robert Stalnaker (1978) and David Lewis (1983b, Ch 13). For some imaginative applications and developments of the approach shared between Lewis and Stalnaker, see Langton (2009), including the chapter jointly written with Caroline West.

presumed authority if you are to stop me from changing the common ground in this way.

No one is an island and, as these observations show, no speaker holds just by insular attitudes. Conversation is essential for gaining the benefits of mutual reliance that we have been emphasizing throughout, but it imposes costs on those of us who submit ourselves to its discipline. It means that as members of this or that group, any one of us may have to avow beliefs and desires on behalf of many as well as on our own behalf alone. And it means that as members of this or that group, each of us has to accept that we cannot excuse a failure to live up to any successfully co-avowed attitude by appealing to a misleading mind—that is, by claiming that the spokesperson involved got our attitude wrong.

4.3 *The confidence co-avowal requires*

The linkage with purposeful conversation—palpably attractive, even unavoidable conversation—explains why we members of Erewhon, like human beings anywhere, will have a powerful motive for presuming to make co-avowals. But it is one thing to show that we have a means and a motive for doing this. It is quite another to show why we may be expected to have sufficient confidence about the attitudes we share with others to be ready to essay a co-avowal. What could give me confidence enough to be ready to speak for you and others as well as myself in presuming to avow a belief or desire that we share?

This problem is particularly challenging, because I would find myself in a sorry position if I could not muster such confidence. Fearful of aspiring to speak for a group without winning the support of others— fearful perhaps of being mocked for my pretensions—I might be led to avoid conversation altogether, or at least to avoid taking the lead in any conversation. If I alone were reduced to this state of diffidence, I would suffer greatly in the extent to which I could initiate efforts to gain information from others and establish a productive pattern of mutual reliance. And if each of us were reduced to this state of diffidence, then the prospect of mutually profitable reliance would vanish altogether.

The requirements of confidence

In order to avow a belief in my own name—or at least an expensive avowal that boosts the credibility of my words— I have to think that the data supporting the proposition believed are sufficient to elicit that belief and that my sensitivity to those data is secure against distraction and disturbance. And in order to avow a desire in my own name, incurring a parallel expense, I have to rely on the desiderata at the origin of the desire being sufficient and, again, on my sensitivity to those attractors being secure against distraction and disturbance.

This suggests that if I am to be able to avow a belief or desire on behalf of you and others as well as myself, then I must be able to assume that you have access to the same data and desiderata as I do, that you are disposed to respond to them in the same way, and that you are equally secure in your responsiveness to them. But how could it be reasonable on my part, or on the part of anyone else in the conversational group, to rely on our being exposed to the same data and desiderata and to be responsive to them—securely responsive to them—in the same manner?

It is relatively easy to see how I could reasonably assume that we are exposed to the same data or desiderata. There is good empirical evidence that human beings are disposed by nature, not just to attend to this or that body of fact, but to exercise joint attention: to focus on certain matters in shared awareness that they are available at the same time to others, albeit from different perspectives (Seemann 2011; Tomasello 2014). That being so, I will often be in the position to recognize that as I can access a certain body of data or a certain set of desiderata, so you can do this, and so you and I can do it jointly.

Many of us will have access to some data not available to others, as when I alone have evidence that p and q, you alone have evidence that p and r. But even in such a case, it may be manifest that we both have evidence that p. Again, many of us will recognize special desiderata that are not available to others, and perhaps not available by a sort of necessity: the welfare of your child may matter to you in a way it cannot matter to me, and vice versa. But that is consistent with there being common desiderata or attractors that are manifestly effective for both of us: say, that peace or prosperity should be commonplace or, indeed, that parents be allowed to care for their own children in a special way.

It is one thing, however, to assume that I and you and others may often face a manifestly common body of data or common set of desiderata. It is quite another to suppose that we are each disposed to respond to that common base in a common manner: to suppose that as the data or desiderata are likely to lead me, so in general they are likely to lead you. Is this further assumption a reasonable one to make, in particular a reasonable one to make about those of us in Erewhon?

Confidence about common responsiveness

Suppose that the data you rely on in forming a belief are not good or complete by my lights. Or suppose that the desiderata you are moved by in forming a desire are not attractors that I can see as relevant, even allowing for differences of taste and background, or that they are only a proper subset of the desiderata I take to be relevant. This will be no problem so long as I can point out my worries about the idiosyncratic or incomplete basis on which you form your attitudes and you respond appropriately. You may change the attitude in response to my complaint, or you may show me that the basis is not as quirky or patchy as it seemed. Seeking a saucer of mud, in the example cited earlier from Elizabeth Anscombe (1957), you show me that for you it is an important reminder of mortality.

But suppose that you are not disposed or able to do this and continue to display a form of sensitivity to data or desiderata that is completely alien to me. Suppose that without giving me reason to assign different meanings to your words, you present to me as someone for whom the effect of data is not the same as it is with me; or as someone for whom the role of desiderata is played by different properties from those that make any impact on me. Whether on a wider or a narrower front, you and I do not work with the same logic of attitude-formation. Or the logics with which we operate overlap only in part.

How should I be expected to respond if you were as alien as this? I could not relate to you as in practice human beings generally relate to one another. I could only see you as someone to whom I had to adjust as I might adjust to a force of nature, not as someone conversable, as it was put earlier: someone I can reach in the space of words. I would be likely to be bewildered and at a loss. In the end, indeed, I might even be forced to assume that in a narrower or a wider domain you are a subject for treatment, as Peter Strawson (1962) puts it, not a partner with whom I can expect to interact conversationally.

Strawson suggests that human beings treat the option of seeing another person in this manner—seeing them from within a dehumanizing, objective stance—as a last resort, only embracing it out of desperation. They insist instead on looking in every case for grounds to see their interlocutor as someone intelligible on lines familiar to them: someone with whom they could participate in profitable conversation, given the chance to do so. This commitment to finding one another conversable is sustained successfully in the practices of many societies, since the last-resort option is only occasionally forced upon people. And that success suggests that human beings do generally conform to the required pattern in the way they form their beliefs and desires under the impact of data and desiderata.

If this is correct, then it is natural to assume that we in Erewhon, like human beings everywhere, will generally have the capacity as interpreters to find conversable sense in what we say to one another and in how we behave; we will be able to avoid having to regard one another as subjects for treatment rather than as potential interlocutors (Pettit and Smith 1996). Our human nature is likely to have given us the common sensitivity to data and desiderata that would ensure such mutual conversability and intelligibility. And if that sensitivity were not wholly supplied by nature, we would each have a motive to simulate or internalize it in order to establish ourselves as someone on whom others can rely: someone with whom they can do business (McGeer 2007).

These observations suggest that not only should you and I be able to establish that the same data or desiderata are available to each of us, we should also be able to rely on sharing in a common pattern of sensitivity to those data and desiderata. Thus, we can assume that where certain shared data lead one of us in the formation of belief, there they will also lead others; and that where commonly engaging desiderata push any one of us in forming our desires, there they will also push others.

The possibility of confidence

As we in Erewhon have a motive to essay co-avowal, then, and a means of satisfying it, these observations suggest that we will also have the confidence to do so. We can assume a common logic of attitude formation and, recognizing the data and desiderata that are broadly at our common disposal, we can presume on speaking for others as well as ourselves in avowing corresponding beliefs or desires. Or at least we can presume on doing this when we satisfy a further condition. This is that we can also assume that those of us who accept a co-avowal made on our behalf will recognize the possibility of distraction and disturbance, as we recognize that possibility in the case of individual avowals and pledges, and will be on guard against it.

Distraction in this case, as in others, will be illustrated by any factors that can cause oversight or inattention. And disturbance can be introduced by any influences that are liable to lead us not to live up to a co-avowed or co-accepted attitude; that do not provide us with what we could treat as a changed-mind excuse; and that we can neutralize or avoid, if only we make the effort.

The disturbers in the case of co-avowed or co-accepted attitudes will include, not just the sorts of intrapersonal factors mentioned in the individual case—the momentary illusion or impulse, for example—but also disturbers of an interpersonal character such as the premature rush for consensus, which will weaken the force of the data and desiderata shared in common with others. Individuals can expect to be able to make avowals in their own name only if they guard against the disturbance relevant in the individual case. And equally they can expect to be able to co-avow or co-accept attitudes on behalf of a plurality only if they and those they speak for guard against the relevant disturbers.

By the account offered in the last chapter, it is a sort of maker's knowledge that gives me enough confidence to be able to avow or pledge an attitude in my own name. The line developed here shows that it is something of the same sort that can give me enough confidence to essay the co-avowal of an attitude for a group.

Suppose I recognize that a body of data or desiderata that is available to me in common with you and others is sufficient to elicit a certain belief or desire, that you are disposed to respond to it in the same way as me, and that we are each on guard against distraction and disturbance. In consciously deferring to those data or desiderata, making up my mind on the attitude to form, I am positioned to be confident that I hold that attitude. And in consciously recognizing that you and others are responsive in the same way to the same data and desiderata, I am positioned to be confident that you and others hold that attitude, too.

Certainly, I can be confident that you hold the attitude once I or someone else essays a co-avowal and calls attention to the supportive data or desiderata. I do not make up the group's mind in this sort of initiative, but I am part of the exercise in which we together make up that mind. I have a co-maker's knowledge, as it might be put, of our each holding the attitude.

4.4 Bounded and unbounded co-avowal

With any conversation of the kind under consideration, there is always going to be a group of individuals who are taken as parties to the conversation, and there is always going to be a presupposed ground that is taken to be common to those parties. But conversations may vary, depending on how the group of participants is identified and how the ground they share in common is delimited. The main variation is between conversations in which the group or the ground is fixed in advance, on the one side, and conversations in which they are allowed to change, on the other. Conversations in which the group or the ground is fixed in some measure may be described as bounded or closed; conversations in which they are each allowed to shift may be cast as unbounded or open: they are pursued as conversations in which anyone may seek to have a say, on any proposed basis.

Bounded conversation

There are two sorts of bounded exchange, as these comments indicate. In a first variety, I and other speakers may seek accommodation with all the members in a given, pre-determined group, being prepared to make compromises—even compromises that disregard what one or another of us sees as relevant data or desiderata—in order to establish common ground between us. In a second variety, I and other speakers may treat some ground, not the membership of our group, as given and pre-determined—this, perhaps, because each of us takes it to be revealed doctrine—and not be prepared to give up that ground for the sake of keeping dissenting members on our side or of attracting new members. In the one case, we keep the members fixed, except perhaps under strict rules of succession or admission, and let the ground move; in the other, we keep the ground fixed, at least in some purportedly core part, and let the membership move instead.[5]

Conversations in Erewhon are unlikely to be bounded on the doctrinal front, unless we indulge in religion or politics. If we go in for the formation of a quasi-religious faith or aspiration, we may establish an orthodoxy that we put beyond question within the society or within one or another sub-culture. And if we in a particular caste or clan wish to maintain our identity against others, we may establish a belief in our superiority, or a desire for our pre-eminence, as something that no one dare deny, or at least no one in the relevant party. But in the absence of such contingent pressures, we will hardly want to immunize any particular ground of belief or desire, securing it against drift and development.

But if conversations in Erewhon are unlikely to be bounded in respect of ground, they are very likely to be bounded in respect of the group involved. If I am interested in resolving certain differences with others, what will be important for me is to find common ground with those

---

5. We might also aspire not to let either group or ground move. But that would put very firm limits on where conversation can take members. It would prevent them either from altering the membership or from reforming their core tenets.

others, or at least with most of them. And the same is going to be true if I am interested in coming to an agreement about certain matters or in organizing an expedition of some sort. In each case, the members of the relevant group will be fixed and the task that I and others will face is that of establishing common ground within the grouping. We may be able to achieve such common ground, however, only at the cost of personal compromise. It may be that by my lights or yours, some members are insufficiently cognizant of relevant data or desiderata or insufficiently responsive to them. But in the name of sticking together, we may have no option but to cut down the grounds endorsed in co-avowal and to tailor our joint commitments accordingly.

Unbounded conversation

Conversation is unbounded when it is not constrained either in respect of group or in respect of ground. As a contributor to such a conversation, I will start from presumptively solid common ground and speak to unspecified others, expecting them to share that ground or to provide considerations that require me to revise it. The others invoked as audience may constitute a present or just a prospective group: say, an audience that I might hope to reach by setting things down in writing. But in doing this I will remain open to change in two ways: first, by not fixing the membership of the group in advance; and second, by not fixing in advance the ground to be found in common with that membership.

In unbounded conversation, I will be happy to let the ground that is co-avowed with others shift from its initial or any later shape insofar as others change my perception of relevant data or desiderata. Equally, I will be happy to let the membership include any others who accept the common ground or are persuasive in arguing for a change, and to exclude any others who reject the common ground but do not provide persuasive arguments in their defense. And as that is true of me, so it is also true of every other participant.

On the unbounded model of conversation, as on the bounded model, I put forward the claims I make on ground that I assume will be available to others. But the others I address in the unbounded case, whether in speech or writing, or indeed any other medium, may extend indefinitely. I put forward my claims as presuppositions and proposals that I think any presumptively conversable others should find sufficient. But of course, I remain constantly open to the possibility that I may be led by one of those others to change the ground held fixed between us and to amend the attitudes we co-avow or co-accept in an unbounded way.

Once the idea of an unbounded conversation is available to me, it will give me a novel way of thinking about what I do in avowing a belief on the basis of data that are presumptively relevant for everyone or in avowing desires that happen to be based on desiderata that are presumptively relevant for all. In avowing a belief, to stick to that case, I will normally put it forward as securely supported by the data available to me. But that means that there will be no block to thinking of it as a belief that others may be expected to endorse on the basis of those same data, assuming that the data are complete and reliable. Anticipating that others will go along with me in responding to such data, I will be able to think of my utterance as purporting to be a co-avowal made on their behalf as well as on my own. And insofar as I remain open to opposition and correction by others—this might happen, for example, if they could show that my data are inadequate—I will be more or less bound to think of it in that way.

In some avowals, of course, I may speak in a confessional or autobiographical mode, conveying my beliefs or desires to you on the assumption that you are primarily interested, not in what I say, but in the fact that it is I who say it. But in most avowals, I will not assume such a narcissistic stance. I will speak in a dialectical mode that invites any interlocutors, real or imagined, to accept what I say or to challenge me where they disagree. And when I make avowals in this spirit, I speak as a member of a potential conversation, presuming to co-avow beliefs or desires that I think should command the assent of any others in the imagined or actual community of interlocutors.

As I speak in a dialectical rather than an autobiographical mode, I aspire to find a viewpoint that others can share and to contribute to an ongoing conversation. Indeed, I may even think of that conversation continuing into the future or continuing from the past. It was in this spirit that, expelled from office, Machiavelli would end a day on his farm by entering the courts of ancient men, as he famously records, and feed on the food of their conversation. And it may be in this spirit that more recent authors like Richard Rorty (1980) have invoked the conversation of humanity as an ongoing enterprise in which each of us wittingly or unwittingly participates.

Bounded conversation is likely to be common in Erewhon, as noted earlier, but unbounded conversation will be common, too. Indeed, it will be inescapable. Whereas co-avowal in the name of a bounded group is contingent on happening to belong to such a group, unbounded co-avowal is as unavoidable as individual avowal. Or at least it is as unavoidable as the sort of individual avowal that is based on grounds that are relevant for all; this includes the avowal of any belief on the basis of unquestionable data, and the avowal of any desire on the basis of desiderata that are not peculiar to me or mine.

The presumption to unbounded co-avowal is going to be implicit in any exercise of talking things through—and by extension thinking them through—from a standpoint that is taken to be available to anyone. It will materialize, for example, as we talk and think about the movements of the animals we hunt, the seasonal patterns in the plants we harvest, the attraction of eating meat over vegetables, the honor due to our elders, and the destiny we face after death. The possibility of writing, or otherwise communicating over spatial and temporal distances, is bound to make unbounded conversation more accessible and attractive. But no human beings, not even those of us in a relatively undeveloped Erewhon, could fail to indulge in such exchange.

4.5. Co-avowing and co-pledging intentions

Desires and intentions

As appeared in discussing individual pledging, there is an important difference between intending and desiring. I count as acting on an intention just in case I form the intention—whether or not I pledge it—and then act accordingly. It does not matter, as it would in the case of desire, that no independent desiderata remained effective as between the time when I formed the intention and the time when I acted on it.

A disposition to act in a certain way can constitute a desire, in the sense assumed here, only if it is supported by certain independent desiderata. If they are removed but the disposition is preserved, then what remains does not count as the desire. A disposition to act in a certain way can constitute an intention, however, even if it survives the removal of independent desiderata; all that is strictly required is that it should continue to dispose the agent to act appropriately.

As the presence of a continuing set of independent desiderata may not be necessary for intention, so it may not be sufficient. A given set of desiderata may fail to elicit intention, to put the point more sharply, while succeeding in eliciting a corresponding desire. This difference stems from the fact that, plausibly, there are forms of disturbance, associated with weakness of will, that may undermine intention without undermining desire. Suppose some of our compatriots in Erewhon have had their homes destroyed in a river flood. Desiderata that would elicit a desire to provide relief for one or another victim—this, leading to expressions of sympathy and so on—might not succeed, say because of attendant costs, in eliciting an intention to give relief.

The problem with co-avowing or co-pledging intentions

This sufficiency consideration marks a contrast between desires and intentions as candidates for co-avowal and indeed co-pledging. In order for me to have grounds for essaying the co-avowal of a desire in a certain group—say, a desire to provide relief for the flood victims—it will be sufficient that some strong desiderata are manifestly available to all of us. But while the desiderata may actually prompt an intention on the part of each of us to provide some relief, it would be misleading of me to rely on those desiderata as a basis for presuming to co-avow or co-pledge an intention to help.

Assume that it is a matter of common awareness that disturbances may undermine an intention to help without undermining a desire to help. To claim to be able to co-avow or co-pledge an intention to help will communicate in that case that I have a firmer basis for doing so than just the presence of relevant desiderata. The message conveyed will be that I am authorized, presumably in advance, to avow or pledge an intention on the part of each to provide relief to the flood victims. [6]

The lesson of these observations is that purporting to co-avow or co-pledge individual intentions that others share with me is going to make sense only in the special circumstances in which I have their prior authorization to speak for them. For that reason, as mentioned earlier, the focus in this account of speaking for others—that is, others as a plurality, not a corporate body—will be on beliefs and desires and, since they do not allow of co-pledging, on the co-avowal of such attitudes.[7]

The points just made apply only to the co-avowal and co-pledging of individual intentions that a number of people—a plurality of agents, as we have put it—happen to share. But people may cooperate in the formation of joint intentions and there is room for any one of them to co-avow or even co-pledge such an intention without prior authorization. This possibility is worth documenting for the sake of completeness, although it will not be of particular relevance in the remainder of the book.

6. One possible exception might occur in the case in which I publicly co-avow or co-pledge an intention on the part of each to provide relief, making it manifestly the case that it will be embarrassing, even perhaps shameful, for anyone for whom I purport to speak in public either to object to what I say or to fail to deliver on the intention ascribed. A similar point applies to publicly essaying the co-avowal or co-pledging of joint intentions of the kind discussed later in the text.

7. Suppose, contrary to the assumption on which this argument rests, that intention is manifestly as sensitive as desire to certain desiderata, so that nothing is likely to disturb the effect of desiderata in eliciting intention, if nothing disturbs their effect in eliciting desire. Even in this case, the message of my claiming to co-avow or co-pledge an intention will be that I have the prior authorization of others to do so. For why otherwise would I go beyond essaying a co-avowal of desire and attempt to co-avow, indeed co-pledge, an intention?

Joint intentions

Apart from the individual intentions I may share with others to help out the victims of the flood, there are also joint intentions I may share with them. And there may be ground for essaying the co-avowal or co-pledging of a joint intention of this kind—say, to get together in building a dam against future floods—even when I lack prior authorization.

The category of joint intention is probably best introduced by identifying the elements it requires in a typical case. When we form a joint intention in the group, such as the intention to cooperate in building a dam, that will usually be because it is obvious that none of us can build the dam on our own, at least not with hope of any great success. And in such a case, it will normally be a matter of common awareness between us that further conditions are fulfilled as well: first, we all individually desire the achievement of the result; second, there is a manifest plan—a rough specification of roles—whereby we can achieve it together; and third, we are individually ready to play our particular parts in enacting the plan and achieving the result.[8]

A joint intention will lead us to perform a shared action in a case like this—to play our individual parts in bringing off the action—insofar as one or more of us takes the lead and the rest follow. In an earlier example, you and I and the friend who joins us will enact a joint intention to go hunting when we follow someone's lead in acting on the basis of what our conversation makes manifest: that we all want to go hunting; that we can hunt together by making our way to the southern side of the woods; and that we are all ready to take part in such an expedition. In the example of building the dam, I may get things going in a similar manner, if there is a plan for damming the river that is manifest to all; or if I can make a plan manifest by pointing out that we can stop the

8. This draws on the account of joint intention sketched in the first chapter in order to illustrate the creature-constructive methodology; this is modeled on Bratman (2014). But for purposes of the present narrative, any of a variety of accounts of joint intention might be adopted instead; for some important alternatives, see Tuomela (2007); Searle (2010); Gilbert (2015).

flooding, say by moving rocks and debris into a position where they will stop the river overflowing.

Whenever a joint intention has been formed among the members of a group, that will put any one of us in a position to presume on the authorization of others and to essay a co-avowal or a co-pledge of our joint intention to follow the assumed plan and pursue the desired result. And in the absence of an objection from others, I will be deemed to have been successful in co-avowing or co-pledging the intention. Thus, I may seek to reassure the flood victims that they won't suffer a similar disaster later by announcing that we intend to build a dam or by pledging on our joint behalf that we will get a dam built.

Corporate bodies

In the case of the hunt or the dam, I get together with others to pursue an episodic, more or less isolated purpose. But joint intentions also appear, and perhaps appear most commonly, in the case in which we incorporate as a multipurpose group agent: say, as a disaster-relief organization. Forming joint intentions is not sufficient for incorporation, but in standard cases, it is certainly necessary (Pettit and Schweikard 2006).

When we come to constitute a corporate agent, we each manifestly accept certain procedures for resolving various issues in any of a range of relevant circumstances: say, various sorts of disaster. These, typically, will be issues to do with what the particular problems are that we face in such a scenario; how they should be prioritized relative to one another; what it is we might in principle do by way of response; how therefore we should act; and so on. We will perform across that range of situations like a single agent, with certain more or less fixed goals or desires; with certain beliefs established among us and with procedures in place for updating those beliefs to take account of novel opportunities and obstacles, for example; and with a capacity to act in pursuit of those goals under the guidance of our beliefs (List and Pettit 2011; Pettit 2014a).

If we do constitute a corporate body of this kind, mimicking the performance of an individual agent, there are an open number of joint intentions that any one of us may presume to co-avow or co-pledge without fear of opposition. It will be possible for any of us—not just anyone in the position of an official spokesperson—to presume to co-avow or co-pledge the group's intention to pursue its general goals or indeed to pursue the more specific goals that are selected under its decision-making procedures.[9]

The ensuing narrative will have little or nothing further to say about the co-avowal and co-pledging of joint intentions, whether on the part of unincorporated or incorporated groups. This, as will appear in the next chapter, is because it is the avowals and co-avowals of beliefs and desires that put us within reach of prescriptive concepts of credibility and desirability.

Many exercises in the co-avowal of beliefs and desires naturally lead to the formation of joint intentions, however, and pave the way for their co-avowal and co-pledging. Thus, the conversation that leads you and me and our common friend to go hunting will usher in an action that expresses a joint intention, by the conditions gestured at earlier. And so, it will put any one of us in a position to presume to co-avow or co-pledge that intention without fear of contradiction.

As that is true in this case, so it will be true in the case of any purposeful conversation that is designed to resolve differences and identify solutions. Much of our life in Erewhon will presumably revolve around such exercises, as we discuss when to plant as well as where to hunt, what to do about defending ourselves against predators, and how to organize our communal festivals. The co-avowal and co-pledging of intentions may not be important for the purposes of the narrative: that is, for making sense of how prescriptive properties become accessible, prescriptive concepts available. But they must still bulk large in the social life of Erewhon that the narrative presupposes.

9. With any such group agent, of course, there will also be beliefs and desires that it forms as a body, whether in general or in this or that situation. And it will also be possible for any of us to essay a co-avowal of any such attitude.

Chapter 5: Discovering Desirability

According to the argument in the preceding chapters, a simple, reportive community like Erewhon would not be a steady or stationary society. It would contain within itself the seeds of its own transformation, providing us as members with the means, the motive, and the confidence to take us beyond merely giving reports on ourselves and our attitudes. On pain of having few excuses for failure, we would back ourselves to live up to certain self-ascribed attitudes and commit ourselves, in a strategic sense of the term, to those attitudes. Our commitments would include individual avowals and pledges of attitude, as well as co-avowals and co-pledges that we make in company with others.

Nothing in the developments reviewed so far takes us into the realm of ethics. At the point reached in the narrative, we do not yet make judgments of desirability, or indeed any prescriptive judgments, and we do not hold one another responsible for living up to them. The challenge now is to carry forward the narrative and show why the commitments that we make in avowals and pledges are liable and indeed likely to take us into prescriptive and ethical space. This chapter argues that we are in a position where it is natural to begin to think in terms of desirability, in particular moral desirability. And the next chapter shows that having come to make judgments in that mode, we are also going to be in a position to hold one another properly responsible to such judgments.

The argument in this chapter is that once we can avow and co-avow belief, we will be able to access the concept of credibility and, more pertinently to the purpose of the narrative, that once we are able to avow and co-avow desires, we will be able to access concepts of desirability, including the concept of moral desirability. And with that conceptual access, we will be able to make suitable judgments of desirability and allow them to guide us in action.

The notion of a judgment that makes an appearance here can be equated with the act of making up your mind that was discussed in chapter 3. Whenever you avow a belief that p, claiming to be able to foreclose the misleading-mind excuse, you rely on having made up your mind that p. For present purposes, a judgment that p—and, to anticipate, a judgment that something is desirable—is just the act of making up your mind that p. While it is associated with the individual avowal of a belief, it may presumably materialize internally without an avowal actually ensuing. In this sense, you may make a judgment that p without asserting a word.

The argument of the chapter develops in five sections. The first analyzes the notion of moral desirability in order to make clear what the narrative is required to show. The second looks at how the social world is bound to appear to us from within the standpoint of avowing belief and desire, and the third at how it is likely to appear to us from within the standpoint of co-avowing those attitudes. The upshot of those discussions, as charted in the fourth section, is that while such perspectives support a single concept of the credible, they provide us with access to a variety of desirability concepts. The fifth section then argues that in face of that variety we are more or less bound to evolve a concept of the desirable that integrates or transcends such different standpoints and that this concept is effectively equivalent to the concept of the morally desirable.

5.1 Desirability characterized

Desirability, moral and non-moral

That something is desirable may be taken to mean that you are permitted to desire it or, perhaps more strongly, that desiring it is recommended. But here it will be taken to mean, more strongly still, that you ought to desire it: that desiring that alternative is prescribed, not just permitted or recommended. The fact that you judge that something is desirable in that prescriptive sense usually presupposes that it is one option in a set of alternatives, and in judging it to be desirable you rank it above the others; it is not just desirable in a generic way but, specifically, more desirable than those other options. The option that counts as most desirable may be a simple option like X or Y or Z in a three-way choice or, in the case of a tie, a disjunctive option like X-or-Y; in this case, some independent factor—perhaps just a mental toss of a coin—may be allowed to determine which disjunct to realize.[1]

How to distinguish moral desirability from other forms of desirability? Three features characterize it broadly, as noted briefly in chapter 1. The first of these features is that judgments of moral desirability are fixed by considerations that are relatively unrestricted in the range of interests served; they contrast on this front with judgments of prudence that target a particular person's interests, for example, or the judgments of patriotism that target those of a particular country. It is a mark of moral desirability, shared with certain other forms of desirability as well, that the features that determine whether an alternative is suitably desirable are not restricted to particular interests and beneficiaries.

The second mark of judgments of moral desirability is that they are grounded in features that are relatively unrestricted in standpoint, not just in the range of interests involved. Other concepts of desirability are generated by practical standpoints like those of law and etiquette, or by the epistemological standpoint from within which it is desirable

---

1. An option is a possibility that will be realized, given how things are in the world, depending on what you want (Pettit 2018a). This means that an option will be disjunctive in the fashion of X-or-Y in any case, like that envisaged in the text, where you rank the disjuncts equally and are happy to allow chance, or some such arrangement, to select between them. What of the case in which you can opt to do something that will result in X or in Y, depending on chance, but you cannot opt for X or for Y independently? In that case, X and Y will count as possible outcomes of the basic option, and that option is likely to be identifiable other than just in disjunctive terms as X-or-Y.

to believe that which the evidence supports, or by the standpoints associated with a set of projects—perhaps self-interested, perhaps disinterested—embraced by a certain individual or group. The concept of the morally desirable is not tied in the same way to such perspectives. This shows up in the fact that human beings routinely transcend such standpoints in moral judgment, debating the moral desirability of standing by a certain practice of law or etiquette, of allowing only the evidence to determine our attitudes, or of seeking to advance this or that project.

These comments bear on the first two marks of judgments of moral desirability: that they are grounded in features involving a relatively unrestricted range of interests and a relatively unrestricted standpoint. The third distinctive feature is that not only are judgments of moral desirability relatively unrestricted in their grounds, they are also relatively authoritative. Judgments of moral desirability are typically assigned a weight that allows them to adjudicate between judgments of desirability dictated by rival interests and standpoints.

There are likely to be many judgments of desirability that conflict with one another because they reflect different ranges of interests or different standpoints. The third mark of moral desirability is that it is taken to be sufficiently authoritative to clinch the issue of what should be prescribed in such conflicts. Or at least to clinch the issue of what should be prescribed for ideal subjects. For, to anticipate discussion in the next chapter, what a judgment of moral desirability holds out as the preferred alternative may be beyond the capacities of relevant agents to the point where they are not fit to be held responsible for a failure to adopt it; the alternative, as it is often said, may be supererogatory, not a matter of obligation.

Is moral desirability equivalent, then, to overall desirability? No, because by most accounts the considerations relevant in moral judgments are ones that bear on certain conflicts; according to perhaps the most salient account, they bear on conflicts between the interests of different persons. That something is overall desirable, then, does not necessarily entail that it is morally desirable; considerations that give it this overall status may not be relevant to conflicts of that sort. And that something is morally desirable, being supported by considerations relevant in conflicts between persons, does not necessarily entail that it is overall most desirable.[2]

By some accounts, the conflicts relevant to issues of moral desirability are restricted to conflicts affecting different human beings, by others they may extend to conflicts affecting any sentient beings, perhaps to conflicts where non-sentient nature or the divinity is involved, and even to conflicts, usually cast as prudential, between the interests of a person at different stages of their life. It is not necessary to decide between these accounts at this point, although it is worth noting that in the narrative developed later, conflicts affecting human beings or persons are given a certain priority.

The morally desirable and the morally obligatory

The concept of the morally desirable plays a central role in ethics or morality because of its connection with the more frequently invoked notion of moral obligation. But the connection may be understood in either of two ways.

The morally obligatory option, on one pattern of usage, is identical with the morally most desirable alternative, simple or disjunctive. But on the pattern to be adopted here, it is the morally most desirable option that it would be wrong or blameworthy for the agent not to take. On this construal, the morally most desirable option of all will not be the obligatory option if it counts as supererogatory: that is, if it is so demanding that regardless of its desirability, it would not be appropriate to blame the agent for failing to take it.

Why not identify the obligatory option with the morally most desirable of all the options rather than with the most desirable option among

2. The first claim is likely to be widely accepted, since there are many sets of alternatives where moral considerations or reasons are irrelevant in ranking the members, so that the member that is overall most desirable may not be morally desirable. The second claim is at the center of a controversy about whether, as it is put, there could be most reason overall to do something that runs counter to moral reasons. For rival responses, see Portmore (2014), who answers in the negative, and Dorsey (2017), who answers in the positive.

'erogatory' alternatives—that is, among alternatives that would not be supererogatory choices? Either equation would work for purposes of the narrative, but it makes more sense to let obligation be understood on the second pattern. This construal has the advantage of marking clearly the accepted distinction between an option that is right in the strict sense of being morally obligatory and right in the wider sense that allows it to be supererogatory.

On this way of construing the notion of obligation, it is impossible to give an account of how we might get to make use of the concept in Erewhon, prior to having an explanation of how we might get to hold one another responsible for how we perform. The concept of obligation can only emerge properly, then, at the point in the narrative where it becomes intelligible why we should get to hold one another responsible, and the narrative will reach that point only at the end of the next chapter.

At that point, we will be able to understand, not just why certain options are obligatory but also why others are prohibited or permitted. An option will be prohibited if it is obligatory to avoid it, and an option will be permitted if it is not obligatory to avoid it and, at least in the sense in which "permitted" means "merely permitted", not obligatory to take it. Up until the point at which the concept of the obligatory is introduced, however, the focus will be exclusively on the concept of desirability, in particular moral desirability.

What role does judging that something is desirable, and in particular morally desirable, play in our thinking? There are three generic constraints that all judgments of desirability must satisfy and two specific constraints that judgments of moral desirability must satisfy in addition. The generic constraints reflect the role that any judgments of desirability must play in relation to desire, paralleling the role that judgments of credibility generally play in relation to belief. The specific constraints reflect assumptions about what judgments of moral desirability in particular should be taken to assert; whether the constraints are also satisfied by other judgments of desirability is not an issue that will be addressed here.

Three generic constraints

The first generic constraint on judgments of desirability is that the desirability of any possible scenario relative to alternatives is grounded in the independent features of the alternatives on offer: ultimately in features that do not themselves have any prescriptive significance. As it was said earlier, the desirability of a scenario is fixed by how far it satisfies suitable considerations, restricted or unrestricted. That scenario cannot cease to be more desirable than competitors without a change in the distribution of independent properties across alternatives; fix those properties, and the relative desirability of the alternatives will be fixed, too.

Why believe in the supervenience of desirability on other properties—its grounding in other properties—as this constraint is often described? The answer is, because it is encoded in the ordinary use of language. When I hold one alternative to be more desirable than another, it is always appropriate to ask about what makes it more desirable: what distinguishes it in independent terms from the other alternatives. And that question is appropriate only on the assumption that desirability is grounded in independent properties.

The second generic constraint on desirability judgments is that it is always possible that while one alternative in a choice is desirable—and even while I judge it to be desirable—I actually desire another. This may be because I am subject to any of those familiar influences that can disturb the effect of the desideratum registered in the judgment: say, the influence of impulse or whim. This constraint scarcely needs defending, since conflict of that sort between judgments of desirability and actual desires is a datum of common experience.

The third constraint is that in any such case of divergence, it is going to count as a rational failure on my part—a failure to function properly—if, other things being equal, I act on my desire and against my judgment of what is desirable. Other things will not be equal, if I do not have the capacity to do what I judge to be desirable, for example; or if there are other judgments of desirability still in play; or, to go to an extreme possibility, if the judgment does not catch and I actually hold the contrary belief.[3] Absent such possibilities, however, the idea is that I will not function properly if I fail to let the judgment of desirability govern what I do. The idea is plausible, since it will be perfectly reasonable to ask me to explain myself in any situation in which I fail in that way.

These constraints may be named after what they impose or allow: grounding in the first case; divergence in the second; governance in the third. As they apply to any form of desirability, so they apply to moral desirability in particular and, by extension, to the obligation that it makes it possible to define.

The first, grounding constraint shows up in the fact that if I am told that one option is morally desirable, and another not, it always makes sense to ask about what is the difference—the independent difference— between them. The second, divergence constraint is reflected in our pervasive sense that we may often desire what is not morally desirable, even what we judge to be not morally desirable. And the third, governance constraint applies with particular force, since the judgment of moral desirability does not leave room for the idea that it is no more authoritative than certain rival judgments that remain in play. The constraint means that when we judge something to be morally desirable, and things are otherwise equal, then it ought to have the role of guiding us, and if necessary correcting us, in the formation of desire and intention.

Two specific constraints

Where the three generic constraints reflect the role that judgments of desirability in general are expected to play in relation to desire, the two specific constraints reflect an assumption about what judgments of

3. This, by a plausible analysis, is what happens when Huck Finn judges that he ought to report Jim, the runaway slave, but does not do so: this, presumptively, because of actually believing that it is desirable not to report him (see Arpaly 2003; Joshi 2016).

moral desirability should be taken to assert. The assumption reflects widely supported intuitions about judgments of moral desirability, but it also has a methodological appeal, since it makes the exercise on hand more difficult rather than less difficult to complete. The assumption raises rather than lowers the bar to be crossed in providing a plausible explanation of how we residents of Erewhon could come to master and apply the concept of the morally desirable.

The first of the specific constraints is that when I judge that one among a set of alternatives is morally desirable—when I assent to the proposition ascribing such desirability to it—the property that I ascribe is not the property of being morally desirable$_{me}$, where this is distinct from the property, morally desirable$_{you}$, that you would ascribe if you were the one assenting to the proposition. The constraint is that 'morally desirable' is not indexical in the manner of 'mine' or indeed 'now'; it does not assume a different referent, depending on the identity of the utterer or of the context of utterance. Thus, when I say that it is morally desirable for a person to do something and you deny that that is morally desirable, we are not talking past one another, addressing different properties in our respective claims.

Where the first constraint holds that judgments of moral desirability do not vary in content as between speakers, the second holds that neither do they vary in truth-value by virtue of being about moral desirability. The first constraint is that you and I address the same proposition when, given the same context, I say that something is morally desirable and you deny this. The second is that in such a case, at most one of us is correct about that proposition. It cannot be that from my standpoint as an assessor—from the position that my evidence gives me—the alternative at issue truly is morally desirable, and from yours it truly is not; if it is morally desirable from one position, it is morally desirable from all. There may be nothing incoherent about the claim that truth-value may be assessor-sensitive, so that a given proposition should be deemed true from within one position of assessment and false from within another (MacFarlane 2014). But, so the second constraint holds, this is not the case with propositions about moral desirability as such.

The two specific constraints satisfied by the notion of the morally desirable enable it to play a communal role in identifying a property such that people are capable of recognizing it in common, of taking their own guidance from it, and of using it in critique of one another's performances or proposals. The concept is tailored by its satisfaction of the constraints to assume an important coordinating part in regulating people's relationships with one another.

The fact that the concept of the morally desirable satisfies the two specific constraints implies that the concept of obligation in the sense endorsed here—the concept of the most desirable alternative among 'erogatory' options—satisfies them, too. And that implied claim is independently plausible. If the obligatory is to serve its characteristic community-wide role in assessing options and actions, and in determining the responsibility of different agents, then it must be non-indexical and non-relative; it must allow different people to address the same content on the basis of the same criteria of assessment.

Given this understanding of what it is to judge that something is morally desirable, it is possible to explore how far we, the people of Erewhon, equipped with the committal practices of avowal and pledging, are likely to come to form such judgments. The argument to be offered is that making avowals and co-avowals—in particular, avowals and co-avowals of desire—is going to provide me and others in the community with a perspective from within which it is natural to begin to think in terms of the desirable and in particular of the morally desirable. Pledges do not figure much in this account, but they play a crucial role in the next chapter, helping to explain why it is also going to be natural for us to hold one another responsible to certain standards, including standards of moral desirability.

5.2 *The view from within avowal*

The robustly persuasive and attractive

When I speak for myself in Erewhon, making a potentially expensive avowal of a belief or a desire—in particular, the sort of belief or desire that is likely to be relevant in continuing interaction with others—I rely on a solid basis for holding the belief or desire, and I guard against the effects of distractors and disturbers. The basis for belief is provided by the data I take care to survey, the basis for desire by the desiderata I carefully register. Given that I guard as needed against distraction and disturbance, data that argue that p elicit a relatively dependable disposition to act and adjust as if it were the case that p; and the desiderata that draw me to R elicit a relatively dependable disposition to act and adjust as if R were indeed attractive. I may later change my mind about whether it is the case that p or whether R is really attractive, as other data or desiderata come into play. But short of such an alteration, I will continue to believe that p and desire R. Assuming that the data or desiderata remain in place, and that I remain a competent subject, I will hold by that belief or desire robustly over variations in other factors, in particular variations in the distractions or disturbances that might affect me.

Given that basis for confidence about the belief or desire, I step out of the contingencies of the here and now when I avow the attitude. Taking the basis in data or desiderata as sufficient to elicit a dependable attitude, at least given a guard against distraction and disturbance, I treat the belief or desire as something I can stand by with relative assurance. I treat it as firmly enough entrenched for me to be able to put aside the possibility of appealing to a misleading-mind in order to excuse a miscommunication.

No matter how effective my protection against distraction and disturbance, of course, I still have to recognize that I may occasionally fail to display the attitude ascribed. Thus, persuaded by the data to avow that the gambler's fallacy is a fallacy, I still have to recognize that regardless of taking precautions against disturbers, I may lose sight of this truth in the excitement of the casino, and that if I do, I will not be able to excuse myself by saying that I changed my mind. Again, persuaded by the desiderata at hand to avow the desire to tell my friends the truth about some embarrassing episode, I may still have to recognize that, regardless of how far I guard against disturbance, the shame of telling the truth face to face may inhibit me from owning up to the episode with someone who is particularly judgmental: and this, without being able to excuse my failure by a change of mind.

Think now about how I must view such disturbers, when in the wake of a failure I have to admit that they caused me not to live up to my avowed attitude. Given that disturbers, by assumption, are factors against which I can guard, I cannot claim not to have been able to act on the belief or desire or intention in play. But given that I did not change that attitude, I cannot claim that how I acted revealed my true mind. Hence only one alternative remains open. I must disown the action that I took, whether that involved placing a heavy bet on red after a run of blacks, or beating a hasty retreat from meeting with a judgmental friend. I must hold that that action does not reflect who I am. I must present it as the product of contingent influences that I do not identify with: influences that are not expressions of the mind for which I speak.

If I am disposed to take this view in retrospect, that also has implications for the view I must take in advance of any failure. It means that as I avow the attitude in question, backing myself to live up to it, I must not only hold the attitude avowed and be aware of holding it. I must also assume that I hold the attitude as a result of the impact of relevant data or desiderata, not as a result of any other influence, like that of a disturber or indeed a distractor. If I thought that my holding it was the effect of such an influence, then I would not have the confidence required for avowal.

It follows that when I hold an avowed belief that things are thus and so, for example—when I find that scenario relevantly persuasive—I do more than hold by the simple belief that they are thus and so. I hold also by the sophisticated belief that the data support my believing that things are thus and so; it is not because of a lack of evidential care in guarding against distraction, or a lack of executive care in guarding against disturbance, so I assume, that I am led to believe that they are that way. In other words, I hold by the simple belief under the assumption—in general, no doubt, a default rather than a confirmed assumption—that there is nothing suspect at its origin: no distraction or disturbance. If I thought that there was, after all, then that would give me pause about avowing it; I could no longer have the confidence to bet on myself to stick with it.

The same line of thought applies with the desires that I avow. When I hold an avowed desire that things be thus and so—when I find that scenario relevantly attractive—I do more than enjoy an attraction to their being that way. I enjoy that attraction but hold at the same time by the belief that relevant desiderata ground the attraction; that the attraction is not due to any lack of evidential care in guarding against distraction or any lack of executive care in guarding against disturbance. I stand by the attraction, perhaps letting it shape my actions, under the default or perhaps confirmed assumption that there is nothing suspect at its origin. If I thought that a lack of care played a part in the attraction, then, as in the case of belief, that would give me pause about avowing the desire; I could no longer have the confidence to bet on myself to stick with that desire.

Enter prescriptive concepts

These observations imply that, like everyone else in Erewhon, I have to treat the data on which I rely in avowing belief, and the desiderata on which I rely in avowing desire, as enjoying a certain privilege. Certainly, I have to do this in the case of the expensive avowals in focus here. Insofar as I am invested in the practice of avowal, and more generally in the role of spokesperson for myself, I have to see the data and desiderata as generators of attitude that I can safely mobilize. I have to see them, indeed, as the only generators of attitude on which I can rely in avowals, contrasting them with the contingent, erratic factors that may enter as a result of a lack of evidential or executive care. They represent the forces that must hold sway within my psychology—and the only forces that must hold sway there—if I am to be a reliable spokesperson for myself.

What am I to think, then, if I realize that the relevant data support a belief that p but, for whatever reason, I do not hold this belief, or even hold by the belief that not-p? What am I to think if I realize that the relevant desiderata support the desire for R but, for whatever reason, I do not harbor this desire, or even harbor a desire for not-R?

As someone committed to speaking for my attitudes, and to holding those attitudes for which I speak, I have no option but to think in each case that by a principle implicit in that practice, the actual state of my belief or desire is not what it should be. And equally, I will have no option but to seek, if possible, to let the relevant data or desiderata elicit the missing attitude instead. It may not be futile to seek this result. The recognition of my failure—the recognition that I cannot claim to speak for myself, if the actual state of my belief or desire remains as it is—should supplement the relevant data or desiderata in eliciting a change of attitude. It should activate a natural desire to give careful attention to those factors, guarding against distraction and disturbance.

But not only must I take a critical view of a current failure that I recognize in the formation of my attitudes; I must also take a critical view of a past or prospective failure on my part or indeed of any similar failure on the part of another person. Thus, suppose I now recognize that I formed a belief or desire in the past that, because of a lack of evidential or executive care, was not supported in the manner appropriate to the practice of avowal—in the manner that made it fit for avowal. In that case, I must judge that my attitude was not then as it should be. And suppose I recognize that despite being committed to avowing it, you hold a belief or desire that is not supported by data or desiderata in an avowal-fit manner. In that case, too, I must think that your attitude is not as it should be.

The upshot is that as commissive creatures who avow our beliefs and desires to one another, claiming to be able to speak for such attitudes, we must treat our beliefs as attitudes for which we can speak when, and indeed only when, the propositions believed are persuasive in a way that makes them fit for avowal; and we must treat our desires in the same way when and only when the prospects desired are attractive in a parallel avowal-fit manner. This is going to be a matter of common awareness in Erewhon, given that the importance and price of claiming to be able to speak for ourselves is obvious: the evidence supporting the claims is salient for all, the evidence that that evidence is salient is itself salient for all, and so on in the usual pattern (Lewis 1969).

The content of these claims will find natural expression among us in talk of what I or anyone else ought to believe or desire. What I ought to believe qua someone who avows beliefs—qua someone who claims to be able to speak in avowal for myself—are just those propositions for which there are data enough to elicit belief, when I exercise any evidential and executive care that may be needed. What I ought to desire qua someone who avows desires are just those prospects for which there are desiderata enough to elicit desire when I practice similar forms of care. And I must acknowledge those claims about what I ought to believe and desire as general truths that hold in abstraction from the precise identity of the relevant data or desiderata.

Thus, the persuasive, as determined within the practice of avowal, will present as what I ought to believe; the attractive, as determined within the practice, will present as what I ought to desire. That which is persuasive and attractive within this practice is going to be persuasive and attractive robustly over variations in any factors other than the relevant data or desiderata. In particular, it is going to be persuasive or attractive over variations in the distraction and disturbance that evidential and executive care are designed to protect me against. It will be robustly persuasive, as it may be put, or robustly attractive.

It will be plausible for all of us in Erewhon, then, that we each ought to believe that which is robustly persuasive, desire that which is robustly attractive, and avoid beliefs and desires that fail these conditions. And this will be plausible as an abstract truth of principle, so that we must admit that we ought to respond in this way to anything, and only to anything, that proves to be robustly persuasive or attractive for us, even if we do not currently recognize that it is persuasive or attractive.

This holds of us, as mentioned, insofar as we are creatures who are invested in speaking for ourselves in avowal of our attitudes. Is that a significant restriction on the principle? Not really. At least not, on the assumption that as we learn to treat others as interlocutors, and find that they treat us in the same way, we will treat ourselves as potential interlocutors to ourselves. According to this assumption, having learned what it is to be on the hook with others, we invent a parallel hook on which we will find ourselves if we self-ascribe a desire or belief for which we can see no robustly supportive data or desiderata.

The assumption means that even beliefs and desires that are irrelevant in our relationships with others, even indeed beliefs and desires whose absence in us others are not in a position to test for, will fall under the principle that lets the robustly persuasive guide belief and the robustly attractive guide desire. Thus, to revert to earlier examples, the principle will govern the avowal of a belief that I once saw a mathematical equation in the clouds, a belief that Mogli is probably honest, a desire to fly, or an intention, if p or q or s, to X.

Is the assumption plausible? Yes, because the categories of the robustly persuasive and attractive are applicable to all beliefs and desires, and I am in a position to apply them in my own case, even when others cannot readily do so. But why apply them in my own case? Because doing anything else would involve treating like cases differently. It would involve a failure in my own case to invoke categories that I invoke in relation to others, expect others to invoke in relation to me, and treat as relevant when others invoke them in that way. It would mean assuming the role of interlocutor in relation to others while rejecting that role in relation to myself.

This assumption will not play a crucial role in the evolving narrative, but it may be adopted as a plausible generalization; it will be relevant to the discussion of the linkage between morality and personhood in the first section of the final chapter. Not only should the beliefs and desires that are relevant in our relationships with others be guided by the robustly persuasive and the robustly attractive, then; all our beliefs and desires, even ones that do not figure in our avowals to others, should be guided in this manner.[4]

With the developments charted in this discussion, we in Erewhon have entered prescriptive space. We are in a position to access the idea of what I or anyone else ought to believe—what is credible for me—and

---

4. There is an important issue as to how such prescriptive principles relate to constraints on credence and utility supported in one or another form of decision theory. For some consideration, see Pettit (2016b).

the idea of what I or anyone else ought to desire: what is desirable for me. And those concepts are prescriptive insofar as they satisfy the grounding, divergence, and guidance constraints mentioned earlier.

First, whether something is credible or desirable relative to me is going to be grounded in its relations to data or desiderata; these will explain why a proposition is credible, a prospect desirable. Second, what is credible and what I judge to be credible may diverge from my actual beliefs, what is desirable and what I judge to be desirable may diverge from my actual desires, since distraction or disturbance may play a role in generating my actual attitudes. And third, assuming other things are equal, it would be a functional failure not to let what I judge to be credible govern or determine what I believe, or not to let what I judge to be desirable govern what I desire. It would involve an inconsistency with what I assume in following the practice of avowal.

Other things will not be equal, and this third lesson will not follow, as mentioned earlier, if the judgment of credibility or desirability is not the only one in play. This observation is important, as it turns out that there are judgments of credibility and desirability that answer to practices of co-avowal as well as the judgments of credibility and desirability that answer to the practice of individual avowal. In order to mark this contrast, what is credible or desirable in light of the practice of individual avowal will be cast henceforth as what is individually credible or desirable, leaving open the possibility that it is not credible or desirable in other ways.

Avowals of individual credibility and desirability

With access to the concepts of the individually credible and individually desirable, I and others in Erewhon can form beliefs to the effect that something is credible or desirable in that way. And, of course, we will avow such a belief in asserting that something is individually credible or desirable; that assertion will communicate the belief pragmatically rather than report on its presence. Avowal is a potentially recursive operation such that we may avow a belief in a content—that something is credible or desirable in some way—whose very availability to us as a content to be believed itself presupposes the prior use of avowal. While the standpoint of avowal enables us to gain access to the concepts of the individually credible and desirable, applying these to what we find robustly persuasive and attractive, it enables us at the same time to avow beliefs in propositions that ascribe those very properties of credibility and desirability.

How in Erewhon might I avow a belief in the individual credibility of a proposition 'p' or in the individual desirability of a prospect R? The usual linguistic devices will be at my disposal. I may express such a belief, as just noticed, by asserting that it is credible that p, or that R is desirable. But I may also self-ascribe such a belief, and still retain the force of an avowal, by saying that I believe that it is credible that p or that R is desirable. And equally I may resort to remarks that serve in context to explain, not why I believe that p or desire R—I may not actually do so—but why it is credible that p or why R is desirable: I may say, for example, "The data stack up in support of 'p,'" or "R would be a lot of fun."

These observations show that, like others in Erewhon, I would naturally be led, just in virtue of making personal avowals, to develop a prescriptive viewpoint on myself. I cannot practice avowal without privileging a robust personal standpoint, as it may be described: the standpoint in which I am responsive to the robustly persuasive in the case of belief, and to the robustly attractive in the case of desire. This standpoint is ideal in the sense that, by assumption, it is free from those distracting or disturbing factors that might warp the influence of suitable data on belief, suitable desiderata on desire. And so, assuming that standpoint, I can prescribe for how my actual self ought to perform.

I can prescribe that actually I ought to stick with a belief that the gambler's fallacy is a fallacy when I go to the casino, or that actually I ought to speak truthfully in face-to-face meetings with my friends. And, should it prove impossible to guard against such disturbing influences, I can prescribe that I ought to avoid occasions when they arise. I ought to avoid exposing myself to the disturbers, as I ought to avoid exposing myself to the distractors, that undercut the effect of data or desiderata. I ought to avoid visiting the casino, or I ought to avoid difficult face-to-face encounters.[5]

5.3 The view from within co-avowal

My individual perspective in avowal lets me identify the robustly persuasive and attractive, and leads me to give it prescriptive status, treating it as representative of the individually credible, on the one side, the individually desirable on the other. But my perspective in co-avowal and co-acceptance allows me to do something parallel at the social level and complicates the concepts to which I and others in Erewhon will enjoy access.

The complication is exacerbated by the fact that co-avowal may be bounded or unbounded, as appeared in the last chapter, and that bounded co-avowal may take as many different forms as there are different bounds. In the discussion that follows, the unbounded case will be given priority, since conversation of this kind is tied up with individual avowal and, as noted, enjoys a certain inescapability for human beings. That discussion will address the co-avowal of belief first, the co-avowal of desire second, and in each the lessons it teaches will be drawn first for unbounded conversation and co-avowal and then for bounded counterparts.

From within the unbounded co-avowal of belief

Suppose that I essay the co-avowal of a belief that p, opening up a potential, unbounded conversation with others. Suppose that some others go along, acquiesce in the co-avowal, and essay further co-avowals themselves. And imagine then that in an exercise involving various

---

5. This is to say that the ideal self may advise that the actual self should behave in a manner that takes account of difficulties the ideal self does not itself have to deal with. On this lesson, which also applies in the idealizations considered later, see Smith (1994).

episodes of rejection, rejoinder, and revision, we come into convergence with one another. The result should be that we will each endorse a set of beliefs that any one of us is in a position—indeed is manifestly in a position—to avow on behalf of all of us and, by aspiration, on behalf of any others who join up. In the domain explored, this exercise will reveal certain propositions as robustly persuasive for us all; and this, as a matter of common awareness from within the standpoint that we share.

It will be manifest to each of us in such a case that due to distraction or disturbance, anyone may occasionally fail to believe what is robustly persuasive within this group. But, recognizing what the interpersonally tested data elicit, we must each be disposed to disown any such failure: that is, to treat the distraction or disturbance as warping the performance required of us within the standpoint presumptively shared with an open number of others.

This means that what is robustly persuasive from the common standpoint of this open group is a prescriptive category on a par with what is robustly persuasive from an individual standpoint. The practice of co-avowal will require each of us to believe that which we take to be robustly persuasive for all and ready for co-avowal by any one of us. What is robustly persuasive in this way constitutes the commonly credible, as we in Erewhon might come to articulate it.

The prescriptive status of the commonly credible shows up in its satisfying the grounding, divergence and governance constraints listed earlier. What is commonly credible is grounded in the evidence that is common to an open group of others. What is commonly credible, and what I judge to be commonly credible, may diverge from what I actually believe under the influence of distracting or disturbing influences. And if my judgment of common credibility is sound, it would be a functional failure on my part not to let that judgment govern my beliefs. Or at least it would be a failure on the assumption that other things are equal, and in particular that there is not some rival judgment of credibility in play.

This last observation is important, since it appears that there is always going to be a rival judgment of credibility in play: viz., a judgment as to what is individually credible rather than commonly credible. So how then are these judgments likely to compare with one another?

It turns out that they relate in a wholly convergent manner. What is individually credible for each of a number of people is bound to be commonly credible. The reason is that the data relevant in my perspective ought to be relevant in everyone else's as well, since evidence for one person is evidence for all. Let two people confront the same body of evidence, where this includes what they know by way of background as well as the data on hand, and it will make little sense to imagine that it might argue for a different belief on the part of each.[6] The data that make something individually credible for me, then, are bound to be able to serve as data that make it individually credible for you, and vice versa. And whatever is individually credible for each member in any such twosome, or in any open group whatsoever, is commonly credible for all.

As the individually credible is bound to be commonly credible, so for similar reasons the commonly credible is bound to be individually credible. All that it means, in effect, for something to be commonly credible is for it to be credible for any individual, no matter who. And if something is credible for any individual, it is going to be credible for me in particular and for you or anyone else in particular.

These observations show that since individual and common credibility converge, there is only one category in play. If something is credible for me or anyone else in particular, it is natural to say that that is because it is credible for no matter who; the general credibility explains the particular credibility, and not the other way around. Thus, the conclusion that individual and common credibility do not come apart may be cast as the claim that common credibility is a master category. This, as will appear later, marks a sharp contrast with the relationship between the individually and commonly desirable.[7]

6. Of course, it may be that the data do not require any particular belief but allow both of our beliefs. For simplicity, as mentioned earlier, I concentrate here on the more straightforward case.

7. This is not to deny that there are some standpoints, say those associated with certain forms of oppression, such that it may take enormous efforts of empathy on

As avowal is recursive, so, too, is co-avowal. Once the category of the commonly credible becomes available in Erewhon, we members can avow beliefs in propositions to the effect that it is commonly credible that such and such simply by asserting that such and such is commonly credible. Indeed, we will presumably be ready to co-avow that belief, since we will surely expect others to go along, provided they exercise any required evidential and executive care. Thus, we can co-avow a belief that something has the property of being commonly credible, despite the fact that property will have become accessible to us only in virtue of having practiced co-avowal with simpler beliefs: beliefs not involving the property in their content. And for reasons familiar from other cases, the fact that we can co-avow a belief in this way means that in suitable contexts we will also be able to avow it by ascribing it to ourselves or by explaining why it is true.

The standpoint from within which I believe—and avow the belief—that something is individually credible is idealized, as appeared earlier; it represents a standpoint from within which I can prescribe for my actual self. We now see that the standpoint from within which I believe—and no doubt avow and co-avow the belief—that something is commonly credible converges with that standpoint. It represents the ultimate point of idealization from which I can prescribe matters of belief for my actual self. There is no tussle between the individually and the commonly credible, and no problem about their offering different guidance on what I should hold.

From within the bounded co-avowal of belief

As the commonly credible will become defined for the members of an unbounded group, so a counterpart ideal—the jointly credible, as it may be put—is likely to be defined for the members of any bounded

the part of outsiders—and a willingness to trust the testimony of those occupying such a standpoint—to grasp what is revealed therein. Similar points apply, of course, in the case of the commonly desirable. See Jones (1999) and, for a general perspective, Fricker (2007).

group—say, a group devoted to some cause or some creed, whether or not organized as a group agent. The considerations that made this plausible in the unbounded case will also make it plausible in this, explaining how we can avow and presume to co-avow a belief in the joint credibility of a proposition, whether by expressing it in an assertion of joint credibility, ascribing the belief to those of us in the relevant group, or explaining why it is true by our lights.

How does the commonly credible relate to what is jointly credible, now from within this group, now from within that? If we are given a motive within a bounded grouping to set aside some beliefs that we take to be commonly credible, that must be because of constraints that are independent of data. This may be the desire to find a compromise among a fixed set of members, including some who by our lights are not suitably attentive to the data. Or it may be the desire to stick with a certain core of doctrine, regardless of how far it outruns the presumptive data, even perhaps conflicts with the data.

If a consideration unrelated to data constrains the category of the jointly credible, however, keeping it apart from the commonly and individually credible, then that undermines any hold it can have on us. It means that insofar as it does not coincide with the commonly credible, the idea of what is jointly credible for us in a particular group directs us only to things such that we have to act as if we believed them, assuming we wish to maintain our connection with other members of the group. Thus, we cannot take the category seriously in the determination of belief.

There is a noteworthy difference in this respect between the bounded group that organizes itself for action, incorporating in the manner of a group agent—say, a voluntary association, a company, or a church—and the bounded group that does not. In each case, members may have to set aside some of the beliefs they themselves take to be commonly credible. But where only contingent pressures will have this effect in the unincorporated group, the requirements of group agency make it more or less inevitable in the incorporated case. Any group agent has to establish a coherent set of judgments designed to guide all its members when they act in the name of the group; and it will have to do this, inevitably, regardless of their particular opinions (List and Pettit 2011).[8]

When we speak here of the jointly credible—a similar lesson applies to the jointly desirable—what we have in mind is what is credible for each one of us, as members of a bounded group. And whether the group be incorporated or unincorporated, it should be clear that the notion of the jointly credible can have no serious hold on us as individuals. The idea of the commonly credible—the idea of what is credible in light of data available to all—retains its status as the master category. This, as will appear, marks a deep contrast between the idea of the credible and the idea of the desirable.[9]

From within the unbounded co-avowal of desire

We now turn from the co-avowal of belief to the co-avowal of desire. Suppose that I presume to co-avow a desire for R, aspiring to speak to an open audience in an unbounded conversation on the topic. And suppose that those who pay attention, at whatever time and place, acquiesce in that avowal, essay further co-avowals themselves, and come to identify a shared set of desires in an exercise involving rejection, rejoinder, and revision. Each of us at that point will be in a position—indeed manifestly in a position—to avow those desires on behalf of the group and, by aspiration, on behalf of others whom we allow to join us. Within the domain explored, this exercise will reveal certain scenarios as robustly

8. If that new subject is to be conversable itself, of course, operating like one of us, then it must presumably submit to the discipline of common credibility. Otherwise it could not present as a subject that others can understand and rely on (Buchak and Pettit 2014). The difficult issues that this raises, however, are beyond the reach of the current discussion. One case in which they arise is when a corporate group seeks to develop group judgments of desirability, including multilateral or moral desirability; although that case is not considered here, later discussion indicates that it is possible.

9. The treatment here ignores the fact that it may prove to be desirable, in whatever mode, to hold a belief in what is not commonly credible. We ignore such practical or state-centered reasons, as distinct from theoretical or object-centered reasons, for holding by certain beliefs (Parfit 2001).

attractive for all of us: they will appeal to us in light of desiderata that we are each disposed to acknowledge, absent distraction and disturbance, from within the common standpoint we assume.

What sorts of scenarios are likely to prove robustly attractive, and fit candidates for co-avowal, from within this standpoint? The issue is more complex than with the robustly persuasive. What count as data for one count as data for all. But what attracts one person may fail, indeed fail with a certain inevitability, to be attractive from a standpoint shared equally with others. I may desire my daughter's welfare on the basis, precisely, that she is my daughter, where others will only desire her welfare as they might that of a random person. With such an agent-relative desideratum in play, what is robustly attractive from within my individual standpoint may not be robustly attractive from within a standpoint that I purport to share with others. From within my individual standpoint, my daughter's welfare may be robustly attractive, even at a cost to the welfare of other children; from within a common standpoint, the welfare of all children will presumably count in the same way.

Returning to the question raised, then, what scenarios are likely to show up as robustly attractive, and fit candidates for co-avowal, from within the standpoint of an open group? The answer is, those scenarios that are attractive in virtue of promising to realize agent-neutral desiderata: that is, desiderata we are each liable to care about in a similar manner. Plausible neutral attractors may make it robustly attractive for all of us that social norms like truth-telling or non-violence should obtain; that our species should survive into an indefinite future; that there should be no unnecessary suffering; and so on.

We each have to recognize that we may fail to live up to what is robustly attractive from a common standpoint, due either to distraction or disturbance. Disturbers will include the self-centered preferences that may detach us from the common point of view as well as the wayward impulses that may affect any one of us individually. But when we take something to be commonly attractive, we must assume that, as we guard against distraction, so we are each going to guard against disturbance, disowning any desires that they might introduce and seeking to stay faithful to the shared standpoint.

This means that like that which is robustly persuasive for the open group, that which is robustly attractive for the open group is a prescriptive category, directing us to what is desirable from within a standpoint that we share with an indefinite number of others; this is the category of the commonly desirable, as we in Erewhon may think of it. The commonly desirable satisfies the grounding, divergence, and governance constraints associated with all prescriptive categories. It is going to be grounded in the desiderata—the agent-neutral desiderata—that make something robustly attractive to me and others qua members of an open group. It may come apart from what I actually desire—say, as a result of distraction or disturbance—even when I purport to occupy a common standpoint with others and to think as the member of an open-ended group. And assuming other things are equal, my identification with that standpoint rationally or functionally requires me to let my judgment of the commonly desirable guide or dictate what I actually desire.

But are other things likely to be equal? In particular, is the judgment of common desirability likely to converge with that of individual desirability? Not as a general matter. In any case, where I or you or anyone else makes a judgment as to what it is commonly desirable to do, we are each liable to make a different judgment about what is individually desirable. How, then, are these judgments likely to relate to one another? It turns out that they are liable to diverge and that neither has a clear priority in relation to the other.

The individually desirable and the commonly desirable may often coincide, of course. It may be both individually and commonly desirable, for example, that I should tell the truth to others; this may be robustly supported by desiderata relevant in each standpoint. But in many cases, these standpoints are likely to offer inconsistent prescriptions. The role of agent-relative desiderata in determining what is individually desirable means that what I would prescribe from an ideal, individual standpoint may diverge from what I would prescribe from the ideal, common standpoint. And of course, it also means that what I prescribe from my ideal, individual standpoint may differ from what you prescribe from yours.

The consequence of this is that neither the individually desirable nor the commonly desirable can play the role of the unconditionally desirable, at least not in any context in which both are relevant, as they will often be. The categories target what is robustly productive of desire, in the one case, under the characterization of robustness that goes with my practice of individual avowal, and in the other, under the characterization that goes with our practice of common co-avowal. Those perspectives may come apart in a way in which the corresponding perspectives in the case of belief do not. And so, neither can direct us toward a master category akin to the category of the commonly credible.

As avowal is recursive, so, too, is co-avowal. Once the category of the commonly desirable becomes available in Erewhon, then, we members are likely to form beliefs in propositions to the effect that this or that scenario is commonly desirable. And when we assert that a scenario is commonly desirable, we will avow our belief in its desirability rather than merely reporting on it. Others may be expected to go along with such an assertion, of course, if the scenario is commonly desirable and they are not evidentially or executively careless. And so, our assertion will naturally purport to have the status of a co-avowal of the belief, not simply an individual avowal.

As I may avow a belief in the individual desirability of a scenario by expressive, ascriptive, and explanatory devices, so I may resort to such devices in avowing or presuming to co-avow a belief in its common desirability. Depending on context, I can avow or presume to co-avow a belief in the common desirability of a prospect, R, by saying that it is desirable or commonly desirable; by saying that we desire it or believe that it is desirable or commonly desirable; or by explaining its desirability appropriately: say, by reference to how much fun it would be for everyone or to how it would give us each a fair return.

From within the bounded co-avowal of desire

According to the emerging narrative, I am naturally led by the practice of making individual avowals of desire, to develop one prescriptive point of view: a personal standpoint from which I can judge my actual performance, letting what I desire be assessed in terms of whether it is individually desirable. And in the same way, I am led by the co-avowal and co-acceptance of desire that I practice in unbounded conversation, to develop a second prescriptive standpoint on desire: a common standpoint from which I can judge what I desire, letting it be assessed in terms of whether it is commonly desirable.

But this, of course, is not all. The discussion so far has focused on what is likely to count as attractive from the point of view of an unbounded group and on what is commonly desirable in the sense of being robustly attractive from within the perspective of the group. But the argument developed in the case of that group supports parallel conclusions for this or that bounded group. As the perspective of the unbounded group will direct us to the category of the commonly desirable, so the perspective of any bounded group will point us toward the category of what is jointly desirable for members of that group in our part as members; this will be identified by what is robustly attractive to us in that role.

We the members of Erewhon, like the members of every society, are likely to find ourselves in any of a number of bounded groups; indeed, our own community, should we come to discover neighboring societies, would also constitute one example. And within such a partial grouping, as within the unbounded community imagined, we will each conduct conversational exchanges with others in which we co-avow and co-accept a range of desires that reflects the properties that matter from our shared standpoint, identifying scenarios that we will see as jointly attractive.

These properties will include group-relative properties that matter to us greatly as members—the welfare of our caste, the prosperity of our clan—but may not matter much to us in other roles. And so, for each such grouping, there is likely to be a notion of the jointly desirable that operates prescriptively but is in potential conflict with rival forms of desirability. It will satisfy constraints like those of grounding, divergence, and governance. And it will be a property such that any one of us can avow a belief in its presence, and presume to co-avow the belief within suitable contexts. We may do this by expressing the belief in an assertion that something is jointly desirable. Or we may avow it, for the same reasons as in other cases, by ascribing it to ourselves or by explaining why it is true.

The category of the jointly credible, as noticed earlier, is not of much significance, since it is only in virtue of constraints unrelated to data that the jointly credible might not coincide with the commonly and individually credible. The jointly desirable has a very different status, since it is group-relative desiderata, and not independent factors, that may force it apart from the commonly and the individually desirable. Thus, the divergence from individual and common forms of desirability, like the divergence between the individually and commonly desirable—and like the divergence between what is jointly desirable from the viewpoint of different groups—is not just salient but highly significant. This divergence in desirability, contrasting as it does with the convergence in credibility, is at the focus of the discussion in the remainder of the chapter.

5.4 A breakthrough and a shortfall

A conceptual breakthrough

If the argument so far is sound, then, in the wake of the developments charted, I and you and others in Erewhon will enjoy a conceptual breakthrough but suffer at the same time a conceptual shortfall. The conceptual breakthrough occurs in the areas of both belief and desire, the shortfall is confined to the area of desire alone.

The breakthrough is that we will become able to think in prescriptive terms, enjoying a position from within which we can distinguish between things as we actually believe or desire them to be and things as we ought to believe or desire them to be. How we ought to believe and desire things to be, in this way of conceiving of them, is how we would hold or want them to be, if we conformed to the constraints associated with a position we privilege: if we let the associated data or desiderata robustly determine the attitude. Depending on context, this is the position of the avowed self, or the self that is projected in one or another form of co-avowal. It is the position of the self as spokesperson for itself, now in one context, now in another.

It is a real gain for us in Erewhon to be enabled on this basis to think and talk in prescriptive terms, avowing beliefs as to what is credible and we ought to believe, what is desirable and we ought to desire. Once equipped with this capacity, there are two selves that we each confront: first, the self we project in our role as spokesperson for ourselves, more or less regularly living up to it; and second, the self we display in our actual behavior, when we fail to live up to the self for which we speak. As agents who speak for ourselves, we naturally identify with the bespoken self and, taking it as our point of view, look on the attitudes of the failing self as attitudes to reject. From the perspective of the bespoken self, we must each think that what that failing self thinks and feels and does is not me; it is not who I am.

In the life that we enjoyed prior to making commitments, we might have responded to incentives to prove reliable to others; we might have generated aggregate social patterns like those of general truth-telling; and we might have been in a position to recognize that result and to treat the patterns as social norms to guide ourselves by. And equally, in that life, we might have been in a position to be frustrated at our having failed to prove reliable, say, because of not guarding against distraction and disturbance, and at consequently losing out in the reputation stakes. But still, we would have felt that frustration from the point of view of a single agent or self. It would have distanced us from what we did but not from the beliefs and desires that those doings fail to reflect, and not in that sense from the self that we ideally are.

This would have been so even if it is assumed, plausibly (Tomasello 2016), that natural selection would have favored the appearance of ever more altruistic desires and ever more allo-centric beliefs. On this assumption, we would not have needed to think strategically in order to establish mutual accommodation and reliance; we would have become spontaneously more disposed to take one another's welfare into account, and to adjust to one another's testimony. But no accretion of such desires or beliefs, however other-regarding it made us, would have provided for a critical, prescriptive viewpoint on ourselves. None would have given us an alternative self with which to identify (Pettit 2018b).

All of that changes once we begin to practice acts of avowal and pledging, and gain access to the concepts of credibility and desirability that they bring on stream. Those shifts enable us to recognize that how we are may or may not be how we are committed under relevant practices to being, and that when we do not conform to the requirements of those practices then we display a sort of failure. We fall short in ourselves of the self we spoke for; we believe what is not credible, or desire what is not desirable, by the lights of that bespoken self. And when we recognize the actuality of failure, we simultaneously grasp the possibility and attainability of success. We see it as within our grasp: what we can become, if only we allow the bespoken self to help shape the self we actually are.

The perspective of the bespoken self is also, it should be noted, the perspective of the beholden self. For the self that we speak for in avowing or pledging, co-avowing or co-pledging, is a self that we have given others the right, under the rules of relevant practices, to expect us to display. If we do not display that self in action as well as word, then the rules of avowal or pledging give them the right to ignore certain excuses—to treat us as uncooperative parties—and consciously or unconsciously to impose associated reputational costs.

This conceptual breakthrough ought to be welcome in itself, opening up a wholly new way of thinking, and holding out the possibility of a new sort of personal aspiration and criticism. But it ought also to be welcome insofar as it is bound to serve our interest in being able to rely on others and to get others to rely on us. For with the extra resources available in any given context, we will each have an enhanced capacity to assure others of our reliability. I will be able not just to avow or presume to co-avow a belief that p or a desire for R, but to avow or presume to co-avow a belief that p is credible or that R is desirable. And in reaching for such an extra means of communicating my belief or desire, inviting you to rely on me, I will signal that I must pay an even heavier reputational cost, should I fail in the absence of excuse to live up to what I say.

A conceptual shortfall

But while the breakthrough into prescriptive space is a huge benefit for us, the people of Erewhon, it conspicuously gives us less in the area of desire than it does in that of belief.

The fact that the commonly credible is a master category in relation to the individually and the jointly credible has two welcome results. First, I need not be divided within myself as a result of being disposed to avow or co-avow different beliefs when different perspectives are available; the only belief to which I am going to be committed as a general matter is the belief that I take to be commonly (and so individually) credible. And second, I need not be divided from others, at least not as a matter of necessity, as a result of being disposed to avow that belief; the belief to which I am committed on any relevant topic is a belief, being commonly credible, to which anyone, plausibly, should be committed. The first lesson is that I can be unified within myself in the domain of avowed belief, the second that I can take my avowed belief to be universally compelling, not just compelling in my particular case.

These implications of unity and universality are available in the case of belief because the data that are given a special role in avowal and co-avowal are the same data across those practices. They are the same data across the practices of individual, joint, and common avowal. And they are the same data across the different positions that you and I and other people may occupy. Not only do they enable me to form a single mind on the issues answerable to the data, they also enable me to make persuasive sense of that mind—specifically, of the beliefs I hold—in terms accessible to others.

Such unity and universality of perspective fail in the area of desire. This, as emphasized at various points, is because the desiderata that engage me in individual, joint, and common practices may vary considerably, as may the desiderata that engage you and me and others in our individual or joint practices. And that is so, despite the fact that we need not be exclusively self-centered in the desiderata that engage us in practices of individual avowal, nor particularly group-centered in those that engage us in practices of joint avowal.

The desiderata that move me in the individual avowal of desire, however altruistic I am, will certainly include agent-relative attractors—that the action will help my child or, more altruistically, enable me to keep a pledge—and may be the only set to do so. The desiderata that engage me or you in joint avowal will certainly include group-relative attractors—that this will promote a shared interest—and may be the only set to do so; again, this will be so, however oriented we are toward the interests of others. And the desiderata that I mobilize in common avowal will include neither. They will be restricted to agent-neutral, group-neutral properties: properties like that of promoting truth-telling, reducing pain or ensuring peace.

As I may be moved by different desiderata in practices of individual or joint avowal, so you and I and other persons may be moved by different desiderata. Being differently motivated as individuals, we may weigh various desiderata differently, whether they be agent-relative or agent-neutral in character. And being differently motivated as members of distinct groups, we may also give different weights to various group-relative or group-neutral desiderata.

The lack of unity in the case of desirability will show up wherever different perspectives are relevant on a decision I face, and different sets of desiderata compete for determining the desirable option. One of my alternatives in such a context may be individually desirable, another commonly desirable, and yet another desirable from the joint stand-point of some contingent grouping. In a time of need, for example, it may be individually desirable that I devote my efforts to my children, jointly desirable from the standpoint of my neighborhood that I devote them to the welfare of those who live nearby, and commonly desirable that I put them at the service of people in general.

In any such situation, it may be clear to me how I should choose under one hat, and clear to me how I should choose under another. And so, it may be clear to others that I will be ready to avow a desire for one option under the first hat, a desire for another under the second. But this will be of little use to me or them. I will want to determine which option is desirable for me, independently of the hat I wear. And others will want to know which option is desirable for me, independently of that hat. Otherwise, I will be inscrutable to both myself and others. I won't know, and they won't know, where I stand.

Even if we could resolve the problem raised by this lack of unity, the lack of universality in the case of desirability would still constitute a difficulty. Resolving the problem of unity, it might be the case for each of us that in any conflict between what we find individually, jointly, and commonly desirable, there is always or generally a fact of the matter as to what is overall most desirable for us personally. But that would still leave the problem of universality in place; indeed, as will appear, it may make that problem even more challenging that it might have otherwise been.

The universality problem is that there is no shared currency of what is desirable for anyone—no accepted idea of multilateral desirability— that might enable us to present ourselves as disposed to do what is desirable in that sense. There is no currency that can serve on the side of desire in the way that the currency of common credibility can serve on the side of belief. Thus, we lack an idea of desirability that would enable us to support our commitments to behave in a congenial manner that is acceptable on all sides and to persuade others of our reliability on that front.

This universality problem will be made worse, if we have evolved a notion of what is personally most desirable, solving the unity problem. For this idea will naturally suggest the thought that we will each do what is personally most desirable. And that will be troubling in two ways. First, it may make it seem unlikely that we will reliably stick to the commitments we have made and behave in a manner congenial to others. Second, even if this is not so, others won't be in a position to assure themselves readily that it is not so; it will be hard for them to tell what is personally most desirable for us in this or that situation.

An idea of multilateral desirability would enable us to get over both of these difficulties. By seeing that a certain option was multilaterally desirable—desirable on many, indeed all sides—others could be fairly confident that we will take that option: after all, it would be bound to appeal on our side as well as on theirs. And they would be able to see whether something is multilaterally desirable without conducting a psychological investigation of our particular dispositions; a given alternative would presumably be desirable for us in that way insofar as it would be desirable—presumably, more or less clearly desirable—for just about anyone in our situation.

5.5 Toward the morally desirable

How we could repair the shortfall

Is there a likely means of resolving these problems of disunity and non-universality? In particular, is there a way in which we might construct a concept of multilateral desirability? There are some obvious steps whereby we could resolve both of these problems, and it is worth looking at these before going on to ask about whether we in Erewhon would be likely to take those steps.

The unity problem arises from the fact that different, if overlapping, sets of desiderata support that which is desirable from the individual, the joint, and the common perspectives. But there is a salient way in which we might hope to resolve this, which is to put those desiderata together and determine what they support in aggregate.

Many desiderata are going to be involved in a number of practical perspectives, as when a property, P, that makes something robustly attractive within my individual point of view also makes it robustly attractive within one or another joint viewpoint or within the common viewpoint of an unbounded group. That means that a desideratum like P can weigh against one set of desiderata within one viewpoint, against others in another, in determining perspective-specific desirability. And this shows that there is no problem in principle with thinking that desiderata that figure in different viewpoints may weigh against one another in determining what is desirable from a viewpoint that transcends particular perspectives: that is, what is personally most desirable overall.

The desiderata that weigh against one another within any particular viewpoint may not uniquely determine a desirable alternative from that perspective but will presumably do so in many cases. Similarly, the desiderata from different viewpoints that weigh against one another in determining desirability of a kind that transcends viewpoints may not always identify a single alternative as the one that is personally most desirable overall. But there is no reason to think that they will not be able to do this in the majority, perhaps the vast majority, of cases.

If any one of us can aggregate different desiderata to determine what in many cases is desirable overall by our lights, then we can achieve unity in our judgments of desirability. Consistently with this resolution of the disunity problem, however, I might give a totally different extension to the emerging concept of desirability from that which you or others give it. I might let the desiderata aggregate to support one set of options in a range of relevant choices; you might let them aggregate to support quite a different set. In that case, the concept of such unified desirability would be idiosyncratic to each of us: in effect, I would work with a unilateral concept of desirable$_{me}$ and you with a unilateral concept of desirable$_{you}$.

While the move described might get rid of disunity, then, it would not provide the means of overcoming the lack of universality and delivering a fully multilateral concept of desirability. Indeed, as we saw, getting rid of the disunity, and developing the concept of what is personally most desirable for someone in a given situation, might make the need for a multilateral concept of desirability even more pressing. We might feel unsure about being able to rely on others to act congenially if they are moved by what is personally most desirable for them. And in any case, we might find it difficult to determine what is personally most desirable for this or that individual; that might require an exploration of their personal psychology.

As the disunity problem is resoluble with the means at our disposal in Erewhon, however, so the non-universality problem ought to be resoluble, too. We will be able to resolve it by restricting the desiderata relevant to determining what is multilaterally desirable to properties such that we can welcome the prospect that they should move others as well as ourselves. Where the resolution of the first problem would require us to look in aggregate at the desiderata mobilized under different practices, the resolution of the second would require us to filter the desiderata, putting aside those that put people in inescapable competition with one another.

The desiderata excluded under this filter may include both of two kinds of properties, which we may describe respectively as rancorous and rivalrous attractors. Rancorous attractors are ones that make something attractive to me or to my group, but only at the cost of imposing harm on other individuals or groups. They would make an action attractive despite its harming others: say, despite its meaning that we hurt them physically, seize some of their property, or threaten their lives. Rivalrous properties are ones such that as a result of scarcity, the fact that some individuals or groups enjoy them in their own case necessarily means that others cannot enjoy them in theirs. These properties would make an action attractive for its giving me an advantage over others, although it would not require us to harm them directly.

Thus, to illustrate rivalrous properties, we may each find esteem or power or wealth attractive from our particular individual or group viewpoints—we may see it as an agent-relative or group-relative good—despite the fact that the more we enjoy such a benefit, the less others can do so. Everyone can seek to be famous or influential or to be better off than others, of course, and it may be a non-rivalrous attractor that they should do so. But not everyone can win that prize, since as a matter of logic not everyone can be famous or influential, and not everyone can have more goods than others. And so, it cannot be a non-rivalrous attractor in a certain arrangement that it would deliver such a benefit for me or for any other individual.[10]

What are the non-rancorous, non-rivalrous desiderata that would pass the filter for multilateral desirability? They are certainly going to include the agent-neutral, group-neutral desiderata that would make a scenario attractive from no matter what perspective or standpoint: desiderata like truth-telling or peace or prosperity. But they can also include agent-relative or group-relative desiderata that count as concordant or non-competing.

These are relativized properties such that it is possible for each of the relevant agents or groups to instantiate them at once, and to do so without necessarily reducing the level of satisfaction in other agents or groups. Plausibly, they may include the property of my children doing

---

10. We might prescribe that people should each seek fame or influence or a greater share of some goods than others—this, because we think that the competition would have a result that is commonly desirable—while fully recognizing that they cannot

well, my keeping my pledges, some group to which I belong prospering, my actively pursuing such an agent-relative or group-relative result, and even my pursuing some rivalrous prize in an open competition.

In a term from R.M.Hare (1952, 1981), all such concordant agent-relative desiderata, like all agent-neutral desiderata, are universalizable properties. They are such that if we prescribe realizing or pursuing them for ourselves, then without any inconsistency we can prescribe their realization or pursuit for anyone in a similar position to ours. Thus, we can universally prescribe in a suitable context that each of us should pursue or realize a certain agent-neutral good. And, despite the agent-relativity involved, we can universally prescribe that each of us should look after our own children, keep the pledges we make, look after particular groups to which we belong, pursue those ends as best we can, or pursue even a rivalrous end in a suitably open competition.[11]

If we were able to develop a concept of the multilaterally desirable, following steps like these, would it be likely to make various options substantively desirable? Would it be likely to make them desirable enough on every side for each of us to expect others to be moved by the fact that an option has that feature? Assuming, in line with our narrative, that we in Erewhon manifestly stand to benefit from being able to rely on others and to get others to rely on us—assuming in that sense that we are invested in relationships of mutual reliance—it is very likely that we will each be responsive to what we see as the multilaterally desirable. Indeed it is likely that any option that is multilaterally desirable will generally prove to be also the personally most desirable option for us to take.

---

all attain that prize. The property of seeking the prize is non-rivalrous, the property of winning the prize is rivalrous. The distinction is similar to that drawn by Derek Parfit (1984, 53) between prescriptive theories that are 'directly collectively self-defeating' but not 'indirectly collectively self-defeating'.

11. Hare himself fails to recognize that certain agent-relative desiderata can pass his universalizability test, so that he takes it to support the view that only the commonly desirable can play a role in determining what he thinks of as moral desirability. He is in that sense a classical consequentialist.

These observations show that a concept of the multilaterally desirable is bound to be available, at least in principle, within Erewhon. It may be that we depend on practices of avowal and co-avowal to access concepts of the individually, commonly, and jointly desirable. And it may be that none of those concepts has the status of a master category, as the concept of the commonly credible has that status in the case of belief; it may be that they leave us each short of a unified or universal concept of desirability. But that would still allow us, in the case of any choice, to aggregate and unify the desiderata relevant to different modes of desirability, to filter out those desiderata that make universality inaccessible, and to let the resulting set determine the multilaterally desirable alternative.

Why we would repair the shortfall

Is there any reason to think that we would introduce the category of the multilaterally desirable in Erewhon and thereby overcome the problem of non-universality? Is there reason to think that that category would emerge more or less spontaneously among us? Or is there reason, at the least, to believe that we would be motivated as a community to invoke it as a solution to a collective problem: to contract, as it were, into such a resolution?

There is certainly reason why we might be motivated as a community to introduce the category, since doing so would establish a firm prospect of overcoming various conflicts over desirability, as the master category of common credibility entrenches a prospect of overcoming conflicts on issues of credibility. It would point up the problems that the absence of that category creates among us and motivate a search for the more or less obvious sort of solution just sketched. And it would do so in the presence of conceptual resources that made the required sort of contract accessible.[12]

---

12. Invoking a contract at this point would not presuppose the sort of desirability concept it seeks to explain; it would differ in that regard from the contractual stories that were contrasted in chapter 1 with stories of unplanned emergence.

But there is no need to invoke such a collective move in order to make sense of why we might get to think in terms of the multilaterally desirable. For there is a fairly plausible story to tell about how we might generate the category spontaneously: how we might generate it, first, by adjusting to the challenge of disunity and generating in response a unified concept of the personally most desirable; and then, by adjusting to the problem of non-universality, generating in the process a concept of what is multilaterally rather than just personally desirable.

We can easily imagine, taking the disunity problem first, that you will naturally put pressure on me to say where I stand when the different options I face appear to score differently in different modes of desirability. Suppose that it seems to be individually desirable for me to take one option, jointly desirable for me to take another, and commonly desirable for me to take a third. Suppose, indeed, that I myself openly acknowledge this situation, as I will presumably have to do. In such a situation, you will be likely to despair of determining where I stand if I do not go beyond those particular perspectives to say what is desirable for me in a more outright fashion. And since the likelihood of your despairing of me will be clearly repugnant from my point of view, it must be a matter of manifest expectation that I will come off the fence in any such scenario.

What holds for me in this sort of situation will hold equally for you or anyone else. There will be enormous pressure on each of us, therefore, to acknowledge that not only is there an issue as to which of a number of scenarios is most desirable in the individual or joint or common mode; there is also a question as to which is most desirable in a manner that transcends those modes. But if I or you or anyone else responds to that pressure, we will each make room for a concept of what is overall desirable for us, regardless of practical perspective. And, the pressure and the response being manifest, we will do so as a matter of common awareness across the community.

With access to the concept of what is personally most desirable for each of us, the problem of non-universality will be particularly pressing. For we may begin to feel that we do not have sure ground for relying on someone else to act in a congenial way, even someone who has made an explicit commitment to us, unless we can see that acting in that way is personally the most desirable option available to them. And we will not be in a ready position to determine that one or another option satisfies this condition: that would seem to require a customized sense of their particular psychology.

There are some cases, of course, where we might find our way beyond this problem of non-universality. These are cases in which the alternative that is desirable$_{me}$ is manifestly also desirable$_{you}$. This convergence would be bound to attract notice, leading us to cast the option as desirable from a shared, interpersonal perspective—desirable$_{us}$—and inviting the thought that it may even be desirable$_{all}$. Any option that was desirable$_{all}$, of course, would count as multilaterally desirable: it would satisfy all relevant desiderata for each, including all that are non-rancorous and non-rivalrous, and would be bound to prove desirable on all sides.

Of course, cases where the notion of the desirable$_{us}$ clearly applies— and, potentially, the notion of the desirable$_{all}$—are bound to exceptional. But the experience of such cases in Erewhon is bound to underline for us the attraction and the possibility of finding an interpersonal perspective, and achieving convergence, in other cases too.

In those cases, achieving full convergence will be problematic just insofar as we are each exposed to the effect of rancorous or rivalrous desiderata, and are liable to seek ends that require directly harming others or to pursue essentially competitive goods for ourselves like esteem or power or wealth. But that means that the search for an interpersonal, convergent perspective will naturally lead us to focus on that which is attractive for each of us on a non-rancorous, non-rivalrous basis. That basis ought to be enough to secure the universal attraction of various options, given that we are invested in building relations of mutual reliance with one another.

Thus, the search for a convergent, universal perspective would be likely to lead us, by this account, to make use of a notion of multilateral desirability that applies to anything that is supported on the basis of non-rancorious, non-rivalrous desiderata. And that notion would be a salient and appealing candidate for playing in most cases the role that the concept of the desirable$_{us}$ or the desirable$_{all}$ can play in some. The concept would be salient insofar as such relationships of mutual reliance could clearly prosper only if we suppressed the attraction of rancorous and rivalrous properties. And it would appeal to each of us insofar as we could plausibly invoke it to support our disposition to behave in a manner congenial to others—say, to live up to our commitments—and to persuade others of our reliability on that front; the support provided would be persuasive in virtue of our manifest investment in relationships of mutual reliance.

If this line of thought is sound, then the sorts of pressures that lead us in Erewhon to make use of avowals and pledges in communicating our attitudes, and the sorts of pressures that lead us therefore to think in terms of the credible and the desirable, are likely to provide us with prompts that push us eventually into invoking a concept of multilateral desirability. The concept will be a resource that is going to be more or less manifestly available to us and that we can use to the manifestly attractive effect of assuring others of our broadly congenial dispositions. Thus, the trajectory that the narrative has traced leads us plausibly, if not inexorably, towards that concept.

Assuming that concept gets established in the community, it will enable us to form beliefs in common about what is multilaterally desirable in this situation or that, and about what options are multilaterally desirable. And, of course, it will also enable us to avow and presume to co-avow a belief that an option is multilaterally desirable, whether by expressing the belief in an assertion that it is, or by ascribing the belief to ourselves, or by explaining why it is true. Avowal and co-avowal are recursive operations, as already emphasized, so that the fact that the concept of the multilaterally desirable would not be available in the absence of such practices is quite consistent with our being able to rerun the practices with beliefs that presuppose the availability of that concept.

The range of the multilaterally desirable

How substantive is the agreement we are likely to achieve about the multilaterally desirable option in any choice: say, in a choice between alternative actions that an agent might take or between alternative arrangements that we as a community might establish? Agreement will be easily achieved in cases in which one option in the choice satisfies all the non-rancorous, non-rivalrous desiderata that are satisfied by others and satisfies them in a higher measure; or, satisfying some of those desiderata in at least equal measure, satisfies others better. And it will be relatively easily achieved in other cases to the extent to which the weightings we attach to the different relevant desiderata are in more or less the same range.

The relevant desiderata that we recognize in certain choices may be weighted differently, of course, and may block the emergence of full-scale convergence. In many cases, this will generate a range of different views but still allow continuing discussion that is aimed at clarifying the issues involved and perhaps reducing differences of weighting. In other cases, however, the weightings may be so divergent that, no matter how much clarification is achieved, divergence is going to prove unavoidable. In those cases, it will be indeterminate whether this or that option in a choice is multilaterally desirable.

Notwithstanding such failures of convergence on the extension of multilateral desirability, however, we may expect to achieve actual agreement over a broad range of issues, even if we are likely to leave some questions unresolved or treat them as irresoluble. Thus, it is likely that we in Erewhon will agree about the multilateral desirability of many types of choice, or at least about the desirability of most instances of those types.

Consider choices of the kind that are generally resolved by social norms of the kind introduced in the second chapter. Each of us is likely to be sensitive to the desiderata relevant to the multilateral desirability of conforming to such a norm. We are likely to agree that it is multilaterally desirable to tell the truth, abstain from violence, avoid fraud, and so on. Those norms will represent standards such that, as a matter of common awareness, we all take conformity to be multilaterally desirable, at least in most contexts: specifically, in contexts where their demands are clear and conformity is not likely to trigger any exceptional, multilaterally undesirable costs.

Standards that are shared in this sense may be supererogatory: they may require a capacity for self-sacrifice—a degree of heroic virtue— that few of us will be expected to possess. While we may well share some supererogatory standards of multilateral desirability in Erewhon, we are also likely to share standards that we take people generally to be able to meet. These will include standards like those that preclude lying, violence and fraud, which are certainly within our normal capacity to follow—otherwise they could not get established under reputational pressures—and within our normal capacity as a matter of common belief. They will count in that sense, not only as shared, but as routine standards of multilateral desirability.

When standards of multilateral desirability are shared and routine in this sense, they will constitute norms of desirability, as the notion of a norm was defined in chapter 2. Being shared and routine, people will generally conform to what they present as multilaterally desirable patterns; conforming to those patterns will generally be expected to have reputational benefits, therefore, not conforming to have reputational costs; this expectation will help to support the general pattern of conformity; and all of this is likely to be a matter of common awareness. This is to say that many of the purely social norms mentioned in chapter 2 are likely to double as norms of multilateral desirability in Erewhon: that is, as norms such that following them requires understanding what it is to be desirable in that sense.

The discussion in chapter 2 showed how pre-social norms that are supported by reputational forces, without our necessarily recognizing them or tracking them, will become properly social norms once they satisfy a common awareness condition. At that point, we will see meeting their requirements as a condition for full acceptance in the community and can invoke that condition as a desideratum of complying. When social norms double as norms of multilateral desirability, the difference made is that we can now see meeting their requirements, not just as a condition for social acceptance, but as a condition for satisfying the demands of multilateral desirability. The reputational forces will remain in place as an engine motivating conformity, as will the social desideratum of conformity. But the norms will gain a new aspect under which conformity to them appeals: one that is provided by the idea of the multilaterally desirable.

There are also likely to be norms of multilateral desirability established in Erewhon that reflect practices of avowal and pledging that had not yet appeared in the narrative of chapter 2. Given the importance assigned on all sides to these practices, and given their central role in social life, we are all likely to regard it as multilaterally desirable that people should live up to the unquestioned demands of their avowals and pledges: that they should display fidelity to their commitments. And equally, we are certainly likely to regard such fidelity as lying within people's normal capacity to follow. Standards of fidelity will be both shared and routine in the society, and will constitute further norms of multilateral desirability.[13]

The norms of multilateral desirability that prevail at any one time in Erewhon may not coincide with those that prevail in another society or in Erewhon at another time. It is very likely that conversation about matters of multilateral desirability may affect the standards that the members of any society are likely to endorse in a shared manner at any time. And it is equally likely that as conformity to any such pattern rises, the disesteem for not conforming will increase, and conformity may become motivationally more accessible, with the result that an aspirational ideal may turn into a routine standard. The assumption made about Erewhon is that there will almost certainly be some standards of multilateral desirability that are shared and routine at any period, not that any particular set of standards will achieve this status or that they will remain in place for all time.

Multilateral and moral desirability

These observations argue that as we in Erewhon would each come to access a range of practice-specific concepts of desirability, so in all likelihood we would evolve a unified, universalized concept of multilateral

---

13. This illustrates yet another aspect of the recursion stressed at various points. We may depend in Erewhon on the practice and concept of avowing and pledging in

desirability. This would give us a master concept of desirability to rival the master concept of common credibility and would ease the path to mutual reliance. The argument marks a crucial development in the narrative, for the concept of the multilaterally desirable coincides broadly with the concept of the morally desirable, as that was outlined earlier.

Thus, the concept invokes considerations that are relatively unrestricted in the range of interests invoked, relatively unrestricted in the standpoint adopted, and consequently fit to play an authoritative role in adjudicating certain clashes among other judgments of desirability. The concept of multilateral desirability is unrestricted in the range of interests that it reflects since it is designed not to reflect just the particular interests of one individual or grouping. It is also relatively unrestricted in the standpoint adopted, since it is designed to unify the perspectives offered by different practices for any individual, and to universalize the perspectives of different individuals. And being designed to adjudicate conflicts between the rival interests and investments of different people, it is bound to have the authoritative cast associated with the concept of moral desirability.

The notion of the multilaterally desirable not only connects with morality in this manner; it also converges with the concept of moral desirability in more detailed ways. It satisfies the three generic constraints satisfied by any concept of desirability, including the moral. And it conforms to the two specific constraints associated with the concept of moral desirability in particular.

The generic constraints are those of grounding, divergence, and governance. If one option in a choice counts as multilaterally desirable and others not, then there must be a difference in the desiderata that ground their relative desirability. If an option is desirable in that sense, or even if I judge it to be desirable in that sense, it may still be that what I desire diverges from that judgment as a result of a distraction or disturbance that I fail to resist: say, the disturbance generated by a rancorous or

order to develop the concept of multilateral desirability. But that does not prevent us from applying that very concept to those practices.

rivalrous attractor. And my functioning properly as an agent among agents—as someone invested in relationships of mutual reliance—requires that the judgment of multilateral desirability should dictate or govern what I actually desire in relevant contexts. This will be so, at any rate, when other things are equal: for example, when the multilaterally desirable is not beyond my capacity and, to anticipate discussion in the next chapter, I am fit to be held responsible for pursuing it.

The first of the specific constraints on the concept of the morally desirable requires that you and I should have the same content in mind when we judge that it is desirable for anyone, whether anyone in general or anyone in a certain position, to choose a given option. And the second requires that it should be true or false that the option is desirable—assuming the issue is determinate—so that there is no possibility that it might be true by your criteria as an assessor, false by mine.

Is the concept of the multilaterally desirable likely to meet these constraints? It must do so if it is to get us out of the problem raised by rival personal standpoints, satisfying an important part of its design specification. If it is to facilitate interpersonal understanding and reliance in the required manner, then it must rule out both the relativity of content that the first constraint forbids and the relativity of truth-value that the second constraint outlaws. It must direct us to a range of issues that we may hope to explore and resolve in common.

These considerations argue that the concept of multilateral desirability, which would be likely to evolve among us under the pressures described, can be identified with the familiar concept of moral desirability. In at least this respect, then, we in Erewhon would be more or less bound to develop an ethical way of thinking and prove ourselves an ethical species.

The convergence of the idea of multilateral desirability on the idea of moral desirability is hardly surprising, at least on many received accounts of what it is to take the moral point of view. David Hume gave an account of this point of view that makes a nice connection with the multilateral idea (Sayre-McCord 1994). Asking what someone does in adopting the language of morals and using it to assess others, Hume (1983, s9.6) answers: "he expresses sentiments, in which, he expects, all his audience are to concur with him. He must here, therefore, depart from his private and particular situation, and must chuse a point of view, common to him with others: He must move some universal principle of the human frame, and touch a string, to which all mankind have an accord and symphony."[14]

The developments charted in this chapter do not yet give us the concept of moral obligation, which figures even more prominently in ethics than does that of moral desirability. But if we come in addition to develop the idea of responsibility, we are also going to be in a position to introduce a concept that plays the role of the obligatory, under the construal adopted here. It will be morally obligatory for someone to choose a certain option under that construal if it meets two conditions: it figures among those options that fall within the domain where the agent is fit to be held responsible, and it is morally the most desirable of those options. This means that we will have access to the concept of moral obligation—and to the related concepts of moral prohibition and permission—if it is possible for us to gain access to the notion of responsibility. And that possibility is the topic of the next chapter.

14. I am grateful to Ralph Wedgwood for drawing my attention to this Humean passage.

Chapter 6: Discovering Responsibility

The observations made so far provide solid ground for thinking that we in Erewhon would evolve a conception of multilateral desirability akin to the established category of moral desirability. We would inevitably develop practices of avowing and pledging, co-avowing and co-pledging our attitudes. Those practices would make the introduction of various concepts of desirability more or less inevitable. And, confronted with conflicts between those notions, we would be pushed to develop the concept of what is multilaterally desirable: that is, desirable in a way that transcends the perspectives of different persons. This, plausibly, converges on the concept of the morally desirable that figures prominently in common usage.

If it is to give us a potential explanation of the emergence of ethics, however, the narrative must also explain how we in Erewhon can come to think in terms of responsibility as well as desirability. It must explain why we who have evolved the concept of the morally or multilaterally desirable would go on to hold one another responsible to certain judgments and standards of moral desirability. It must offer an account of why we would censure those who flout such moral judgments or standards and commend those who conform.

As argued in the last chapter, the concept of multilateral or moral desirability will apply with a particular salience in Erewhon to certain shared and routine standards, like those exemplified in social norms against lying, violence, and fraud, and against infidelity in avowals or pledges. Such standards will constitute properly moral norms: that is, norms that presuppose the availability of the concept of moral desirability among practitioners.

The account to be given of why we would hold one another responsible to moral norms of this kind might also be invoked to make sense of how we could hold one another responsible to certain social norms or standards, whether of prudence or patriotism, law or epistemology. But the focus here will be on holding one another responsible for conforming to moral norms in particular. The focus will be entirely on moral responsibility, as it may be put, where this is understood as responsibility to moral standards, not as responsibility of any inherently special, moral character; responsibility, so it is assumed, amounts to more or less the same thing, regardless of the standards involved.

This chapter takes up the responsibility challenge in three sections. The first section explores what is involved in holding someone responsible for an action, in particular an action that breaches moral norms, distinguishing between three messages that are conveyed by holding the person responsible. While that first section analyzes how we in the ordinary world hold one another responsible, the second section looks at why we in Erewhon are likely to hold one another responsible to moral norms—shared and routine moral standards—after the same fashion: specifically, in a way that conveys the same three messages. The final section turns to general issues about responsibility and freewill, showing how the theory supported by the narrative about Erewhon relates to contemporary rivals.

6.1 Responsibility characterized

Setting the scene

As in the case of desirability, it is essential in pushing forward the narrative to have a good sense of what fitness to be held responsible connotes in everyday usage and practice; otherwise, it will not be clear what is needed for the narrative to be successful. There are various accounts in the literature of what it means to hold someone responsible for having done something, and there will be some mention of these in the final section. But rather than going into the debate between different approaches at this point, the line taken here will be to begin from an account that has two virtues, one substantive, the other methodological. On the substantive side, the account satisfies many of the common connotations of saying that someone is fit to be held responsible for an action. And on the methodological, it offers a rich account of those connotations that makes the task to be discharged by the narrative about Erewhon more rather than less difficult to accomplish; it does not tilt the scales in favor of success.

What responsibility connotes in ordinary usage is best articulated for the scenario in which I hold you responsible for something I see as an undesirable choice—an offense or misdeed, as we may now say—and blame you for what you did. This is a case in which the implications of being fit to be held responsible are sharp and the costs high, so that the received understanding of fitness to be held responsible is likely to be at its clearest there. And if it proves possible to articulate the concept of responsibility for this scenario, then the lessons should carry over to the case in which I hold you responsible for having done something good rather than something bad.[1]

Fitness to be held responsible as conceptualized here is a role property that consists in your being such that, under the rules of the practice, you are an appropriate target for being held responsible. Fitness to be held responsible consists in your satisfying the messages or thoughts I convey about you when I hold you responsible. It may be realized in different individuals on the basis of varying neural configurations, as indeed it may be realized in different corporate bodies on varying organizational bases (Pettit 2007c). But the idea of fitness to be held

---

1. They may not carry over smoothly, since doing good often makes more robust demands than doing bad (Pettit 2015a, c). This asymmetry between good and bad generates a similar asymmetry between holding someone responsible for good and holding them responsible for bad. The topic relates to the disposition-dependence of many of the goods you can bring about, which is discussed briefly in chapter 7, section 5. The complexity will not be pursued further here.

responsible can be defined in a way that abstracts from how it is realized or grounded in such different agents. [2]

Suppose, then, that I hold you responsible for a misdeed of some kind. Let this be an action like telling a lie, when there are no special considerations that might have made it desirable to hide the truth. And let the context of action be one in which telling the truth, by common assumption, does not require heroic virtue but only a routine form of sensitivity to the desirability of truth-telling.

On the account to be adopted here, there are three aspects to holding you responsible in this way or, alternatively, to treating you as fit to be held responsible. They come out nicely in three distinct messages that I convey by way of holding you responsible for a misdeed when I say: "You could have done otherwise; you could have told the truth." To hold you responsible, of course, is not necessarily to make any such utterance. But it is actively to assume an attitude that you could use those words or similar expressions to convey. It is actively to form a thought that you would be likely to communicate in that way, if it was possible to do so—for example, it did not concern someone in the distant past—and was not too difficult or costly (Watson 1987; McKenna 2012).

"You could have done otherwise": the literal content

The literal meaning of "You could have done otherwise," naturally understood, is just that you might have done otherwise: that it was possible, however unlikely, that you should have responded to the desirability of telling truth; there was nothing that stood in your way. But is the possibility of having done otherwise always going to obtain when

2. While different in the concrete version to be defended, the approach taken here broadly conforms to the abstract framework for conceiving of responsibility that Gideon Rosen (2015) describes as the alethic conception as distinct from the fittingness or moral conception. It denies that the relation in virtue of which it is appropriate to hold you responsible is primitive or sui generis, as in the fittingness view, or that it is a matter of the fairness of holding you responsible, as in the moral. It holds that what makes it appropriate to hold you responsible is just the truth of the thoughts or messages that adopting such a stance conveys.

I think you are blameworthy? Yes, it is, contrary to a familiar line of thought (Frankfurt 1969).

Suppose we blame you for misleading me by telling a lie or, assuming this conveys the same message, by staying silent. And suppose we continue to blame you, after learning that you could not have done otherwise than mislead me; this, because, unbeknown to you, there was someone on standby, ready to intervene by preventing you from telling the truth. Blaming you in such a situation seems reasonable. So, does it show that we may reasonably blame you for doing something, even when it is not the case that you could have done otherwise?

No, it doesn't. You could still have tried to tell the truth rather than misleading me spontaneously; you could have taken steps that required the standby agent to intervene. And in at least that sense, if not in the sense of actually telling the truth, you could have done otherwise than you did.

You could not have done otherwise even in that sense, of course, if, as is sometimes supposed, the standby intervener would have stopped you, not just from telling the truth, but from trying to tell the truth. But if you could not even have tried to tell the truth, you would not have enjoyed agency in the proper sense and I would not have grounds for blaming you; you would be wholly exempt, by ordinary criteria, from censure.

This shows that with any misdeed for which I hold you responsible, there must be some sense in which you could have done otherwise, some sense in which that possibility holds. And that being so, we may set aside the complexities of the sort of case in which doing otherwise means just trying to do otherwise. We may stick with the standard sort of example in which I blame you for misleading me by saying, correctly, that it was possible for you to have told the truth.

What sort of possibility should we take this remark to ascribe? Not just logical possibility, for sure, but something like physical, psychological, and social possibility: in short, possibility of an agential kind. After all, we would not think that you could have done otherwise under the construal relevant to holding you responsible for an offense, if there were any physical, psychological, or social obstacles that got in your way. The agential obstacles that are generally taken to undercut the point of saying that you could have done otherwise in such a context are related to exemption and excuse in the senses introduced earlier. That you could have done otherwise, construed to fit that context, means in its literal signification nothing more or less than that exempting and excusing factors were absent.

That exempting factors were absent means that you were not subject to any general agency-debilitating condition like paranoia or obsession or delusion or something of that kind. On the assumption that these come only in non-partial forms, which is maintained for convenience throughout this study, any such condition would remove altogether the possibility of your having done otherwise and exempt you from being held responsible (Watson 1987; Wallace 1996; Gardner 2007).

That excusing factors were absent—that is, unforeclosed, excusing factors—means that you were not confronted by specific, situational obstacles, epistemic or practical, that stopped you registering or acting on the desirability of truth-telling. On the assumption that these, too, come only in non-partial forms, any such factor would have blocked the possibility of your doing otherwise than telling a lie.

"You could have done otherwise": three connotations

The literal content of saying that you could have done otherwise, by this account, is fairly platitudinous: that you were not subject to any exempting or excusing influences, so that there was nothing about your situation that ruled out acting other than how you did. Uttered by way of holding you responsible for a misdeed, however, I convey much more than this mere possibility in saying that you could have done otherwise: that you could have told the truth, responding to the desirability of that option (Nelkin 2011). As I communicate indirectly or pragmatically that I believe that p when I assert that p, so there are at least three messages about my attitude that I communicate in a pragmatic manner when I say that you could have done otherwise.

These messages are pragmatic because I convey them, not by virtue of the semantic content of the remark, but by virtue of the pragmatic significance of my uttering the sentence in the context of responding to a misdeed. In that sense, the messages are conversational implicatures (Grice 1975a). They are messages that I take to be manifestly available to you as audience insofar as you see me as a normal interlocutor and as someone, therefore, who has something more interesting to convey—something more relevant in the context (Sperber and Wilson 1986)—than the platitude associated with its semantic content. This is the platitude according to which you might have responded to the desirability of telling the truth in the sense that there was nothing like an exemption or excuse to stop you doing so.

Saying that you might have told the truth in this vein pragmatically conveys the following three attitudes over and beyond the belief that that possibility was open: first, a recognition that you had the capacity to tell the truth; second, a retrospective exhortation, to introduce a notion explained later, to have told the truth; and, third, a reprimand for not having told the truth. I recognize that despite not having acted like someone with a capacity or disposition to respond to the considerations that made truth-telling desirable, you did indeed have such a disposition at the time of choice. I exhort you to have told the truth, displaying an impatience at your failure; I hold by an attitude after the action that I might have expressed beforehand by saying that you can and ought to tell the truth, thereby urging you to do so. And finally, I reprimand you for not having told the truth; I present you as someone who is on the hook, without any exempting or excusing consideration to invoke.

The first connotation: recognizing capacity

If I say "You could have done otherwise" in response to a misdeed, then I credit you with a capacity or disposition to have done otherwise in the situation where you made your choice. I assume that you had that capacity and simply failed to exercise it. I do not conclude from your failure to act as appropriate that you must have lacked the capacity to act appropriately. Rather, I judge that you had that capacity but failed to manifest it in your behavior.

Does the capacity I credit you with in saying that you could have done otherwise consist just in the fact that you were not subject to any physical, psychological, or social obstacle, of the kind that would exempt you or excuse you from being held responsible? No, it does not. The claim that you were not disabled in the excused or exempted fashion—that it was agentially possible for you to have done otherwise—is involved in the literal content of the words: You could have done otherwise. But the first connotation of using those words in holding you responsible is that you had the capacity to have done otherwise in a much more demanding sense than this.

It may be agentially possible for you to give away all your worldly goods, surplus to strict need, to those who are poorer than yourself. But I would hardly hold you responsible for not doing so. There is a sense of capacity in which we take this to be beyond your capacity, so that if you did it, and I approved, then I would regard it as an exercise of heroic virtue. When I hold you responsible for failing to do something, however, I must think that there is a more substantive sense in which it lay within your capacity. Thus, when I hold you responsible for telling a lie by saying that you could have told the truth, I must take those words to convey something more than the fact that it was a bare, agential possibility that you might have told the truth: that there was no exempting or excusing factor to stop you.

Intuitively, I must convey the message that you were such that it was not only possible for you to register and act on the desirability of telling the truth; it was also to be expected that you would do so. Your makeup and milieu did not rule out telling the truth but, much more importantly, they actually ruled it in: they made it into a matter of natural expectation. You may not have told the truth in the actual situation, then, but the implicature is that you would have told the truth across many of the variations on that situation in which the considerations of desirability that support telling the truth remain saliently in place, and exempting and excusing factors continue to be absent. You had the capacity to tell the truth in that demanding sense of capacity, albeit you failed to exercise it.

The message, in other words, is that it was not barely possible for you to respond to the desirability of truth-telling and speak the truth, as the absence of exempting and excusing factors would imply. It was dependably or robustly possible for you to do so. You were disposed to tell the truth robustly over variations of circumstance that continued to keep that desirability in place, and did not introduce excusing or exempting circumstances; in particular, you were disposed to tell the truth over variations in which different sorts of distractions or disturbances were in play. You were disposed to tell the truth so robustly, indeed, that your failure to do so must count as something of a fluke (Smith 2003; Hieronymi 2007; McGeer and Pettit 2015).

The message holds, it appears, even in the case in which you are a stranger, or are someone who lied to me in the past. If I am to hold you responsible for lying to me now, then, regardless of your missing or miserable record, I must credit you with a capacity to have told the truth. Otherwise, I would have to think that you were not properly responsive to the accepted desirability of truth-telling. And in that case, I could hardly hold you to the truth-telling standard, and blame you for not living up to it.

You might be someone, it is true, who is unresponsive to the accepted desirability of truth-telling. In that extreme case, I might blame you in the absence of exempting or excusing factors for having allowed yourself to become unresponsive or for not doing anything to regain responsiveness. But given that you are now someone incapable of robustly telling the truth, it would be misleading of me to blame you for the particular lie you told, as if that were something out of the ordinary. What I would do, rather, is to excommunicate you, as we might say, from the moral community: to denounce you as someone wholly insensitive in the relevant, truth-telling domain.

As exemption and excuse exculpate you in one sense, excommunication would exculpate you in another. But the sort of exculpation it provides is even worse than blame or censure: it represents the sort of reaction that is appropriate for the irredeemably evil person. To blame you for telling a lie is to display a positive attitude of respect insofar as it involves crediting you with a robust capacity to tell the truth, albeit a capacity you did not exercise on the occasion in question. To excommunicate or denounce you is to put you beyond even the pale of routine culpability; it is to cast you in the very lowest regions of Dante's hell.

That we assume a rich capacity to have done otherwise in anyone we blame for not living up to a shared, routine standard—and so a standard to which they themselves subscribe—is supported by the fact that, absent any excusing or exempting difficulty, such an offender is unlikely to claim that it would have required heroic virtue on their part to abide by the standard. They are unlikely to avoid regular blame or censure, in other words, when that means inviting excommunication instead. And that is to say that they may be expected to lay claim implicitly to having the robust capacity to have done otherwise—in our example, to have told the truth. If we make a default assumption that an unexcused, unexempted offender had the robust capacity to have told the truth, then, that only reflects an implicit invitation on their part to be ascribed such a capacity.

Still, it may seem rash of me to assume in every case in which excuse and exemption are unavailable that, despite having told a lie, you had the robust, situation-specific capacity to tell the truth. It may seem reckless to make the default assumption that you were sufficiently responsive to the desirability of truth-telling to make it surprising that you should have lied. In mitigation of this difficulty, however, there are three softening qualifications that may help to give the assumption some plausibility.

A first is that, while it is convenient to speak of the presence of such a capacity as an on-off matter—and while this way of speaking will be maintained here—it may be somewhat misleading. Having the required capacity does not mean responding invariably to the relevant considerations, at least in the absence of excuse and exemption. It means responding more or less dependably to those considerations, where the threshold at which the response counts as suitably dependable need not be set at the highest level.[3]

3. For a discussion of how to think about variation on this front, see Pettit (2015c, Appendix II).

A second softening qualification is that when I take you to have the capacity to respond to the desirability of truth-telling, and to be able to avoid lying, I do not have to think that it will be easy for you to respond in that way. I may think that you can respond appropriately, not because doing so comes naturally to you, but because you can get yourself to respond in that way. You can take measures to guard, for example, against being distracted from the desideratum of telling the truth or against any disturbance of the motivating effect of that desideratum. For example, you can remind yourself of the reputational costs of failure, letting this reinforce the attraction of truth-telling and strengthen your will. Your capacity to respond to the desirability of truth-telling in a case in which you actually lie would then consist in the disposition to be moved in part by such costs, and so to tell the truth, in relevant variations on the actual circumstances.[4]

A third softening qualification of the capacity I credit you with when I say that you could have told the truth will be relevant in later discussion. I need not think of this as a capacity that you had on an enduring basis, independently of the effect I attribute to my having encouraged you to speak the truth—or to someone else's having done so—or independently of the fact that you had been reminded about the costs that lying would impose on a third party. I may think, in other words, that, while you had a dependable disposition at the point of action to tell the truth—a disposition that was partly grounded in the encouragement you received or of the reminder you had been given—that disposition was not of the standard, durable type; it was not necessarily a disposition that was already in place, prior to the effect of those pressures.[5]

4. On the idea of being able to get yourself to do something, see Estlund (2014) and Southwood (2017).
5. In this case, I ascribe a disposition to tell the truth dependably or robustly but a disposition that may fail to be durable—that is, fail to be robust in the independent sense of surviving robustly over the ravages of time and other disruptive factors that do not count intuitively as distractors or disturbers. See Pettit (2015c); McGeer and Pettit (2017).

The second connotation: exhorting the agent

Saying that you could have told the truth in censuring you for lying implies, as mentioned, that it was something of a fluke that you failed to exercise that capacity. But in saying that you could have done otherwise, I do not mean to communicate just that it was a fluke that you did not tell the truth. That would be to console you rather than to speak in censure. Blame or censure involves quite a different attitude toward your failure to exercise your truth-telling capacity: a form of impatience with your failure; a refusal to accept it as a brute, regrettable fact. And the second connotation of saying that you could have done otherwise in such a case is to communicate that distinctive attitude. [6]

How to describe the attitude involved? Perhaps the best way to approach the issue is to consider the attitude that I or anybody else takes toward you prior to action, when we enjoin you to tell the truth, perhaps spelling that out by saying in an encouraging way: you can tell the truth. Such an injunction or exhortation says or supposes that you ought to tell the truth or that there is reason for you to tell the truth. But it does not have merely the force of a positive evaluation of that action. It does not amount just to saying that it would be better if you told the truth, where that has no action-directive significance for you now: i.e., where it has the same merely evaluative force as saying that it would be better if you had learned the local language or had received a scientific education. When the words "You ought to tell the truth" constitute a mere evaluation, it makes sense to add: "but I realize that you won't." Where they constitute an exhortation or injunction, such an addition would make no sense; it would undermine the force of the utterance.

The attitude I take toward you in the wake of your failure to tell the truth is best cast as a counterpart of this exhortatory attitude. When

6. Victoria McGeer and I (2015) take the problem of explaining why "You could have done otherwise" does not just amount to saying it was a fluke that you did not do otherwise to constitute "the hard problem of responsibility." The line taken in the text broadly follows the approach that we adopt in the paper of that name.

I say that you could have told the truth, I convey the message that it would have been appropriate for me or anyone else to have exhorted you to tell the truth prior to your utterance; it would have been appropriate, indeed, for you to have exhorted yourself to do so, seeking to get yourself to tell the truth. I retrospectively ratify that exhortatory attitude, implying that at the time of action you were a fit target for exhortation. You had a capacity to tell the truth that was sufficiently robust to have made sense of anyone's exhortatory efforts to get you to tell the truth. You were suitably exhortable in the domain of the action you took.

In communicating this message, I refuse to be resigned to the negatively evaluated fact that you hid the truth, as I might be resigned to the weather having turned foul or the dog having misbehaved. I invite you to look at what you did, as we might say, and to recognize with me that it was within your power to have done otherwise; the suggestion is that this was not just a possibility, even a robust possibility, as it was just a possibility that the weather might stay fine or the dog mind its manners. The message is that whether you were to reveal or hide the truth was up to you—it was a matter of your choosing—and you blew it; you made a choice contrary to what I or you or anyone else might have reasonably exhorted you to do in advance.

This message may be described as one of retrospective exhortation, where that is understood as a message of ratifying the exhortatory efforts that someone might have made prior to the action. In retrospective exhortation, I express the sort of attitude toward what you have done that I would have expressed prior to the action if I had said in the normal exhortatory way, "You can do it—you can tell the truth," or if I had implied this by enjoining you to do it. Speaking in retrospect, I cannot aspire to get you to change what you did, of course, but I can communicate that you did it in the presence of resources that would have made you a fit target of exhortation before the action. Fitness to be held responsible for an offence ex post goes with fitness to be exhorted not to do it ex ante.

The third connotation: reprimanding the agent

The third effect of saying that you could have done otherwise in the case of a misdeed is to reprimand you: to communicate an unwelcome attribution of failure. Not only do I recognize your capacity to have responded to considerations of desirability and told the truth, treating this as a robust possibility. And not only do I display an exhortatory attitude, expressing impatience rather than resignation at how you behave. I also indict you for the failure to have told the truth. In remarking that you could have done otherwise, I highlight your failure in a presumptively unwelcome, penalizing manner and thereby reprimand you for not having told the truth.

In communicating this reprimand, I present it as deserved in a straightforward sense, if not deserved in every sense possible (Pereboom 2014). I communicate as part of the implicature that you were not subject to any exempting or excusing obstacle that might let you off the hook and that you were not lacking in sensitivity to relevant considerations of desirability. And I convey thereby that you have no basis for complaining about the reprimand. In presenting that reprimand, of course, I may also support further sanctions of custom or law, whether these are justified on consequentialist, contractualist, or other grounds (Scanlon 1998, Ch. 5). But we may put aside penal sanctions here, concentrating only on the sort of reprimand or censure that they normally presuppose.

The task ahead

As remarked earlier, I express and communicate my belief that you could have told the truth—that there was nothing relevant to stop you doing so—when I report that possibility. By the implicatures just examined, however, I also convey a great deal more about my attitudes when I make this remark in the wake of an offense. As the words express a belief that you might have told the truth in such a context, so they will also express a recognition of your dispositional capacity to have told the truth, a retrospective exhortation to have told the truth—that is, a retrospective ratification of the exhortatory attitude—and a reprimand for having actually told a lie. They represent you as someone with a rich capacity to have told the truth, someone who is suitably exhortable on that front, and someone who is subject to an unwelcome ascription of failure that they have no grounds to complain about.

With these aspects of the responsibility practice spelled out, the question to be explored is whether I and you and other members of Erewhon are likely to hold one another responsible for living up to certain standards of moral desirability. There is good reason, it turns out, to think that we would evolve this sort of practice. In particular, there is good reason to think that we would come to use the remark "You could have done otherwise," or some cognate utterance, with the three connotations described.

As the discussion has focused on cases in which I hold you responsible for misdeeds rather than for good deeds, so it has focused on cases in which I hold you responsible, not on cases in which I hold myself responsible. But the points made about those interpersonal cases apply straightforwardly in the intrapersonal cases, as well. Insofar as it makes sense for me to recognize your capacity to have told the truth, to exhort you retrospectively to have told the truth and to reprimand you for actually having told a lie, so the same exercise can make sense in relation to myself. I can remonstrate with myself as I can remonstrate with you about any failure, recognizing my own capacity in the relevant domain, exhorting myself to have exercised it, and reprimanding myself for not having done so. The narrative will not address this first-personal case directly, but it supports the same lessons there as it supports in the case of holding another person responsible.

Responsibility and regulation

Before developing the narrative to take account of responsibility, it is worth observing that the practice of holding one another responsible is very different from the blind regulation that was discussed in chapter 2 in the account of pre-social norms. The observation applies to the practice of holding one another responsible to any suitable standards, such as social norms, not just with the practice of holding one another responsible to moral standards. But we concentrate here on the moral practice.

Blind regulation would consist in the fact that if you do not tell me the truth in any instance, that is likely to give me a bad opinion of your reliability as an informant, to lead me to speak ill of you, and to impose a reputational cost. And the prospect of such a cost is likely to lead you, instance by instance, to tell the truth in making reports and to conform to similarly welcome patterns like abstaining from violence or coercion or theft.

In the scenario envisaged with a pre-social norm like telling the truth, we each have an interest in proving ourselves to be reliable truth-tellers; unless we do so, we cannot expect to be able to rely on others or to get others to rely on us. This interest leads us each to tell the truth in general, seeking to win a reputation for having the disposition to tell the truth reliably. And that means that just by being there as an audience for one another, ready to pass judgment on whether someone is a careful and truthful speaker, we provide an incentive for one another to tell the truth. We regulate or police one another into telling the truth and may be expected to elicit thereby a general pattern of truth-telling.

The practice of holding one another responsible for doing something like telling the truth will certainly have a similar, regulative rationale. In recognizing your capacity to have done otherwise than tell a lie, in exhorting you retrospectively to have told the truth, and in reprimanding you for not having done this, it should be clear in ordinary practice that I am working with the assumption that I can thereby influence and even reform you.

I may not blame you with an explicitly reformative intention; my intention may be just to draw your attention to the failure, presenting it as one you could and should have avoided. But there would scarcely be any point in holding you responsible for any failure of this kind, if I thought that there was no possibility of getting you to change. This is an observation supported even in a tradition that insists on the distinction between practices of holding others responsible and efforts to reform them. As P.F. Strawson (1962, 25) says, if "our beliefs about the efficacy of some of these practices turn out to be false, then we may have good reason for modifying or dropping some of those practices" (McGeer 2014).

But notwithstanding this regulative rationale, the practice of holding you responsible for telling the truth is distinct from the reputational regulation exemplified in the pre-social case. As emphasized in discussing that case, I and others may exercise such regulation without being aware of the general pattern that we thereby elicit in our aggregate behavior toward one another. And so, it may be an exercise in which none of us intentionally takes part. Not recognizing what I am doing in regulating you, I cannot do it intentionally; it is not something I desire as such, for example, nor is it a foreseeable effect of something that I desire as such.

When I hold you responsible for living up to a standard like truth-telling, I do so with an awareness of the overall pattern associated with the standard and out of a desire that mere regulation need not involve. Thus, if I censure you for not acting as the desirability of truth-telling requires, I censure you consciously and intentionally. This will certainly be so if I express the censure in words, as in saying "You could have done otherwise," "You could have told the truth." But it will also be the case if I just assume an attitude of censure, in which assuming an attitude is a mental act. It barely makes sense—although it may convey something metaphorically—to imagine that I might censure you but only unconsciously or unintentionally.[7]

But while regulating one another reputationally into certain patterns of behavior falls short of holding one another responsible to corresponding standards, that regulative regime may continue to play an important role in supporting a responsibility practice. This will appear in the story to be told of how we in Erewhon might come to hold one another responsible. The narrative assumes that we are subject to a

---

7. I may blame you unintentionally, if not unconsciously, in the sense in which blame involves just an attitude but not necessarily an action, not even the internal or mental act of assuming or taking up an attitude. I use the word "censure" here to refer essentially to the action of holding responsible; and this, in either an external or internal sense.

reputational discipline in which, as a matter of common awareness, we expect one another to be suitably reliable: in particular, reliable in telling the truth. The existence of this background pressure is bound to increase the prospects for our regulative success in holding one another responsible for telling the truth and for conforming in other ways to the moral standards that we take for granted.

This observation connects with a point registered at different points in earlier discussion. The motivating engine that drives us to conform to many moral or indeed social norms may continue to be substantively reputational, even as we steer by a distinct justifying rationale for conformity. The steering thought in the social case is that conformity is a precondition for communal acceptance, in the moral that it is required as a matter of moral desirability. In holding one another to moral norms, as in holding one another to social norms, it is plausible that we expect the rationale invoked to be effective in good part by virtue of the reputational effects that are going to be salient on all sides.

6.2 *Recognition, exhortation, reprimand*

Holding one another responsible in Erewhon

Why might we be led in Erewhon to go beyond mere regulation and to hold one another responsible for living up to certain moral standards, in particular standards that are shared and routine? In order to answer this question, it will be enough to show that if in response to breach of a norm we make a remark like "You could have done otherwise"—the literal content of the remark will allow us to do this in the absence of excuse and exemption—then that will have the three connotations or effects associated with holding you responsible. If the remark reliably has such effects when made in response to a breach, then it must constitute an act of holding you responsible for the offense.

The three connotations may be described as the recognition effect, the exhortation effect, and the reprimand effect. The discussion that follows explores each of these in turn. While they may be triggered by a breach of any shared and routine standards, the focus will be on the breach only of moral norms: that is, the shared and routine standards of moral desirability that get to be established among us in Erewhon.

The recognition effect

According to the first connotation, the remark, "You could have done otherwise", when uttered in response to a moral offense, does not merely record the fact that you might have done otherwise, given the absence of excuse or exemption. It conveys the message that you were disposed in the situation of choice to respond robustly to the relevant considerations of moral desirability: that is, to register and act on them in most variations on the actual circumstances—in particular, ones introducing various distractors or disturbers—in which the considerations remained present and there was no exemption or excuse. And so, it would communicate that your failure to respond appropriately in the actual situation was more or less a fluke; it was out of character.

But why would the remark be expected to attract this reading among us? Why would I not be moved by the evidence of your failure to conclude that, actually, you were not suitably responsive to our shared moral standards? It was possible, to be sure, that you might have responded to the standards, given the absence of exemption and excuse. But why should I think that this was a suitably robust possibility; why should I think that you would have responded to the standards in a wide raft of variations on the actual circumstances? Why should I ascribe a capacity to respond to those standards and conclude merely that you failed to exercise it? Why should I treat your behavior as a departure from normal: a contingent failure?

It would certainly be reasonable to treat it as a contingent failure if you had already demonstrated that capacity over a range of similar cases. But even in the absence of demonstrated capacity, as appeared earlier, we in the ordinary world assume as a default that you have such a capacity when we hold you responsible to shared, routine standards like those that support telling the truth. Indeed, we make this default assumption with others in general, even with strangers and even with those who have lied to us in the past. So, is it possible to explain why we who live in Erewhon might support a default assumption of this kind?

Plausibly, it is. In order to provide the required explanation, however, it is essential to develop our earlier account of pledging and to defend a general thesis that applies in any instance of pledging. This will be described here as the anti-expulsion thesis.[8]

According to the anti-expulsion thesis, if pledging is to have a useful place in Erewhon, then we must generally take one another to have the capacity to live up to our pledges. In particular, we must not expel someone from the ranks of those who can live up to their pledges just because they fail on a particular occasion to do so. We may become more wary about assuming the ability to live up to their pledges in those who fail time after time, eventually excluding them altogether from the ranks of those with whom we can do business. But we should be slow to resort to such expulsion.

The reason for this is grounded in our nature as beings who need to be able to rely on one another in various ways, if we are to prosper and thrive. If we were disposed to expel one another from the ranks of the potentially reliable in response to any single failure to prove reliable, or even to any handful of failures, then we would be likely to deprive ourselves of the benefits of mutual reliance.

Assuming that everyone is going to fail occasionally to live up to a pledge, a disposition to expel someone on the basis of a single offense would eventually lead each of us to expel most others from the circle of the potentially reliable. And as we would each expel others from that circle, so we would each be expelled ourselves. As a community we would be led inevitably toward a social wasteland. It might not involve the war of all against all that Hobbes (1994, 13.9) imagined, but it would still be likely, in his words, to make life solitary, poor, nasty, brutish, and short.

---

8. A comparable claim applies also in the case of avowing, but this will not be of concern here.

Back now to the question raised. Why might we make the default assumption in Erewhon that when you offend against a shared, routine standard of desirability, and there is no exemption or unforeclosed excuse available, the offense is not due to a lack of the capacity to respond to such a standard but just to a failure to have exercised the capacity? The answer can be set out in a schematic argument, which relies for its conclusion on the anti-expulsion thesis just defended.

The argument goes as follows:

- We, your compatriots, will manifestly expect you, as we will expect others in general, to acknowledge and abide by the unquestioned requirements of shared, routine standards of desirability, at least in the absence of exemption or of unforeclosed excuses; that is what makes the standards shared and routine.
- We will take you in effect to have pledged fidelity to any such standard for, as we see things, you will have made the pledge in a virtual manner by not saying "Nay" to that manifest expectation—that is, by not denying that the standard is shared or routine.
- I would be refusing you the status of a potentially reliable pledger, if I were to conclude from one failure, or even a few failures, that you did not have the capacity to prove faithful.
- But it would be unappealing to refuse you this status in view of the anti-expulsion thesis; expelling you from the community of those capable of living up to pledges would rule out the prospect of future benefits and, as a general strategy, it would be destructive of mutual reliance.
- Therefore, in the case of shared, routine standards of moral desirability, we in Erewhon must be expected to make a default assumption that in any non-exempt, non-excused offense, you possessed but failed to exercise a robust capacity to conform.

This argument shows that, absent exemption or excuse, I am likely to respond to a failure on your part to conform to a shared, routine standard of truth-telling, not by questioning your capacity to conform, but by insisting that you had that capacity and that you failed to exercise it. And I am likely, moreover, to give this response a default status, displaying it when I meet you for the first time, for example, or even when you have lied to me on previous occasions. I might be driven to withdraw the assumption, of course—I might be forced to treat you as an unredeemable liar, for example—if your failure was repeated time and time again. But the cost of expelling you in this way from my circle would be enormous, and so I would be likely to embrace it only as a last resort. It would amount to excommunication, as that was described earlier.

To resort to excommunication would be to treat you in effect as unconversable, or at least unconversable in the domain of the failure (Pettit and Smith 1996). For it would mean that I could not take you to be someone with whom it is possible to interact normally in that domain. I would recognize no basis for relying on your words, no basis for entering into a relationship where your reports, avowals, and pledges guide me in my actions and expectations in relation to you.

The situation would be close to that in which I take you to be exempt from responsibility and unfit to be treated as a proper interlocutor. I might think of trying to engineer this or that response in you—I might deal with you as a subject for treatment (Strawson 1962)—but I could not seek to induce the response by pointing to its desirability under a routine, shared standard. In what follows, the assumption will be that we rarely resort to excommunication in Erewhon and that this makes sense; we are rarely confronted with the sort of unresponsiveness to shared, routine standards that would warrant excommunication.

The exhortation effect

If these considerations are sound, then when I say that you could have done otherwise in response to a misdeed, in particular some misdeed in which you were not subject to a suitable exempting or excusing condition, then I should be taken to convey by those words that you had the capacity to do otherwise. You were someone disposed to register considerations of desirability robustly—considerations derived, within the focus adopted here, from shared, routine standards of moral desirability—and to act robustly as they require: robustly, in particular, over variations in distraction and disturbance.

On the account offered earlier, however, those words should convey a second message, too, if they are to represent an instance of holding you responsible. "You could have told the truth," for example, should communicate a retrospective exhortation or injunction to have responded as the considerations of desirability required, not a resigned acceptance of a failure that I evaluate negatively. It should retrospectively ratify the exhortatory efforts I or anybody else—or you yourself—might have made to get you to tell the truth. It should express the same attitude that I might have expressed prior to the action by saying in the normal, exhortatory way: "You can do it: you can tell the truth."

Is it possible to explain why in Erewhon the words would communicate this second message? Yes, it is. Suppose that I say that you could have done otherwise in wake of a misdeed such as telling a lie, where it is granted that the action offends against shared, routine standards of desirability, and that it was performed in the absence of an exemption or an unforeclosed excuse. Is there any reason to think that in Erewhon these words would naturally have a retrospectively exhortatory significance: that they would express the sort of attitude that a prospective exhortation would have conveyed? For reasons related to the reputational discipline that operates there, it turns out that there is.

By the argument presented in support of the recognition effect, we in Erewhon are each pledged to live up to shared, routine standards of desirability like that of truth-telling. As assumed, these standards unquestionably require us, now here, now there, to act appropriately and to live up to them in that sense. We are pledged to live up to that sort of standard in the same way that we are pledged to act on any more specific intention to which we may have expressly committed ourselves. But just as reflecting on something that holds of pledging in general helped to explain why saying "You could have done otherwise" has the recognition effect, so reflecting on another general feature of pledging can help to explain why those words have the exhortation effect, too.

As the anti-expulsion thesis helped in the previous case, so a similar lesson—the empowerment thesis, as it will be dubbed—can help in the present instance. The thesis is that we each empower one another in the practice of pledging. We help to elicit a capacity in one another to live up to our pledges and to get us each to exercise that capacity as appropriate.

Consider a situation in which you pledge to do something, inviting me implicitly to rely on your doing it. In any such case, it is manifest that you will be likely to suffer a serious reputational cost if you fail to perform as pledged: a cost in my opinion of you and in the opinion of any others who witness or learn of the failure. In the event of failure, we may not expel you from the community of the potentially reliable, but we will call you out as someone who proved unreliable in practice, someone who failed to exercise a robust capacity to prove reliable. The pledge means that you will not be in a position to excuse your failure by appeal either to a misleading or to a changed mind. Thus, when you make a pledge, you must do so in awareness that the stakes are high and that you will almost certainly suffer ignominy in the event of failure.

How can you be confident enough to make such a pledge? By the analysis offered earlier, you may draw some confidence from the general fact that there are lots of desiderata that make it attractive to act as the pledge requires. But since those desiderata may not remain relevant at the time for action, you must draw confidence in particular from the fact that acting on the pledge—proving faithful to your word—has a powerful reputational payoff. It promises to establish with a special force that you can live up to your word, earning you a very attractive reputation with anyone who learns, even learns after the event, about your performance.

But not only is it the case that you can draw enough confidence from the reputational discipline under which you operate to be ready to pledge yourself in this or that respect. We others must also draw confidence from the role of that discipline in your psychology, if we are to be ready in general to rely on the pledges you make. For why else would we be prepared to rely on you? After all, it will be obvious to us, as it is obvious to you, that living up to the pledge may prove independently very unattractive and that only the reputational discipline may be there to keep you in line.

By the narrative developed so far, pledging emerges in Erewhon side by side with avowal and becomes a stable feature of the society. On this assumption, your confidence, and our confidence, that you can remain faithful to your pledges is vindicated. We are vindicated in the belief that by being there to observe how you perform in keeping your pledges, and to form a judgment about your reliability, we can help to establish your capacity to live up to those pledges and to elicit its regular exercise.

What we others do for you, of course, we all do for one another. And that is just to say that the empowerment thesis is sound. We play a powerful role in getting one another to establish and exercise the capacity to live up to our pledges. By being there to impose reputational costs on any failure, we help to police one another, if only in the fashion of blind regulation, into acting as we pledged ourselves to act. We provide an environment for one another that scaffolds our capacity to live up to our words. That capacity is grounded, not just in how we each are in ourselves, but in how it is with those around us; it has an ecological, and not a purely psychological character (McGeer 2013; McGeer and Pettit 2015).[9]

The empowerment thesis explains why exhortation or injunction can play an important role in interpersonal interaction. The soundness of the thesis is a matter of common accessibility and awareness: the evidence supporting it is salient; that the evidence is salient is itself salient; and so on. And that means that, being aware of my reputational, empowering role, I can actively build on that role by encouraging you to live up to a pledge. I can exhort or enjoin you to be faithful to the pledge, and do so with a manifest rationale. By encouraging you, I express the

---

9. The idea of an ecological capacity is borrowed from Vargas (2013). The ecological idea ought also to appeal to Pamela Hieronymi (2007, 111) insofar as she takes the following to be true of moral capacities as well as capacities of other sorts: "Typically, our capacities develop as demands are put upon us to exercise them well—beyond our current ability," where "the demands one is under remain insensitive to one's own particular shortcomings; one's capacities develop as one tries to meet them."

expectations that I and presumably others hold and I make the reputational cost of a failure particularly salient.

Suppose you have pledged to join others in some venture, then, and that you now shrink from the prospect. You may have pledged to go on a hunt but recoil from doing so, as in an earlier example, because the weather has turned foul. I may insist that you still have the capacity not to backslide, saying, "You can do it; you can live up to your word." Or I may presuppose the presence of that capacity, as in saying, "You ought to keep your word and join the hunt." And by making such an utterance, I may expect to have some effect in reminding you of the costs at stake and in bolstering your capacity to do what I am saying or implying that you can do. I may expect to empower you, if you need empowerment, and to help to get you to the point where acting on the pledge comes within your reach.

This lesson about the role of exhortation carries over from ordinary pledges to virtual pledges to live by shared, routine standards of desirability. By the argument run in support of the recognition effect, you are pledged in this way to be faithful to such standards. And so, I or anyone else may sensibly exhort or enjoin you to live up to any shared, routine standard of desirability. I will do this whenever I tell you what you are now required to do under such a standard, or when I just say that you can live up to the current requirements of the standard. I will play a role in helping you to conform to the standard, whether or not my help is needed; my words will have the empowering force of an exhortation.

These observations make it possible, finally, to explain why in an appropriate context the remark "You could have done otherwise"—in our example, "You could have told the truth"—has the character of a retrospective exhortation. They make sense of why those words express the sort of attitude toward you that anyone would have expressed prior to the utterance, if they had exhorted you to tell the truth.

If my saying "You can tell the truth" has the force of an empowering exhortation when uttered prior to a choice, then saying "You could have told the truth" in the wake of the choice is going to communicate that the ex ante exhortation was appropriate; it is going to ratify that exhortation ex post. The alternative to the ex post remark would be to say "It's not the case that you could have told the truth," which would certainly convey the message that the earlier exhortation had been inappropriate. If it is not the case that you could have told the truth at the time of choice, after all, then it was misconceived on my part to tell you, with whatever exhortatory or injunctive intent, that you could do so.

Why would I reject that alternative in the wake of the choice, then, and say that despite failing to do so, you could have told the truth? I say this, presumably, because I maintain the same attitude toward you that I expressed in the original exhortation. The remark can only communicate that it was appropriate on my part to have enjoined you earlier to tell the truth; telling the truth at that time was within your reach, at least in the presence of my exhortation.

If this is right, plausibly, then whenever I say that despite a failure, you could have told the truth, I communicate that an earlier exhortation to tell the truth would have been appropriate. That will be the case, presumably, whether or not I or anyone else actually exhorted you at that time to tell the truth. And so "You could have told the truth," uttered in a suitable context, must have the force of a retrospective exhortation, as that is understood here. It does not just express the belief that you had the capacity to tell the truth: i.e., that it was possible for you, robustly over distraction and disturbance, to have told the truth. It conveys an impatience with your having failed to exercise the capacity, given the status you enjoy of someone embedded in our culture of mutual exhortation and regulation. Insofar as we see you as someone party to that culture, who was susceptible to prospective exhortation to tell the truth, we see you as a person with whom it makes sense to ratify that exhortation retrospectively.

This lesson extends to every case in which you offend against a shared, routine moral standard. In any such event, my saying that you could have done otherwise will not just express a belief in your capacity to have done otherwise—this, in the robust, dispositional sense of capacity mobilized by the first connotation—but also an exhortatory form of impatience with your failure to have exercised that capacity. The words will identify you as one of our mutually regulating kind and will convey an exhortation to have done better as surely as they will convey a recognition of your dispositional capacity to have reached that level of performance.[10]

The reprimand effect

The observations so far show that assuming that no one is excommunicated, I and you and others in Erewhon would routinely satisfy the first two conditions associated with holding someone responsible. I would be in a position to give default recognition to your capacity, absent exemption or unforeclosed excuse, to respond to the considerations of desirability that require you to tell the truth; and to do this, even in the wake of failure. And I would be in a position to speak with an exhortatory force in saying in the wake of any such failure that you could have done otherwise. The final question is whether I could also be taken to reprimand you by making such a remark, expressing an unwelcome opinion of your performance and communicating at the same time that this opinion is deserved.

By the account developed so far, my saying you could have done otherwise in the wake of a misdeed like telling a lie presupposes that it was manifestly appropriate for anyone prior to your action to have exhorted

10. The line taken makes good sense of the reactions we might have even in Frankfurt (1969) cases of the kind mentioned in Chapter 2 and earlier in this chapter. Suppose I know, but you don't, that there is a back-up agency in place to ensure that you will tell the truth, even if you decide to lie or to mislead me otherwise. Still, I may exhort you to tell the truth, wanting you to do so spontaneously, and not as a result of that agency. Or suppose I know, and you don't, that there is an agency in place to ensure that you will mislead me, even if you decide to tell the truth. Still, I may exhort you to tell the truth, wanting you at least to try to tell the truth: wanting you to mislead me, not willingly, but only as a result of the intervention of that agency. If I hesitate in either case to exhort you to tell that truth, that will only be because the exhortation would communicate a false message: that there is no one around to force your hand. But if I do exhort you in that way ex ante, saying "You ought to tell the truth", then I will be able to say something similar ex post, communicating in the first case, that you ought to have told the truth willingly; in the second, that you ought at least to have tried to tell the truth.

or enjoined you to respond to considerations of desirability and tell the truth: this, assuming that the option of telling the truth was supported by a shared, routine standard of desirability. But if it was manifestly appropriate for anyone to have enjoined you to respond to considerations of desirability and to tell the truth, then in the wake of the failure, it is manifestly appropriate for me to register that you acted in violation of such an injunction. And that is something, plausibly, I can be taken to register in saying that you could have done otherwise. In the context, this amounts to registering that you did not act as it would have been appropriate for anyone to enjoin you to act. In saying that you could have done otherwise, I stand by the appropriateness of the exhortation or injunction and mark your failure to satisfy it.

This in itself is to impose a recognized penalty on you. For it is to express a bad opinion of your failure to act as you might appropriately have been enjoined to act: i.e., your failure to do what it would have been morally desirable for you to do. In effect, it is to issue a reprimand for the way you behaved. And not only does the remark constitute a reprimand; it also communicates that the reprimand is deserved in a straightforward sense. In saying that you could have done otherwise, conveying the message that you acted against an appropriate injunction, I assume that you were not subject to an exempting or unforeclosed, excusing condition and that you were not lacking in sensitivity to the relevant considerations of moral desirability. And in assuming the absence of such factors, I emphasize that there is nothing, under our practices, that might lead me to withdraw the reprimand. I put you on the hook and deny you any basis on which to complain about my reprimand.

But will the reprimand count as deserved in this sense if there is a naturalistic explanation for your having failed to exercise a relevant, robust capacity, say, the capacity to tell the truth? Or will the availability of such an explanation support the claim that despite the absence of excusing or exempting factors, still it is not fair to blame you? It might seem so. *Tout comprendre c'est tout pardonner*, as it is said; to understand everything is to pardon everything. But however things seem, they are not so. Explanation does not undermine reprimand.

One sort of explanation for a failure is readily squared with maintaining that a reprimand is deserved. This is the kind that invokes a familiar sort of distraction or disturbance to make sense of why you failed to tell the truth. Thus, I might explain your lying to me by your having been subject to one or another temptation—say, to impress an audience—and your having proved weak of will. And I might explain any of a range of similar failures by appeal to factors like inattention or laziness. These explanations are fully consistent with maintaining the reprimand, since they are factors that we will take you, like more or less anyone else, to be capable of overcoming. In particular, they are factors that it will make sense for us to exhort you to overcome, the assumption being that you are able to respond to the considerations we put before you in the course of exhortation.

But there is another sort of explanation that we must recognize for any failure on your part to exercise a capacity to tell the truth, whether or not this also involved a failure to overcome distraction or disturbance. On naturalistic assumptions of the kind maintained here, the failure must have been sourced in some natural antecedent, probabilistic or deterministic. Some breakdown of normal functioning—say, an unknown glitch or brute chance—must have led you to behave out of character and not exercise your capacity. Does the availability of this sort of explanation, which we may or may not have the neuroscientific knowledge to detail, suggest that a reprimand is out of place? No, it does not.

Under the practice documented in this narrative, we invite each other to rely on us to keep our pledges—and, in the relevant case, to live up to shared, routine standards of desirability—in the absence of exemption or excuse, assuming in ourselves an appropriate sensitivity to considerations of desirability: the sensitivity presupposed in the notion of a robust capacity. And we do this with confidence, since it is a matter of common belief among us that the reputational force mobilized by the invitation can generally lead us to be able to keep the pledges we make; if this were not a matter of common belief, then our relying on one another's pledges would be inexplicable.

If the practice allowed us to get off the reputational hook, however, just by citing a non-exempting, non-excusing cause of the failure—just by invoking an unknown glitch or brute chance—this common belief would break down. For then the cost attendant on a failure would always be avoidable and we would lose any reason to expect, or expect others to expect, that the reputational discipline would make us into reliable pledgers. To think that you could get out of a pledge—including a virtual pledge to live up to a shared, routine standard of desirability—by citing a non-exempting, non-excusing cause of failure would be to display a misunderstanding of how things work in the practice of holding one another responsible, as that has crystallized in the course of the narrative.

By the account supported in the narrative, there are two assumptions built into the practice. The first is that regardless of our capacities, we cannot expect to regulate one another into conformity with any pledge, and so into conformity with any shared, routine standard of desirability, if there are exempting factors or unforeclosed, excusing factors present. And the second is that in the absence of such factors, and regardless of whatever other causes may be at work, we can expect to be able to exercise a significant regulative influence on one another. The factors that count as exempting or excusing, and the factors that count as mere distractions or disturbances, may shift from time to time, and may differ from those recognized in other societies; different cultures of expectation and regulation may cast somewhat different factors in these roles. But it is crucial to the practice of holding one another responsible to accepted standards that some causes of failure are treated as regulation-resistant and others as regulation-susceptible; exempting and excusing causes are treated as resistant to the effects of regulation, other causes as susceptible to those effects.[11]

Why, then, should you be expected to pay the costs associated with a misdeed that is due to a regulation-susceptible factor—say, a brute

---

11. I am indebted to Victoria McGeer for introducing me to this way of thinking about the regulative significance of excusing or exempting causes on the one side, non-exempting and non-excusing causes on the other. On this issue, and on the treatment of responsibility in general, I stick closely to our joint work in McGeer and Pettit (2015).

chance or an unknown glitch? Why should you be expected to treat a reprimand as deserved? In a word, because the glitch or chance counts as an influence that you are able, by received ideas, to overcome. You have all the motivation required to carry you past it, given the reputational force field in which you live. Factors that count as regulation-resistant, and that we regard as exempting or excusing, are influences that you are unable, despite your assumed sensitivity to considerations of desirability, to overcome in the same way. It is not because they obstruct the operation of an allegedly uncaused will, or anything of that non-naturalistic kind (more on this later) that they are special. They are special because they stand out among natural causes by virtue of the fact that there is not much that you can do, and not much that we can get you to do—this, by issuing appropriate exhortations and reprimands—that would lead you to overcome them.

The regulative aspect of the practice of holding responsible connects with the empowerment thesis mentioned earlier and with the ecological character of the capacity I ascribe to you when I say, given the absence of exemption or unforeclosed excuses, that you could have responded to the desirability of truth-telling. And it connects also with the earlier observation that the capacity I ascribe to you in making such a remark may be a capacity that you have only as an addressee of the sorts of expectations that the remark expresses. The capacity may depend for its existence and effectiveness on the presence of a community in which we hold one another to a standard like truth-telling. The theme will return in the next section in the course of a comparison between the approach to responsibility supported here and other approaches in the literature.

Back to obligation

The upshot of these considerations is that when uttered in a suitable context, the assertion in Erewhon that you could have done otherwise is going to serve the three functions required under a practice of holding an offender responsible; it will support the recognition, exhortation, and reprimand effects. This concludes the narrative explanation of how, having developed the idea of desirability, we would go on in Erewhon to hold one another responsible for living up to shared, routine standards of moral desirability.

But there is still one loose end to tie up. By most accounts, it is the concept of the obligatory that is central to ethics, not the concept of the morally desirable. And by most accounts, it is standards of obligation, not standards of desirability, that ought to figure in our practice of holding one another to account. So how does obligation fit into the picture?

On the line adopted earlier, it is obligatory for an agent to choose one option rather than another just when it is the morally most desirable alternative among 'erogatory' options: i.e. options that are undemanding enough not to count as supererogatory. Thus, with any choice that violates a shared, routine standard of desirability, we will be in a position to think of the option of living up to that standard—meeting its unquestioned requirements in this or that situation—as obligatory. For given the routine nature of the standard, living up to it will count by definition as a suitably undemanding option. And given the shared status of the standard, living up to it will be the morally desirable thing to do, by perceptions that we share with the agent.

With the concept of the morally obligatory in hand, as mentioned before, we will also have access to the concepts of the morally prohibited and the morally permitted. An option will be morally prohibited if it is morally obligatory to avoid it. And an option will be morally permitted on a first usage, if it is not morally obligatory to avoid it and, on a second, if in addition it is also not morally obligatory to take it. On the first usage, the fact that an option is permitted does not rule out its being obligatory; on the second, it does: the option, as it is said, is merely permitted.

However important the category of the obligatory is in Erewhon, there is no reason to think that it will take over completely within our discourse. Certain standards might be shared across the community, without being routine enough to count as obligatory. They might manifestly require such a level of effort and difficulty that we would not be prepared to blame people for failing to conform to them; they might be taken to fall outside people's robust capacity. Such standards would count as supererogatory ideals, not matters of obligation. It is important to keep them in the picture if only because, as already noted, today's supererogatory ideals may become tomorrow's standards of obligation—this, as a result of a changing sense of moral desirability, and a changing pattern of mutual, empowering expectation.

6.3 *Theories of responsibility*

Two other approaches to responsibility

It may be useful in conclusion to try to relate the theory of responsibility supported by this narrative to more familiar accounts. The theory supported is naturalistic in the sense that it is compatible with the assumption that all the entities in the world, including human beings, belong to the domain charted in the most basic natural sciences and are subject to the laws established there. The narrative provides a presumptively naturalistic explanation of how we in Erewhon could have come to develop the concept of moral responsibility, as it provides a naturalistic explanation of how we could have come to develop the concept of moral desirability. And so, it does not take that concept to ascribe a non-naturalistic property; in particular, it does not take our fitness to be held responsible to presuppose a non-natural, scientifically alien freewill.

The theory supported in the preceding narrative contrasts in the first instance, then, with the family of non-naturalistic or libertarian views that posit such a freewill. A libertarian theory would represent the capacity to respond to standards of moral desirability as a sui generis capacity on your part to intrude yourself into the causal chain preceding any action—a causal chain involving the immediate neural antecedents of behavior—and to make your behavior conform to what those considerations support. It constitutes a capacity, on this sort of account, to inhibit the neural chain that might take you in an unwanted direction and so to control things according to your will. The capacity postulated is non-natural, for it implies that the causal network that operates at a level accessible to natural science does not constrain you in any choice, or even expose you to the vagaries of objective chance. It leaves you with leeway to act according to your own will and so, if that be your will, to act according to the perceived demands of moral desirability.

The presence of such a capacity, according to libertarian views, means that whatever you do, you do as a result of what you as a person—you as identified with your will—want to do, not as a result of causal laws and pressures that operate on you or within you. Hence the capacity makes sense of why we might say in advance of action that you should and can do something like tell the truth: you can exercise your will, notwithstanding any causal obstacles, so as to respond to the considerations that support that option.

That being so, libertarian views also make sense of why we might say in the wake of an offense that you could have done otherwise, conveying an injunction to have done otherwise, and not just a negative evaluation of the choice you made. The idea is that despite the fact that natural antecedents may have prompted the misdeed, you had the capacity to override those influences and act as the relevant standard requires. Thus, when we exhort you to have done otherwise, we seek to remind you of that capacity and of your failure to have exercised it.

No naturalistic theory can live with such an image of the person and so it has to offer a very different sort of account of what it is about you or anyone else that allows us to think that, absent exemption or unforeclosed excuse, you have or had the capacity to live up to standards of moral desirability, responding appropriately to their requirements. The account has to cohere with an image of the human being as a creature, like any other animal, that is organized out of cellular—and ultimately, molecular, atomic, and sub-atomic—matter; and a creature, therefore, that operates under the force of the laws that govern such matter at the most fundamental level. It has to make sense of your capacity to live up to moral standards on the assumption that its exercise does not involve a rupture in the regular causal order.

One candidate analysis, once popular among naturalists, is conditional in form. It holds that to have the capacity to respond appropriately to considerations of desirability is to be such that if you want or try to respond to those considerations—if that causal antecedent is in place—then you will respond to them. But no such analysis can be satisfactory (Chisholm 1982). For it may be true that if you wanted or tried to respond to such considerations, you would respond appropriately, without its being true that you could want or try to do that. You may be a psychopath who satisfies the condition given but could never want or try to respond to relevant considerations. And in that case, we would scarcely credit you with the capacity to respond appropriately.

The theory of responsibility supported in the narrative of this chapter offers a naturalistic account that avoids that problem, while still making sense of what we do in holding someone responsible. But this theory should be distinguished, not only from the non-naturalistic family of approaches, but also from an alternative family of naturalistic views that also seek to avoid that problem (see Clarke, McKenna, and Smith 2015).

Reconstructing this family of approaches in a way that abstracts from different versions, they all suggest that to say you could have done otherwise in censuring a lie is to hold that you were not exempt from being held responsible—you were not subject to a debilitating disorder, for example, or compulsion—and that you could have had a better attitude, displaying it in telling me the truth (Wallace 1996). There may be no relevant sense in which you could have acted otherwise in the situation of choice, according to this sort of view; the general assumption is that you could have done otherwise in that sense only if you had a non-natural power of will. But there is a sense, so the idea goes, in which you could have displayed a better attitude. There is a possibility, perhaps even a robust possibility, that you might have become sensitized to the salient desirability of truth-telling, might have developed a suitable attitude toward truth-telling, and might have been led therefore to tell the truth in the situation on hand. You could have been otherwise, even if you could not have acted otherwise; you could have been generally good willed.

Proponents of this approach typically assume that the relevant attitude is characteristic of your makeup and properly attributable to you, an idea that was introduced by Gary Watson (1996); see, too, Wolf

(1990). Most now follow T.M. Scanlon (1998, 20) in assuming further that the characteristic, attributable attitude must be "judgment-sensitive," that is, responsive to reasoning and such that we may expect it to be present in anyone who reasons properly, making appropriate judgments of desirability; see, for example, Smith (2005).

According to this approach, then, three facts make it appropriate to hold you responsible for telling a lie. First, that it was possible for you, perhaps even robustly possible for you, to have had a better attitude and, absent exempting or excusing obstacles, told the truth in the context in question. Second, that this possibility would have materialized if you had been generally more sensitive—say, more sensitive over the course of your life, or over some relevant period—to the considerations of desirability that supported truth-telling in appropriate contexts. And third, that there was nothing in your character or circumstances that put such sensitivity beyond your reach: it would have been available to you had you been conscientious about the meaning and implications of judgments of desirability that you were in position to make.

The crucial difference between this attitude-centered account, as it may be called, and the action-centered account supported here is that on the former account there is no sense in which it is appropriate to exhort you to have acted differently in the particular choice indicted. Why exhort you to have done something that was the product of naturalistic cause or chance, so the idea goes, and not something that you had the non-naturalistic power, regardless of such antecedents, to control? Despairing of finding sense in such a possibility, the focus in the approach is on the fact that you could have had a different sort of attitude and could have been a different sort of person: for example, you could have been someone of goodwill toward others. And so blame is associated with finding fault with you for the sort of attitude you displayed—for your lack of goodwill—rather than for the particular action you took (Scanlon 2008). The idea, presumably, is that the problem raised by the assumption that you could have done otherwise is not raised by the assumption that in the appropriate sense you could have had a better attitude and could have been a better person.

Recasting the theory supported here

The theory supported by the narrative of this chapter focuses on the action that you performed rather than just on the sort of attitude you displayed and the sort of agent you proved yourself to be. But it holds that this focus is consistent with believing that you, like any other human being, are subject to the laws that govern the natural world. In particular, as emphasized earlier, it is consistent with believing that the action I censure you for performing was the product of a natural cause or natural chance. All that it presupposes is that the action was not occasioned by a factor of a suitably exempting or excusing kind.

The theory is that the capacity that makes you fit to be held responsible for a misdeed like telling a lie is a disposition on your part, in the absence of a suitable exemption or excuse, to respond robustly to relevant considerations and tell the truth. But it denies that when I say that you could have done otherwise and told the truth, the principal message is that it was a relative fluke that you told a lie. For the theory insists, at a second level, that in saying you could have done otherwise, I speak from the viewpoint of an exhortatory interlocutor, reaffirming the injunction to tell the truth that someone might have addressed to you before you spoke. And that means at a third level that the remark that you could have done otherwise constitutes a reprimand and, given the absence of exemption or excuse, a deserved reprimand that you are unable, under the relevant practice, to deflect.

This action-centered theory endorses a purely naturalistic metaphysics, making sense of how I can hold you responsible for a particular misdeed by appeal to the exhortatory or regulatory perspective I adopt in doing so. Your failure to live up to a standard like that of telling the truth will look from within the exhortatory perspective as an instance in which I or anyone else—or perhaps even you yourself—might well have gotten you to tell the truth by being there before the choice to force your attention on the standard, to encourage you to conform to it, and to make manifest the cost of failing. When I say that you could have done otherwise, I stand by the appropriateness of such an ex ante injunction and give natural expression to my disappointment or impatience at your not having been moved by the considerations that it would have made salient: at your not having responded to the expectations that my remark expresses.

Looking on your failure from a regulatory perspective, then, I cannot simply treat it as an occasion for resignation to brute fact or as an opportunity for indicating how you might have been a better agent in various ways. I can treat it only as an occasion for reminding you in an exhortatory spirit of what you could have done. Thus, I will naturally be led to use the only sorts of words available to me after the fact—words such as "You could have told the truth"—to give expression to the evocative or injunctive aspiration with which I might have said before the action: "You can tell the truth."

On this approach, my saying "You can tell the truth" prior to your acting does not merely register that, absent suitable exemption and excuse, you are disposed to tell the truth in many variations on the situation that continue to provide the same support for truth-telling. Uttered in the relevant context, "You can tell the truth" helps to elicit the very capacity it ascribes. The remark is not a descriptive utterance like "You have a ruddy complexion" that records a state of affairs that obtains independently of whether or not it is made. And nor is it a performative utterance like "I resign" that brings about the very state of affairs that it records (Lewis 1983b, Ch. 12). Rather, it falls somewhere in between the two. It is an evocative or exhortatory remark that helps to bring about—but does not guarantee to bring about—the state of affairs that it records (McGeer and Pettit 2015).

Saying "You could have told the truth" in wake of a lie amounts to treating you as an addressee of exhortation in the same way that anyone might have treated you prior to your offense. What the words convey is not, as in a non-naturalistic theory, that you had some special, non-natural ability that no causal factors could have withstood. What they communicate, rather, is that at the time you spoke you were a fit target for exhortation and injunction, unhindered by exempting or excusing factors, and that your actual failure to tell the truth does not negate that. The words convey something about you that depends on your relationship to me and others and something, in particular, that allows me to remonstrate with you about your failure.[12]

Defending the theory against the alternatives

How does the theory supported here compare with alternatives? It scores in a general metaphysical fashion over any non-naturalistic approach, since it presupposes nothing that is inconsistent with the scientific image of the world. This is not going to be a knock-down consideration for those who are prepared to countenance a non-natural, contra-causal sense of freewill. But it is a decisive objection from the point of view adopted in this work.

How does the naturalistic approach compare with the attitude-centered, naturalistic alternatives? There are three respects in which it ought to prove more appealing.

First, unlike those views, it preserves the idea, central to a long tradition, that in holding someone responsible for an offense we blame or censure the person, not for the attitude they displayed—or not just for that attitude—but for the deed they actually performed. We may condemn the careless driver who is about to drive through a red light for the attitude they take to traffic regulations, even if seeing a police car inhibits them. And we may equally condemn the careless driver who actually drives through, and perhaps injures a pedestrian, for their attitude. But we will also condemn the second driver for what they did. So, blaming that driver for that action cannot just consist in blaming them for their attitude.

Second, the current account gels more comfortably with the assumption, central to long religious tradition, that if you are fit to be held responsible for an offense, then you must have acted with full knowledge of the guilt and full consent of the will (Pettit 2007c). Those

12. The approach counts, in a term from Bernard Williams (1995), as a "proleptic" theory insofar as it makes sense of blaming someone on the basis of the general effect of blaming in making a person responsive to others; faithful to the etymology of the word, it broadly involves treating something anticipated as already attained.

conditions are intuitively satisfied if you stand in such a relationship to us that I can meaningfully credit you with a robust capacity to have registered and acted on the arguments against the offense and can meaningfully enjoin you to have performed better, treating you as a fit target for retrospective exhortation. But it is not clear that they will be satisfied just on the basis that you might have had better attitudes and might have been a better person.

But apart from these two, quite specific problems, there is a general question as to how far the attitude-centered approach scores above the current account in the very regard that may have seemed to make it more appealing. It supposes that there is nothing problematic about my claim that you could have had a different attitude. But that supposition itself raises a challenging query. Do I say that it was possible for you to have had a different attitude—say, for you to have been goodwilled—merely in the sense that this was not ruled out, and may even have been ruled in, by natural facts about your makeup and milieu? Or do I say this with an implicature of retrospective exhortation?

If I make just the first, non-exhortatory claim in holding you responsible for telling a lie, then holding you responsible in that way amounts merely to putting you among the goats rather than the sheep—distancing myself from you as from someone with whom a profitable relationship is unlikely (Scanlon 2008). But that really doesn't answer to the phenomenology of blame, since it communicates distaste rather than impatience, frustration, and resentment (McGeer 2013). It represents a radically revisionary account of what it is to hold someone culpable for what they did and to censure them for it.

Perhaps the intent of the approach, however, is that I make the second, exhortatory sort of claim in saying that you could have had a better attitude. Perhaps the idea is that in saying this I mean also to imply that retrospective exhortation, or some such attitude, is appropriate. T.M. Scanlon (1998, 22) seems to support such a reading when he says that because the attitude for whose absence we blame you is "judgment-sensitive"—dependent on your judgments about reasons—it is "up to you." And Angela Smith (2005, 263) supports a similar reading when she says that on the approach that she shares broadly with Scanlon, you are "active, and responsible, for anything that falls within the scope of evaluative judgment." The fact that the attitude was up to you, or that you were active and responsible in endorsing it, would suggest that retrospective exhortation is indeed appropriate. But the mere fact that the attitude might have been different—or even that it is surprising that it wasn't different—does not suggest anything of the kind.

On the account presented here, it is likely to make perfectly good sense for those of us in Erewhon, or for those in the actual world, to blame one another for attitudes as well as actions. This will make sense if it is a matter of common belief that we are virtually pledged to follow certain epistemic standards—shared and routine standards—in how we form our beliefs, desires, or intentions, say, standards bearing on the import of certain data or desiderata. I may blame you for not living up to such a standard in the formation of your attitudes, say, for not being prepared to accept that a certain massacre occurred, or for not reacting with distaste to someone's cruelty. I may treat you as someone fit to be exhorted, retrospectively as well as prospectively, to respond attitudinally to compelling evidence of the massacre or to the unambiguous specter of cruelty.

But if the claim that you could have had a better attitude is supposed to be heard in this exhortatory way, then the grounds for adopting the attitude-centered theory disappear. If retrospective exhortation is allowed to give a richer sense to the claim that you could have had a better attitude, why shouldn't it be allowed to give a richer sense to the claim that in the actual behavior adopted, you could have done otherwise than you did? I conclude that as the approach defended here scores over non-naturalistic theories of responsibility, so, too, it has a clear advantage over naturalistic theories of an attitude-centered sort.[13]

---

13. The action-centered approach also scores over the attitude-centered approach in other ways. It makes better sense of the idea that you may blame yourself for a failure, expressing an exhortatory attitude toward yourself. And it makes good sense of the fact that we blame corporate bodies for offenses committed in their name, recognizing that there is ground for exhorting them prospectively and retrospectively to a better level of performance (Pettit 2007c; List and Pettit 2011).

Three qualifications

In order to round out the account of responsibility supported by the narrative of this chapter, it may be useful to comment on three ways in which it is less committal than may initially appear. The first comment, which builds on some remarks earlier in the chapter, is that the capacity or disposition it postulates need not be as demanding as it seems. The second is that I may ascribe the capacity to you and others, yet hold that you are not so deserving as others of being penalized for a failure to exercise it. And the third comment is that there is a sense in which I may hold you responsible even in the absence of the capacity normally postulated.

Taking up the first comment, the capacity or disposition I ascribe when I hold you responsible for telling the truth may require that you are likely to exercise it across relevant scenarios only at a relatively high level of dependability, not without exception. Again, the requirement is not that it is easy for you to tell the truth, only that you can get yourself to tell the truth: this, perhaps, by means of self-exhortation, and with the help of exhortation from others. Finally, the capacity that you are required to have need not be a durable disposition; it may depend for its appearance on contingent enabling conditions such as the level of exhortation to which you are exposed.

Just as you may have the capacity to live up to certain standards of desirability only in a relatively undemanding sense, so, to move to a second comment, your possession of that capacity may be consistent with not penalizing you as harshly as others for a failure to exercise it. While ascribing the capacity, and treating you as a conversable subject, I may recognize that there are factors that make its exercise and nurture particularly difficult. You may be lacking in opportunities to live up to those standards, say by avoiding crime, without losing out significantly in other respects; you may be exposed to very few role models who manage happily to live by those standards; or you may be embedded in a sub-culture where rival, in-group standards are given precedence.

Such problems would not constitute exempting conditions, by any account. Nor are they likely under any approach to count as excuses that would let you off the hook for a failure of conformity; they will not count as regulation-resistant factors that would make exhortation pointless. But consistently with the theory endorsed, I may still think it important to take them into account in judging whether it is reasonable to impose extra sanctions of norm or law, whether on consequentialist, contractualist, or other grounds.[14]

The third comment on the line taken here is that I may often go through the motions of holding you responsible, when as a matter of fact I do not think that you currently have the capacity to live up to the standards I invoke. I may do this, because of a plausible belief that the best way to make you fully responsible in the longer run—think, for example, of the adolescent child—is to treat you as if you were responsible. The belief guiding my attitude is not that you are responsible in the sense of being fully fit to be held responsible but, in a criminological phrase (Garland 2001), that you are "responsibilizable." You are capable of being made fit to be held responsible by being held responsible, so that holding you responsible has a sensible developmental rationale (Pettit 2007c).

14. The line in this paragraph reflects lessons that I have learned from Benjamin Ewing (2016). That line is particularly appealing on the assumption made throughout the text, that exempting and excusing factors do not come in degrees.

Chapter 7: Morality Reconstructed

The narrative developed in chapters 2 to 6 invites us to see the ethical concepts with which we work in the actual world as concepts of a kind with those whose emergence in Erewhon the narrative tracks. After all, the concepts of desirability and responsibility that the narrative seeks to explain conform, as we argued, to the way we ordinarily understand desirability and responsibility. And so, the assumption that something similar to what explains the use of those concepts is also likely to explain our actual use of corresponding concepts is parsimonious and plausible.

The claim is analogous to a similar thesis about the standard genealogy of money. That genealogy tells us how what we recognize as money could have emerged under standard economic assumptions in a barter society, and would have been conceptualized appropriately as a medium of exchange, a metric of value, and a means of storing wealth. And it gives us ground as theorists for thinking that as the concept employed in the story predicates only an economically unproblematic property—the bearer of the appropriate role—so our familiar concept, which responds to similar prompts and serves similar purposes, can be taken to ascribe the same unproblematic sort of property.

We have offered a narrative in the preceding sections of how ethics could have emerged under standard naturalistic assumptions. And that narrative serves the same function in rendering ethical concepts naturalistically unproblematic that the other narrative serves in rendering the concept of money economically unproblematic. The concepts of moral desirability and responsibility that members of Erewhon would have come to develop are expressively equivalent to our concepts of moral desirability and responsibility, being subject to similar prompts and serving similar purposes. And as the naturalistic explanation of the emergence of the Erewhonian concepts implies that those concepts presuppose only naturalistically intelligible entities, so it suggests that the same must be true of our familiar concepts.

The aim of this final chapter is to endorse that suggestion and to explore how the narrative about Erewhon would lead us to think on a variety of issues raised by ethics in the actual world. In the esoteric jargon of the discipline, the issues to be discussed involve moral metaphysics, moral semantics, moral epistemology, moral psychology, and ground-level moral theory, or, if you prefer, normative ethics.[1]

Moral metaphysics identifies for us the sorts of properties and other entities that are presupposed by moral or ethical discourse. Moral semantics explains how the moral or ethical terms we use relate to such properties and entities. And moral epistemology tries to make sense of how we can learn about those features of the world, if there is learning to be had. Moral psychology explores the place of moral judgments in the economy of our makeup, tracing their connection to the desires that move us to action and the dispositions that establish our character as agents. And moral theory or normative ethics looks for patterns in the judgments we form as we determine what it is obligatory to do individually or with others, and tries to build on those patterns to establish an overall vision of the ideals and principles that should inform our behavior.

We look in this chapter at the views we are likely to adopt in these different areas, if we endorse the narrative presented as an account of how ethics could have emerged naturalistically and take it as a guide to the role and nature of ethics in the actual world. The chapter outlines a plausible reading of the significance of ethical concepts in all five areas and should help both to illuminate the significance of the narrative and to vindicate the claim that it offers a useful guide to the role and nature of ethics or morality.

---

1. For an overview that illuminates many of these areas, see Miller (2013).

The lessons for the five areas are drawn in broad strokes. They support an anthropological account of the presuppositions of moral thinking; a realism about the semantics of moral language; an account of moral learning in which the participants in moral practice enjoy an important priority over analysts; a story about our moral psychology that makes sense of how we are guided in action by moral judgments and dispositions; and a sketch of moral theory under which it is understandable why there should be divides like those that distinguish consequentialist from non-consequentialist thinkers.

The chapter is in six sections. The first three deal with moral metaphysics, moral semantics, and moral epistemology, and the last two with moral psychology and moral theory. The fourth, intervening section looks at how the sparse vocabulary with which we have been working—essentially, a vocabulary of desirability and responsibility—can be extended to make room for other familiar moral terms or concepts.

The discussion of moral metaphysics in the first section, as promised in the introduction, defends one of the motivating claims of the study, according to which it is in virtue of the commissive practices at the origin of morality that we human beings come to constitute functioning persons. The connection between being moral and being a person is of central importance, because it underpins a plausible answer to the age-old question as to why we should be moral.

7.1 Moral metaphysics

A naturalistic metaphysics

The most important issue in moral metaphysics bears on whether moral or ethical thinking presupposes properties or other entities that are non-natural in character. They would be non-natural in character, by the broadest possible criterion, if they were incapable of being squared with the view that natural science promises to reveal the material out of which all the items in the universe are composed and the forces to which they are subject.

Non-natural posits have no place or role in the theory of ethics supported by our reconstructive analysis. According to that analysis, all that ethics presupposes in the world are the beliefs and desires that dispose us toward different options and a language capable of expressing them; the practices of avowal and pledging generated by our wish and need to be able to rely on others and to get others to rely on us; the patterns of desirability, in particular the pattern of moral desirability, that become salient from within the perspectives of those social practices; the habit of treating one another to be pledged to live up to shared, routine standards of moral desirability; and the associated disposition, in the absence of recognized excusing or exempting conditions, to hold offenders responsible to moral standards: to treat them as having had the capacity to conform, to exhort them retrospectively to have conformed, and to put them on the reputational hook for their failure to do so.

This brief overview should make clear that on the theory emerging from our reconstruction, there is nothing to the metaphysics of morals that need scandalize naturalists. There is nothing presupposed in the picture presented that cannot in principle be located within the world that natural science describes (Jackson 1998).

The account on offer does not give us naturalistic reductions of moral or other prescriptive terms to decidedly natural counterparts. But the fact that the residents of Erewhon could have come to master such terms in the absence of non-naturalistic entities implies that they do not posit or presuppose anything of that kind. And the expressive equivalence between those terms and terms in actual usage, which is borne out in the course of the narrative, means that the same is plausibly true of our own talk of desirability and responsibility.[2]

---

2. The approach assumes that while the inhabitants of Erewhon are intentional, linguistic subjects, and are able to practice a form of theoretical and practical reasoning, those capacities are naturalistically intelligible. But that assumption is independently plausible, as we argued in chapter 1. Even those who reject that claim may still find interest in the approach, however, since they can see it as showing that it is only in the area of such basic capacities that we need to postulate a breach of naturalism.

A social metaphysics

The metaphysics of morals that our narrative supports is distinctive, not just in being naturalistic, but also in making interaction and community central to the explanation of ethics. It is only because of their role in supporting avowals of desire, for example, that certain desiderata get to be identified as sources of desirability. And it is only because of the assumptions built into practices of avowal and pledging that agents get to be identified as fit to be held responsible for living up to the demands of desirability.

The suggestion is that in the absence of such social engagement with one another we human beings might be incapable of developing suitable concepts of moral desirability and responsibility. If the inhabitants of Erewhon gain use of those concepts only in virtue of social interaction, it is plausible that our mastery of expressively equivalent concepts should be rooted in our reliance on similar practices.[3]

The social character of this moral metaphysics is particularly striking, because it is vindicated in a narrative that ascribes a broadly rational, opportunistic psychology to the members of Erewhon. Psychological evidence and evolutionary theory combine to suggest that by nature we as a species are disposed to be significantly helpful and cooperative in our dealings with one another (Tomasello 2014, 2016). But despite the fact that the narrative works for methodological reasons with a more opportunistic image, for reasons discussed in chapter 1, it supports a view of morality in which social practices of avowal and pledging, co-avowal and co-pledging, play an absolutely central part.

Avowals, pledges, and persons

It may be surprising that we depend for becoming ethical or moral agents on the practices of avowal and pledging and that it is only in the

---

3. In taking this social approach, the narrative supports a theory within the sort of space opened up in the eighteenth century by Adam Smith's (1982) *Theory of Moral Sentiments*. Here the perspective for moral judgment is provided, not by the impartial spectator—this, by many versions, can be the idealized self—but by the impartial interlocutor.

presence of such practices that the properties of desirability and responsibility become accessible. For all we have said up to now, the appearance of practices of avowing and pledging attitudes, however central to our narrative about Erewhon, may look like a historical contingency. And we may be inclined to be incredulous at the idea that such a contingency should be essential to the emergence of one of the central facets of humanity: our having access to moral concepts and our using those concepts in regulating our lives together.

As against this challenge, to take up one of the three motivating themes mentioned in the introduction to the book, it is important to emphasize that the practices of avowing and pledging attitudes are much more than historical accidents. They are central to our counting, not just as agents, but as persons; as agents of a markedly different kind from the mute agents that other animals constitute, even animals of great cognitive skill and deep social character.

To be an agent is to be a system that embodies certain purposes, forms certain representations about its environment, and pursues those purposes according to those representations: according its perceptions, for example, of the opportunities available for realizing its goals and the best means at hand for doing so. On this account, even sophisticated robots and most other animals are agents. At least when things are not rigged against their functioning well—at least, as it is said, when circumstances are normal—such mechanical or organic systems readily present as oriented toward certain goals, as forming representations about relevant opportunities and obstacles, and as trying out one or another apparent route for satisfying their goals until, ideally, they identify one that succeeds. The pattern is present in the robot that tidies up a room, in the fly that seeks a way out of the bottle, and in the dog that hears the family come home and takes appropriate steps to greet them.

When we seek to make sense of any mute agent, robotic or organic, we assume that it forms representations that are fairly reliable and that the actions it takes are reliable ways of advancing its goals according to those representations. And then, working from the evidence at its disposal and at the modes of action it adopts in presumptive pursuit of its goals, we characterize its attitudinal or intentional profile. We develop a sense of the desires that move it toward certain goals, of the beliefs that guide it in those movements, and of the intentions it forms in light of those beliefs and desires. We adopt the intentional stance and look for patterns that reveal such attitudes (Dennett 1987).

We human beings are certainly agents in the abstract sense of conforming to this broad template. But we are very special agents, for two reasons supported in the narrative of Erewhon. First, we interpret ourselves to others, communicating to them the sorts of attitudes we maintain and not just leaving them to work out those attitudes from inspection of our surroundings and our actions. And second, we communicate those attitudes with the special authority that goes with being ready to foreclose misleading-mind and even changed-mind excuses for not acting as we advertise—that is, that goes with being ready to avow and even pledge certain of those attitudes.

The first feature that marks us off from other natural agents is that we are creatures of the word: as Aristotle emphasized, animals that have speech (Taylor 2016). The second feature is that we rely on the word to communicate our attitudes in such a way that we speak for ourselves, not about ourselves; we act as spokespersons for ourselves, not reporters on ourselves.

Thomas Hobbes (1994) drew on a medieval tradition about legal persons to argue that we human beings count as natural persons just insofar as we are spokespersons for ourselves. In the medieval tradition, the corporate body is a person—an artificial, not a natural, person—insofar as the members are represented by a voice, emanating from an individual or from a process of accommodation between individuals, whose ascriptions of attitude to the corporate whole they individually authorize. They agree or pledge to act as is required of them individually in order that the group should live up to the attitudes ascribed to it by the authorized voice (List and Pettit 2011; Pettit 2014a).

Hobbes argued that as a group becomes an artificial person through organizing its members in this fashion, an individual human being becomes a person in much the same way. You are a person, so the line goes, insofar as you can utter words—in effect, make avowals and pledges—that you authorize in the way the members of a group authorize a corporate voice. Those words may be uttered actively or, as we know, virtually: you may speak for yourself, not just when you actively avow or pledge an attitude, but also when you fail to reject an avowal or pledge with which you are manifestly credited. But in either mode the words speak for who you are and do so in such a way that you must count as a salient failure if, without a suitable excuse, you do not live up to the words endorsed.

In supporting this line, Hobbes mentions that the word "persona" refers to the mask worn by ancient actors. This is the mask through which an actor would speak for a character, where "per" means through, and "sonare" means to sound or speak. His idea is that to be a natural person is to give yourself a character in the same way, holding out an image of who you are and inviting others to rely on your acting in accordance with that image: this, you say, is who I am; this is the self you are entitled to take me to be. On this conception, the concept of a person, as John Locke puts it later in the seventeenth century, is essentially forensic: it is tied up with the idea of being someone who assumes responsibility for their attitudes and actions and can be held responsible for them by others. "Where-ever a Man finds, what he calls *himself*," Locke (1975, s 26) says, "there I think that another may say is the same *Person*. It is a Forensick Term appropriating Actions and their Merit."[4]

The connection between your being a person and speaking for yourself in avowals and pledges turns in a particularly decisive way, of course, on how far you speak for yourself reliably when you invoke master categories of credibility and desirability. The master category in the case of belief, as we saw, will be that of common credibility—that is, credibility for anyone, it does not matter who. And the master category in the case of desire, at least insofar as we are committed to living together in mutual reliance, will be that of multilateral or moral desirability. It is only by recourse to such patterns, as we saw in chapter 5, that you can achieve and display the unity that resolves divergence across practices,

---

4. Carol Rovane (1997) usefully emphasizes this Lockean theme.

and the universality that ensures the possibility of reconciliation between individuals.[5]

Could we achieve the status of persons without relying on the interpersonal relations exemplified by our avowing and pledging attitudes,
in particular moral attitudes? Could we achieve this status, for example,
not by virtue of how we can bind ourselves to others in avowals and
pledges, but by virtue of how we can bind ourselves to ourselves? Not
plausibly. We cannot make a promise to ourselves, because we can always let ourselves off the hook; "he that can bind can release," as Hobbes
(1994, 26.6) says. We can speak for ourselves to others, as avowals and
pledges make clear, but we cannot speak for ourselves in the same way,
when we speak to ourselves. Or at least we cannot do so other than in
a parasitic way: in the way that we make suitable avowals and pledges
to ourselves, when we consciously try to simulate the position of an
independent interlocutor. Thus, we cannot rely on relations with ourselves, only on our relations with others, as the basis on which to gain
the standing of persons.

Once we see that the practices of avowing and pledging attitudes
are intimately connected with achieving the status of a person—an
adult, able-minded person—then it should cease to look surprising that
those practices are also implicated in our coming to invoke the ideas of
moral desirability and responsibility, and to regulate ourselves by them.
Morality and personhood, so it now appears, are two sides of one coin. On
the account developed here, they come in a package deal. We are a moral
species on the same basis, and to the same extent, that we are a species
who achieve the status of persons, not just that of sophisticated agents.

Why be moral?

One of the oldest challenges in the metaphysics of morals is to give
an account of moral desirability and responsibility under which it

---

5. By the account given, there is a sense in which speaking for yourself involves
constructing a self (Velleman 2000); but the construction involved is not the explicit,
narcissistic sort of narrative exercise criticized in Strawson (2005).

becomes possible to make sense of why the morally desirable—or at least the morally obligatory—should have a hold on us. What is it about the morally desirable and obligatory that explains why it has such a grip that we feel guilt and shame about our failures to live up to it, and a sense of peace with ourselves, even perhaps some pride, when we succeed?

This question is distinct from the question as to why morality directs us to standards of behavior that we expect to matter for society. That question is relatively easily answered, on almost any account. On ours, for example, such standards will all count as multilaterally desirable— that is, desirable in a way that is relatively unrestricted in the range of interests engaged and the standpoint adopted. Being collectively beneficial, standards of this kind are likely to be manifestly shared and routine in any functional society.

The question 'Why be moral?' bears on why you yourself ought to live up to the demands of morality, given that, however socially beneficial they may be, they are personally burdensome. The question arises in particular if you can breach them, avoiding the burden they impose, without others detecting the breach and without suffering any reputational cost. The question assumes its sharpest form when it is the case that not only are others unlikely to detect the breach, they are even unlikely to be made worse off by it. For an example, we might imagine a death-bed promise, unwitnessed by anyone else, to undertake some strenuous activity—say, to climb a challenging mountain—in memory of the deceased.

There is a plausible, if not invariably persuasive answer to the question of why be moral, on the approach adopted here. To fail to be moral, on your own recognition of moral demands, is to fail to perform in the manner of an integrated person; it is to display an attitude of which you must think, if only in your private reflections: that is not who I am. Being moral on the emerging account, then, is just a matter of being faithful to the self you speak for, the self you proclaim yourself to be. Whether or not Shakespeare (2014, Act 1, sc 3) endorsed the sentiment, Polonius got it right in *Hamlet* when he enjoined his son: "This above all: to thine own self be true." The demands of morality are nothing more or less than the demands of personal integrity: personal wholeness and unity.

Our answer to the question of why be moral is particularly appealing, since it avoids a dilemma often raised for purported answers. This, in a traditional format, is that answers either cite causally instrumental reasons for being moral—say, reasons of prudence—reducing morality to something else; or they cite intrinsically moral reasons for being moral, making morality into a self-evident or intuitive system of demands (Prichard 1912). Our answer does not claim that moral demands are self-evident, since it ties them to the achievement of an integrated self. But nor does it instrumentalize morality in the alleged manner, since the integration of self that it underpins is not a causal result of being moral. It is something constituted by fidelity to perceived moral demands, not something that is brought about as a contingent, downstream consequence (Pettit 2018).

Being moral in the sense that ties it to living up to an integrated self does not necessarily involve abiding by only or even all the moral standards that are shared and routine in your society. It is quite possible, for all we have argued, that you may reject some of these, at least in your own case, and live by other judgments of presumptively multilateral desirability. You may even make a claim like that which Bernard Williams (1981) imagines Gauguin endorsing, that your artistic potential and its requirements justify abandoning your family.

Even if you do adopt such a view, however, the current account implies that it will still involve a claim, however persuasive, to endorse commitments that are universally accessible—capable, as you think of them, of being explained and justified to others. Thus, as you will see things, Polonius was also right in articulating an implication of following his injunction to be true to yourself: "And it must follow, as the night the day," he said, "Thou canst not then be false to any man."

The issue of why be moral is sometimes cast as an issue, coarsely, between rationalism and sentimentalism. Rationalism would suggest that reason alone requires us to be moral, disciplining our spontaneous desires; sentimentalism, that it is also necessary that we be moved by certain distinctive desires or, more broadly, sentiments. The alternative suggested by our remarks might be described as personalism. This would tie the moral imperative to the need to function properly as a person among persons and a person in relation to yourself: that is, as someone who actively or virtually makes certain general or particular commitments, purportedly acceptable to others, and who proves capable of living up to them.[6]

7.2 Moral semantics

On expressivism and error theory

Consistently with the metaphysics assumed in the theory defended here, it might be the case that a debunking theory of moral semantics such as expressivism or error theory is actually correct. According to the expressivist account, what we do in holding or avowing moral beliefs—in making moral judgments—is to express our feelings or emotions, our plans or prescriptions, about the subject matter under consideration. We do not assert anything truth-conditional about that matter—that is, anything that is apt to be true or false—but express such attitudes in the direct manner in which we express a belief that p by asserting that p.

On the sort of theory envisaged, my saying that something is desirable—or, in explanation of its desirability, that it would be fun or would make for greater fairness or whatever—is not primarily designed to make an assertion that is true or false; or at least true or false in the regular sense that applies with straightforwardly non-prescriptive statements. And if the theory is extended to ascriptions of responsibility, which it usually is not, my saying that you are fit to be held responsible for one or another deed is equally resistant to analysis as a truth-conditional assertion.

The idea is that in each case I aim to communicate my attitude of approval or disapproval, commendation or condemnation, and not

6. The term "personalism" is used in a different but related sense in Schroeder, Roskies, and Nicholls (2010). It has also been used, of course, to tag other philosophical schools.

primarily to convey anything about the world; if I do convey some-thing about the world—say, that a widely accepted precondition of fun or fairness is satisfied—that is a secondary aspect of the message. One distinctive feature of the view is that while I am said to aim voluntarily at communicating my attitude in this manner, choosing my words to suit that aim, I am said to do so without necessarily forming a belief about the presence of the attitude I express, and certainly without com-municating that I hold such a belief.[7]

While this position has been developed in some very sophisticated versions (Blackburn 1984; Gibbard 1990, 2003), it gives rise to a range of difficulties, not least the difficulty of assuming that I can voluntarily express an attitude other than a belief without forming or expressing any belief in my having that attitude (Jackson and Pettit 1998; Pettit 2006a). Those difficulties apart, however, expressivism gives an account of moral utterances that struggles to make sense of some salient phe-nomena such as the fact that we treat the utterances as assertions that can be true or false and that we embed them comfortably in more complex assertions: say, in arguing that if an option is desirable, we should recommend it, or that if someone is responsible for an offense, then we should impose a sanction (but see Schroeder 2008). Hence, we should have resort to expressivism only in the absence of a theory that can save those phenomena, making straightforward sense of the appar-ently truth-conditional character of moral judgments.

Moral error theory does save those phenomena but only in a second-rate fashion. According to this theory, we do indeed treat our moral ut-terances as truth-conditional, taking them to assert that things are thus and so. But, and this is where those utterances are given second-rate status, we are mistaken to do so (Mackie 1977; Joyce 2006). The idea

7. This aspect of expressivism is meant to distinguish it from what G.E. Moore (1911) described as subjectivism: the theory that in saying that something is de-sirable, for example, I communicate—in effect, I just report—that I hold a favor-able attitude towards it. For an argument that expressivism is less satisfactory than subjectivism, at least under a variation in which reporting a favorable attitude is replaced by avowing that attitude, see (Jackson and Pettit 1998).

is that we take the properties presupposed by moral or ethical talk, in particular by talk of desirability and the like, to be inherently prescriptive and so take them to be properties that cannot be given a place in a world that answers to the scientific image. Assuming that that image of the world is sound, then, whatever we purport to say in moral or ethical judgments is undercut by the absence of the properties whose instantiation it presupposes.

What to do when we recognize this error? The best line, according to this approach, is to treat moral discourse as having an essentially fictional but still useful character. This is to treat moral judgments as telling us that it is as if certain options were desirable or undesirable in the non-natural sense, and to encourage people to choose the would-be desirable alternatives and to avoid the would-be undesirable (Appiah 2017).

Moral realism

The theory supported by our reconstruction of morality makes it unnecessary to resort either to expressivism or to error theory. For on that theory the properties that become salient to people from within practices of avowing desire—in effect, robustly attractive desiderata—are excellent candidates for properties that judgments of desirability predicate. While such properties make options desirable only relative to practices of individually, jointly, or commonly avowing a desire, they can also serve under suitable filtering to make certain options mulitilaterally or morally desirable.

A similar lesson holds for sentences that employ one or another term for an agent's being fit to be held responsible. Sentences used to assert that someone is responsible for an action—for example, responsible for having told a lie—can be taken to ascribe the property that is salient to us insofar as we adopt a regulative, exhortatory perspective on the person. This is the property, roughly, of having breached a shared, routine standard of truthfulness while having a suitably robust capacity to tell the truth and being effectively exhortable to do so.

This means that while the metaphysics presupposed in the theory postulates nothing of a non-natural character, it still leaves room for a moral semantics that makes judgments of desirability and responsibility capable of having truth-conditions—apt to be true or false—and enables them, when suitable conditions are fulfilled, to record truths about the world. In allowing those judgments to be truth-conditional, it supports a form of cognitivism, as it is often described; and in allowing that the judgments ascribe bona fide properties, so that there is no bar to their truth, it supports a full-scale realism. It means that there may be a fact of the matter as to whether certain actions are desirable, certain agents fit to be held responsible, and that we seek to track such facts in our corresponding judgments.

Real properties

But are we really entitled to think that the properties ascribed under this account by judgments of desirability and responsibility are bona fide properties? Yes, we are entitled to do so, on a plausible pattern-based view of what such properties involve.

Any property is associated with a potentially infinite range of instances and counter-instances: instantiations and non-instantiations of the abstract entity involved. Those instances will display a pattern just insofar as it is possible on the basis of a proper subset of instances to determine other instances; it is possible, in other words, to extrapolate from the examples provided by that subset to other examples where the pattern is present (Jackson, Pettit, and Smith 1999).

Thus, there is a pattern in the number sequence 1, 2, 3, 5, 8, 13, etc. insofar as it is possible by inspection of existing members to extend it: we extend the sequence, registering a new member, by adding the previous two. There is a pattern in the class of regular geometrical figures, as we describe them, insofar as a finite range of examples and counter-examples is enough to make it possible, even for a geometrically uninformed perceiver, to determine whether novel figures belong to the class. And there is a pattern in the set of activities we regard as games insofar as a sample of those activities makes it possible to identify other activities, even unfamiliar ones, as games, too.

On the pattern-based view of properties, there is a property realized in each of these cases insofar as there is a pattern present that determines the extrapolation to new instances. The crucial point is that in none of the examples is the set of members a random class; in each, it offers us a basis for projecting the class to include further items. Otherwise put, the class is capable in principle of being represented in a more compact fashion than by just listing its members (Chaitin 1975, 1988; Dennett 1991).

The pattern-based theory is generous but not overly generous in the range of properties that it countenances. It is more generous than the sparse theory that would require a special sort of commonality in the instances of any property, not just a commonality sufficient to support a projectible pattern. But on that theory, only properties that are special in some way—fundamental or primary or natural or whatever— can count strictly as properties (Lewis 1983a; Sider 2011). Common or garden-variety features of things would fail, counterintuitively, to have that status.

Generous though it is, however, the pattern-based theory is not so tolerant as the abundant theory according to which every set of items, no matter how artificial and gerrymandered, realizes a common property. Random sets certainly do not instantiate a property on this theory; properties are present just in patterned sets or classes. Thus, there will be a property present in any set of items of which we can successfully predicate something, insofar as predication is constrained by the nature of the things it gathers together. Such properties might be cast in older terminology as *predicabilia,* or predicables.

Since regular predication is constrained by the nature of the things it collects and classifies—since it does not proceed on the basis of objectively unconstrained decision—the unity of a predicable, or of any patterned property, does not lie in the eye of the predicator. Thus, there must be an objective commonality or unity in the nature of those items that underlies this constraint. But this is not to say that all properties are equally significant in a scientific or god's-eye view of things.

A property will be of greater or lesser significance, plausibly, depending on the range of interactions between bearers and the environment that it explains: that is, depending on how wide its cosmological role (Wright 1992). The mass of something will be more significant that its solidity, and the solidity of something will be more significant than its color, given that the mass of the object explains a wider range of interactions than its solidity, and its solidity than its color.

While having the status of objective properties, desirability and responsibility are on the less significant end of this cosmological spectrum. But that is hardly surprising. The role they play in the world is restricted to their impact on creatures like us, who seek to track them in making judgments about what to desire or who to hold to account. And they are properties that we take to explain our convergence in such judgments, when we do independently converge; that is why we look for purportedly perturbing factors to explain any divergence that does emerge between us.

Admitting indeterminacy

On this account, there will be a determinate fact of the matter as to whether this or that option is desirable, this or that agent fit to be held responsible, in most cases. But this need not be so in every case. Some questions of desirability or responsibility may not be resoluble in the ordinary fashion, even in principle; there may be no determinate fact of the matter at issue. This is a more striking possibility in the case of desirability, and we may stick to that case here.

Judgments of desirability in every category are based on the desiderata or properties that make relevant alternatives more or less robustly attractive. The desiderata that make an option individually desirable for an agent are those agent-relative and agent-neutral desiderata that aggregate to make it more robustly attractive than any alternative for that particular agent. Those that make an option jointly desirable for a more or less bounded group are the group-relative and group-neutral desiderata that aggregate to make it more robustly attractive for that group. Those that make an option commonly desirable are the agent-neutral properties that aggregate to make it more robustly attractive from the common point of view of people in general. And the properties, finally, that make an option multilaterally or morally desirable are those in all relevant categories that aggregate to make it more robustly attractive from the point of view privileged in ethics: one that transcends different practical and different personal perspectives, filtering out competitive or discordant desiderata.

In the view supported by the reconstruction offered, the desiderata that play a role in determining any form of desirability, and moral desirability in particular, are required on pain of mutual unconversability to be recognized as relevant on all sides. But there is no obstacle to those desiderata being weighted differently by different people. When an option counts as desirable, it will be supported under all the weightings of desiderata supported by conversable agents. But people's weightings may sometimes diverge in a way that creates conflict over whether an option is desirable. And in that sort of case, the prospect of indeterminacy arises: the prospect that there is just no fact of the matter as to whether or not that alternative is desirable.

The fact that desirability and obligation are determined by desiderata that are recognized on all sides means that it is always going to be possible to compare the options in any choice with one another— say, options X and Y—looking at how they each score on the desiderata relevant.[8] But the fact that people may weight those desiderata differently means that, despite the fact that X and Y are comparable options, X may score over Y on some weightings, Y may score over X on others, and X and Y may be equivalent on others again. In such cases,

---

8. Is there a problem raised by the fact that in comparing X and Y, one set of desiderata may be relevant, while in comparing Y and Z or X and Z, another set may come to be relevant? Not if we re-individuate the options, so that when an alternative described as X engages different desiderata in comparison with Y from those that it engages in comparison with Z, then there are two distinct options in question: X' and X", as we may call them. Take an example that arises with binary choices between certain pieces of fruit, where I pick first, and you get what I leave. Suppose in a relevant choice that I prefer a big apple to an orange; that I prefer an orange to a small apple in another choice; and yet that I prefer a small apple to a big apple in a

the alternatives are on a par, as Ruth Chang (2002) puts it; the relations between them mean that we cannot deny they are comparable, yet we cannot treat either as scoring above or at the same level as the other (Rabinowicz 2012).

This observation about the prospect of parity means that on the theory of morality emerging here, we can be realist about moral properties like moral desirability and obligation without thinking that there is always a fact of the matter as to whether one or another alternative is the desirable or obligatory option in a given choice. This possibility may obtain with choices between different actions but also with choices between different social rules, and different political arrangements. It will materialize in any situation in which there are non-negotiable differences in the weightings given to different desiderata and those weightings fail to converge on an ordering of the alternatives; some go in one direction, some in others.

7.3 Moral epistemology

The primacy of practices

How do we learn about what is desirable—particularly, morally desirable—according to the theory supported by the reconstruction offered? And how do we learn about when agents are fit to be held responsible in the choices they make?

We can identify the morally desirable option in any choice by looking at how the desiderata mobilized by different practices and relationships— the desiderata that can make something robustly attractive—combine to make that option multilaterally desirable. We can learn whether or not the agent is fit to be held responsible for choosing or not choosing that

---

third. Is this inconsistent on my part? No, because the desideratum of politeness is relevant in the third case but not in the other two; taking the big apple in that case is a different option from what it is in the first. For a discussion of this case and the re-individuation strategy, see Pettit (1991b) and Broome (1991). For more far-reaching, alternative treatments of relevant issues, see Temkin (2012) and Buchak (2015).

option by determining whether they were actively or virtually pledged to take it and how far, under our regular practices, they can be held to those pledges. And we can identify it as a morally obligatory option, by the fact that it is the most desirable option among those for which the agent is fit to be held responsible.

According to this view of things, moral learning can come about only among those who are inducted into suitable practices. On the one side, they must be inducted into the practice of avowing and co-avowing desires, recognizing the properties that can serve to make something robustly attractive, and coming to recognize associated patterns of desirability, in particular multilateral desirability. And on the other side, they must be inducted into the practice, first, of making pledges, including the virtual pledges associated with shared, routine standards of desirability; and, second, of holding one another responsible to such pledges, conveying the recognition of a suitably responsive capacity, an exhortation to exercise it, and a reprimand for any failure on this front.

By this account, the primary or canonical mode of forming judgments about desirability and obligation, and the appropriate mode of resolving issues of responsibility, will be by tracking the patterns salient under the relevant social practices and by letting the properties that gain salience determine our responses. This mode of forming judgments will be canonical, in the sense that any other modes of doing so will presuppose it. They will presuppose it in the way in which the color-blind person's judgments of color, however based, presuppose that some people make judgments of color on the basis of sensations that the color-blind person lacks.

How practices reveal properties

By the account supported, the practices at the origin of ethics provide the means, presumptively the only means, whereby you can come to understand properties like those of desirability and responsibility in a proper manner. This does not make ethics special, since being inducted into a suitable practice—learning the rules of the practice—is typically the only means whereby you can properly identify the patterns and properties associated with the practice. If you have not learned the rules of chess, to return to an example used in chapter 1, you may fail to see the patterns in castling or check-mating; and, even if you do register underlying physical patterns, you will not appreciate their significance. But once you do know how to play chess—once you know at least the rationale and rules of the game—you will have no difficulty in understanding what castling and check-mating involve. Without a knowledge of those rules, you could have only the parasitic understanding that they are properties to which players respond in such and such a fashion; you could only have an understanding akin to the color-blind person's understanding of color.

As your understanding of properties like castling and check-mating is derived from practice, requiring you at least to know the rules of chess, so on the present account the same is true of your understanding of matters of desirability and responsibility. Being inducted into suitable practices, at least in the sense of knowing the rules, enables you to access properties like those of desirability and responsibility. And it is hard to see how you could properly or non-parasitically grasp those properties without familiarity with such practices.

Thus, being inducted into the practice of making avowals of desire ensures that you will be able to recognize the pattern among potential attractors that identifies some as having the capacity to make bearers robustly attractive. And being inducted into the practice of identifying the multilaterally desirable alternative in any choice ensures that you will be able to recognize the pattern that selects the desiderata suited to determining what is desirable in that presumptively moral sense. Again, being inducted into the practice of holding others responsible for their choices ensures that you will be sensitive to the pattern displayed among agents who are fit for censure or commendation for what they do. And, finally, being inducted into the combination of those two practices ensures that you will be suited to determine the pattern present in those options that count as obligatory.

The connection between the practices of avowal and pledging and the properties of desirability and responsibility is that the practices reveal the properties. This marks a deep contrast with cases in which practices serve, not to reveal corresponding properties, but to construct and define them.

Think of how the property of the fashionable is associated with the practice of haute couture, where the recognized authorities decide season by season on what is fashionable. Or think of how the property of being cool, as that is identified idiomatically, looks like a construct of the same sort: a property that belongs or fails to belong to something, depending on what the relevant authorities—the cool crowd—decide.

In the case of the fashionable and the cool, the properties are defined as the counterparts of the practices, and what drives those who converge in their use of the predicates is quite independent of the nature of the properties themselves. The driving force is typically a wish to coordinate—ultimately to coordinate with the formal or informal authorities—for the sake of coordination, or for the sake of an associated form of acceptance. And it is only in light of successful coordination that properties present themselves as candidates for predication, now in this instance, now in that.[9]

On the account supported by the Erewhon narrative, we do not define properties of desirability and responsibility as the counterparts of the practices, letting their extension vary with wherever the practices move under independent pressures. And similarly, we do not coordinate in predicating such properties just for the sake of coordination, and certainly not for the sake of coordination with any authorities. Rather, we coordinate as a result of finding that in seeking out the robustly attractive, and in determining who it makes sense to take at their word, we triangulate reassuringly on more or less common properties of desirability and responsibility. Those properties are revealed in the practices, not defined or constructed by them.

This aspect of how our practices relate to those properties shows up in how you would respond to any divergence between your claims

---

9. David Hume (1965) suggested in the eighteenth century that we coordinate for coordination's sake in settling matters of aesthetic taste, thereby making the tasteful look dangerously like the fashionable and the cool. But see Sainsbury (1998) for a different perspective on Hume's view.

and those of others. Whether in Erewhon or in the actual world, you would treat any divergence as evidence that you or others are not seeing things properly and try to determine, in negotiation with others, where the problem arises: whether on your side, or theirs. You may not always succeed in achieving convergence with others, of course, as you may not succeed in any area of inquiry. But if you do not resolve the issue, then, short of positing indeterminacy of the kind allowed earlier, you will have to hold that at least one side is misled on the issue.

The relationship between participating in suitable practices and discerning properties of desirability and responsibility is broadly similar to the relationship between being able to have color sensations in response to the surfaces of objects and being able to gain access to a property like that of being red or green or whatever.[10] Redness as we conceive of it in surfaces is a categorical property, not something defined by reference to our sensations. But it is our sensations that enable us to access it properly, at least as we correct for problems of color perception in negotiation with others. We rely on one another as a reality check that enables us to triangulate on redness. And we rely on one another in a parallel way to triangulate on properties like desirability and responsibility.

The sorts of observations invoked here are often taken to support an analysis of color according to which something is red or green if and only if it looks red or looks green to normal observers—that is, to observers not subject to the problems of color perception identified in interpersonal negotiation. But, as supported here, that analysis does not pick out conditions by which ordinary users are guided in applying color concepts and predicating color properties. Rather, it directs us to conditions under which ordinary users get to master color concepts; it identifies their acquisition conditions, not their application conditions. (Pettit 1993, Ch. 2; Jackson and Pettit 2002; Pettit 2002, Pt. 1). Were we

10. A difference, passed over here, is that whereas participating in a practice comes in degrees—it may involve full induction in the practice or just getting an initial sense of the rules—having access to color sensations is an on or off matter; your color sensitivity may vary in degrees, of course, but there is a bright line between having color sensations of some kind and having none at all: being fully color-blind.

to try to construct a parallel analysis linking ethical properties with the practices invoked in the genealogy, that analysis would direct us equally to conditions for the acquisition of ethical concepts, not conditions that guide their application.[11]

In finding our way about in a colored world, we sometimes recognize that our color perceptions are playing tricks on us: say, because we are wearing rose-tinted glasses. But the common or default option is to authorize those perceptions, letting them serve as presumptive representations of how things are. This is our canonical way of judging color, as we put it earlier, and the canonical way of detecting desirability and responsibility operates on parallel lines. In finding our way around the social world, we routinely authorize our suitably supported desires, taking them to reveal desirability in one or another mode. And in the same manner, we routinely authorize our exhortatory and resentful responses, taking those proactive and reactive attitudes to reveal someone's fitness to be held, or to have been held, responsible.

There is a difference between green and red surfaces that can be registered in science; by most accounts, it is a difference in their spectral reflectance: that is, in the ratio at which they reflect incident light at various frequencies. In the same way, there is undoubtedly a difference between desirable and undesirable scenarios, and between agents who are fit and those who are unfit to be held responsible, that can be characterized in the neutral scientific view. But as the color difference shows up as such only from the perspective of a creature with appropriate sensations, so the difference in desirability and responsibility shows up as

---

11. Conditions of application and acquisition ought each to be a priori defensible. But where someone who understands a concept might be expected to have an intuitive or immediate grasp of its application conditions, this is not necessarily the case with its acquisition conditions. Reconstructive analyses are likely to deliver only conditions of acquisition or mastery, not conditions of application, when the concepts involved are practice-dependent. Once grasped, however, an acquisition-conditions analysis may begin to guide the sophisticated in applying the concept and thereby impact on the habits of others. The genealogy of money may have had this effect, giving us the concept of a medium of exchange that serves as a metric for pricing goods and services, and a means of storing wealth.

such only in the perspective of creatures who make and hold one another to commitments.

This, of course, is hardly surprising. Color, desirability, and responsibility are not properties with a wide cosmological role, to revert to an idea introduced in discussing moral metaphysics. The only part of any significance that they play in the causal network of the cosmos is in relation to creatures of our narrow species. It is no wonder that as those properties only matter in the view from our kind, so they only get to be registered properly from within that viewpoint.

In defending a naturalistic metaphysics of morals, we argued for a metaphysical monism: that is, for the claim that reality is unified and does not divide into quite different realms, as in a divide between natural and normative properties. But what we see now is that a metaphysical monism is consistent with an epistemological pluralism or perspectivism (Pettit 2000). This is the claim that in order to survey what there is in the world, in intuitively the most illuminating way, it is necessary to move between different perspectives, as in the perspectives associated with the practices of avowal and pledging. The view from nowhere—the view from the widest scientific or objective perspective—does not reveal all that there is, at least not in a way that gives due importance to each and every facet of reality (Nagel 1986). Being restricted to understanding the world from that perspective would be like being restricted to understanding color from the perspective of the color-blind.

The issue of moral deference

Like any account of the epistemology of ethics, our account must confront the issue of moral deference, as it has come to be known. In morality, there are often recognized authorities—ecclesiastical, political, or cultural—who rule on what is acceptable and what is not. Given that, by our account, they cannot have the status enjoyed by authorities on the fashionable and the cool, there is a question about how you should respond to the discovery that their judgments diverge from yours. Should you hold your ground, perhaps after thinking about what they have to say? Or should you defer to their judgments, even when your own inclinations lead elsewhere?

Unless you are subject to some cognitive or affective pathology, it is hard to see why, on our account, you should defer. Absent any defect, you will have access to the patterns in desiderata that determine moral character. Thus, it would be servile, even self-abasing, to rely on the judgment and testimony of others rather than relying on that access. It would be like relying on the judgments of color that somebody else makes, despite having perfectly good color vision yourself. The same goes for resolving issues of responsibility as distinct from desirability, but it will be easier to stick to the desirability case.

Keeping to that case, then, how should you respond to the fact that you yourself are inclined to make one judgment in a certain choice—say, that option X is the desirable, even obligatory option in a set of alternatives, X and Y—and someone with recognized authority is inclined to make the opposite judgment? The divergence should certainly prompt you to seek out relevant facts that you may have overlooked or misread, as a result of distraction. Again, if you think you may be subject to a disturbing blind spot or unconscious bias, say, because of your gender or your power, the divergence might reasonably prompt you to recalibrate the weight you give to certain desiderata and to suspend or reshape your judgment (Jones 1999; Fricker 2007). But absent any such unsettling effect, why should you allow the testimony of any other person to elicit a change of mind? To do so would be to let your moral judgment drift away from its moorings in your sensibility: your appreciation of the force of relevant desiderata.

This is not to say that deference to the testimony of others in any domain of judgment is generally reprehensible. The point to recognize is that there is something special about moral judgment insofar as the grounds that determine how you should go, assuming a relatively reliable sense of background facts, are ones that may be expected to show up in your personal sensibility.

It is often observed, plausibly, that claims to aesthetic knowledge—say, the claim to know that the *Mona Lisa* is an extremely beautiful painting—are essentially experiential (Pettit 1983). It would be ludicrous to make that aesthetic claim and then, in support of the assertion, to invoke the authorities you had read, admitting that you yourself had never seen the painting or even a reproduction of the painting. On the account defended here, the linkage between moral judgment and personal sensibility supports a similar, independently plausible observation.

In order to vindicate a claim to know that something is desirable or obligatory, it would make no sense to invoke the authority of others. The claim to know that the *Mona Lisa* is a beautiful painting carries the implicature that you have seen and savored it, since that is the canonical mode of aesthetic judgment. And the claim to know that one or another option is desirable or obligatory, at least on the account of morality emerging here, carries a parallel implicature to the effect that you have registered and weighed the desiderata that support it. You might claim to know on the basis of authority that something is "desirable," where the scare quotes indicate that you mean desirable-according-to-the-authorities. But you could not plausibly invoke that ground for making a claim about what is desirable with the quotes off.

Moral ignorance

The moral epistemology emerging under this account of morality raises the related question as to whether we can excuse you for an offense by citing moral ignorance. Assume that when we take something to be desirable or obligatory, we hold that it is desirable or obligatory in itself, not just relative to us. The question is whether we can exonerate you from blame on the basis that while you committed an offense, say, by doing something cruel or domineering, or by enslaving others, you were ignorant of the moral valence of the property involved. You realized that you acted in a cruel or domineering fashion, or that you did have slaves, but you just did not see what is so bad about being cruel or domineering or about having slaves (Rosen 2004).

Given the salience of relevant desiderata in any culture, and given the role of those desiderata in grounding your judgments of desirability and obligation, it is hard to see how we who belong to the same world could allow moral ignorance to excuse a wrong action. But that consideration does not apply across cultures or epochs, and so there remains an issue as to whether we can allow moral ignorance to excuse what we see as wrongful behavior on the part of those at other places or in other times.

This issue is connected with the question as to whether it is possible to envisage a development in the recognition of desirability and obligation over time, whether within a culture or across cultures. For if such development is possible, then it may well be plausible to think that we should not blame those in another culture, past or present, for acting in a way that presents as an offense only in light of the development. By the observations made so far, development in moral cognition does seem to be possible, and so it seems possible in principle that we may have to refrain from blaming those at another place or time for acting in a way that we would find culpable in our own.

There are two ways in which development might make moral ignorance into a plausible excuse. One is by the identification of a desideratum that was previously unregistered but, once identified, gains recognition on all sides. Thus, it may be, as is sometimes said, that the idea in Abrahamic religions of charity toward the poor, even the unknown poor, was unrecognized in some other traditions. If that is so, then it would seem out of place to censure those in such other traditions for a lack of charitable assistance to the poor. The recognition of this possibility is consistent with arguing for conversability across cultures, since in forming our own judgments of desirability we might rely on a desideratum that plays no role in another culture; while we think it could be introduced there, we acknowledge that as yet it has no presence in that culture.

Another mode of cognitive development in moral matters is easier to imagine. This would consist in transferring a recognized desideratum from one domain to others, and using it in those domains to argue for quite novel modes of behavior or organization. This has surely occurred in many of our own cultures with the invocation of a notion of equality to support mutual acceptance among religious or ethnic groups, equal provision for women as well as men in public life, and equal recognition of the claims of people of different sexual orientations. It would seem reasonable to suspend the censure we would heap on contemporaries for intolerant or disrespectful behavior, in thinking about those in places or times where the ideal of equality is given much more restricted application.

The two sorts of developments envisaged would offer us grounds for excusing those not exposed to such changes for making mistakes about desirability in their moral judgments and for acting as those judgments allowed. Thus, we might think that it would be inappropriate to blame people in the past for cruelty to children, for being domineering in the treatment of a subordinated class, or even for holding certain others in slavery. We may have no doubts about how offensive such behavior is, regardless of the culture in which it occurs, but hold that we cannot plausibly blame people for that behavior in cultures in which it was just not so obvious that it was offensive.

It is worth noting that the two sorts of developments invoked here might also direct us to excuses for offensive behavior that stem, not from moral ignorance, but from the difficulty that the perpetrators, unlike us, would have faced in eschewing such behavior.

Suppose that while the desideratum of dealing well with those in a certain group—say, a certain caste—was indeed available for recognition by certain individuals in a past culture, it was not registered generally or generally given weight. In that situation, it would not have been reputationally costly for others to treat members of that caste badly, and it might have been downright idiosyncratic, even derisible, to treat them well.

In such a moral ecology, to reintroduce an idea invoked in the last chapter, giving favorable treatment to those in the downtrodden caste might have been supererogatory and even extremely heroic; it might have been a form of treatment that would have been too demanding to expect even among those aware of the relevant desideratum. And if that is the case, then, while we may think ill of such agents in retrospect, it would seem harsh and judgmental to impose on them the sort of censure that we readily impose on our contemporaries.

7.4 Expanding moral concepts

The discussion has focused so far on two families of concepts central to morality: on the one side, concepts of desirability; on the other, concepts related to issues of responsibility. And by putting those concepts together, it has introduced the concept of the obligatory and its relatives—the concepts of the prohibited and the permitted—as well as the concept of the supererogatory. An obligatory option in a choice is the most desirable of those options that are within the agent's power and domain of responsibility; a prohibited option is one that it is obligatory to avoid; and a permitted option is one that it is not obligatory to avoid, whether or not it is obligatory to take it. A supererogatory option, however, is one that scores high in desirability but is too demanding on the agent's capacity for us to regard it as the obligatory option in the choice.

But moral thinking deploys other concepts beyond these. It makes much use, for example, of the concepts of reasons, duties, and rights. A natural question, then, is how far these can be given countenance within the framework emerging from our reconstructive analysis of ethics. By many accounts, the notion of reasons—prescriptive reasons or, as it is usually said, normative reasons—is the most basic in ethics, and this is the first concept we discuss.

The notion of a reason

The concept of a prescriptive or normative reason, at the most general level, is that of a consideration or fact that counts in favor of something (Scanlon 2014, 30). The most obvious role for the concept of a reason within the theory supported by our narrative is in the formation of desire. Desiderata are candidates for the role of reasons—that is, good supportive reasons—in relation to desire. A desideratum D— strictly, the presence of a desideratum, D—will constitute a reason for an agent A to desire a prospect R, relative to an avowing practice, P, just insofar as it makes that prospect robustly attractive. Provided the agent is not evidentially or executively careless, and guards as needed against distraction and disturbance, the presence of the desideratum more or less ensures that the prospect will continue to be attractive.

This formula allows us to think that reasons may vary with the practice in the background. Thus, we can distinguish between reasons that are meant to be relevant from the viewpoint of an avowing agent or a co-avowing group, bounded or unbounded. We can distinguish between such reasons and the reasons that make something personally most attractive for an individual and or make it multilaterally attractive. And, extending beyond cases considered in the narrative, we can distinguish between such overall and multilateral reasons and reasons associated with a certain range of interests, like those of prudence or patriotism, and reasons associated with a certain standpoint, such as that of law or etiquette.

The formula also allows us to distinguish between the reasons that there actually are for an agent A to desire prospect R, and the reasons that A—or indeed anyone else—thinks, perhaps wrongly, that there are to desire R. And it can allow that the actual reasons and the self-ascribed reasons for A to desire R may come in any of four combinations. A may have reason to desire R and recognize that reason; A may have reason to desire R and fail to recognize or mistake it; A may not have reason to desire R and think that there is such a reason in place; and A may not have reason to desire R and recognize that such reason is indeed lacking.

As there is room for introducing the idea of a reason for desire, within the theory supported by our narrative, so there is room also for introducing the idea of a reason for belief. But of course, reasons for belief will only be of interest relative to the master category of unbounded co-avowal. Any datum that would make it robustly persuasive that p will constitute a prescriptive reason to believe that p.

This account of reasons for desire and belief can make room for the fact that reasons may not always be taken to be conclusive. A desideratum may make something robustly attractive within a practice, even make it attractive multilaterally, only in abstraction from its other properties, not all things considered. And in that event, it will constitute just a pro tanto reason for desire, not a reason simpliciter or pro toto (Broome 2013, 5). And a datum may make something robustly persuasive, all things considered, only in abstraction from other evidence. It may constitute just a prima facie ground for holding the appropriate belief.

When there is reason for an agent A to desire a prospect R, in whatever mode, that explains why R is correspondingly desirable for A. It explains why the property of being robustly attractive figures in the desirability role: that is, why it should be grounded in other properties, why it may diverge from the actually attractive, and, other things being equal, why it should have prescriptive priority over the actually attractive.

Whenever there is a reason for A to desire R, not only is R desirable for A, there is also a reason for A to believe that R is desirable: there is evidence available to A that R is desirable. But there will be evidence that R is desirable because there is reason to desire R; it will not be the case, as is sometimes maintained, that there is a reason to desire R because there is evidence that R is desirable (Kearns and Star 2008). The reason to desire R does not consist in the evidence of R's desirability

As there are reasons for desiring certain outcomes, under the approach supported by our narrative, so there will be reasons for holding someone to an avowal. These will consist in the presence of those capacities, in the absence of excusing and exempting factors, that make it useful to take someone at their word, even in the wake of particular failures to act on their word. And as reasons for desire go with reasons to believe in desirability, so reasons to take someone at their word will go with reasons to believe that they are fit to be held responsible. But the main focus in this discussion is on desirability.

Whenever something is desirable it counts as good, whenever something is multilaterally or morally desirable it counts as morally good. Thus, the account we have given of reasons for desire, and their connection with desirability, amounts to a fitting-attitude theory of the good. The theory holds that the notion of reason is prior to the notion of good or desirable, and that the good is that which there is reason to desire—that which is fittingly desired. Fitting-attitude theories of the good normally deny that the fittingness of the appropriate attitude—in our case, desire—is naturalistically reducible or explicable; they treat it as analytically primitive (Scanlon 1998). But the account supported here, of course, is entirely naturalistic in character.[12]

Primitive reasons, fundamental rights

For all that has been said so far, there might be little further use for the notion of reasons in moral reasoning. With the notion of desirability introduced—and introduced on a basis that we use the notion of a reason for desire to explicate—we might carry on in moral guidance, assessment, and censure without having any further use for the idea of a reason. All there might be reason to do, for example, is that which counts as desirable. Thus, we might be able to say everything ethically worth saying in the terminology of desirability and responsibility and in the related terminology of the obligatory and the supererogatory (Chappell 2012).

But now we face a challenge for our account of the role and nature of morality. For how are we to make sense within that account of the many further ways in which moral theorists, and agents more generally, speak of reasons? How are we to explain how they can assume that there is often a reason to do something that does not consist in its being desirable to act that way? And how are we to explain the distinctions they take such reasons to display: distinctions such as those among reasons that permit, reasons that justify, reasons that mandate, and reasons that exclude the consideration of other reasons (Raz 1999)?

The challenge to provide such an explanation is parallel to a challenge to provide a similar explanation for why a parallel notion of rights also figures prominently in moral discourse, whether in the seminar or on the street. By many lights, there are things that you can claim from

---

12. Consistent with that naturalistic character, it is plausible to identify reasons for desire with values, to introduce a term that we do not use much here. Certain desiderata will count as values for an agent just insofar as they constitute reasons for that agent to hold corresponding desires: they constitute robust attractors. We will probably be ready to describe them as that person's values—as properties that the person values—only if they are recognized as robust attractors and actively play a role in the formation of their desires (Scheffler 2010).

others, and that others can claim from you, as a matter of basic, intuitive moral right: that is, on a basis that is not plausibly explicated in terms of how it is desirable or obligatory for people to act. Rights in this sense seem to provide the grounds on which claims can be made, so that those claims are supported on a basis other than the fact, if it is a fact, that it is desirable or obligatory that they should be satisfied.

The fact that reasons and rights—and perhaps related notions, too—figure in this way has led many thinkers to treat the reasons as primitive, the rights as fundamental. If reasons and rights do have this status, of course, then our account of ethics is radically incomplete. But the problem turns out to be resoluble. For we can understand why reasons and rights figure as they do in moral discourse—and why some might be tempted, therefore, to treat them as primitive or fundamental—against a background of accepted rules of behavior. And the narrative described here makes good sense of why we should be ready to build such rules into the background of moral thought.

Explaining reasons and rights

We saw in chapter 2 that interactions among agents who seek to prove reliable and congenial partners will give rise to regularities of behavior like truth-telling, non-violence, and the like, and that these regularities are likely to become a matter of shared awareness, constituting social norms. With the notion of moral desirability available, as we noted in chapter 5, it is more or less inevitable that these social norms are going to assume the status of shared and indeed routine standards of multi-lateral desirability: established rules of moral behavior. And it is equally inevitable, as we saw, that they will be supplemented with similar standards of fidelity in avowals and pledges. These will all be rules whose unquestioned requirements, now in this case, now in that, we may expect one another to satisfy and to be virtually pledged to satisfying.

Once moral rules are taken to be manifestly in place, it is possible to explain why we should have an immediately accessible sense of reasons and rights that command our response, and do so without restating demands of desirability.

Assuming a shared commitment to moral norms, be it active or virtual, we can each identify anything that a rule unquestionably requires as something that there is a mandatory reason to realize, anything that the rules support in a weaker way as something we have justifying reason to realize, and anything that is consistent with the rules—whether by design or default—as something that we have a permissive reason to do. Assuming a shared commitment to the priority of some rules over others—say, the priority of moral norms over conventions of etiquette—we can even take the requirements of those rules to constitute reasons for excluding a consideration of the requirements of the other rules. And we can view the rule-based requirements in these different ways without thinking of them as restating the demands of desirability.

Assuming a shared commitment to moral rules, we can also see why that might give us each a ground for making claims on others, without taking that to say just that it is desirable or obligatory for others to treat us in the appropriate way. We can see why we might treat those rules, and the claims or rights they give us, as independent grounds that explain why it is desirable or obligatory for others to act in that manner. Legal rules give us legal rights against one another that are matters of immediate recognition. And in the same way, social norms that are established among us on a moral basis can give us moral rights against one another that we recognize as immediately demanding.

It may be objected that we can also invoke the concept of such an immediately accessible right in the absence of supportive rules. Thus, we can say of a community where women have a second-class status under the morally accepted norms that still they have the same rights as men. But that sort of comment is easily accommodated on the lines suggested. For it can be made, not against the background of actual rules, but against the background of a plausible, presumptively desirable extension of that set of rules.

Living in a society whose actual rules about relationships between men and women give them equal status, for example, it is fully understandable why we should take those rules as background in speaking about the rights of women in an otherwise similar society that lacks those rules. Taking those rules as background, we may say that women have the same rights as men in the society lacking the rules as well as in our own society. But when we say that we are not appealing to a fundamental, rule-independent notion of rights; we are saying in effect that that society ought to have rules, like the rules in our society, under which women would have such rights: that that would be desirable.

On the emerging picture, then, the primary concepts in the moral world may be those of desirability and responsibility, with the associated notions of the obligatory and the supererogatory. But, given that there are shared, routine standards in play among us—standards of moral desirability to which we hold one another responsible—it is entirely understandable why we should begin to employ notions of reasons and rights, rather than the notion of desirability, in ruling on how we and others ought to behave.

This way of accommodating reasons and rights has the great virtue of being able to make sense, within a broadly naturalistic frame, of how we gain access to such concepts. It does not have to appeal to intuitions about primitive reasons or fundamental rights such that it is hard to see how we, the products of a natural evolution, could manage to have and share them. We come to develop the required concepts and make intuitive judgments about their application in the context of the shared, routine standards that are likely to emerge in any society, as they emerge in Erewhon.

The Cheshire cat fallacy

This account of how we come to employ the language of reasons and rights also suggests a debunking explanation of why they may appear to be primitive or fundamental and of why non-naturalists may be misled by that appearance. They may well seem to be primitive or fundamental as the result of what might be called the Cheshire cat fallacy.

As Alice seemed to see the grin of the cat remain in the absence of the cat itself, so those who think they register primitive reasons and fundamental rights may be subject to a similar illusion. They may focus on reasons and rights that are grounded in existing norms—or in projected standards that are taken as ideal—and attend to these phenomena in neglect of the very framework of rules that they presuppose. And as a result of that neglect, they may come to think of the reasons and rights as commanding our allegiance on their own merits, not because of the appeal of the presupposed norms. They may come to think of them as primitive or fundamental.

This suggestion is reminiscent of a proposal made by Elizabeth Anscombe (1958; for comment, see Doyle 2018). One strand in her famous lecture on modern moral philosophy is the idea that the discipline has been betrayed by two simultaneous moves. First, by dropping "the conception of God as a law-giver" (6). And, second, by continuing nonetheless to give terms like "should" and "ought" and "needs," to cite her examples—and, we might add, related concepts like those of "reasons" and "rights"—the sort of sense they would have had under such a law.

This, as she casts it with some irony, is to give those terms "a special so-called 'moral' sense—i.e. a sense in which they imply some absolute verdict (like one of guilty/not guilty)" (5). In making these remarks, Anscombe treats the shoulds and oughts and needs postulated by her opponents as no more real than the grin of the Cheshire cat. "It is as if the notion 'criminal' were to remain," she says, "when criminal law and criminal courts had been abolished and forgotten" (6).[13]

7.5 Moral psychology

The moral psychology implicit in any account of ethics describes the role of moral judgments and associated dispositions in motivating human agents. There are three respects in which the view of morality supported by our narrative has lessons in this domain.

---

13. A genealogy, as it is understood by Bernard Williams (2002), may move with benefit from a counterfactual story, revealing the nature of a practice, to a historical story in which the focus is on misinterpretations of the practice, or deviations from it. This suggestion about the influence of the Chesire cat fallacy, however speculative and undocumented, might be taken as that sort of historical comment.

Judgment internalism

A first lesson it teaches bears on the common claim that making the judgment that an option is desirable, or perhaps that it is obligatory, is internally connected with being motivated in some measure to take that option; or, more weakly, that it is internally connected in the case of well-functioning agents with being motivated appropriately (Darwall, Gibbard, and Railton 1992; Smith 1994). The viewpoint upheld here supports such a form of judgment internalism, as it has been called, but only in a distinctively weak version.

From that viewpoint, making a moral judgment in favor of one or another option amounts to seeing why, or thinking you see why, the option is desirable. And seeing why it is desirable involves identifying one or another desideratum that the option or a prospective outcome of the option apparently instantiates. But a desideratum is nothing more than a property that tends to make a bearer attractive, and attractive in a relatively robust manner. And so, it is natural to think that when I make a moral judgment in favor of an option, purporting to identify a relevant desideratum, I will tend to be attracted to that option. Thus, there will be a non-inductive connection between making the judgment and feeling the attraction (Jackson and Pettit 1995).

While the connection will occasionally break down, of course, it will do so because of special factors. Perhaps because I am not functioning rationally. Or because the judgment is elicited inappropriately and I actually disbelieve the proposition.[14] Or because I am not in one of those disengaged moods in which attraction flags; I am faced by a desideratum that would normally move me but, because of a sort of evaluative malaise, I feel nothing (Stocker 1976).

We saw earlier that the canonical way of registering desirability in an option is to be attracted to it, authorizing that desire by default—this,

---

14. This is the possibility illustrated earlier by the case of Huck Finn. A plausible analysis holds that when Huck Finn judges under cultural pressures that he ought to report Jim, the runaway slave, he actually believes that it is desirable not to report him (see Arpaly 2003; Joshi 2016).

in the way we register the redness of an object by experiencing a red sensation and authorizing it by default. On that picture, authorizing the attraction presupposes its presence and amounts to not explaining it away as the effect of irrationality or anything of that kind. And on that picture, it is manifest that there will be an internal, more than merely inductive, connection between making the judgment and feeling the attraction.

Moral fetishism

A second lesson in moral psychology that is taught by the theory supported here is that the primary concern in moral judgment and responsiveness should be with the desiderata that explain why an option is desirable, in particular multilaterally desirable. Those desiderata direct me to premises on the basis of which I may conclude that this or that alternative is that which I should take, being morally desirable or obligatory. But the premises they lead me to focus on should continue to play a role in my psychology, even after they have supported one or another practical conclusion about what to do.

According to this lesson, there is a contrast between the role of premises in drawing theoretical conclusions, say, about matters of empirical fact, and the role of premises in drawing practical conclusions. Suppose you are interested in forming beliefs about some theoretical issues and that you identify various considerations that serve as premises for drawing an appropriate conclusion on some question. It may be useful to remember those premises for purposes of pedagogy and persuason, even for purposes of retaining an assurance about the conclusion. But there would be nothing inherently amiss about acting on the conclusion, whether in deriving further entailments or in deciding what to do, without paying continuing attention to the premises that support it.

Suppose by contrast that you are interested in forming beliefs about some practical issues and that you identify considerations that serve as premises for drawing an appropriate conclusion, and making a corresponding choice. You might draw the conclusion in a case like this that such and such an option is morally desirable or obligatory. Would it be appropriate in this practical sort of decision to treat the premises as dispensable in the manner in which that would be appropriate in theoretical judgment? Arguably not.

This would not be appropriate in the sorts of agents projected in the current account, whose primary concern is to do what suitable desiderata dispose them to desire: to do what relevant reasons require them to do. As an agent of that type, you will be invested both in acting as those desiderata motivate and require you to act and, at the same time, in making a judgment on what they actually require: a judgment, as it may be, that such an action is morally desirable or obligatory. Since the motivation that goes with such a judgment derives from the moving power of the desiderata, it would be bizarre of you to let those desiderata disappear completely from the picture once the judgment is formed and to rely on being moved from that moment onward only by a desire to do whatever you take to be morally desirable or obligatory.

To rely for moral motivation on the desire to do what is morally obligatory or desirable—or at least to rely only on that desire—would involve a sort of fetishism about obligation or desirability (Smith 1994). As the first lesson for psychology was that we should be internalists about the connection between moral judgment and motivation, the second is that we should not be fetishists of this kind, linking moral motivation exclusively or primarily with a desire to do whatever has the best claim to win in moral argument.

Thus, to focus on obligation, the point in ethics is not to work out what is obligatory, perhaps in detachment from the desiderata that make it so, and then to desire and pursue the obligatory as such. It is, rather, to be sensitive to the relevant desiderata—say, to the kindness or fairness that make the option desirable—and to let those properties move you, as they should, at the same time that they lead you to form a judgment of obligation. You should not be fixated as such on doing what you judge to be obligatory—of course, this may figure as one of your concerns—but should remain sensitive to suitable desiderata and should be led on the basis of that sensitivity to do what those desiderata identify as obligatory.

Reason-responsiveness

The third lesson taught by the narrative developed here connects with the first two but is of more general significance for moral psychology. Let it be granted that the focus in moral psychology should be on the desiderata—the desirability-makers—that are selected as relevant under practices of avowal and pledging: practices that give you the regulative ideal of a suitably bespoken, suitably beholden self. Those desiderata will serve in at least two distinct roles: first, to provide guides for individuals in their behavior and, second, as we may assume, to support those standards that get established as shared, routine norms; these will count as moral norms if conformity is generally morally desirable. Those two roles give us a distinction between two levels, as we might put it, of moral performance.

In their role as guides, the desiderata will present us with reasons for why we should take one or another option in a choice, inviting us to be responsive to those reasons. In their role as supports for suitable moral norms they will present reasons for why such norms should have a claim upon us. Thus, we may assume that reasons of honesty and fidelity, respect and friendship support norms of truth-telling and promise-keeping, respectful behavior and meeting the demands of our friends. But it turns out that in requiring that we conform to such norms, they will require less than they require in guiding us: that is, in serving as reasons to which we are responsive.

Taking the desiderata or reasons as guides, and responding as they require, we will deliver the treatment they support on a robust basis. If we deliver the treatment actually on the ground that it is required by the relevant desideratum, it will follow that we would deliver it in any variation on the actual circumstances where that reason remains in place and there is nothing to deflect its influence: no other desideratum to eclipse its claims, manifestly trumping them, and no excusing or exempting factor that would block our capacity to act on those claims. In other words, taking a desideratum as a guide will amount to delivering the behavior it supports, not just in the actual circumstances, but robustly over variations on those circumstances where the desideratum remains present and its effect is not deflected. These variations will include scenarios, for example, where various distractions or disturbances threaten to put us off our stride.

If our only concern is to satisfy a supported norm, however, all that this strictly requires of us in action—all that it requires if we are not to count as offenders—is that we actually conform to that norm: we actually act as its requirements dictate. Conforming to the standard involved may only involve conforming to it contingently, not robustly. It does not require that we conform both in the actual circumstances and in any variations on those circumstances where the reason for conformity—the relevant desideratum—remains in place and is not deflected by an eclipsing consideration or an excusing or exempting factor.

Of course, we might conform to the norm on a suitably robust basis, and that is what we will do insofar as we are pledged, at least virtually, to conform to it. But we will keep on the right side of the norm—we will not expose ourselves to censure—so long as we attain at least the lower level of performance. We will act in accord with the requirement of the supportive reason in the actual circumstances—the norm spells out that requirement—but we may not act that way because that is what the reason requires: we may do so out of purely self-interested motives.

The difference between the two levels of moral performance, contingent and robust, marks a very salient divide in the case of at least some desiderata, including those associated with truth-telling and promise-keeping, respect and friendship. If you conform to one of those norms in dealing with me, you will give me the good of telling the truth, keeping a promise, showing the restraint associated with respect, or offering the favor that friendship supports. But, for all that conformity requires, you may act in that way out of opportunistic self-interest. And in that case you will not give me the intuitively richer good of your honesty or fidelity, your respect or friendship.

Thus, I do not enjoy the richer good, just because it happens to be in your interest to treat me favorably, restrain yourself respectfully, keep a promise or tell me the truth. While I might certainly be glad of the fact that I receive the sort of treatment from you that is required by the norm, it would be absurd to say that I enjoy the rich good of your friendship or respect, your fidelity or honesty. Those goods are robustly demanding and require you to act out of responsiveness to the relevant reason—to act, as we say, out of the disposition of friendship or respect, fidelity or honesty—not just to meet the requirement of the reason in the actual circumstances: specifically, not just to conform behaviorally to the corresponding norm.[15]

The two levels of moral performance that we have been distinguishing correspond to two sorts of beneficial effects that your actions may have. On the side, their contingent effects in the actual circumstances: the truth-telling or promise-keeping, the restraint or the favor that you display. On the other, the robust effects whereby you give me the benefit of your honesty or fidelity, your respect or friendship. The first set of effects depends only on the nature and consequences of what you do, considered independently of the disposition at its origin; for all that they require, the disposition may be just personal opportunism. The second set of effects materializes, however, not only in virtue of what you do, but also in virtue of the disposition out of which you act: in virtue of your responsiveness to the relevant reason; those effects, in a phrase, are disposition-dependent.[16]

According to this argument, then, it is important for the moral effects of your action, and hence its moral quality, that you act out of

15. For a full discussion of the issues that arise here, and for a contrast in this regard between what is required for doing good and what suffices to do evil, see Pettit (2015a, c; 2018a, c). The claim about the disposition-dependence of effects like those associated with honestly, fidelity and the like is generalized in Pettit (2015c; 2018a) to a claim about the disposition-sensitivity of all of the benefits your actions may bring about; see too Pettit (2018c). The idea is that for any benefit you produce, the more robustly you produce it—the more you act out of a disposition to produce that benefit—the more good you do.

16. As (Pettit 2015c) argues at length, there is a tendency in contemporary moral philosophy to focus on the disposition-independent effects of behavior only; this derives from a focus on the permissibility of actions under suitable rules, and not on the totality of their good effects. Even virtue theorists, who stress the importance of our character as agents, do not generally relate this character—our dispositions—to the valuable effects of our actions.

appropriate dispositions; only by doing that can you hope to realize the rich goods illustrated. Of course, dispositions like honesty and fidelity, respect and friendship, may often come into conflict, with the rival options in a choice competing in the desiderata they display; considerations of friendship may prompt you to take one option, considerations of fidelity to take another, and so on. And in that case, your dispositions cannot spontaneously issue in choice. You will need to take thought over what is best supported overall: that is, what there is most reason to do in light of your judgment of moral desirability or obligation.

This observation raises a question as to whether you would not do better to make that sort of overall judgment in every case—or to follow a rule dictating the sort of judgment appropriate in any case—and to let your virtuous dispositions, whether of attachment or honesty or respect, come into play only in wake of that judgment. While much contemporary philosophy appears to support such a line, assuming that moral judgment should always have a guiding role in action, there is reason to think that it is misconceived (Pettit 2015c, a, 2018).

The line proposed would be perfectly sensible if the virtuous dispositions envisaged were required merely to play the post-judgmental role of facilitating you in doing what you take in judgment to be the morally desirable or obligatory choice: to assist you in acting as a friend, where friendship scores over rival considerations; to support you in acting respectfully, where it is respect that wins out in judgment; and so on. But that approach misses out on the fact that in relevant cases the dispositions play a much richer role. It is only if a suitable disposition is at the origin of the favor you give me, or the respectful way you behave—that disposition, and not the judgment that, in the circumstances, that is the morally desirable or obligatory thing to do—that I enjoy your friendship or respect. The dispositions must move you to action if you are to confer such benefits on me, not just serve to oil a movement that is independently sourced.

We have already noted that acting out of personal opportunism in telling the truth, keeping a promise, acting respectfully or giving you favor, is inconsistent with giving me the benefit of your honesty or fidelity, your respect or friendship. The point here is that acting on the basis that overall the desiderata relevant to moral desirability support such a form of treatment is also inconsistent with giving me the sorts of rich goods listed. I do not enjoy your friendship unless you favor me for my own sake, not for the sake of meeting your obligations. I do not enjoy your respect unless my being an autonomous agent is enough on its own to prompt your respectful restraint. And I do not enjoy your fidelity or honesty if you need to think about all the moral pro's and con's before deciding whether to keep a promise or tell me the truth.

The point here connects with the discussion of fetishism. If you were to pledge conformity to whatever you judge to be morally desirable or obligatory, then when that judgment supports giving the sort of favor associated with friendship, or treating me respectfully, or telling me the truth, it might seem that you are going to give me friendship, respect or honesty. But strictly, that is not the case. For your reason for acting in that way is not a reason of friendship or respect or honesty. It consists in the desideratum of doing whatever is overall desirable or obligatory.[17]

This observation raises a question about the respective roles of disposition and judgment in the moral life. On the one hand, it seems that you have to act spontaneously out of certain dispositions in order to generate the disposition-dependent goods associated with them. On the other, it appears that, because of potential conflicts between any such good and other goods, you have to be open to suspending spontaneity and making a considered judgment on what is morally supported in

---

17. Friendship or respect or honesty only require you to act on the corresponding reason when that consideration is not eclipsed by others, as we put it. But that does not mean that it requires you to act in that way only when it is morally desirable to do so. We can imagine a situation where certain considerations argue against acting as friendship or respect or honesty requires but do not eclipse reasons of friendship or respect or honesty; none trumps a relevant reason so saliently that no one could take you to fail the demands of friendship or respect or honesty by letting it inhibit your response. In that sort of situation, it might not be morally desirable for you to act as friendship or respect or honesty requires, if other things were equal. But other things will not be equal insofar as it is not morally desirable for you to take the steps that would be required to ensure that you act in the morally desirable way. On these issues see Pettit (2015c).

aggregate. And so, it appears, a dilemma looms. If you act spontaneously on the dispositions, you may end up acting in a way that the desiderata do not support overall. If you suspend spontaneity in favor of being guided by your overall moral judgment, you may end up losing out on disposition-dependent goods altogether.

A plausible solution to this problem involves two elements (Pettit 2015c). The first is to give a default privilege to dispositions like friendship and respect, fidelity and honesty, being poised to act as they prompt. And the second is to be ready at the same time to suspend this response and resort to considered judgment whenever the red lights go on or the alarm signals sound: that is, whenever situations cue you to think that there are rival desiderata in play and that reflection is required.

Such a cue can be provided in any of a variety of ways. For example, by something unusual in the prompt, as when a friend asks you to help move a body, not an apartment (Cocking and Kennett 2000). Or by something novel about the situation, as when you have reason to think you may be succumbing to undue pressure from others. Or by a tension in your own dispositions, as when friendship pulls you one way, honesty another.

This solution proposed should not be disturbing, for it supports a line in moral psychology that empirical research tells us is a common pattern anyhow. What the proposal suggests is that in seeking to act morally, you should allow spontaneity to rule by default and only introduce the inhibiting effects of judgment when there is independent reason to think that is necessary. And this, in more familiar terminology, is to suggest that you should let spontaneous system-one thinking operate in the absence of special cues—red lights or alarm signals—and to resort to system-two reflection only under the impact of such prompts (Kahneman 2011).

7.6 Moral theory

On the approach supported by our narrative, there are two fundamental issues to determine in any moral choice: one, what is the morally most desirable option; and two, what is the obligatory option. The obligatory option, in our use of the term, is the morally most desirable alternative among options for which you or anyone else might reasonably be held responsible; that is, the morally most desirable among 'erogatory' as distinct from supererogatory options. In this final section of the chapter, we may set aside the issue of obligation, as doing so will keep things simpler, and take moral theory to focus on moral desirability alone.

The central question in moral theory or normative ethics is how to identify the ways in which reasons—in our terms, suitably filtered, suitably aggregated desiderata—combine to identify one or another option as the morally desirable one to choose. That question naturally breaks down into two issues. One bears on what sorts of reasons should be allowed as inputs into the process of determining the desirable option. And the other bears on the nature of the aggregating process that should serve in any choice, whether between personal actions or institutional arrangements, to identify the desirable option on the basis of those inputs.

Those issues are at the heart of some of the main debates in moral theory. In this final section, we first look at how the account of morality supported by the narrative explains why there should be a divide between consequentialists and non-consequentialists, without offering conclusive support for either group. And then we look at two different perspectives on moral theory that the account also leaves open, whatever position we adopt in that debate. This last divide marks off responsibility-first from desirability-first theorists, to introduce names for the two sides, where those on either side may embrace or reject consequentialism.[18]

It is important that the account of ethics supported by the narrative explains why people should divide in these ways, without forcing us in any particular direction. That is what a theory about the role and nature of morality should be expected to do. The account seeks to make sense of the ethical toolkit, and it would be surprising if it played the additional

---

18. While the two divides are strictly independent, as this suggests, those identified later as responsibility-first theorists do generally tend to be non-consequentialists.

role of explaining how we should use that toolkit in moral theory. We should not expect it to be able at the same time to guide us adequately in moral theory. We should expect that the pursuit of normative ethics would require reflection on richer sources of evidence about what properties matter naturally to us as human beings and are fit to assume the role of prescriptive reasons for action.

The consequentialist debate

Traditionally understood, consequentialism is a genus illustrated canonically by one particular species, utilitarianism: that is, the doctrine that the morally desirable option in any choice is that which promotes overall happiness, however that is interpreted. Understood in this way, consequentialism endorses the view that the considerations that serve as ultimate inputs to the process of moral argument should be agent-neutral. Like the happiness of all, they should not privilege the concerns of the person for whom they serve as reasons—they should not constitute agent-relative reasons—as in reflecting the needs or the duties of me or mine when I am in the relevant position. And understood in this way, the approach is distinguished also by its understanding of the process in which the morally desirable, or at least the morally obligatory, is determined. It takes the process to be promotional.[19] As utilitarianism argues for the promotion of happiness overall, so it argues for the promotion of agent-neutral value, where this is taken to involve universal good, not the good of a particular entity. The idea of promotion may be variously interpreted, but that complication need not concern us here.[20]

Consequentialism, in the emerging account, is a mixture of neutralism about the relevant inputs and promotionalism about the aggregation of

19. I put aside satisficing consequentialism, as it often called; for a debate on its merits, see Slote and Pettit (1984).

20. For the record, I think that we should take the idea in an expectational sense, so that for an agent to promote any form of value is to maximize its subjectively expected realization, perhaps after some correction for the effect of manifest evidential failures on the subject's expectation.

those inputs in the exercise that determines the most desirable alternative. But the neutralism is enough to characterize the doctrine. For it turns out that it entails promotionalism. Try to hold on to neutralism while rejecting promotionalism, and you will end up having to reject the neutralism, too. Thus, we can identify consequentialism with neutralism alone.[21]

To try to hold onto neutralism while rejecting promotionalism would be to claim that, in at least some cases, the desirable option for an agent to take or support bears a non-promotional connection with agent-neutral good: plausibly, it instantiates or honors that good—or bears witness to it—over time (Pettit 1991a). For example, it might be desirable by this account to instantiate non-violence yourself, so far as this proves possible, even if doing so means that non-violence overall is not thereby promoted: even if it means that you do not oppose the violent and consequently that aggregate violence increases. But such a theory is extensionally equivalent to a theory that argues for the promotion of value in a sense in which it may be agent-relative. It would recommend, in our example, that an agent should promote his or her instantiation of non-violence—as distinct from the overall instantiation of non-violence—over time (Pettit 1997a).

Neutralism, then, is the core element that matters in consequentialist theory. And this lesson is underlined by the fact that all non-neutralist—and so non-consequentialist—theories can be cast as joining consequentialist theories in endorsing promotionalism. Where consequentialists argue that the most desirable alternative in any choice is always to promote only agent-neutral value, non-consequentialists can be taken to maintain that, in at least some cases, the desirable option

21. Of course, it is possible to link the term "consequentialism" with promotionalism rather than neutralism, and that has become a fashion in the wake of Dreier (1993). See, for example, Portmore (2014). This linkage means that consequentialism is no longer exemplified by classical utilitarianism. And it means that there are grounds for thinking that all theories can be "consequentialized" (Dreier 1993; Pettit 1997a); but for some complications, see Brown (2011) and Dietrich and List (2017, s6.1). That is why I prefer to link consequentialism—big "C" or classical consequentialism—with neutralism.

may be to promote a mix of agent-relative and agent-neutral value; at the extreme limit, perhaps, a mix in which agent-neutral value goes to zero. They differ, not on the question of whether to promote, but on the question of what to promote: whether agent-neutral value only, as consequentialists hold, or a mix that includes agent-relative value, as non-consequentialists maintain.[22]

The issue in the consequentialist debate

The question addressed by the two approaches turns on the sorts of desiderata or reasons that ought to be taken into account in the determination of the most desirable option in any set of possible actions or arrangements. The reconstruction defended argued that a suitably filtered subset of all the desiderata that might be mobilized in any choice are the candidates for consideration in determining what is multilaterally desirable. But it left open the question as to precisely which sorts of desiderata ought to be given weight.

According to consequentialism, only the desiderata mobilized as reasons for ascribing common desirability—only the agent-neutral desiderata relevant in the open or unbounded co-avowal of desire—serve to determine what is morally desirable and obligatory. According to non-consequentialism, this is an unnecessary restriction and the desiderata mobilized as reasons for individual and joint desirability, which can certainly be agent-relative, may sometimes serve in the determination of what is morally desirable and obligatory.

Our reconstruction of morality not only identifies the basis on which consequentialists and non-consequentialists divide; it also helps to explain why people are attracted to different sides. Let it be assumed that

22. This appealing account breaks down if non-consequentialists are allowed to treat the distinction between a person over time—between you-at-this-time, you-at-that-time, and so on—as enjoying the same significance as the distinction between you and other persons; the fact that you-now seek to instantiate non-violence cannot be represented as your seeking to maximize your instantiation of non-violence over time. But this complication may be set aside, since non-consequentialists generally reject the time-relativity envisaged.

the main point of arguing that a certain action or arrangement is morally desirable, or at least obligatory, is to justify where you stand on the choice to others: in particular, to an open set of others, not just to those in a particular group. The assumption makes good sense on the narrative about Erewhon, where we each seek to present ourselves as reliable interlocutors, responsive to desiderata mobilized in different social practices, and disposed to seek a mutually appealing resolution of conflicting demands.[23]

Given this assumption, consequentialists and non-consequentialists can be seen as offering different accounts, each with its own appeal, of what is required for interpersonal justification.

Consequentialists assume that you can justify your preferences to others—say, over your own actions or over communal arrangements—only on the basis that they are supported by common ground between you: that is, by the ground associated with desiderata derived from purportedly open, co-avowable desires; in a word, by agent-neutral desiderata. This restriction on the basis of justification need not make it impossible, of course, to justify favoring your family, for example, or prioritizing your own keeping of a promise. One of the many ways in which such a justification might be provided is by appeal to the fact, invoked in the last section, that when you act out of love for your family or fidelity to a promisee, that action brings about a special form of disposition-dependent and agent-neutral good.

But, however permissively the consequentialist restriction is construed, non-consequentialists reject it. They hold that your preferences may be justified to others on a basis other than that provided by agent-neutral desiderata: specifically, on the basis of agent-relative desiderata that are neither rancorous nor rivalrous. These are desiderata that you would be happy for others to act on in their own case; they are concordant, agent-relative attractors that do not put you in inevitable

---

23. It fits well with the view, advanced in particular by T.M. Scanlon (1998), that a prominent motive for morality is to be able to put yourself in the right with others—not just particular others but others in general—answering any complaints that they may have against you.

competition with others. Thus, an option you take may be justified by ground appealing only to you—say, that an alternative will foster your family's welfare or that it will enable you to keep a promise—so long as that ground is concordant with ground available by your lights to others: that is, so long as you would be happy for any other in a similar situation to choose the corresponding option on the ground that it would foster their family's welfare or enable them to keep a promise.

Where consequentialism holds that there is no interpersonal justification without common ground that is identical in content between different parties, non-consequentialism maintains that interpersonal justification may also be achieved on concordant ground that is identical only in its character. That ground may have a different content as between you and me, but it points in your case to something that appeals to you, in my case to something that appeals to me. It is isomorphic between us in the sense that it engages the same sorts of considerations in each case and that we are each content for the other to act on that ground, whenever it is relevant (Pettit 1997a).[24]

On this account of the two doctrines, the narrative presented here leaves the debate between consequentialism and non-consequentialism open. True, we argued in chapter 5 that while the agent-neutral desiderata invoked in unbounded co-avowal have a strong claim to be treated as relevant in determining the multilaterally desirable, so do those agent-relative desiderata that are concordant or non-competitive. But that argument was designed to indicate only the plausibility of recognizing relevant desiderata over and beyond the agent-neutral ones. It was not meant to establish a case against the consequentialist restriction.

Responsibility first or desirability first?

As our account of the role and nature of morality explains why there should be a divide over the consequentialism issue, so it explains why there should also be a division in moral theory between those who take

---

24. As mentioned earlier, agent-neutral desiderata and concordant, agent-relative desiderata have the common feature of being universalizable (Hare 1952, 1981).

a responsibility-first approach and those who prefer a desirability-first alternative. This division cuts across the divide between consequentialism and non-consequentialism and, as in the case of that divide, the narrative explains how it is likely to arise without committing us to one or the other side. The division of perspectives is not regularly marked in moral philosophy, let alone given a name, but it constitutes just as important a fault line in the terrain as the more commonly discussed divide.

Let it be assumed, as our narrative would explain, that we operate with concepts of desirability, in particular moral desirability, and associated practices. And let it equally be assumed, on the same basis, that we operate with concepts of responsibility, in particular moral responsibility—that is, responsibility to suitable moral standards—and associated practices.

It may seem natural to think that in working out a normative ethics, we should begin with the identification of morally desirable standards and then identify those standards to which we can hold one another, and indeed ourselves, responsible: that is, the standards that it is within our capacity to follow. This, in effect, is the approach suggested in our narrative about Erewhon. But an alternative approach, consistent with that narrative, would reverse this order. It would begin with the practice of holding one another responsible and argue that if we are to be faithful to this practice, we must recognize various desiderata as robustly attractive, and recognize them in particular as attractive in the multilateral manner of moral desiderata.

The responsibility-first approach

This responsibility-first approach would suggest that in constructing a normative ethics, a good strategy is to build it in the first place around the desiderata that are endogenous to the responsibility practice. To prioritize these would be to take the standards of multilateral desirability associated with abiding by the practice—standards that are bound to be shared and routine—and to construct an ethics around the demand that we should treat one another in accord with those endogenous standards.

At least we should do this in the first place, for the approach would also allow that there may be other suitable attractors, and other moral standards, that are exogenous to the responsibility practice but also impose demands on us.

Assuming that every adult, able-minded human being is fit to be held responsible in various domains, the responsibility-first approach assumes that it is multilaterally or morally desirable that every such subject should be treated in accord with the standards endogenous to the practice. We saw earlier that wherever certain shared, routine standards apply, it is possible to speak of the rights that participants enjoy— and the corresponding duties that they incur—under those standards or rules. The responsibility-first approach naturally focuses in the first place, then, on people's rights against others, and their duties toward others, that the standards support.[25]

What are the rights, and correlative duties, that the responsibility-first approach would be likely to identify? In particular, what are the rights that go with being participants in the practice of holding one another responsible for purported misdeeds? What are the rights that distinguish us as mutually engaged moral subjects?

On the one side, we must each have the right under the responsibility practice to hold one another responsible for what we do or do not do in certain domains—this, under culturally variable standards of desirability, multilateral or otherwise—and, by implication, the right to be taken seriously in this exercise. In that sense, we must each have the status, acknowledged as a matter of common awareness, of being someone to whom others are answerable.

On the other, we must each have the right to dispute in various ways the charges that others bring against us, whether by challenging the

---

25. It may treat those rights or duties—and in effect, treat the agent-relative good of your granting those rights or abiding by those duties—as fundamental, thereby embracing non-consequentialism. Or it may hold, in a consequentialist spirit, that the ground for such fidelity to rights and duties derives from the agent-neutral desirability of the practice that grounds them.

presupposed standards of desirability, by questioning the claim that we had actually breached the standards, or by invoking a purportedly relevant ground of excuse or exemption. In that sense, we must each have the status, again acknowledged as a matter of common awareness, of being someone entitled to engage as conversable interlocutors in any debates over matters of answerability.

There are different ways in which this responsibility-first approach might be implemented, each invoking a somewhat different basis for identifying the rights that we have as participants in the practice of responsibility. Most of the ways in which it is implemented have a non-consequentialist cast, although this is not essential to the approach.

One version of the approach holds that the rights of participants—and, by implication, their duties—all derive from a fundamental right on the part of each that others should justify to them, as to equals, the treatment they impose (Forst 2012). Another holds that the rights and duties under the practice are just those reciprocal rights and duties that are required by any form of discourse in which each seeks an overt form of influence over others that they would be happy for others to seek over them (Benhabib 1990; Habermas 1990). Yet another maintains that the rights established ought to reflect the authority we grant others, as a matter encoded in our reactive emotions and practices, to hold us to account for how we deal with them (Darwall 2006).

The responsibility-first approach naturally distinguishes between two branches of normative ethics, one of which might be described as constitutional ethics, the other as practical ethics. Constitutional ethics would bear on the standards that ought to be established among people, if they are to assume their place within the practice of mutual responsibility. Its subject matter is the endogenous standards of the practice that ought to be established among people, giving them suitable rights against one another and suitable duties toward one another.

Practical ethics would bear, by contrast, on the exogenous standards of multilateral desirability that are independently plausible. These standards might involve the proper treatment of those who are not adult or able-minded, the proper treatment of other species, the proper treatment of corporate bodies, the treatment of adult, able-minded individuals in ways that are not endogenously constrained, and the treatment that we owe ourselves.

For responsibility-first thinkers, standards endogenous to the responsibility practice have a natural priority over exogenous requirements. Let there be mistakes about endogenous matters, so the idea goes, and the very enterprise of pursuing ethical debate, and imposing ethical judgments, may be compromised; it may give undue influence to some or it may encourage an inadequate level of reflection. Let there be mistakes about exogenous standards or judgments only, and that enterprise will remain capable of putting these right in time.

The desirability-first alternative

With these points in place, it should be clear what those thinkers who reject the responsibility-first approach are likely to think. They may hold that questions about how to treat participants in the practice of mutual responsibility are particularly important. But unlike their opponents, they will not be committed methodologically to taking that view. On their approach, there are no prior constraints on what to conclude when we inquire about the most desirable action to take in any situation or the most desirable arrangement to establish in a society.[26]

Thus, if adult, able-minded human beings are to be credited with more important claims than other members of the species, or than the members of other species, then that has to be established in one and

---

26. The divide in ethics is similar to a divide in the theory of justice between what by analogy we might describe as a democracy-first and a fairness-first approach. By analogy with a responsibility-first ethics, a democracy-first theory would prioritize those demands of justice that must be fulfilled, arguably, by any society in which people share equally in control of their state. Habermas (1995) broadly defends such a theory, Rawls (1995) opposes it. For a defense of the democracy-first view—an argument, as it is put, for the priority of political justice over social justice—see Pettit (2015b).

the same process of moral argument. There is nothing about the way that the books are kept that gives those agents a natural, constitutional priority. A prominent example of a desirability-first approach is the sort of utilitarian theory that would argue for the supreme importance of happiness, and treat the relative importance of human beings and other animals in the promotion of happiness as an open question (Singer 1981). But the approach might also assume other forms, including the form of a non-consequentialist theory that ascribes rights to animals, casting it as agent-relatively desirable that we should each honor those rights.

As the consequentialism divide has dominated much recent moral theory, so the same is true of the division we have just been discussing. It is easy to confuse the divide with the consequentialist one, taking the responsibility-first approach to be essentially non-consequentialist. This is because it is tempting to treat the rights associated with endogenous standards of responsibility—and, in effect, treat the agent-relative good of your granting those rights—as fundamental or natural rights, and therefore as constraints that are not grounded in agent-neutral desirability.

It is important to see that this temptation is resistible. By the account presented here, the rights we ascribe are grounded in sets of shared, routine standards or rules, or in plausible extensions of those rules, as your right to move the bishop on the diagonal is grounded in the rules of chess. The rights we have against one another under the responsibility practices are grounded in the shared and routine standards endogenous to that practice. And so, it remains an open question whether or not we should treat them in a consequentialist spirit as having a hold on us only because of the agent-neutral desirability of that practice. Consistently with putting responsibility first, we might think that this is justified by agent-neutral rather than agent-relative good.

The point of introducing this division between moral theories into the discussion, like the point of introducing the division between consequentialist and non-consequentialist theories, is not to resolve the issue between them. Rather, it is to emphasize that without resolving the issue, the theory of the role and nature of morality supported by our narrative serves the useful function of explaining why the debate should take place. That theory is meant to explain why our species should have come to think in ethical terms—why it should have evolved a basic ethical toolkit—and it is a merit in the theory that it makes sense of why we differ about the use of that toolkit in the construction of a normative ethics.

Conclusion: The Claims in Summary

The introduction to this book gives an account of its three guiding theses. First, the methodological claim that a good way of making sense of morality may be to provide an account of how it could have emerged, similar to the familiar, counterfactual genealogy of the origin of money that economists invoke to explain what money is. Second, the anthropological thesis that habits of mutual reliance, essential to human survival, are likely to make it more or less inevitable that creatures like us, possessed of natural language, should have developed practices of avowal and pledging and thereby put themselves within reach of ethical space. And third, the metaphysical thesis that if it is practices of this kind that lie at the origin of ethics, then being moral is tied up very closely with performing as a person—with being an agent capable of speaking for himself or herself—and that a reason to be moral is that that is the only way of achieving integration or integrity as a person.

Rather than rehearse those themes again, it may be more useful to provide a rough summary of the main claims that we have maintained across the seven chapters. The summary is designed to provide a reminder of the ground covered, of course, often skipping over various aspects of the terrain. It is not meant to offer a free-standing alternative to the lengthy argument pursued in the foregoing pages.

Chapter 1 Reconstructing Morality

The focus in this book is on ethical or moral concepts and, in particular, concepts in the family of the desirable and the responsible. The aim is to make sense of how those concepts, despite their being prescriptive, could

300 • The Birth of Ethics

have application in a naturalistic world that answers to the scientific, non-normative image. And the method is to resort to a style of analysis that we characterized as reconstructive rather than reductive.

The introduction argued that ethics requires not just the appearance of altruistic patterns of motivation and behavior but also the generation of those patterns by intuitively moral or ethical ways of thinking. Focusing in particular on the ethical concepts of desirability and responsibility, as the whole book does, it argued that these are distinctively prescriptive notions: this, in the sense that when we assume that you are fit to be held responsible for certain options in a given choice, we prescribe that which we take to be the most desirable of those alternatives. Moral desirability is distinct from a range of other prescriptive concepts, such as those of prudential or legal desirability, insofar as it is unrestricted in the range of interests reflected and in the standpoint adopted, and serves to provide a relatively authoritative resolution of differences.

The first section of the chapter looked at the precise requirements of the sort of naturalism that the book aims at vindicating. It distinguishes the naturalism sought from naturalistic accounts of a debunking kind, such as expressivism and error theory; it seeks a naturalistic realism about ethics. The idea is to vindicate a realism about ethical judgments that makes them out to be generally truth-conditional and capable in many cases of being true.

But where standard approaches to that goal seek to provide a reductive analysis of ethical concepts, the method adopted here is reconstructive. This begins from a naturalistic narrative in which creatures like us might have gotten to introduce concepts like our ethical concepts, using them under similar prompts to serve similar purposes. And then it argues on the basis of that narrative, first, that their concepts correspond to our more familiar concepts and, second, that those concepts—and, given that correspondence, our concepts—must predicate broadly naturalistic properties.

The reconstructive project aims at satisfying the same sorts of aims as the reductive. But it has two advantages, one general, the other specific to domains like the ethical. As a general matter, a reconstructive analysis of concepts is methodologically more accessible than a reductive one; it does not require us to provide naturalistic paraphrases of problematic concepts, only a naturalistic account of how people might have come to have a referring use for similar concepts. And it has a particular explanatory value in the case of concepts, like those of moral desirability and responsibility, that co-exist and presumably co-evolve with certain practices; it is more readily adapted to making sense of concepts of those kinds.

The second section of the chapter looked in greater detail at the project of reconstruction, casting it as a story about how the members of a pre-ethical society called Erewhon—an anagram of "nowhere"— might spontaneously develop moral practices and concepts. We looked at two conditions for the success of the sort of reconstruction sought, one associated with the starting point, the other with the process of development, and we then set up a contrast between the emergence story attempted and other projects.

In the starting point of the narrative, the residents of Erewhon must have the characteristics we would expect in conspecifics, even conspecifics who lack ethical and prescriptive concepts. We stipulated in particular that they have intentional and linguistic competence, but that they use the language only for the basic purposes of conveying and sharing information about the common environment they inhabit. We assumed that such competence makes naturalistic sense and argued that, while it may require the capacity to conduct theoretical reasoning—say, reasoning in accordance with modus ponens—such reasoning does not necessarily presuppose access to a concept of epistemological desirability: a notion of what it is desirable to believe in light of the evidence.

Turning from starting point to process, we noted that the narrative about Erewhon will only be persuasive insofar as it meets the following conditions. First, it explains the cascade of transitions that eventuate in ethical conceptualization and regulation without postulating any naturalistic miracle; second, it explains the cascade without positing a lucky fluke; and third, it does so without being less parsimonious than any naturalistic alternative—without introducing an idle wheel.

The second, lucky-fluke condition is the most demanding of these. In order to avoid such flukes, the narrative about Erewhon must avoid rigging the books unrealistically in favor of the emergence of ethics. And that constrains, first, the psychological profile that it ascribes to the members of Erewhon and, second, the account it offers of their social circumstances. The psychological profile and the social account must be realistic or, if they depart from realism, they must do so in a way that makes the development of moral concepts and practices less likely rather than more likely.

The psychological profile that the narrative ascribes is rational, on the one side, and self-regarding, on the other. The assumption of rationality is quite realistic, since it is limited in range to reciprocation and has routinely confirmed benefits. And while the self-regarding aspect may not be realistic, given the extent to which human beings are spontaneously cooperative, it represents a worse-case scenario that makes the emergence of ethics more rather than less surprising.

Turning to social circumstances from psychology, the narrative assumes that Erewhon is isolated from other societies and that it does not suffer from excessive inequalities of power. This is because it would be hard to predict how things might transpire, in the absence of these assumptions.

The assumption of isolation is reasonably realistic—many human societies must have existed in relative isolation—and does not rig the books objectionably. And while the assumption of relative equality of power may seem to favor ethical development, there are two things to say in its support. The first is that it is realistic insofar as it fits with the fact that human beings have lived with great inequality only since the agricultural revolution. And the second is that even a highly unequal society is likely to contain an elite of relatively equal members, so that the narrative can serve the required purposes as a story about how ethical concepts and practices might emerge within the elite membership and be available for extension to all.

The assumption of isolation does raise the question as to whether the project pursued here can have anything to say on the extent and significance of cross-cultural variation in moral views, particularly its significance for realism about values. While the narrative does not directly support a line on this issue, it is consistent with admitting substantial variation across cultures but supporting at the same time a naturalistic realism about ethics.

Turning to the contrast with other projects, the narrative about Erewhon is designed to provide an upshot that differs markedly from that which game theory, contractual theory, and a sort of prudential theory would provide. Game theory would explain the emergence of broadly altruistic behavior but would not explain the role of moral concepts. Contractual theory would explain the reliance of Erewhonians on morality but, in the form considered here, only by presupposing that they had a concept of morality prior to the contract and knew what they were agreeing to. And prudential theory would fail in the same way, postulating a process of prudential reasoning that would lead people to conclude that morality is the best policy.

The third section of the chapter aimed to illustrate reconstructive analysis in practice, both outside philosophy and within. Outside philosophy, a very revealing example is provided by the standard economic analysis of money. This proceeds by asking us to imagine a purely barter society, to recognize the problems that people would face in seeking exchanges with one another, and to see that a natural solution to that problem would emerge as people came to think that one or another commodity—say, gold or cattle or cigarettes—was attractive to most.

Under this solution, the selected commodity, and IOUs in that commodity, would enable people to use it in exchange for just about anything, to invoke it in measuring the exchange value or price of different things, and to accumulate purchasing power by building up their holdings. The story would explain in individualistically unproblematic terms why participants would come to have the concept of something that plays that role. Thus, it would give us ground for recognizing that their concept is expressively equivalent to our concept of money, being guided by similar prompts and serving similar purposes. And, equally, it would provide us with a base for arguing that as their concept ascribes an individualistically intelligible property, so the same is plausibly true of ours.

The aim in this book is to do for ethics what that sort of narrative does for money. But the project undertaken has many philosophical analogues, too, as the chapter illustrated with cases drawn from different areas of contemporary philosophical inquiry. Likewise, it employs a methodology akin to the methodology of creature-construction that is often invoked in contemporary work.

A creature-constructive analysis of joint intention and action, to take one example of the approach, would make that phenomenon individualistically intelligible by showing how people might display such a pattern on the basis of intending to play their respective parts, as a matter of common awareness, in a more or less salient plan. Without assuming that this is exactly what happens in ordinary life, it suggests that the concept of joint intention and action that people would develop in the model narrative is expressively equivalent to the concept we employ and that as the model concept predicates an individualistically intelligible property, so our concept may be taken to do the same.

The methodology employed here has the same rationale as creature-construction but differs in the strategy adopted. It begins from a process imagined among agents in the past, not from one enacted in the present. And it postulates adjustments that emerge without planning or foresight rather than developments that the agents intentionally introduce. The core aim, however, is the same in each case: to reveal the nature of the properties ascribed in relatively problematic concepts by looking at an unproblematic explanation of how those concepts might have arisen in the first place, targeting corresponding properties.

Chapter 2 Ground Zero

This chapter looked in the first part at what has to be present in the Erewhon with which the narrative begins, in the second part at what is saliently absent there, and in the third at reasons to think that that absence might be reparable.

The argument of the first part was that, assuming we have natural language at our disposal, we inhabitants of Erewhon are bound to exchange information with one another about our surroundings, and that in pursuing this goal we will establish a social norm of truth-telling. That norm will materialize just to the extent that four conditions are satisfied. First, almost everyone tells the truth. Second, almost everyone expects to be reputationally benefitted as a result of telling the truth, and reputationally damaged as a result of failing to do so. Third, this expectation helps to explain why we each tend to tell the truth. And fourth, all of that is a matter of common awareness; we are each aware that the conditions are satisfied, each aware that each is aware of this, and so on. Other social norms like those against violence or fraud are likely to materialize on a similar basis.

The achievement of universal truth-telling in the absence of the common awareness condition would not be conscious or intentional. It would constitute a pre-social regularity that emerges, as by an invisible hand, from the self-seeking adjustments we individually make toward one another in our interactions; while we might be said to regulate or police one another into conformity at this stage, we would do so in a blind fashion.

With common awareness in the picture, however, the truth-telling norm will be able to serve a proper, social role in indicating to each of us that we must abide by it if we are to gain full acceptance in the community. Thus, we can each see it as a rule to guide us: a pattern that we must satisfy, on pain of social ostracism. And in the same way, we can see norms like those against violence or fraud as rules of the same social sort. The norms can gain this novel appeal, even while the main motor of conformity remains reputational in character.

The second part of the chapter argued that there are two salient sorts of absences in the mutual exchange of information that by this account we in Erewhon practice. One is our failure to communicate our attitudes to one another by avowing them, the other our failure to do so by pledging them.

If we report on our attitudes in the same way that we report on the world, then we leave open misleading-mind and changed-mind excuses for failing to tell the truth. We allow ourselves to explain any misreport in a face-saving way—in a way that saves our reputation for reliability—by claiming either that we were misled about our attitudes or that our attitudes had changed since the time when we observed them and made our report. Avowing an attitude rather than reporting it would foreclose the misleading-mind excuse, and pledging an attitude rather than reporting or avowing it would foreclose the changed-mind excuse as well.

Avowals would seem to be within reach of human beings, including those of us in Erewhon, insofar as we are presumed to have a special sort of access to some of our attitudes. And pledges would seem to be within our reach insofar as we are taken in addition to have a special sort of control over certain attitudes. The special access would enable us to set aside misleading-mind excuses in the communication of an attitude, and it would combine with the special control to make it possible to set aside changed-mind excuses, as well. Later chapters argue that we do indeed have special forms of self-access and self-control but argue for this result without invoking any non-naturalistic properties: without postulating anything like a Cartesian consciousness or a libertarian freewill.

The third part of the chapter argued that not only are avowals and pledges saliently absent at this stage in view of our capacities for self-access and self-control; they are surprising absences, given they are not as hazardous as they may at first appear to be. Misleading-mind and changed-mind excuses are both epistemic in character, since they aim to explain why I as speaker may have failed to process correctly the information that I communicate about my attitudes. But the path to avowing and pledging attitudes is eased by the fact that, regardless of the epistemic excuses that those speech acts foreclose, they may still allow a speaker to excuse a miscommunication by invoking a practical excuse or, more radically still, an exemption from being put on the reputational hook.

Where excuses would imply that my capacity to tell the truth was impeded in some way, an exemption would imply that it was temporarily or even permanently impaired. Epistemic excuses invoke an impediment that purportedly affected my ability to process information correctly; practical excuses invoke an impediment that blocked me from transmitting it faithfully. A practical impediment explains why, in the case of an avowal, my words did not match the attitude registered—"I was coerced into misleading you"—and why in the case of a pledge my behavior and intention failed to match the words—"I broke a leg."

Epistemic and practical excuses, as well as exemptions, may be partial or complete but, in this text, they are taken for convenience to be complete. And for the sake of convenience they are also taken to be wholly synchronic. A synchronic excuse—like not having been fully aware of things on which you reported—will not be face-saving if it is present only because of a diachronically prior condition, say, getting drunk, that itself explains why you were not fully aware of things. In this text, excuses and exemptions will all be taken to impose only synchronic requirements, not requirements of a diachronic kind as well.

Avowals and pledges, as presented here, are commitments in the game-theoretical, not the moral, sense of that term. When I avow or pledge an attitude, I back myself to display the attitude communicated, betting that I will not fail to do so. The stake in that bet is that if I do fail, then I cannot have recourse to a misleading-mind excuse in the one case, a misleading-mind or changed-mind excuse in the other. The two chapters to come explore the variety of commitments that we in Erewhon will be motivated to make as we move on from ground zero; they involve avowals and pledges that we make to others and co-avowals and co-pledges that we make in tandem with others.

Chapter 3 Committing to Others

This chapter began from a society in which we inhabitants use natural language to report to one another about aspects of our shared environment. We generally tell the truth in such reports, since not doing so would be likely to damage our reputation, jeopardizing our ability to rely on the reports of others or to get others, when we wish, to rely on our reports to them. And whether or not we give reports on our individual attitudes as well as on our shared environment, we do not avow or pledge those attitudes.

With this as background, the first move in the chapter was to point out that when it comes to communicating any of our beliefs to others, there is inevitably a means available for avowing it rather than reporting it; that is, for communicating it in a way that forecloses resort in the event of a miscommunication to a misleading-mind excuse. This consists in communicating a belief that p, not by reporting it in words like "I believe that p," but by expressing it in the simple assertion "p." And not only do we in Erewhon have a means of avowing such a belief; we will also often have a motive for doing so. Assume that the content of the belief is not qualified probabilistically in the manner of "it is probable that p." An avowal of an unqualified belief will be more risky than a report; it will reduce the possible ways of getting off the reputational hook in the case of a miscommunication. But for that very reason it will also be more credible and more attractive.

But could I ever have the confidence required to be able to avow a belief? The argument was that I can achieve such confidence insofar as I am careful to identify data that support the fact that p and that I can rely on those data to keep my belief in place, absent new discoveries. By virtue of knowing that I am deferring to the data, I can generally know that I believe that p. This is so, at any rate, so long as I am on guard against any potential distraction from those data—anything leading to oversight or inattention—and against any potential disturbance of their effect.

Their effect will be disturbed if it is affected by a factor that tends to suspend the belief; does not provide a changed-mind excuse for the failure; and yet is capable, with effort, of being neutralized or avoided. An example might be the illusion in the casino that suspends my belief that the gambler's fallacy is a fallacy without leading me to treat the suspension as a change of mind. In order to have confidence that I hold the belief that p, I must take care, where needed, not only to guard against distraction from the data that support the proposition, but also to guard against such sources of disturbance.

These observations explain why we in Erewhon are likely to find avowing beliefs feasible and attractive: in particular, more attractive than reporting them. But analogous observations explain why we would also move to avowing rather than reporting certain desires and intentions. There will be the same motive available for doing this as that which obtains in the case of belief: the fact that it promises to make our words more expensive and credible. Or at least there will be a motive of that kind with desires that connect closely with action, and with desires and intentions that are not conditional, and it is attitudes of that kind that are in focus here.

We cannot communicate a desire or intention that q by saying "q"; doing this expresses a belief that p, not any sort of desire or intention. So how do we manage to avow desires and intentions? The chapter argued that once the avowal of beliefs gets established in the community, it will become a matter of common assumption that when I do not go out of my way to indicate otherwise, I can avow the belief that p just by ascribing it to myself, or by explaining its presence, and that I can rely on analogous measures to avow desires and intentions. I can avow such an attitude by saying simply that I desire or intend such and such or by citing facts that would explain its presence.

But could I ever have enough confidence about having a desire or intention to be willing to risk avowing it? The argument was that as I can rely on relevant data to keep a belief in place, absent any distraction or disturbance, so something parallel holds in these cases. I can rely on relevant desiderata to keep a desire or intention in place, absent any distraction and absent any disturbance—say, any disturbance by a brute impulse or compulsion. I can be more or less sure of desiring a prospect R, then, just insofar as I exercise due care, whenever it is needed; I exercise evidential care in guarding myself on the first front and executive care in guarding myself on the second.

The invocation of desiderata in a parallel role to that of data is supported by a common line on what is required for human beings to be mutually intelligible or conversable. The idea is that just as someone would not make proper sense by our lights, if the beliefs they advertised were not supported by recognized data, so they would not make proper sense if they advertised desires or intentions—say, in Elizabeth Anscombe's example, the wish for a saucer of mud—that were not supported by familiar desiderata.

The chapter concluded with an argument that not only would we members of Erewhon be likely to develop practices of avowing rather than reporting certain attitudes, we would also be likely to develop practices of pledging. A pledge would make my words even more expensive and credible than an avowal, since it would set aside the changed-mind excuse as well as the misleading-mind excuse. The possibility of pledging would be attractive with any attitude, because of this increase of credibility, but we saw that it would not be available with beliefs or desires; I could not have the confidence that the data or desiderata supposed by those attitudes would remain constant.

But how could I muster the confidence required to be able to pledge an intention, foreclosing the changed-mind as well as the misleading-mind excuse? In brief, because pledging an intention would generate its own support. It would mean that a later change of mind would be very costly, showing that I was not a person of my word. And so, it would enable me to be confident that if in suitable circumstands I make a pledge of intention, I will stick by it even in the presence of considerations that might otherwise have caused me to let it go. At any rate, I can have such confidence if, as needed, I am evidentially careful to guard against distraction from that desideratum and executively careful to guard against disturbance of its effect.

Chapter 4 Committing with Others

This chapter began from a picture under which we members of Erewhon will not only act as reliable informants in making reports to one another, we will also commit ourselves to one another in the sense associated with avowing and pledging attitudes. We will communicate various beliefs, desires, and intentions in a way that shuts down the possibility of excusing a miscommunication by appeal to having been misled by our own minds. And we will communicate some intentions in a way that shuts down, in addition, the possibility of excusing a miscommunication by appeal to having changed our minds.

The chapter introduced a new dimension to the sort of commitments we enter into by arguing that we would also be drawn in Erewhon into speaking, not just for ourselves, but also for ourselves and others; these include others with whom we have no prior relationship: we need not be members, for example, of the same organization. Setting aside intentions, it argued that we would be drawn into making avowals of beliefs and desires on behalf, now of this group, and now of that; we would presume to co-avow such attitudes, as it was put. If I successfully co-avow a belief or desire on behalf of a group, acting under appropriate constraints, then no members of the group will seek to excuse not living up to my words by claiming that I got their attitudes wrong.

The first section of the chapter showed that in Erewhon we would certainly have a means of such co-avowal available. It would be possible for me or anyone else to co-avow beliefs or desires that a certain number of others share with me either by being authorized in advance to speak for the group or by presuming on such authorization and then being vindicated by a lack of objection. In the first case, people would individually pledge to be bound by the words of the spokesperson; in the second, they would be pledged in a virtual fashion—that is, not by saying "Yea" to the the spokeperson's assumption of authority, but by failing to say "Nay" in a context in which that was an available option.

Drawing on an existing literature, the second section went on to argue that in any conversation, whether in Erewhon or elsewhere, we participants invariably presume in this way on the authorization of others, seeking to build up a body of presuppositions that we manifestly share and that any one of us may presume to co-avow on behalf of all or co-accept in response to the co-avowals that others essay. We in Erewhon would invariably have to practice conversation in sorting out the various issues we confront, and in seeking to establish a pattern of mutual reliance and cooperation. And the appeal, indeed the unavoidability, of conversation would mean that we had a motive to make co-avowals as well as a means of doing so.

But how could we ever find the confidence to be able to speak for others as well as ourselves? The third section of the chapter argued that we could have this confidence in virtue of being able to recognize that in a certain group we are each manifestly confronted with the same data or desiderata and are each manifestly responsive in the same way to such inputs. But while it is intelligible that we might be able to see that we are confronted with the same inputs, how could we be sure of being responsive in the same way to them? The answer offered was that similar responsiveness is required for mutual conversability and that this assumption, being central to human interaction, is vindicated by people's success in working with it.

The fourth section of the paper opened up a topic that is of importance in chapter 5, which looks at how the practices reviewed so far in the narrative would lead us in Erewhon to find a use for the concept of desirability. It argued that, consistently with all that had been said up to then, there are two contrasting sorts of conversation and co-avowal possible, one bounded and the other unbounded. In one, the group involved or the ground invoked in the conversation is taken as relatively fixed, so that there are inherent limits on where it may lead. In the other, both the group and the ground are open to change and the conversation aims at establishing matters of common belief, or even common desire, that are supposed to be able to command the acceptance of just about anybody.

While many conversations in Erewhon are likely to take the bounded or closed form, as we seek to drive deals with one another for this or that purpose, the idea of unbounded or open conversation will also be firmly in place. It will be there to provide a picture of what any one of us is doing in making avowals of beliefs on the basis of data that are necessarily relevant on all sides or of desires that are grounded in desiderata that are contingently relevant for all. Such avowals will constitute would-be co-avowals to the extent that, by our lights, the beliefs and desires are attitudes that just about anyone should hold and, presumptively, the avowals do not give rise to opposition and correction.

The final section of the chapter turned to a topic that will not be of further concern in this study: the co-avowal and co-pledging of intention. The negative thesis in this section was that we will only have a motive to presume to co-avow or co-pledge the individual in-tentions we share with others in special circumstances in which we have prior authorization to speak for them: this, for example, in co-avowing or co-pledging our individual intentions to provide some help for victims of a river flooding. Intentions are subject to forms of disturbance, as in weakness of will, that do not affect desires in the same way. Thus, while there may be desiderata present that would be likely to elicit a common intention to provide assistance for the flood victims, and while these would support my essaying a co-avowal of the corresponding desire, it would be misleading to rely on them as a basis for claiming to co-avow or co-pledge the intention. By doing so, I would mislead an audience into thinking that I had prior authoriza-tion for making such a claim.

The positive thesis in the last section was that when I and others form a joint intention to do something together, that will provide a basis for essaying a co-avowal or co-pledge of that sort of intention. A joint inten-tion, say to build a dam to stop the river flooding in the future, will ma-terialize, roughly, when it is a matter of common awareness that we all desire that result, that there is a manifest plan for achieving it together, and that we are all ready to join with others in implementing that plan.

In this example, the joint intention bears just on a particular episode, but we will also sustain many joint intentions when we form organized agencies—for example, to build on the example given, a disaster-relief body. Any one of us will be positioned in such a case to essay the co-avowal or co-pledge of general intentions associated with the formation of the group or more specific intentions to go along with the application of this or that organizational procedure.

The observation about joint intentions is important, since much of our life in Erewhon involves forming and acting on such intentions. But insofar as it relies on commitment with others, the ensuing narrative will focus on the attitudes of belief and desire and on their co-avowal. As the following chapter argues, such co-avowal plays an important part in explaining how concepts of credibility and desirability come within our reach.

Chapter 5 Discovering Desirability

The practices of avowal and co-avowal, pledging and co-pledging, that we in Erewhon are more or less bound to evolve, by the argument of earlier chapters, presuppose nothing more than strategic adjustments that we each make with a view to securing the benefits associated with mutual reliance. We develop the adjustments out of a wish to prove ourselves reliable in our communications with one another, making it possible to rely on others when we need to do so and to get them to rely on us when that is in our interest.

Beginning from that starting point, this chapter sought to establish that the practices of avowing and pledging, co-avowing and co-pledging—and, in particular, the practice of avowing and co-avowing beliefs and desires—put us within reach of prescriptive ideas. They enable us to gain mastery of concepts of credibility, desirability, and, in particular, moral desirability.

The concept of moral desirability, as it figures in ordinary moral discourse, is relatively unrestricted in both the range of interests registered and the standpoint adopted, and plays a distinctively authoritative role in adjudicating between conflicts about desirability. It does not focus just on what is desirable for the interests of a particular agent, as does prudential desirability. It does not target just what is desirable from the standpoint of a particular practice like law or etiquette, or from the standpoint of particular projects, or even from the standpoint of evidence and epistemology. And because it is unrestricted in these ways, it can play a relatively authoritative role in negotiating conflicts.

Like other concepts of desirability, the idea of moral desirability in ordinary exchange satisfies three generic constraints. The judgment of moral desirability is grounded in independent properties of that to which it applies; it may diverge from what the agent actually desires; and it would be a rational or functional failure on the part of an agent not to let it determine or govern actual desire—this, at any rate, when a variety of other things are equal. And, whether uniquely or not, the concept of moral desirability meets two more specific constraints as well. It is non-indexical, in the sense that the content of moral judgments does not vary with who is making it. And it is non-relativized, in the sense that the truth-value of the judgment does not vary with who is assessing it.

With these clarifications in place, the chapter sought to argue that the avowal and co-avowal of belief explains why we in Erewhon would develop the notion of credibility, and the avowal and co-avowal of desire why we would develop the notion of desirability, in particular moral desirability.

Let me avow beliefs on the basis of robustly supportive data—data that keep a belief in place provided I guard against distraction and disturbance—and it will be manifest that such data make propositions credible, presenting them as things I ought to believe. If, other things being equal, I do not believe such robustly supported propositions—if I drift as a result of independent influences into other beliefs—then that must count as a failure from my viewpoint as someone invested in the avowal of belief. It will be manifest that in that sense I ought to believe such propositions.

Again, let me avow desires for certain scenarios on the basis of robustly supportive desiderata—desiderata that keep a desire in place provided I guard against distraction and disturbance—and it will be manifest that such desiderata make scenarios desirable, presenting them as things I ought to desire. If, other things being equal, I do not desire such robustly attractive prospects—if I drift under independent influences into other desires—then that, too, must count as a failure from my viewpoint as someone invested in the avowal of desire. It will be manifest that in that sense I ought to desire such prospects.

As individual avowal enables us each to develop the concept of the individually credible or desirable, so co-avowal enables us in a corresponding way to develop the concept of the commonly credible or desirable and the jointly credible or desirable. What is jointly credible or desirable will be a function of the data or desiderata that are relevant to one or another bounded grouping, so that any of a variety of propositions or scenarios will have this characteristic. What is commonly credible or desirable will be a function of the data or desiderata that are relevant to anyone, no matter who they are and no matter where they belong.

The notion of the commonly credible coincides with that of the individually credible. What is individually credible has to be commonly credible, since otherwise some of the data invoked in its support are not data that others can countenance and, data being common across persons, the proposition would not be properly credible at all. And what is commonly credible has to be individually credible: to be commonly credible is to be credible for anyone, it does not matter who; to be individually credible is to be credible for me or you or someone else.

Since we naturally explain why something is credible for me or for you by the fact that it is credible for anyone, but not vice versa, the category of the commonly credible has the status of a master category. It is also a master category in relation to joint credibility, since the need for compromises means that what is jointly credible may not be properly credible at all; it may be endorsed among the members of a group for reasons strictly independent of the data available.

Things are very different, however, on the desire front. Something may be individually desirable or jointly desirable, because in part of agent-relative or group-relative desiderata: because the scenario would enable me to help my children or keep my pledges, for example, or because it is in our interest as a bounded group. What is commonly desirable, however, may prove desirable in virtue of a different, only partially overlapping set of desiderata. These are agent-neutral and group-neutral desiderata that ought to appeal to everyone, independently of their particular identity or affiliations.

Where there is a single, compelling perspective that commands our allegiance as believers, then, there are many different perspectives that compete for our allegiance as desirers. And that is going to raise a challenge for us in Erewhon.

The master category in the case of credibility gives us a notion that is relevant for me as a believer independently of the perspective associated with this or that practice and independently of my perspective as an individual. It is unified across practices, and applies universally across people. The challenge raised in the case of desire is that, with many practices and persons in play, both unity and universality fail.

What I find desirable will depend on the particular practice from within which I am considering the option or arrangement at issue. And what I find desirable in any such way is unlikely to count as desirable for you. These failures of unity and universality make for a problem. I will be unable to see or present myself in cases of conflicting practices and perspectives as backing a unified judgment of desirability. And even if I get over the unity problem, I will be unable to back a judgment of desirability that I can expect you to back, as well: a judgment of multilateral desirability, as we may call it; my judgment may reflect the impact of agent-relative or group-relative desiderata that have no grip on you.

There is a means available in principle for getting over these problems and, in particular, for developing a suitable concept of multilateral desirability. In order to unify our practical standpoints in the case of any conflict, we could let the distinct, if overlapping, sets of desiderata determine in aggregate what is desirable, independently of practice-related perspectives; this would give us the concept of what is personally most desirable for each. And in order to gain access to a concept of multilateral desirability, we could filter those desiderata, allowing only certain desiderata to count: on the one side, agent-neutral desiderata and, on the other, agent-relative desiderata that are non-competitive or concordant. These desiderata will be non-rancorous insofar as they do not require anyone to harm others and non-rivalrous insofar as they not mean that to the extent that one person enjoys them, others cannot.

There is reason to think that we in Erewhon would get over these problems by converging in the adjustments they prompt; and this, without necessarily planning, or contracting into, a response. Faced with the pressure to say where we stand in the event of disunity, we would make natural use of the concept of what is most desirable for each of us: in my case, what is desirable$_{me}$, in yours what is desirable$_{you}$. That would make it even more pressing to solve the problem of non-universality, since it might not be clear to you and others that I am likely to be moved to act congenially on the basis of what is desirable$_{me}$ and in any case it might not be easy to tell what is and is not desirable$_{me}$.

But those very difficulties ought to prompt the appearance of a concept of multilateral desirability among us.

In some, perhaps exceptional cases, one or another pattern will manifestly be both desirable$_{me}$ and desirable$_{you}$ — desirable$_{us}$ and potentially desirable$_{all}$. In those situations, the pattern will clearly be multilaterally desirable; being supported by all relevant desiderata, it will be supported in particular by non-rancorous and non-rivalrous desiderata. The resolution of differences accessible in such cases will naturally appeal in virtue of our investment in relations of mutual reliance with one another. And so it ought to prompt us to look for a similar, universal or interpersonal perspective in other cases too.

In those other cases, convergence will be problematic just to the extent that people are moved by rancorous or rivalrous desidera to harm or disadvantage one another. And so the search for a universal perspective will prompt us to identify that which is desirable with that which is desirable on the basis of non-rancorous, non-rivalrous properties; in effect, it will lead to the introduction of the concept of the multilaterally desirable.

The notion of the multilaterally desirable allows for indeterminacy in which option realizes the property in some sorts of choices. And short of admitting indeterminacy, it allows for differences of opinion on many questions about what is most desirable in that sense.

Still, however, there are a range of cases in which judgments of multilateral desirability are likely to be shared, being held by all of us as a matter of common awareness. Social norms like those against violence and fraud, reviewed in chapter 2, would be likely to engage shared standards of multilateral desirability. And such standards would also be routine, in the sense of manifestly lying within people's capacity to follow. Thus, gaining a new justifying and orientating rationale, they would come to constitute norms of multilateral desirability. And they would not be on their own in this role. Norms governing fidelity to avowals and pledges, which did not yet figure in chapter 2, would also come to have that status, being suitably shared and routine.

As pre-social norms gain a new social appeal, once they are seen as conditions we must satisfy to gain full acceptance in the community, so social norms will gain a new appeal when they are seen as generally indicating requirements for acting in a multilaterally desirable fashion.

Even while reputational pressures continue to serve as motors of conformity, the norms will attract our compliance on a novel basis, once the idea of multilateral desirability is in place.

The notion of multilateral desirability answers well to the idea of moral desirability, as that was explicated earlier. It does not reflect a restricted range of interests or a restricted standpoint, unlike other desirability concepts, so that it can enjoy a certain authoritative status. And it meets all the constraints we expect the idea of moral desirability to satisfy.

Like any of the desirability concepts considered, it satisfies the three generic constraints introduced earlier: it is grounded in distinct features of the options to which it applies; what I judge desirable may diverge from what I actually desire; and in the case of divergence, it will be a functional failure on my part, as someone invested in relations of mutual reliance with others, not to bring the desire in line with the judgment. The notion of multilateral desirability also satisfies the two specific constraints associated with moral desirability in particular. Being designed to play a role in adjudicating conflicts between people, it must be nonindexical in content, communicating what is desirable in a shared perspective. And for the same reason it must also be nonrelativized in truth-value.

While the notion of the multilaterally desirable may not correspond exactly with the notion of the morally obligatory option in the choice—the option that is morally obligatory for the agent—it is certainly essential to its definition. Under the approach adopted here, the obligatory option is the morally most desirable option that is not supererogatory—not so demanding that we would refuse to hold an agent responsible for failing to choose it. In order to explain how we in Erewhon might develop the concept of the obligatory action in that sense, it is necessary to see how we might develop the practice of holding one another responsible and the associated idea, built into that practice, of an agent's being fit to be held responsible for an action. That is the topic of the next chapter.

Chapter 6 Discovering Responsibility

This chapter began at the point where it is assumed that we in Erewhon have access to concepts of desirability, in particular the concept of multilateral or moral desirability. The challenge it addressed was that of showing that we would naturally develop a practice of holding one another responsible for breaching certain standards of moral desirability: specifically, the shared, routine standards associated with moral norms.

The first section of the chapter was devoted to elaborating the practice of holding one another responsible, and taking one another to be fit to be held responsible, as that exists in ordinary life. The practice is distinct from that of blindly regulating one another in the way in which, according to the second chapter, we regulate or pressure one another into conforming with pre-social norms. When I hold you responsible for doing something—in particular, when I hold you responsible for an offense—I do so with an awareness of the standard to which I am holding you and with the intention of drawing your attention to the failure. And I do this on the basis of a background assumption that holding you responsible can help to keep you to that standard; we would hardly maintain the practice in dealing with one another if we thought that it had no regulatory impact.

The analysis of what is involved in the practice of responsibility may be focused on the case in which I hold you responsible for breaching a relevant standard by saying that you could have done otherwise—for example, that you could have responded to the standard of honesty and told the truth. While that remark communicates literally that it was at least possible for you to have done otherwise—in particular, there were no suitably exempting or excusing factors that got in the way—it carries three distinctive implicatures or connotations in addition. And it is in virtue of communicating those messages that it counts as a means of holding you responsible.

The first connotation is that it was not merely possible for you to have responded to the desirability of truth-telling, it was robustly possible for you to have done so. In other words, you were disposed to respond robustly over variations in distraction and disturbance to the considerations that made telling the truth desirable. Although you actually failed to do so, you would have responded appropriately in most or many of the variations on the situation that kept those considerations in place without introducing exempting or excusing factors. The second connotation is that you should have done otherwise, you should have told the truth, in the sense in which that conveys, not just that you would have been a better person had you done so, but that it would have made sense for anyone to have exhorted you to tell the truth; I ratify ex post the exhortation or injunction to tell the truth that I or someone else, or you yourself, might have issued before you spoke. And the third connotation is that, by my lights, you are culpable; the remark constitutes a reprimand in itself and a reprimand that you, purportedly, are in no position to deflect.

The second section of the chapter argued that the remark that you could have done otherwise, uttered in an appropriate context, would carry the same connotations in Erewhon that it carries in familiar discourse. Given that the remark would naturally carry these connotations, and would therefore contribute to the sort of mutual regulation to which we are committed, the assumption is that this would motivate us to give it currency in that role and to hold one another responsible for living up to shared, routine standards of desirability.

The key to the argument employed in the second section is that each of us is going to be pledged in a virtual manner to live up to shared, routine standards—that is, to act as they unquestionably require, now in this situation, now in that. Since the standards are shared and routine, it will be a matter of common awareness that, like everyone else, you are going to be expected to live up to them. Assume that you acquiesce in those expectations, not denying the shared or routine status of the norms. In that case, you will be pledged in a virtual manner—pledged as a result of your not having said "Nay" to the expectations—to live up to the standards. After all, it will be a matter of common awareness, given their relevance at every time and context, that you will not be able to excuse a failure to live up to them in either of the standard epistemic ways: either by claiming that when you acquiesced in the expectations of others you were misled about your own mind; or that you had changed your mind since acquiescing.

Why, then, would we in Erewhon credit you with a capacity to have lived up to a shared, routine standard like truth-telling when we say, in the absence of a suitable exemption or excuse, that you could have told the truth rather than lying? Because taking any other line in reacting to you would jeopardize the mutual benefit of ongoing relationships; it would amount to denying you the status of someone conversable in the relevant domain. Why would our saying that you could have done otherwise amount to ratifying the exhortation that anyone might have addressed to you, to tell the truth? Because not to reaffirm such a prior exhortation would be to renege on the practice, in which we are all invested, of empowering one another to keep our pledges—this, by being reputational regulators—and, in particular, to live up to shared, routine standards like that of truth-telling. And why, finally, would the remark constitute a reprimand, expressing our censure? Because it indicates that you did not tell the truth and that in the absence of exemption or excuse you cannot avoid paying the reputational cost.

But is the capacity of the remark to constitute a reprimand compromised by the fact that whenever you fail to exercise the capacity to tell the truth, in the absence of exemption or excuse, it must be the case on naturalistic premises that some unknown glitch or brute chance caused the failure? No. The assumption in the practice described in the narrative is that while exempting and excusing factors make it impossible for us to regulate you reputationally, other causes of failure do not. The idea is that your sensitivity to the expectations of others, in particular your aversion to failing to live up to a pledge, is likely to be able to overcome such influences. And so, despite the effect of such an influence in causing you to lie—that is, in causing you not to live up to the virtual pledge to tell the truth—we may reasonably ratify a prior exhortation to tell the truth, and expose you to the associated reprimand.

The third section of the chapter sought to situate the theory of responsibility supported by this narrative among contemporary alternatives. Those alternatives divide broadly into two families, one non-naturalistic, the other naturalistic. The non-naturalistic theories assume that only a scientifically alien form of freewill could underpin our practice, in holding you responsible for a misdeed, to exhort you to have done otherwise—that is, to ratify a prior exhortation to do otherwise. The idea is that in a world where natural cause or chance ruled, it would not have been possible for you to do otherwise. Sharing that assumption but holding on to the scientific image of the world, the established, naturalistic alternatives to the approach suggest that in holding you responsible, we focus on your attitude as an agent, rather than on your action. We take you to task for having the sort of attitude that the action displayed, believing that you would not have had that attitude had you been generally more sensitive to facts about desirability.

The non-naturalistic alternatives to the current theory are unappealing on the grounds that the metaphysics they defend is dramatically out of line with what science appears to teach us about the world. But the naturalistic alternatives are also unappealing. One problem highlighted is that those approaches need to make sense of why we should enjoin offenders to have displayed a different attitude; it will not be enough that they might have had a different attitude, by our lights, and that it would be better if they did. But if the approaches make use of the idea of the exhortatory perspective to solve this problem—as, it was suggested, it makes good sense to do—then the availability of that idea means that there can be nothing against the action-centered approach that they would displace.

Chapter 7 Morality Reconstructed

This chapter attempted to lay out to the lessons for moral philosophy of taking seriously the naturalistic reconstruction offered in the narrative of Erewhon. We saw that the reconstruction has clear implications in five distinct areas and that, while the focus was on the emergence of concepts in the domain of desirability and responsibility, it can also support a derived account of a number of other concepts. The five areas we looked at are moral metaphysics, moral semantics, moral epistemology, moral psychology, and moral theory.

The metaphysical view supported by our reconstruction takes ethics or morality to presuppose nothing non-natural. The only posits of the view that are presumptively capable of naturalistic vindication are the formation of mental attitudes of belief and desire and intention, the existence of natural language as a means of expressing those attitudes, and the appearance of practices in which attitudes get to be expressed in avowals and pledges.

Practices of avowing and pledging are of central importance in human life, because of the way they enable us to perform as persons, speaking for ourselves and then seeking to live up to the selves we speak for. They are particularly important on this front insofar as they involve avowals and pledges related to multilateral or moral desirability, and seek to satisfy demands of unity and universality. And that means that the metaphysics of morality supported here has the special appeal of explaining why we should be moral. The case for being moral—the case for living up to the acknowledged demands of morality, even when no one independently benefits—is that otherwise you will fail to be an integrated person—a person, in quite a literal sense, of integrity.

With this moral metaphysics in place, the theory can make semantic sense of how moral assertions employ terms that pair off with suitable patterns or properties, being able to predicate those properties as in ascriptions of desirability or responsibility. On this view, two things are going to hold: first, the assertions will be true or false, depending on whether or not the bearers instantiate those patterns; and, second, there will be nothing to block the possibility that many are actually true, since the assertions predicate real-world properties, not illusions that cannot belong to anything in our world.

The first implication means that expressivism of any kind is unappealing; we need not see moral assertions as the mere expressions of desires or of any such non-credal attitudes. The second implies that error theory is equally unnecessary; moral assertions do not predicate properties of a kind that we have to regard as illusory from within a naturalistic perspective. More positively put, the first lesson supports a cognitivism about moral assertions, the second a full-scale realism.

The sort of realism supported commits us to the reality of bona fide properties of moral desirability and responsibility, where such properties are associated with patterns we can reliably track and extrapolate. But that realism leaves room for recognizing that there may not be a fact of the matter corresponding to every issue in morality, in particular every issue about which alternative in a set of options is morally desirable.

The desiderata we invoke in support of a moral assertion have to be recognized on all sides, on pain of unconversability, and that means that the alternatives in any such choice have to be comparable; they are capable of being judged, after all, by the same terms of reference. But those desiderata may be differently weighted among individuals to the point that in some choices, they do not single out a winning option or even an equally good set of options; by some weightings, one option may be desirable, by another, a second option, and so on. The options in such a case are not capable of being morally ordered.

The moral epistemology supported by the approach fits well with the moral metaphysics and the moral semantics that it defends. Building on the points rehearsed, it argues that mastery of moral concepts, and access to the properties they ascribe, is dependent on participation in practices like those of avowal and pledging. It is just in virtue of such participation that we can track desirability and responsibility and find terms with which to predicate those properties. Ultimately, it is just in virtue of participation in suitable practices that we can track moral desirability and responsibility.

The idea is not that desirability and responsibility are defined by reference to those practices as the fashionable is defined by reference to the practices that are governed, under independent pressures, by the authorities of haute couture. The idea, rather, is that by participating in the relevant practices, seeking to meet the preconditions of avowal and pledging, we become attuned to properties of desirability and responsibility and gain access to them.

Participating in the practices is as essential to discerning what counts as desirable, and who counts as responsible, as the ability to have color sensations is essential to being able to identify and track different colors. In each case, we rely on negotiating with others to determine when we are subject to blind spots and when we are seeing clearly. We use others to triangulate on genuine instances of the relevant properties.

The desiderata mobilized in practices of avowal and pledging are familiar to all of us, and it is natural therefore to give only a limited role to the idea of a moral authority: someone that you would do well to follow in determining how best to act, rather than relying on your own view. To defer to authorities in the absence of any independent reason to distrust yourself, then, would be to sideline your own sensibility and practice a sort of self-abasement.

Our familiarity with relevant desiderata also argues that within a given culture, moral ignorance is unlikely to figure as an excuse for your doing something that counts as less than morally desirable. But it may figure as a reasonable excuse across cultures, since we can imagine a culture that lacks a concept for some desideratum that we treat as important. And we can also imagine a culture that recognizes a particular desideratum that we also acknowledge but that has not developed to the point of applying it across the full range that we think relevant: it might give an important role to the desideratum of equality, for example, but not recognize its implications across all the divides that are relevant by our lights.

Having discussed issues in moral metaphysics, semantics, and epistemology, the chapter looked at how the reconstruction offered for morality allows us to make sense of concepts other than those of the desirable and the responsible, the obligatory and the supererogatory.

Focusing on the concept of a reason—the concept of a consideration that counts in favor of something—it is clear that a certain desideratum can count for an agent as a reason to desire some prospect, relative to a given practice of avowal, insofar as it makes that prospect robustly attractive. And equally, it is clear that a certain datum can count for an agent as a reason to believe some proposition—specifically, to believe it relative to the privileged practice of unbounded co-avowal—just to the extent that it makes that proposition robustly persuasive.

The theory of reasons for desire implies that when there is reason to desire something in a given mode, then there is reason to believe that it is correspondingly desirable, although it treats this as secondary; that there is reason to desire something—that it is robustly attractive—explains why there is reason to believe it is desirable, not the other way around. As a theory of the desirable or good, it amounts to a fitting-attitude account, holding that for something to be good or desirable is just for there to be reasons to desire it. But unlike other such accounts, it provides a naturalistically intelligible understanding of the reasons presupposed in this definition of the good.

But reasons figure in richer ways within ordinary moral discourse, being taken, first, to offer a form of support for one or another option that does not simply restate a demand of desirability and, second, to do so with varying degrees of force. And apart from featuring reasons in this autonomous role, moral discourse in the seminar and on the street also makes frequent mention of rights, where again these are often presumed to resist analysis in terms of desirability. Can we make sense of why such concepts would figure in moral discourse?

Assuming that there are bound to be shared and routine standards of desirability established in any community, as it was granted earlier, it becomes intelligible why concepts of these kinds should gain currency. There will be a mandatory reason for something that is required by the rules, a justifying reason for anything supported by the rules in a weaker manner, and a permissive reason for anything that is consistent with the rules. And a claim will be a matter of right insofar as people are required by the rules to satisfy it in their dealings with one another. Such reasons and rights will not present as restating demands of desirability but matters of more or less immediate recognition.

This account not only explains why we should have access to moral concepts that resist analysis as restatements of desirability. It also suggests an explanation for why people may think of the reasons and rights involved as primitive or fundamental. They may be guilty of the Cheshire cat fallacy: the fallacy of imagining that in the absence of appropriate rules, the reasons and rights might still remain in place, as the grin of the Cheshire cat remains in place after the disappearance of the cat itself.

The two remaining areas of thought that were discussed in the chapter are moral psychology and moral theory. In moral psychology, our reconstruction of morality suggests that someone who judges that an option is morally desirable or right, responding to appropriate desiderata, is bound to be motivated in some measure to adopt it, at least under certain conditions: viz., that they are functioning normally, that they actually form the belief that the judgment commits them to avow, and that they are not in an apathetic mood. And apart from supporting such judgment internalism, as it is called, the reconstruction also argues against fetishizing the notion of the morally desirable or obligatory, treating it as the main ground for desiring to act accordingly rather than giving that role to the desiderata that support such a moral judgment.

But not only does the approach support judgment internalism and undermine moral fetishism. A third lesson of the approach in the area of moral psychology is that it allows for two levels of moral performance. One is associated with being guided by a reason or desideratum—acting out of responsiveness towards it—such as that which supports telling the truth or acting respectfully. The other is associated with conforming to corresponding norms: the shared, routine standards that the relevant desideratum supports.

If I act out of responsiveness to a moral desirderatum or reason, it will be true, not just that I contingently act as that reason actually requires, but that I would act as it requires robustly over a range of variations on the actual circumstances where that reason remains in place, no rival considerations eclipse it, and there is no excusing or exempting factor that affects me. If I conform to the requirements of the norm that the reason supports—say, a norm of honesty or respect—then then I need not conform robustly: I need not act out of a disposition of honesty or respect but only out of self-interest.

By acting out of responsiveness to a reason, rather than just conforming to the associated standard, I can produce much richer goods: I can give you the benefit of my honesty or the boon of my respect, not just provide you with the benefit of truth-telling or the restraint linked with respect. And so, it appears that the higher level of moral performance requires me to act out of suitable dispositions.

How can I do this without running the risk that my spontaneous dispositions may often lead me to do something that on consideration is not morally desirable? The only solution possible is that while I let the dispositions play a role as default guides to action, I remain alert to red lights: signals, which may take any of a variety of forms, that the situation may be one in which the considerations overall argue for doing something different. It is only when such red lights appear that I should be prepared to resort to full-scale deliberation of the pros and cons of different options and make my decision on that calculated basis.

The final topic covered in the chapter is moral theory. The first item taken up was the issue between consequentialism and non-consequentialism, the second a less well recognized issue between views that prioritize responsibility, as we put it, and views that prioritize desirability. The account of morality supported by the narrative explains why people should take different sides in these debates without providing any grounds for defending either side.

Under the reconstruction of morality presented, consequentialists and their opponents divide on the issue of what desiderata should serve to fix that option among a set of alternatives—these may be personal actions or institutional arrangements—that is morally desirable or obligatory. According to consequentialism, the only relevant desiderata are the agent-neutral considerations mobilized in making co-avowals of desire relative to an unbounded group. According to non-consequentialism, they may also include agent-relative considerations of the kind that may be mobilized in other practices of avowal or co-avowal. But those agent-relative considerations must be concordant: they must be non-competitive desiderata such that each is willing and able, not only to invoke them in support of their own choice, but to allow others to invoke them in the same way.

This reconstruction of the rival doctrines explains why each of these approaches should have its own supporters, on the assumption that the point of morality is to enable people to justify themselves to others. According to the one approach, your justifying your actions to me and others requires showing that the action is supported on common ground between us; according to the other, it may require only showing that it is supported on concordant or isomorphic ground.

The chapter then went on to consider the independent division among moral theories, between approaches that give a priority to the practice of mutual responsibility, and approaches that don't. This is independent in the sense that consequentialists and non-consequentialists may each adopt either a responsibility-first or a desirability-first view.

On the responsibility-first approach, the practice of holding one another responsible constrains judgments of moral desirability, forcing us to prioritize the standards endogenous to the practice: the standards needed if the practice is to prevail among all of those who, as a matter of shared awareness, are fit to be held responsible. The first requirement in ethics, then, is that those endogenous standards should be honored, so that relevant parties enjoy associated rights at one another's hands and assume associated duties in relation to one another.

A second requirement, according to the responsibility-first approach, may be that people should also satisfy any exogenous standards of desirability: any standards unrelated to the preconditions of the responsibility practice. These standards might bear on how adult, able-minded human beings should be treated in endogenously unconstrained ways, or on the proper treatment of other members of our species, of the members of other species, and of ourselves.

The alternative to this responsibility-first approach would treat all issues of desirability as open to the same sort of argument. Denying any priority to the issues endogenous to the practice of mutual responsibility, it would reject the distinction of levels within ethics. It might rate the treatment of adult, able-minded human beings as something of the first importance, but it would not be forced to do so by any methodological assumptions. It would argue for using the same criteria in assessing all ethical questions, and for letting the results fall out as they will.

Like the divide between consequentialist and non-consequentialist theories, this division is explicable on the theory of morality that our narrative supports. But that theory does not require that the issue be resolved in any particular direction. In this case, as in the other, it does all that we might expect of an approach that is meant to illuminate the role and nature of morality. It makes sense of why there should be a debate about the issue.

Comments

Commentary on Philip Pettit's
The Birth of Ethics

Michael Tomasello[1]

Many philosophers on many issues—including Philip Pettit in these thoughtful and very powerful lectures on human morality—subscribe to something like "In the beginning was the word." On most of these issues—including human morality—I myself subscribe to something more like "In the beginning was the deed." The basic point is that language gains its communicative significance from the contexts, the forms of life, within which it is used. From a naturalistic point of view, the forms of life that led to human morality are all and only about cooperation. Cooperation is social action—action whose goal is to influence what others think, feel, or do—and linguistic communication is only one form of social action. And so my claim is that to the degree that Pettit's story works, it is not because of language per se, but rather because of the cooperative social action involved.

Pettit begins his story with an initial step in which individuals go around reporting their experiences to others, for example, "The berries on the hill are ripe." There are social pressures on them to be honest, to always tell the truth, in order to maintain a good reputation. But informing others of things for their benefit is a cooperative social action that may be effected non-linguistically, for example, by pointing to

1. Max Planck Institute of Evolutionary Anthropology and Duke University Department of Psychology & Neuroscience.

relevant referential situations (Tomasello, 2008). And the reputation one creates by engaging in such behavior is not as a skillful language user but as a cooperative one: telling the truth only matters if it either helps or hinders the recipient in her behavioral decision-making. And so, what is actually doing the work in Pettit's account, I would argue, is not language per se, but rather the cooperative intentions and social actions that underlie certain kinds of speech acts.

Of course, Pettit recognizes the important role of cooperation as background for the evolution of human morality. But this recognition receives only unsystematic treatment in his account, and so it stays in the background and its role is never made explicit. A more systematic treatment puts cooperation in the foreground and highlights it as the foundational infrastructure of human moral psychology that imbues speech acts such as reporting with their moral significance.

The primal scene of uniquely human cooperation

In his evolutionary account, Pettit proposes a pre-moral starting state of self-interested creatures, but with some cooperative characteristics (Section 1.2, on "the input condition"). Thus (33), his initial Erewhonians work toward the satisfaction of their desires according to their beliefs with the ultimate goal of promoting their own (and their kin's) welfare. But these are not self-maximizing chimpanzees, because in addition "they have the capacity... to exercise joint attention" and the capacity "to act jointly with one another in pursuit of shared goals." They also, unlike chimpanzees, interact within an essentially egalitarian social system, and "they are able to rely on others, and able to get others to rely on them." And finally, "they are able to build on those capacities and use words in the communicative fashion of natural human language," which usage entails, I would argue, many cooperative structures and motives. If what Pettit is trying to picture here is a step in human evolution that is cooperatively beyond other primates—given that other primates are not egalitarian and have only weak or no capacities for acting jointly, attending jointly, and getting others to rely on them within joint activities—I have a more systematic proposal.

What we need first is an interactive context structured by certain morally relevant features. The most fundamental such feature, as Hume already recognized, is that individuals are dependent on one another for their basic necessities. Although the individuals of all social species depend on group mates in some ways, what is needed is something especially immediate and urgent. The obvious candidate is foraging, because nothing is more immediate and urgent than procuring food. After consuming food, primate individuals have only a few hours respite before they must find and consume more. Foraging thus structures almost all of their waking hours. The key observation in the current context is that, whereas other primates mostly forage on their own (they may travel in groups but still obtain and consume food individually),[2] humans, from at least several hundred thousand years ago, forage together with others collaboratively, procuring resources that single individuals could never procure on their own. Based on observations of contemporary human hunter-gatherers, we may also speculate that in their collaborative foraging, early humans had a large measure of partner choice, with a bias, of course, for choosing good cooperative partners. And so, if collaboration for obtaining one's daily sustenance was obligate (i.e., there were no satisfactory solo alternatives), we have a situation in which choosing a good cooperative partner, and being chosen by others as a good cooperative partner oneself, was a matter of life and death.

Pettit's scenario in which individuals report their observations to others can fit quite well into this scenario, and indeed he points out that mutual reliance is an important feature of Erewhonian life. But when

---

2. The best-known exception is chimpanzees' group hunting of monkeys. But the most plausible interpretation of this behavior is that each individual is attempting to get the monkey for itself—adjusting to the actions of others in the process—and the unintended effect is a kind of surrounding of the monkey. A telling fact is that once they have killed the prey, sharing the meat is difficult (see Tomasello 2014 for a fuller description and defense of this account).

I report to group mates that the berries on the hill are ripe when in fact they are not, the reason my mates become upset with me is because this communicative act leads them to waste their time and efforts. What upsets them is not that I am an inaccurate reporter—they would not care if I report some completely irrelevant fact inaccurately—but rather that I am being uncooperative. If their chasing fruitlessly after ripe berries results in me getting more honey in the opposite direction, then they will become even more incensed that I misled them for selfish reasons. So the social pressure is not for accurate reporting in and of itself, but rather for cooperative, as against selfish, social action. The communicative import of linguistic acts of reporting must involve in some way cooperation, or lack thereof, if they are to be morally relevant.

Tomasello (2016) argues that early human populations adapted to obligate collaborative foraging (with partner choice) by evolving a new social psychology comprising species-unique skills and motivations of joint intentionality. Specifically, individuals became capable and motivated to form with a partner a joint agent "we" that could act together and also know things together in joint attention and common ground with a partner. Early human individuals understood this "we" as comprising "I" and "you," perspectivally defined, each of whom had its own role and perspective in the joint activity. They also understood that the two of them were interdependent in the joint activity, and that they were equal causal agents in the production of the resource. After repeated instances of a particular form of collaboration, such as hunting antelope, partners came to understand together in common ground how each role in this activity had to be performed if there was to be joint success. These role ideals, as we may call them, were agent-independent, or impersonal, in the sense that they were standards that anyone had to meet if the joint agent was to achieve its joint goal, and also in the sense that the roles of the partners could be reversed and the exact same standards would apply to each role.

There are debates about the exact nature of plural agency in general (cf. Bratman 2014 and Gilbert 2015, e.g., as well as List and Pettit 2011), but for current purposes these are not critical. What is critical is that there is something going on that is not just individual agency. This can be clearly seen in comparative experiments in which young children but not great apes do such things as attempt to re-engage a recalcitrant partner (who *should* be doing his part), take leave when they must abandon a collaboration (which they know they *should* not do), and wait to consume the spoils of a collaborative effort until both partners can do so (see Tomasello and Vaish 2013 for a review). Joint agency of this type—individuals sharing a goal while simultaneously recognizing their different roles (the so-called dual level structure)—is morally relevant in a most fundamental way: it creates the possibility of relating to others second personally (as described by Darwall 2006, and others). For current purposes, let us focus on three of its most important features.

First, Pettit claims (47) that a key early step in the evolution of human morality is that individuals discover "that they should embrace ethical standards of desirability and responsibility: they should recognize . . . that morality is the best policy." But in his account, this has to happen by a kind of reciprocity; I cooperate (by speaking the truth) and hope for the same in return. But that is risky business for the first altruist, as the cooperation may never be returned. Much more stable is mutualism, in which we are simultaneously acting together for a common end, and non-cooperation by either of us means failure for both. In this alternative scenario, the standards that first arise are not general prescriptions for behavior, but rather arise only in the local role standards governing collaborative partners; we both come to understand together in common ground what is needed in each role for our success. These initial standards are not really ethical, only instrumental, but they are nevertheless socially shared standards that exclude not only incompetence but also uncooperativeness. The essential point is that in the concrete instrumental contexts of collaborative foraging (e.g., hunting for antelopes, gathering honey), ideal role standards that simultaneously benefit us both arise quite naturally for individuals with a psychology built for collaboration. It is then not a long step to the full-blown ethical standards to come.

Second, Pettit talks very little about such things as equality, fairness, respect, and justice, especially as they manifest in the division of resources (a.k.a. distributive justice). He does mention all of these things,

338 · The Birth of Ethics

but, as with cooperation in general, they are in kind of an assumed background. In my alternative account, in contrast, the complement to working together collaboratively—indeed a precondition for working together collaboratively—is a trust that in the end we will be able to divide the spoils in a mutually satisfactory way. To be ethical, this mutually satisfactory way of dividing of the spoils cannot be done based on some rule of reciprocity motivated by self-interest, but, rather, it must be done for the right reason. And the right reason is that I understand my partner to be equally deserving as myself. Tomasello (2016) argues that the basis for a genuine appreciation of my partner as equally deserving as myself is a cognitive insight, as first stressed by Nagel (1970): I see others as beings like myself. This is not a desire or preference, but an inescapable recognition of the facts of the matter. In the current account, this recognition comes from the basic structure of joint intentionality: our roles are reversible and the standards of each role apply equally and impersonally to us both (not to mention that we are equally important causal agents in producing the resource). The further argument is that this bloodless judgment of equality turns into a judgment of equal deservingness once collaborators feel the need to bond together to exclude do-nothing free riders from the spoils, which they obviously have done nothing to deserve. It is noteworthy in this context that in dividing resources, as a central ethical challenge in the evolution of human morality, language is not centrally involved.

Third, as Pettit and everyone else recognizes, all evolutionary accounts of human morality must provide some kind of reputational pressure on individuals: they must care what others think of them (in a way that chimpanzees and other apes do not seem to). Pettit's account is more or less the traditional one: I care what they think of me. This account is well-known to be unstable in the sense that it is in constant competition with my selfish motives: I will cheat if I can get away with it. But the shared intentionality account includes an interesting variation: I care what *we* think of me. That is to say, once I have formed a joint goal with someone, we together self-regulate the collaboration to make sure that each of us lives up to our role ideals. If either of us reneges, it is "we" who object, or, more precisely, one of us as a representative of our "we." This way of looking at things invokes a kind of Rousseauean mechanism in which I am not only the one being judged, but I am part of the judging collective, as well, which gives the judgment a special legitimacy and so a special force. I live up to the ideal role standards inherent in collaborative activities as a way of cultivating and maintaining my cooperative identity with the "we" in which I am participating. When I judge myself, and perhaps feel guilty, it is because the "I" that is judging "me" (using socially shared standards) has the representative authority of our "we."

Together these three structural features of joint intentionality comprise what I would call the cooperative infrastructure of human morality: socially shared role standards whose observance affects us both, a sense of equal deservingness of collaborating partners (to the exclusion of undeserving free riders), and a concern for how "we" are evaluating me. This way of operating is not yet fully moral, of course, but it nevertheless constitutes what we may call a kind of second-personal morality governing how collaborating individuals, or those considering collaboration, ought to relate to one another if they are to maintain their cooperative identities.

Joint commitment and legitimate protest

Pettit claims that the next step, beyond simple reports, is that individuals begin to avow their beliefs about the world and to pledge their commitment to the truth of their beliefs. Once again, the first point is that avowing and pledging are speech acts aimed, in the end, at cooperation with others and in maintaining a reputation for cooperation. They make defection or deception more costly as the avower or pledger puts her reputation publicly on the line.

In the shared intentionality way of viewing things, it is unlikely that individuals just went around avowing and pledging that they were telling the truth in their reports. More likely, they avowed and pledged their cooperation in the context of partner choice for collaborative activities: "Let's hunt some antelope. I'll be a great partner." Since the partner must accept the offer (either explicitly or by simply beginning the activity), and the acceptance itself in effect constitutes a pledge, what we have is a joint commitment (Gilbert 2015). It is true that a joint commitment requires some kind of intentional communicative act, and so in this case, it may be that language is poised to play a key role. But language itself is not necessary for a joint commitment, specifically in routine activities that are well known in the common ground of the participants. If we have previously net-fished together many times in the stream, a simple head nod at the appropriate time of day in the appropriate direction should suffice.

In any case, an additional key feature of moral relevance in the shared intentionality scenario of obligate collaborative foraging (with partner choice) is the mutual self-regulation created by a joint commitment. As Pettit emphasizes, in making a joint commitment, I put my reputation publicly on the line. But, as hinted earlier, the shared intentionality account also has a somewhat different take on these things: it is not about me giving "them" more reason to believe me, it is about me giving "us" the power to regulate me. A joint commitment thus sets the stage for what Darwall and others have called legitimate protest or moral protest or second-personal protest. If you do not live up to your role ideal, I am not just surprised or puzzled, I positively resent it (since Strawson (1962), the quintessential reactive attitude). I call you on your breach: "Hey, what are you doing?" Because we know in our common ground what you should be doing in your role, I do not even need to tell you the problem. I know that you know the problem and that you will want to correct it, assuming that you want to keep your cooperative identity. If you do not care about your cooperative identity—if you not only cheat but ignore my protest—I will simply leave and choose another partner. So you are faced with the choice of affirming your current selfish identity (in the process of cheating) or reverting to the cooperative identity you expressed when making the joint commitment, in which case you say something like "Sorry, I had a lapse, but now I'm back on board." If you reaffirm the joint commitment in this way, you are in essence saying that my protest is legitimate. You reaffirm that we made a joint commitment to each play our role ideally, and so the protest is warranted; we both agree you deserve it. This is not just cultivating a reputation with others, but, rather, it is preserving a cooperative identity with all of us in the pool of cooperating partners, including oneself.

Importantly, in this way of viewing things we can preserve two of Pettit's deepest insights into how all of this works. First, he notes that in avowing one's beliefs, one is intentionally forgoing the future possibility of making the excuse that I didn't know any better (I mistook my own mind). In the shared intentionality account, a similar function is performed by the fact that the role ideals of our collaborative activity are mutually known in our common ground, most commonly because we have performed the activity together before previously. If we have hunted antelopes successfully three times in the past, performing our roles in specific ways, it is not a valid excuse to say I did the wrong thing because I didn't know any better. Second, Pettit notes that in pledging one's beliefs, one is intentionally forgoing the future possibility of making the excuse that I changed my mind. In the current account, a similar function is performed by the joint commitment. If we both wander over to the stream and start net-fishing, it would be awkward, but I could change my mind. But if one of us has said "Let's go net fishing" and the other has said "Okay," then neither of us can simply change our mind without giving a legitimating excuse (such as "I hear a child calling in distress"). We are committed. And so again in this case we may translate Pettit's insights from his context of reporting beliefs to our context of acting together cooperatively, with the gain being that we now can firmly ground words in actions that matter to both partners.

A key outcome at which Pettit aims in his account is a sense of responsibility. In the shared intentionality account, making a joint commitment to jointly self-regulate the collaborative activity—and to accept as legitimate any criticism for deviation from our mutually known role ideals—is indeed accepting a responsibility, both to my partner and to our partnership. I will responsibly forgo a potentially beneficial selfish activity because my equally deserving partner does not deserve to be treated that way and, in addition, it would ruin our "we." I act as an individual responsible to you and to our cooperative relationship. Nevertheless, despite this nascent sense of responsibility, the early humans we are picturing still have not reached a fully human morality; they are still in the realm of a fairly concrete second-personal morality. The key point is that there is no universality; there is no generalized judgment of "objective" right and wrong. What we have here is "only" ways that individuals relate to one another second-personally.

Scaling up to an objective morality

To reiterate, the early humans who participated in obligate collaborative foraging with partner choice were not fully moral creatures. The complete story must therefore have a large second step in which this early second-personal morality got scaled up to something more "objective." I will be brief.

Once again, at this step we must begin with a new social-interactive context structured by morally relevant features. One possibility (emerging, perhaps, with modern humans some 150,000 years ago or so) is that as human populations began to expand, they began to splinter, with the splintered sub-groups needing to stay together to compete successfully with other expanding groups. The result was so-called tribally structured societies, or cultures, in which different sub-groups were all held together by common ways of doing things; a common set of cultural practices and a common language. To fit in to this tribal structure including in-group strangers, and so to benefit from cultural life (including coordinating with strangers and enjoying protection from other groups), individuals had to conform. Conformity thus came to signal identification with one's cultural group—when the barbarians come, we're all on the same team. And so individuals in cultural groups created group-specific conventions, norms, and institutions to coordinate their activities with in-group strangers and indeed to govern all aspects of their social lives. One set of these could be called moral norms, as they urged conformity to ways of doing things in domains in which there were already second-personal moral practices involving judgments of deservingness. For example, among the most common moral norms cross-culturally are those governing situations in which conflicts and so group disruption are most likely to occur, including such things as how to divide resources, how to settle conflicts, with whom to have sex, etc.

Unlike the earlier collaborative foragers, these modern human cultural beings did not fully control their social commitments. They could still make and dissolve second-personal joint commitments, but their largest commitments were to the norms and institutions into which they were born. Individuals did not view these as external constraints, however, but rather as legitimate guides to thought and action. The culture's norms and institutions were legitimate because individuals identified with the cultural group and its lifeways—we Waziris do things this way and not that way—in effect making themselves co-authors (with their cultural forebears) of these norms and institutions. As in the case of joint commitments, norm-following individuals were self-regulating via a supra-individual social structure, it is just that, in this case, this structure was much more general and beyond the individual's control. Indeed, it was not the case that individuals viewed the norm as emanating from and governing just the members of the cultural group; they viewed conformity to the group's norms as identificational, and so the norms govern the behavior not of a finite set of individuals but rather of "anyone who would be one of 'us'," any rational and moral person (since only our culture is rational and moral).

Social norms of all kinds are transmitted to children in an authoritative and objectified voice: this is how we do things, this is how things are done, this is the right way to do things. And so the process of enculturation served to objectify the group's social and moral norms, thus giving them the kind of universality and absolute authority characteristic of moral rules. This is not to say that individuals lost control of their own individual decision-making in the process. One of the most distinctive features of human morality is the existence of moral dilemmas in which behavior in a certain specific context may be governed by multiple, conflicting norms, or else the prevailing norms may conflict with one's individual second-personal interactions and relationships. As just one example, I may promise my friend to do something, but it turns out that in doing it I would

344 · THE BIRTH OF ETHICS

harm the group. Thus, individuals construct for themselves moral principles that help them in navigating their way through myriad and sometimes conflicting moral demands.

Pettit attempts to capture the generality of moral norms by invoking co-avowing and co-pledging in which individuals make group commitments, or even agree that one individual can make commitments for them. This is completely consistent with the current account; it is just that, again, I would emphasize that the content and context of the co-avowals and co-pledges must, to be moral, be grounded in cooperative interactions and relationships.

Conclusion

Philip Pettit's narrative is among the most insightful and original accounts we have of the evolution of human morality. The weak version of my critique is simply that he has not elaborated to the degree needed the cooperative infrastructure underlying any account based in linguistic interactions. The strong version of the critique is that one simply cannot base an account of human moral evolution in acts such as reporting whose normative dimension is aimed at truth. Evolutionarily, truth is a value in human life to the degree, and only to the degree, that it affects things that matter, such as collaborative success and second-personal relationships. And indeed in the shared intentionality story, cooperative success, sustained over time, is intimately related to how partners view and treat one another and how they expect to be viewed and treated in return.

And so I couch my critique in the form of a friendly suggestion: to provide a convincing account of human moral evolution, Pettit should work harder to ground his language-based account more systematically in the cooperative social interactions that give language its social and moral significance.

Reply

Reply to Michael Tomasello's Commentary

PHILIP PETTIT

It is a privilege for a philosopher's speculations on how ethics might have emerged among our kind to enjoy the notice and commentary of one of the leading figures in the actual prehistory of ethics. My own belief is that philosophy is best pursued, when possible, in interaction with more empirical studies, and I am delighted to have the opportunity to situate *The Birth of Ethics* in relation to Michael Tomasello's work, as that is reflected in his commentary. There are differences between us, to be sure, but they are not differences of the kind associated with blank stares or embarrassed head-scratching. Engaging philosophically and empirically negotiable matters, they are the stuff of which progress in any field is likely to be made.

The two approaches

It is important to understand the difference of aim between Tomasello's (2016) prehistory of ethics, as elaborated recently in *A Natural History of Human Morality,* and my genealogy or reconstruction. His concern is with the historical exploration of the origin of ethics. And so, he looks at the actual situation and psychology of our early forebears—under "an imaginative reconstruction" of these (2016, 154)—and seeks to identify a way in which ethics might possibly have emerged among our ancestors. My concern is with the philosophical explanation of the nature of ethics. And with that in mind, I seek to identify a human situation and psychology, realistic if fictional, that would have reliably triggered its emergence.

While his aim is primarily historical, and mine primarily philosophical, our enterprises are deeply connected. If he is right, after all, then that is likely to have philosophical implications for the nature of ethics. And if I am right, then that is likely to have historical implications for how ethics actually emerged.

What is the main divide between us on the terrain where our claims meet? On the starkest reading—not the only one possible, as we shall see—the difference turns on whether ethics or morality presupposes the use of natural language. If it does not then that has implications for the nature of ethics; if it does, as my argument maintains, then that has implications for the origin of ethics.

Might we claim, even on that stark reading of the difference between us, that we each identify sufficient conditions for the appearance of ethics, without having to reject the claim of the other? No: this easy route to reconciliation is closed. The reason is that if a pre-linguistic infrastructure of cooperation were sufficient for the evolution of morality, then the fact that it might also emerge out of interactions requiring language would not teach any lesson about its essential nature. It would imply, in terminology introduced in chapter 1, that the account I defend, which requires language to exist prior to morality, fails to meet the constraint of being naturalistically economical or parsimonious. Or at least it would imply this, on the assumption, which we may concede for purposes of argument, that the two accounts would direct us to rival candidates for the referents of prescriptive terms.

Tomasello's challenge

Tomasello comments at the end of his remarks that the points he makes might be taken to support one of two challenges for my approach. The first is that it is not possible to "base an account of human moral evolution in acts such as reporting whose normative dimension is aimed at truth" (344). I entirely agree and so don't take this to be a challenge to my position. As he himself says earlier in his commentary, "Pettit recognizes the important role of cooperation as background for the evolution of human morality" (334).

It is the second challenge that I shall take as his core complaint. This, in his own words, is that I have "not elaborated to the degree needed the cooperative infrastructure underlying any account based in linguistic interactions" (344). While I recognize the role of cooperation, as he acknowledges, the complaint is that "this recognition receives only unsystematic treatment . . . and its role is never made explicit" (334).

But this complaint itself can be understood in either of two ways. First, as a moderate claim that while linguistic interactions of some kind are needed for the emergence of ethics—this is not entirely ruled out by a reading of his book—I need to say more on the role of cooperation either to help explain ethics itself or to explain the role of language in relation to ethics. Or second, as a radical charge that once cooperation is placed more systematically and explicitly in the picture than it is under my account, then the need to invoke language in the explanation of ethics vanishes altogether. The radical charge is supported by what I described earlier as the starkest reading of the difference between us.

The issue of how to construe Tomasello's charge is underlined by a remark in his commentary on the division of spoils and the ethical question it must have raised for our forebears. Having sketched his own account of how our predecessors would have come to think ethically about that exercise, and presumably come to regulate it, he makes the following observation. "It is noteworthy in this context that in dividing resources, as a central ethical challenge in the evolution of human morality, language is not centrally involved" (338). On the first reading of his challenge to me, language is involved in the appearance of ethics but is not as important as I make it out to be. On the second, it is not necessarily involved at all.

Before addressing the challenge in either version, I should make two points in clarification of the debate. The first bears on Tomasello's claim that "the complete story" about ethics must go beyond a second-personal morality of the kind envisaged so far to the "common set of cultural practices" and norms that are likely to emerge in any society whatsoever (342). We agree that wherever there is a morality there are bound to be social norms in existence that attract moral approval; this is an important theme in chapters 5 and 6 of my book. Hence, I do not comment in these remarks on the claim about their being necessary for a complete story about ethics; there is nothing there that divides us. I focus instead on the more basic moral ideas—in his view, ideas of a second-personal morality—that moral norms presuppose.

The second point to note is that the question about the relation between language and morality arises, whether language is taken to be essentially verbal or to involve mainly gestural and related signs. My presentation is made on the assumption that those in Erewhon have a verbal language from the very beginning of the narrative, albeit a language mainly used for reporting purposes. While that assumption makes the narrative easier to present, however, it is not strictly essential.

Thus, I can accept a suggestion that Tomasello makes that the avowal or pledge associated with a joint commitment, say to go net-fishing together, may be communicated gesturally; I do not take this to show that "language is not necessary for a joint commitment." "If we have previously net-fished together," he says, "a simple head nod at the appropriate time of day in the appropriate direction should suffice" (340). I agree entirely, since a nod will be of no use whatsoever except among agents who have achieved a means and a medium of communication— some form of language, however rudimentary—in the sense of communication characterized early in chapter 2.

The moderate version of the challenge

I find it more congenial to understand Tomasello's challenge in the first, moderate fashion, if only because it makes the common ground between us quite extensive. And in response to the challenge in that version, I would make three conciliatory points.

The first is that I acknowledge the plausibility of Tomasello's (2016) main claims in the course of my book, accepting that it is likely that mother nature pre-empted calculation about the rationality of

cooperation and that it "selected our forebears for the presence of proximate psychological mechanisms triggering mutual cooperation and reliance quite spontaneously" (41). While having no expertise in the area,
I am happy to go along with the claims he makes about this selection; he
bases those claims mainly on the cooperative dispositions that children
display, even before they reach the age of three.

The second point I would make is that while my narrative about the
fictional world of Erewhon does not assume that inhabitants are born
with this proclivity to cooperation, it makes methodological sense not
to rely on such an assumption. The assumptions about agents and their
circumstances that argue for the emergence of ethics, as I say in the
book, should "offer a firm basis on which to predict the actions and adjustments of the protagonists" (40), and should be "realistic or, if not
fully realistic, . . . should not rig things in favor of the development of
ethical concepts and practices" (42). A willingness to postulate cooperative predispositions might seem to rig things in this way, at least to
many critics, and would not constrain the predictions of the narrative
sufficiently; cooperative predispositions might be posited at will.

Those considerations led me to try to argue for the likely appearance
of ethics under the assumption that the inhabitants of Erewhon are relatively rational and self-regarding in their thinking. A further advantage of that approach, so I suggested, is that ethics must look all the
more central to human life for the fact that it would even appear in a
worse-case scenario. "What nature would generate in the dry wood of
Erewhon, it is all the more likely to have generated in the green wood
of our actual history" (41).

The third point I would make in response to the moderate version
of the challenge softens the second. While the methodology adopted
supports a more individually opportunistic picture of the psychology of
Erewhonians than applies to human beings—this, on Tomasello's own
image of human psychology—the picture adopted does still endorse
many of the elements that he stresses. True, the protagonists in the
narrative, even if they are moderately altruistic, "primarily desire the
promotion of their own welfare and that of their kin" (33). But nonetheless "they are able to rely on others, and able to get others to rely on

them". Moreover, "they have the capacity in pursuing mutual reliance, first, to exercise joint attention, consciously focusing on data they take to be available to all, and second, to act jointly with one another in pursuit of shared goals". And finally, "they are able to build on those capacities and use words in the communicative fashion of natural human language" (33).

The radical version of the challenge

The radical version of Tomasello's charge almost certainly exaggerates the difference between us, but it has the merit of directing attention to a crucial issue in debates about the origin and nature of ethics. This is the question as to whether language is essential to morality.

One reason for thinking that language is not necessary for ethics or morality might be based in a conception of ethics as essentially a matter of behavior or attitude. On this way of thinking, the fact that any creatures behave in a way that answers to recognized, ethical standards, or display a corresponding sensibility, is enough to show that ethics has already made an appearance among them. And it suffices to show this, so the line goes, even if those creatures have no conception of the standards; no idea of their demands across different situations; and no sense of complying with such demands.

Like me, however, Tomasello does not take any pattern of behavior or feeling—even a highly altruistic pattern—to imply in and of itself that the creatures who conform to it have entered ethical space. Thus, agents count as having an ethics, not by virtue of just acting in certain ways, out of certain dispositions, but by virtue of acting in those ways because of thinking in broadly ethical terms. This is implied in his commentary, when he says that "to be ethical," your action toward another "must be done for the right reason" (338). You must act out of "a sense of 'ought'," as he puts it in the book (2016, 84), that does not reflect "just a preference or an emotion."

On the radical version of the challenge, what Tomasello holds is that the pattern of cooperation that he charts in the book, and summarizes in his commentary, is sufficient before the advent of language, or at least independently of language, to make sense of how our forebears would have developed both ethical habits of thought and ethical habits of action—ethical concepts and ethical practices.

The plausibility of this challenge depends on the plausibility of the account at which he gestures in explaining the origin of ethics, where this is read as denying language any role. It may be useful, then, to review the main elements in that account, as summarized in his commentary, and to ask whether a story built around such elements could suffice, independently of language, to explain the emergence of ethics.[1]

1. In the relevant period, from about four hundred thousand to one-hundred and fifty thousand years ago, our ancestors lived in world of obligate collaboration in foraging; unlike other primates, they faced a choice of working together or dying alone.

2. In this world, they were selected for "a new social psychology" in virtue of which they became 'capable and motivated to form with a partner a joint agent "we" that could act together and also know things together in joint attention and common ground' (336).

3. After the experience of one or another form of collaboration, say in hunting antelopes, "partners came to understand together" certain "role-ideals: "standards that anyone had to meet if the joint agent was to achieve its joint role" (336).

4. These "socially shared standards," which were necessary for the success of all the partners in a venture, "exclude not only incompetence but uncooperativeness"; and this, despite the fact that they are "instrumental," "not really ethical" (337).

5. The "complement to working together collaboratively" would have been a form of trust that "in the end we will be able to divide the spoils in a mutually satisfactory way" (338).

---

1. For a consideration of the many more steps of argument itemized in Tomasello's book, and for a critique of the claim that they would have sufficed to ensure the presence of an ethics, see Pettit (2018b).

6. Would this division have been ethical in character? Only if it was established, not in an exercise where the partners each pursue their self-interest, but "for the right reason" required in ethics: viz., that "I understand my partner to be equally deserving as myself" (338).

7. There are two considerations that combine to explain why our ancestors would have been led to divide the spoils of collaboration for the right, ethically relevant reason; these become apparent when we ask about how things present to me or you in the sort of situation they faced.

8. First, in that type of situation, I see others, in line with "the basic structure of joint intentionality," "as beings like myself," playing reversible roles under common role-ideals; I do not acknowledge such equality as a result of "a desire or preference" but by way of observing "the facts of the matter" (338).

9. Second, "this bloodless judgment of equality turns into a judgment of equal deservingness once collaborators feel the need to bond together to exclude do-nothing free riders from the spoils, which they obviously have done nothing to deserve" (338).

10. On this account, the motive that keeps me responsive to the perceived deserts of a partner is not that I want a good reputation with others—not that "I care what they think of me"—but rather that "I care what *we* think of me." For if I offend, "it is 'we' who object, or, more precisely, one of us as a representative of our 'we'" (338–39).

This original and intriguing story, abstracted from *The Natural History of Human Morality*, surely captures important developments among our ancestors that would have contributed to the emergence of ethics. But I find it hard to see why the story, taken independently of linguistic and conceptual initiatives, would have required people to think in the fashion that is distinctive of ethics.

The crucial premise in the argument, involving points 8 and 9, is that the participants in any joint venture would have seen one another as symmetrically positioned with themselves, and would have seen free-riders as different. The crucial move in the argument, then, is the transition from that presumptive fact to the conclusion that participants in the venture would have seen one another as deserving, indeed equally deserving, of a share in the spoils and, by implication, would have seen free-riders as undeserving.

Let that move pass, and the parties involved would certainly have occupied ethical space. They would have access to the ethical property of desert and been in a position to introduce related concepts like those of proper and improper behavior, fair and unfair treatment, just and unjust exclusion. And equally, therefore, they would have been positioned to regulate their own and one another's behavior by deploying such concepts.

But why is the crucial move in the argument supposed to be persuasive? Why does the crucial premise not argue for the development of suitably cooperative behavior without arguing in addition for access to the concept of desert and its cognates?

It may well be unsurprising that in the situation described participants should have become disposed to divide the spoils among themselves, whether equally or not, and to exclude free-riders. They might have been naturally selected for that disposition, for example, assuming that the advantage to the group constituted a selectional pressure; it would have created this sort of pressure to the extent that members survived or failed individually, depending on whether the group as a whole survived or failed. And even in the absence of such group selection, our ancestors might have been naturally selected for the required disposition in the manner in which Tomasello assumes that they were selected in general for cooperative traits.

In any case, putting natural selection aside, we can imagine processes of social selection under which the regularity associated with dividing spoils and excluding free-riders might have emerged and stabilized. Reputational pressures alone would explain why members of the group would have rejected as partners those who had not divided the spoils in the past, for example, or even those who had done nothing to help eject free-riders (Brennan and Pettit 2004).

Tomasello maintains in his commentary that reputational pressure will not support stable cooperation, if it is "in constant competition with my selfish motives: I will cheat if I can get away with it" (339). But that need not be a problem for such a story of social selection.

Selfish motives do not have to be very powerful on his own view of how our ancestors were selected for cooperative dispositions. Besides, he argues that reputational pressure is going to be more stabilizing if it is pressure brought to bear by a collaborative group or community: if it is applied by "one of us as a representative of our 'we'" (338–39). And there is no reason why our story cannot appeal to this, without relying on the prior introduction of ethical concepts. Something close to communal pressure figures prominently in any story, including that which I myself tell, where reputation gets spread by testimony, so that it can become a matter of common belief, manifest to all, that certain individuals are not reliably cooperative.

Thus, there are familiar mechanisms of natural and social selection for why our ancestors in Tomasello's scenario would have evolved suitably cooperative behavior. In particular, there are familiar mechanisms for explaining why they would have tended to divide the spoils of foraging appropriately, and to help to eject free-riders. But there are no mechanisms that I can see to explain why, over and beyond this, they would have begun to think in a novel, prescriptive fashion, developing concepts like that of desert and its relatives. For this reason, I resist the radical version of the challenge discussed.

Detente

It is important to recall at this point, however, that the moderate version of the challenge is much more likely to be that which Tomasello would defend. His central claim, on a plausible interpretation, is that those who make language a prerequisite of morality, as I do, may not recognize that what language achieves in making ethical concepts available, it achieves only because of a dense infrastructure of joint activity. My response, sketched earlier, is that while I might well have given more attention than I did in the book to this infrastructure, I do concede its importance, and I acknowledge it as fully as my worse-case methodology allows me to do.

Not only am I happy to make this concession to Tomasello. I should also acknowledge in conclusion that the sort of narrative I tell might profitably take a different form, in light of the points that he emphasizes about the centrality of joint activity. It is plausible in light of his argument that joint action may come on stream for members of our species as naturally and primitively as individual action. And if we start from a community in which it is second nature, perhaps even first nature, for members to do various things together, then the move to avowal and pledging may be much more straightforwardly explicable than in my account, and the appearance of a prescriptive stance may be much more readily intelligible.

In order to appreciate this, it may be useful to return to some points briefly invoked at the end of chapter 1 about joint action. Many of the things we do with both hands, we do without knowing what we do with either hand taken separately. While we each know how to tie our shoelaces, for example, using both hands at once, few of us know how we move our individual hands in doing so. As this is possible across limbs, something similar is possible across individuals. Thus, while you and I may be able to tango together, we may have little idea of what we individually do in performing the tango (Pettit 2017). Not only may it take two to tango; it may also take two to establish the know-how on which tangoing relies.

Tangoing is a joint activity in which we involve ourselves, at least after practice, as in a basic action; we can do it intentionally, but, as in the shoelaces case, we do not do it intentionally by means of doing anything more basic intentionally (Hornsby 1980). Tomasello's picture of our forebears in the period when ethics arose suggests that joint activities of the same kind may have been absolutely basic for them. They may have found it entirely natural to do various things intentionally together, as children in his studies find this natural, without being able to see the joint action as the aggregate product of what as individuals they intentionally do. Learning would have been required for achieving basic joint activities, of course, but only in the way in which it would also have been required for achieving individual ends.

If we move to a picture in which the protagonists in our narrative about ethics begin from such a scenario, then it may be possible to recast the narrative I tell. The recasting would preserve the role of avowing and pledging, and maintain its importance for the emergence of a prescriptive stance. But it would develop the story without relying as much as I do on charting the rational adjustments of relatively self-seeking agents; it would reduce the part played in my narrative by *homo economicus*. I cannot explore that possibility here, but I see it as a destination that looks more plausible in light of this exchange.

References

Alonso, F. M. (2014). "What is Reliance?" *Canadian Journal of Philosophy* 44: 163–183.

Anscombe, G. E. M. (1957). *Intention.* Oxford, Blackwell.

Anscombe, G. E. M. (1958). "Modern Moral Philosophy." *Philosophy* 33 (124).

Appiah, K. A. (2010). *The Honor Code: How Moral Revolutions Happen.* New York, Norton.

Appiah, K. A. (2017). *As If: Idealization and Ideals.* Cambridge, Mass., Harvard University Press.

Arpaly, N. (2003). *Unprincipled Virtue: An Inquiry into Moral Agency.* Oxford, Oxford University Press.

Axelrod, R. (1984). *The Evolution of Cooperation.* New York, Basic Books.

Ayer, A. J. (1982). *Language, Truth and Logic.* London, Gollancz.

Bar-On, D. (2004). *Speaking My Mind: Expression and Self-knowledge.* Oxford, Oxford University Press.

Benhabib, S. (1990). *The Communicative Ethics Controversy.* Cambridge, Mass., MIT Press.

Bennett, J. (1964). *Rationality.* London, Routledge and Kegan Paul.

Blackburn, S. (1984). *Spreading the Word.* Oxford, Oxford University Press.

Block, N. and R. Stalnaker (2000). "Conceptual Analysis and the Explanatory Gap." *Philosophical Review* 109: 1–46.

Boehm, C. (1999). *Hierarchy in the Forest: The Evolution of Egalitarian Behavior.* Cambridge, Mass., Harvard University Press.

Boix, C. and F. Rosenbluth (2014). "Bones of Contention: The Political Economy of Height Inequality." *Americal Political Science Review* 108: 1–22.

Brandom, R. (1994). *Making it Explicit.* Cambridge, Mass., Harvard University Press.

Bratman, M. (1987). *Intention, Plans, and Practical Reason.* Cambridge, Mass., Harvard University Press.

Bratman, M. (1999). *Faces of Intention: Selected Essays on Intention and Agency.* Cambridge, Cambridge University Press.

Bratman, M. (2014). *Shared Agency: A Planning Theory of Acting Together.* Oxford, Oxford University Press.

Brennan, G., L. Eriksson, R. E. Goodin, and N. Southwood (2013). *Explaining Norms.* Oxford, Oxford University Press.

Brennan, G. and P. Pettit (2004). *The Economy of Esteem: An Essay on Civil and Political Society.* Oxford, Oxford University Press.

Broome, J. (1991). *Weighing Goods.* Oxford, Blackwell.

Broome, J. (2013). *Rationality through Reasoning.* Oxford, Wiley Blackwell.

Brown, C. (2011). "Consequentialize This." *Ethics* 121: 749–771.

Buchak, L. (2015). *Risk and Rationality.* Oxford, Oxford University Press.

Buchak, L. and P. Pettit (2014). "Reasons and Rationality: The Case for Group Agents." *Weighing and Reasoning*. I. Hirose and A. Resner. Oxford, Oxford University Press.

Burgess, A. and D. Plunkett (2013). "Conceptual Ethics (I and II)." *Philosophy Compass* 8: 1091–1110.

Byrne, A. (2011). "Transparency, Belief, Intention." *Proceedings of the Aristotelian Society* Supp Vol 85: 201–221.

Chaitin, G. J. (1975). "Randomness and Mathematical Proof." *Scientific American* 232, May: 47–52.

Chaitin, G. J. (1988). "Randomness in Arithmetic." *Scientific American* 259, July: 80–85.

Chalmers, D. (2011). "Verbal Disputes." *Philosophical Review* 120: 515–566.

Chalmers, D. and F. Jackson (2001). "Conceptual Analysis and Reductive Explanation." *Philosophical Review* 110: 315–360.

Chang, R. (2002). "The Possibility of Parity." *Ethics* 112: 659–688.

Chappell, R. Y. (2012). "Fittingness: The Sole Normative Primitive." *Philosophical Quarterly* 62: 684–704.

Chisholm, R. M. (1982). Human Freedom and the Self. *Free Will*. G. Watson. Oxford, Oxford University Press: 24–35.

Clarke, R., M. McKenna and A. M. Smith (2015). *The Nature of Moral Responsibility: New Essays*. Oxford, Oxford University Press.

Cocking, D. and J. Kennett (2000). "Friendship and Moral Danger." *Journal of Philosophy* 97: 278–296.

Coleman, J. (1990). *Foundations of Social Theory*. Cambridge, Mass., Harvard University Press.

Craig, E. (1990). *Knowledge and the State of Nature*. Oxford, Oxford University Press.

Craig, E. (2007). Genealogies and the State of Nature. *Bernard Williams*. T. Allen. Cambridge, Cambridge University Press: 181–200.

Dancy, J. (2004). *Ethics without Principles*. Oxford, Oxford University Press.

Darwall, S. (2006). *The Second-Person Standpoint: Morality, Respect, and Accountability*. Cambridge, Mass., Harvard University Press.

Darwall, S., A. Gibbard, and P. Railton (1992). "Towards *Fin de siecle* Ethics: Some Trends." *Philosophical Review* 101: 115–189.

Davidson, D. (1984). *Inquiries into Truth & Interpretation*. Oxford, Oxford University Press.

De Scioli, P. and R. Kurzban (2009). "Mysteries of Morality." *Cognition* 112: 281–299.

De Scioli, P. and R. Kurzban (2013). "A Solution to the Mysteries of Morality." *Psychological Bulletin* (139): 477–496.

Dennett, D. (1987). *The Intentional Stance*. Cambridge, Mass., MIT Press.

Dennett, D. (1991). "Real Patterns." *Journal of Philosophy* 88: 27–51.

Dietrich, F. and C. List (2013). "A Reason-Based Theory of Rational Choice." *Nous* 47: 104–134.

Dietrich, F. and C. List (2017). "What matters and how it matters: a choice-theoretic representation of moral theories." *Philosophical Review* 126: 421–479.

Dorsey, D. (2017). *The Limits of Moral Authority*. Oxford, Oxford University Press.

Doyle, J. (2018). *No Morality, No Self: Anscombe's Radical Scepticism*. Cambridge, Mass., Harvard University Press.

Dreier, J. (1993). "Structures of Normative Theories." *Monist* 76: 22–40.

Dworkin, R. (2011). *Justice for Hedgehogs*. Cambridge, Mass., Harvard University Press.

Elster, J. (1999). *Alchemies of the Mind: Rationality and the Emotions*. Cambridge, Cambridge University Press.

Enoch, D. (2011). *Taking Morality Seriously: A Defense of Robust Realism*. Oxford, Oxford University Press.

Estlund, D. (2014). "Utopophobia." *Philosophy and Public Affairs* 42: 113–134.

Evans, G. (1982). *The Varieties of Reference*. Oxford, Oxford University Press.

Ewing, B. (2016). *Punishing Disadvantage: Culpability, Opportunity, and Responsibility*, Princeton University PhD dissertation.

Fine, K. (2012). "Guide to Ground." *Metaphysical Grounding: Understanding the Structure of Reality*. F. Correia and B. Schnieder. Cambridge, Cambridge University Press: 37–80.

Först, R. (2012). *The Right to Justification: Elements of a Constructivist Theory of Justice*. New York, Columbia University Press.

Frankfurt, H. (1969). "Alternate Possibilities and Moral Responsibility." *Journal of Philosophy* 66: 829–839.

Frankfurt, H. G. (1988). *The Importance of What We Care About*. Cambridge, Cambridge University Press.

Fricker, M. (2007). *Epistemic Injustice: Power and the Ethics of Knowing*. Oxford, Oxford University Press.

Fricker, M. (2010). *Scepticism and the Genealogy of Knowledge: Situating Epistemology in Time*. A. Haddock, A. Millar and D. Pritchard. Oxford, Oxford University Press: 51–68.

Gardner, J. (2007). *Offences and Defences: Selected Essays in the Philosophy of Criminal Law*. Oxford, Oxford University Press.

Garland, D. (2001). *The Culture of Control: Crime and Social Order in Contemporary Society*. Chicago, University of Chicago Press.

Gauthier, D. (1986). *Morals by Agreement*. Oxford, Oxford University Press.

Gert, J. (2012). *Normative Bedrock: Response-dependence, Rationality, and Reasons*. Oxford, Oxford University Press.

Gibbard, A. (1990). *Wise Choices, Apt Feelings*. Oxford, Oxford University Press.

Gibbard, A. (2003). *Thinking How to Live*. Cambridge, Mass., Harvard University Press.

Gilbert, M. (2015). *Joint Commitment: How We Make the Social World*. Oxford, Oxford University Press.

Gilovich, T., D. Griffin, and D. Kahneman, Eds. (2002). *Heuristics and Biases: The Psychology of Intuitive Judgment*. Cambridge, Cambridge University Press.

Graeber, D. (2011). *Debt: The First 5000 Years*. London, Melville House Publishing.

Grice, H. P. (1975a). "Logic and Conversation." *Syntax and Semantics Vol 3*. P. Cole and J. L. Morgan. New York, Academic Press.

Grice, H. P. (1975b). "Method in Philosophical Psychology." *Proceedings and Addresses of the American Philosophical Association* 68: 23–53.

Grice, P. (1989). *Studies in the Ways of Words.* Cambridge, Mass., Harvard University Press.

Habermas, J. (1990). "Discourse Ethics: Notes on a Program of Philosophical Justification." *The Communicative Ethics Controversy.* S. Benhabib and F. Dallmayr. Cambridge, Mass., MIT Press.

Habermas, J. (1995). "Reconciliation through the Public Use of Reason: Remarks on John Rawls's Political Liberalism." *Journal of Philosophy* 92: 109–131.

Hare, R. M. (1952). *The Language of Morals.* Oxford, Oxford University Press.

Hare, R. M. (1981). *Moral Thinking: Its Levels, Method and Point.* Oxford, Oxford University Press.

Harman, G. (2000). *Explaining Value and Other Essays in Moral Philosophy.* Oxford, Oxford University Press.

Hart, H. L. A. (1948–49). "The Ascription of Responsibility and Rights." *Proceedings of the Aristotelian Society* 49: 171–194.

Hart, H. L. A. (1961). *The Concept of Law.* Oxford, Oxford University Press.

Hieronymi, P. (2007). "Rational Capacity as a Condition on Blame." *Philosophical Books* 48: 109–123.

Hobbes, T. (1994). *Leviathan,* ed E. Curley. Indianapolis, Hackett.

Hornsby, J. (1980). *Actions.* London, Routledge.

Hume, D. (1965). *Of the Standard of Taste and Other Essays.* Indianapolis, Bobbs-Merrill.

Hume, D. (1978). *A Treatise of Human Nature.* Oxford, Oxford University Press.

Hume, D. (1983). *An Enquiry Concerning the Principles of Morals.* Indianapolis, Hackett.

Jackson, F. (1998). *From Metaphysics to Ethics: A Defence of Conceptual Analysis.* Oxford, Oxford University Press.

Jackson, F. (2004). "What Are Proper Names For?" *Experience and Analysis.* M. E. Reicher and J. C. Markek. Vienna, Kirchberg Proceedings: 257–269.

Jackson, F. and P. Pettit (1990). "In Defence of Folk Psychology." *Philosophical Studies* 57: 7–30; reprinted in F. Jackson, P. Pettit, and M. Smith, 2004, *Mind, Morality, and Explanation,* Oxford, Oxford University Press.

Jackson, F. and P. Pettit (1995). "Moral Functionalism and Moral Motivation." *Philosophical Quarterly* 45: 20–40; reprinted in F. Jackson, P. Pettit, and M. Smith, 2004, *Mind, Morality, and Explanation,* Oxford, Oxford University Press.

Jackson, F. and P. Pettit (1998). "A Problem for Expressivism." *Analysis* 58: 239–251; reprinted in F. Jackson, P. Pettit, and M. Smith, 2004, *Mind, Morality, and Explanation,* Oxford, Oxford University Press.

Jackson, F. and P. Pettit (2002). "Response-dependence without Tears." *Philosophical Issues (supp. to Nous)* 12: 97–117.

Jackson, F., P. Pettit, and M. Smith (1999). "Ethical Particularism and Patterns." *Particularism.* B. Hooker and M. Little: 79–99; reprinted in F. Jackson, P. Pettit, and M. Smith, 2004, *Mind, Morality, and Explanation,* Oxford, Oxford University Press.

Johnston, M. (1992). "How to Speak of the Colors." *Philosophical Studies* 68: 221–263.

Jones, E. E. (1990). *Interpersonal Perception*. New York, Freeman.

Jones, K. (1999). "Second-hand Moral Knowledge." *Journal of Philosophy* 96: 55–78.

Joshi, H. (2016). *Avoiding the One Thought Too Many: Essays on Virtuous Agency*, Princeton, N.J., Princeton University.

Joyce, R. (2006). *The Evolution of Morality*. Cambridge, Mass., MIT Press.

Kahneman, D. (2011). *Thinking, Fast and Slow*. New York, Farrar, Straus, and Giroux.

Kearns, S. and D. Star (2008). "Reasons: Explanations or Evidence." *Ethics* 19: 31–56.

Kelly, E. (2013). "What Is an Excuse?" *Blame: Its Nature and Norms*. J. D. Coates and N. A. Tognazzini. Oxford, Oxford University Press: 244–262.

Kitcher, P. (2011). *The Ethical Project*. Cambridge, Mass., Harvard University Press.

Kripke, S. A. (1980). *Naming and Necessity*. Oxford, Blackwell.

Langton, R. (2009). *Sexual Solipsism: Philosophical Essays in Pornography and Objectification*. Oxford, Oxford University Press.

Lawlor, K. (2013). *Assurance: An Austinian View of Knowledge and Knowledge Claims*. Oxford, Oxford University Press.

Lederman, H. (2018). "Common Knowledge." *Handbook of Social Intentionality*. M. Jankovic and K. Ludwig. London, Routledge.

Lewis, D. (1969). *Convention*. Cambridge, Mass., Harvard University Press.

Lewis, D. (1983a). "New Work for a Theory of Universals." *Australasian Journal of Philosophy* 61: 343–377.

Lewis, D. (1983b). *Philosophical Papers Vol 1*. Oxford, Oxford University Press.

List, C. and P. Pettit (2011). *Group Agency: The Possibility, Design, and Status of Corporate Agents*. Oxford, Oxford University Press.

Locke, J. (1975). *An Essay Concerning Human Understanding*. Oxford, Oxford University Press.

MacFarlane, J. (2014). *Assessment Sensitivity: Relative Truth and its Applications*. Oxford, Oxford University Press.

Mackie, J. L. (1977). *Ethics*. Harmondsworth, Penguin.

Maynard Smith, J. and D. Harper (2004). *Animal Signals*. Oxford, Oxford University Press.

McGeer, V. (1996). "Is 'Self-knowledge' an Empirical Problem? Renegotiating the Space of Philosophical Explanation." *Journal of Philosophy* 93: 483–515.

McGeer, V. (2007). "The Regulative Dimension in Folk Psychology." *Folk Psychology Reassessed*. D. Hutto and M. Ratcliffe. Dordrecht, Springer.

McGeer, V. (2008). "The Moral Development of First-Person Authority." *European Journal of Philosophy* 16: 81–108.

McGeer, V. (2013). "Civilizing Blame." *Blame: Its Nature and Norms*. J. D. Coates and N. A. Tognazzini. Oxford, Oxford University Press: 162–188.

McGeer, V. (2014). "Strawson's Consequentialism." *Oxford Studies in Agency and Responsibility* 2: 64–92.

McGeer, V. and P. Pettit (2015). "The Hard Problem of Responsibility." *Oxford Studies in Agency and Responsibility*. D. Shoemaker. Oxford, Oxford University Press. Vol 3: 160–188.

McGeer, V. and P. Pettit (2017). "The Empowering Theory of Trust." *The Philosophy of Trust.* P. Faulkner and T. Simpson. Oxford, Oxford University Press.

McKenna, M. (2012). *Conversation and Responsibility.* New York, Oxford University Press.

Menger, C. (1892). "On the Origin of Money." *Economic Journal* 2: 239–255.

Miller, A. (2013). *Contemporary Metaethics: An Introduction.* Cambridge, Polity Press.

Miller, D. T. and D. A. Prentice (1996). "The Construction of Social Norms and Standards." *Social Psychology: Handbook of Basic Principles.* E. T. Higgins and A. W. Kruglanski. New York, Guilford Press: 799–829.

Moore, G. E. (1911). *Ethics.* Oxford, Oxford University Press.

Moore, R. (2017). "Gricean Communication and Cognitive Development." *Philosophical Quarterly* 67: 303–326.

Moran, R. (1997). "Self-Knowledge: Discovery, Resolution, and Undoing." *European Journal of Philosophy* Vol 5: 141–161.

Moran, R. (2001). *Authority and Estrangement: An Essay on Self-knowledge.* Princeton, N.J., Princeton University Press.

Nagel, T. (1970). *The Possibility of Altruism.* Oxford, Oxford University Press.

Nagel, T. (1986). *The View from Nowhere.* Oxford, Oxford University Press.

Neale, S. (1992). "Paul Grice and the Philosophy of Language." *Linguistics and Philosophy* 15: 509–559.

Nelkin, D. (2011). *Making Sense of Freedom and Responsibility.* Oxford, Oxford University Press.

Neuhouser, F. (2015). *Rousseau's Critique of Inequality: Reconconstructing the Second Discourse.* Cambridge, Cambridge University Press.

Nietzsche, F. (1997). *On the Genealogy of Morals.* Cambridge, Cambridge University Press.

Olsaretti, S. (2004). *Liberty, Desert and the Market.* Cambridge, Cambridge University Press.

Parfit, D. (1984). *Reasons and Persons.* Oxford, Oxford University Press.

Parfit, D. (2001). "Rationality and Reasons." *Exploring Practical Philosophy: From Action to Value.* D. Egonsson, J. Josefsson, B. Petersson, and T. Ronnow-Rasmussen. Farnham, Ashgate.

Pereboom, D. (2014). *Free Will, Agency, and Meaning in Life.* Oxford, Oxford University Press.

Perry, J. (1979). "The Essential Indexical." *Nous* 13: 3–21.

Pettit, P. (1983). "The Possibility of Aesthetic Realism." *Pleasure, Preference and Value.* E. Schaper. Cambridge, Cambridge University Press: 17–38.

Pettit, P. (1986). "Free Riding and Foul Dealing." *Journal of Philosophy* 83: 361–379.

Pettit, P. (1990). "*Virtus Normativa*: A Rational Choice Perspective." *Ethics* 100: 725–755; reprinted in P. Pettit, 2002, *Rules, Reasons, and Norms,* Oxford, Oxford University Press.

Pettit, P. (1991a). "Consequentialism." *A Companion to Ethics.* P. Singer. Oxford, Blackwell.

Pettit, P. (1991b). "Decision Theory and Folk Psychology." *Essays in the Foundations of Decision Theory*. M. Bacharach and S. Hurley. Oxford, Blackwell; reprinted in P. Pettit, 2002, *Rules, Reasons, and Norms*, Oxford, Oxford University Press.

Pettit, P. (1993). *The Common Mind: An Essay on Psychology, Society, and Politics*. New York, Oxford University Press.

Pettit, P. (1995). "The Cunning of Trust." *Philosophy and Public Affairs* 24: 202–225; reprinted in P. Pettit, 2002, *Rules, Reasons, and Norms*, Oxford, Oxford University Press.

Pettit, P. (1997a). "A Consequentialist Perspective on Ethics." *Three Methods of Ethics: A Debate*. M. Baron, M. Slote, and P. Pettit. Oxford, Blackwell.

Pettit, P. (1997b). "Love and its Place in Moral Discourse." *Love Analyzed*. R. Lamb. Boulder, Westview Press.

Pettit, P. (1998). "Practical Belief and Philosophical Theory." *Australasian Journal of Philosophy* 76: 15–33.

Pettit, P. (2000). "A Sensible Perspectivism." *Dealing with Diversity*. M. Baghramian and A. Dunlop. London, Routledge: 60–82.

Pettit, P. (2002). *Rules, Reasons, and Norms: Selected Essays*. Oxford, Oxford University Press.

Pettit, P. (2004). "Hope and its Place in Mind." *Annals of the American Academy of Political and Social Science* 592: 152–165.

Pettit, P. (2006a). "On Thinking How to Live: A Critical Notice of Allan Gibbard 'Thinking How to Live'." *Mind* 115: 1083–1105.

Pettit, P. (2006b). "Preference, Deliberation and Satisfaction." *Preferences and Well-being*. S. Olsaretti. Cambridge, Cambridge University Press: 131–153.

Pettit, P. (2007a). "Joining the Dots." *Common Minds: Themes from the Philosophy of Philip Pettit*. H. G. Brennan, R. E. Goodin, F. C. Jackson, and M. Smith. Oxford, Oxford University Press: 215–344.

Pettit, P. (2007b). "Rationality, Reasoning and Group Agency." *Dialectica* 61: 495–519.

Pettit, P. (2007c). "Responsibility Incorporated." *Ethics* 117: 171–201.

Pettit, P. (2008a). *Made with Words: Hobbes on Language, Mind and Politics*. Princeton, N.J., Princeton University Press.

Pettit, P. (2008b). "Value-mistaken and Virtue-mistaken Norms." *Political Legitimization without Morality?* J. Kuehnelt. New York, Springer: 139–156.

Pettit, P. (2014a). "Group Agents Are not Expressive, Pragmatic or Theoretical Fictions." *Erkenntnis* 79: 1641-62.

Pettit, P. (2014b). *Just Freedom: A Moral Compass for a Complex World*. New York, W. W. Norton and Co.

Pettit, P. (2015a). "The Asymmetry of Good and Evil." *Oxford Studies in Normative Ethics*. M. Timmons. Oxford, Oxford University Press. 5: 15–37.

Pettit, P. (2015b). "Justice, Social and Political." *Oxford Studies in Political Philosophy*. D. Sobel, P. Vallentyne, and S. Wall. 1: 9–35.

Pettit, P. (2015c). *The Robust Demands of the Good: Ethics with Attachment, Virtue and Respect*. Oxford, Oxford University Press.

Pettit, P. (2016a). "Broome on Reasoning and Rule-following." *Philosophical Studies* 173: 3373–3384.

Pettit, P. (2016b). "Making Up Your Mind." *European Journal of Philosophy* 24: 3–26.

Pettit, P. (2017). "Corporate Agency—The Lesson of the Discursive Dilemma." *Routledge Companion to Collective Intentionality.* M. Jankovic and K. Ludwig. London, Routledge.

Pettit, P. (2018a). "Three Mistakes about Doing Good (and Bad)." *Journal of Applied Philosophy* 35.

Pettit, P. (2018b). "Naturalizing Tomasello's History of Morality." *Philosophical Psychology* 31.

Pettit, P. (2018c). "Defending *The Robust Demands of the Good.*" *Moral Philosophy and Politics* 5.

Pettit, P. (2019a). "Analyzing Concepts and Allocating Referents." *Conceptual Engineering and Conceptual Ethics.* A.Burgess, H.Cappelen, and D.Plunkett. Oxford, Oxford University Press.

Pettit, P. (2019b). "Social Norms and the Internal Point of View: An Elaboration of Hart's Concept of Law." *Oxford Journal of Legal Studies* 39.

Pettit, P. and D. Schweikard (2006). "Joint Action and Group Agency." *Philosophy of the Social Sciences* 36: 18–39.

Pettit, P. and M. Smith (1996). "Freedom in Belief and Desire." *Journal of Philosophy* 93: 429–449; reprinted in F. Jackson, P. Pettit, and M. Smith, 2004, *Mind, Morality, and Explanation,* Oxford, Oxford University Press.

Pettit, P. and R. Sugden (1989). "The Backward Induction Paradox." *Journal of Philosophy* 86: 169–82.

Portmore, D. W. (2014). *Commonsense Consequentialism: Wherein Morality Meets Rationality.* Oxford, Oxford University Press.

Prescott-Couch, A. (2014). "Williams and Nietzche on the Significance of History for Moral Philosophy." *Journal of Nietzsche Studies* 45: 147–168.

Price, H. (1988). *Facts and the Function of Truth.* Oxford, Blackwell.

Prichard, H. A. (1912). "Does Moral Philosophy Rest on a Mistake?" *Mind* 21: 21–37.

Quiller-Couch, A., Ed. (1922). *The Oxford Book of Victorian Verse.* Oxford, Oxford University Press.

Quine, W. V. O. (1970). *Word & Object.* Cambridge, MIT Press.

Quinn, W. (1993). *Morality and Action.* Cambridge, Cambridge University Press.

Rabinowicz, W. (2012). "Value Relations Revisited." *Economics and Philosophy* 28: 133–164.

Railton, P. (2014). "Reliance, Trust, and Belief." *Inquiry* 57: 122–150.

Rawls, J. (1995). "Political Liberalism: Reply to Habermas." *Journal of Philosophy* 92: 132–180.

Raz, J. (1999). *Practical Reason and Norms.* Oxford, Oxford University Press.

Rorty, R. (1980). *Philosophy & the Mirror of Nature.* Oxford, Basil Blackwell.

Rosen, G. (2004). "Scepticism about Moral Responsibility." *Philosophical Perspectives* 18: 295–313.

Rosen, G. (2010). "Metaphysical Dependence: Grounding and Reduction." *Modality: Metaphysics, Logic, and Epistemology*. B. Hale and A. Hoffman. New York, Oxford University Press: 109–135.

Rosen, G. (2015). "The Alethic Conception of Moral Resonsibility." *The Nature of Moral Responsibility: New Essays*. R. Clarke, M. McKenna, and A. M. Smith. New York, Oxford University Press.

Rousseau, J. J. (1997). *The Discourses and other early political writings*, ed. Victor Gourevitch. Cambridge, Cambridge University Press.

Rovane, C. (1997). *The Bounds of Agency: An Essay in Revisionary Metaphysics*. Princeton, N.J., Princeton University Press.

Sainsbury, R. M. (1998). "Projections and Relations." *Monist* 81: 133–160.

Sayre-McCord, G. (1994). "On Why Hume's 'General Point of View' Isn't Ideal—and Shouldn't Be." *Social Philosophy and Policy* 11: 202–228.

Scanlon, T. M. (1998). *What We Owe To Each Other*. Cambridge, Mass., Harvard University Press.

Scanlon, T. M. (2008). *Moral Dimensions: Permissibility, Meaning, Blame*. Cambridge, Mass., Harvard University Press.

Scanlon, T. M. (2014). *Being Realistic about Reasons*. Oxford, Oxford University Press.

Scheffler, S. (2010). *Equality and Tradition: Questions of Value in Moral and Political Theory*. Oxford, Oxford University Press.

Schroeder, M. (2008). *Being For: Evaluating the Semantic Program of Expressivism*. Oxford, Oxford University Press.

Schroeder, T., A. Roskies, and S. Nicholls (2010). "Moral Motivation." *The Moral Psychology Handbook*. J. Doris. Oxford, Oxford University Press: 72–110.

Scott-Phillips, T. C. (2015). *Speaking our Minds: Why Human Communication Is Different, and How Language Evolved to Make It Special*. London, Palgrave Macmillan.

Searle, J. (2010). *Making the Social World: The Structure of Human Civilization*. Oxford, Oxford University Press.

Seemann, A., Ed. (2011). *Joint Attention: New Developments in Psychology, Philosophy of Mind, and Social Neuroscience*. Cambridge, Mass., MIT Press.

Sellars, W. (1997). *Empiricism and the Philosophy of Mind*. Cambridge, Mass., Harvard University Press.

Shakespeare, W. (2014). *Hamlet*. Cambridge, Cambridge University Press.

Shapiro, S. (2011). *Legality*. Cambridge, Mass, Harvard University Press.

Sider, T. (2011). *Writing the Book of the World*. Oxford, Oxford University Press.

Singer, P. (1981). *The Expanding Circle: Ethics and Sociobiology*. Oxford, Oxford University Press.

Skinner, Q. (2009). "A Genealogy of the Modern State." *Proceedings of the British Academy*, Supp. Vol. 162: 325-370.

Slote, M. and P. Pettit (1984). "Satisficing Consequentialism." *Proceedings of the Aristotelian Society*, Supp. Vol. 58: 139–176.

Smith, A. (1982). *The Theory of the Moral Sentiments*. Indianapolis, Liberty Classics.

Smith, A. M. (2005). "Responsibility for Attitudes: Activity and Passivity in Mental Life." *Ethics* 115: 236–271.

Smith, M. (1994). *The Moral Problem*. Oxford, Blackwell.

Smith, M. (2003). "Rational Capacities, or: How to Distinguish Recklessness, Weakness, and Compulsion." *Weakness of Will and Practical Irrationality*. S. Stroud and C. Tappolet. Oxford, Oxford University Press.

Smith, M. (2017). "Constitutivism." *Routledge Handbook of Metaethics*. T. McPherson and D. Plunkett. London, Routledge.

Sober, E. and D. S. Wilson (1998). *Unto Others: The Evolution and Psychology of Unselfish Behavior*. Cambridge, Mass, Harvard University Press.

Southwood, N. (2017). "Does 'Ought' Imply 'Feasible'?" *Philosophy and Public Affairs* 45.

Sperber, D. and D. Wilson (1986). *Relevance: Communication and Cognition*. Oxford, Blackwell.

Stalnaker, R. (1978). "Assertion." *Syntax and Semantics*. P. Cole. New York, Academic Press. 9: 315–323.

Stalnaker, R. C. (1984). *Inquiry*. Cambridge, Mass., MIT Press.

Sterelny, K. (2012). *The Evolved Apprentice: How Evolution Made Humans Unique*. Cambridge, MA, MIT Press.

Stevenson, C. L. (1944). *Ethics and Language*. New Haven, Conn., Yale University Press.

Stocker, M. (1976). "The Schizophrenia of Modern Ethical Theories." *Journal of Philosophy* 73: 453–466.

Strawson, G. (2005). *Against Narrativity*. Oxford, Blackwell.

Strawson, P. (1962). *Freedom and Resentment and Other Essays*. London, Methuen.

Taylor, C. (2016). *The Language Animal: The Full Shape of the Human Linguistic Capacity*. Cambridge, Mass., Harvard University Press.

Temkin, L. (2012). *Rethinking the Good: Moral Ideals and the Nature of Practical Reasoning*. Oxford, Oxford University Press.

Tomasello, M. (2008). *Origins of Human Communication*. Cambridge, Mass., MIT Press.

Tomasello, M. (2014). *A Natural History of Human Thinking*. Cambridge, Mass., Harvard University Press.

Tomasello, M. (2016). *A Natural History of Human Morality*. Cambridge, Mass., Harvard University Press.

Tomasello, M., and A. Vaish (2013). "Origins of human cooperation and morality." *Annual Review of Psychology* 64: 231–255.

Tuomela, R. (2007). *The Philosophy of Sociality: The Shared Point of View*. Oxford, Oxford University Press.

Ullmann-Margalit, E. (1977). *The Emergence of Norms*. Oxford, Oxford University Press.

Vargas, M. (2013). *Building Better Beings: A Theory of Moral Responsibility*. Oxford, Oxford University Press.

Velleman, D. (2000). *The Possibility of Practical Reason*. Oxford, Oxford University Press.

Wallace, R. J. (1996). *Responsibility and the Moral Sentiments*. Cambridge, Mass., Harvard University Press.

Watson, G. (1987). "Responsibility and the Limits of Evil: Variations on a Strawsonian Theme." *Responsibility, Character, and the Emotions*. F. Schoeman. Cambridge, Cambridge University Press: 256–286.

Watson, G. (1996). "Two Faces of Responsibility." *Philosophical Topics* 24: 227–248.

Wedgwood, R. (2007). *The Nature of Normativity*. Oxford, Oxford University Press.

Wiggins, D. (1987). *Needs, Values, Truth*. Oxford, Basil Blackwell.

Williams, B. (1981). *Moral Luck*. Cambridge, Cambridge University Press.

Williams, B. (1995). *Making Sense of Humanity*. Cambridge, Cambridge University Press.

Williams, B. (2000). "Naturalism and Genealogy." *Morality, Reflection, and Ideology*. E. Harcourt. Oxford, Oxford University Press.

Williams, B. (2002). *Truth and Truthfulness*. Princeton, N.J., Princeton University Press.

Winch, P. (1963). *The Idea of a Social Science and Its Relation to Philosophy*. London, Routledge.

Wolf, S. (1990). *Freedom within Reason*. Oxford, Oxford University Press.

Wright, C. (1992). *Truth and Objectivity*. Cambridge, Mass., Harvard University Press.

Zahavi, A. and A. Zahavi (1999). *The Handicap Principle: A Missing Piece of Darwin's Puzzle*. Oxford, Oxford University Press.

Zawidzki, T. W. (2013). *Mindshaping: A New Framework for Understanding Human Social Cognition*. Cambridge, Mass., MIT Press.

Name Index

General Index